Food Safety Standards in International Trade

Food safety has become a major concern for consumers in the developed world and Europe in particular. This has been highlighted by the recent spate of food scares ranging from the BSE (mad cow) crisis to Chinese melamine contamination of baby formula. To ensure food safety throughout Europe, stringent food safety standards have been put in place 'from farm to fork'. At the same time, poor African countries in the COMESA rely on their food exports to the European market to achieve their development goals yet have difficulty meeting the EU food safety standards. This book examines the impact of EU food safety standards on food imports from COMESA countries. It also critically examines both EU and COMESA food safety standards in light of the WTO SPS Agreement and the jurisprudence of the WTO panels and Appellate Body. The book makes ground-breaking proposals on how the standards divide between the EU and the COMESA can be bridged and discusses the impact of EU food safety standards on food imports from poor African countries.

Onsando Osiemo is a legal practitioner and researcher in Nairobi, Kenya. He obtained his PhD in law from the University of Amsterdam. His areas of research are in international trade law and regional integration in Europe and Africa.

'The author deftly exposes current problems with safety standards in food exports from Africa to Europe from a legal perspective, with sensitivity and insight. This book delivers original solutions to these important social challenges and is an invaluable resource for African and European policy makers, academics and the socially concerned'.

Dr Kamala Dawar, *University of Sussex, UK*

'Dr Osiemo has delivered an important and timely study of the comparable impacts of food safety standards in the context of regional trade arrangements: of particular note is his contribution to the debate about such standards in the context of Southern and Eastern Africa'.

Professor Mary Footer, *University of Nottingham, School of Law, UK*

Food Safety Standards in International Trade
The case of the EU and the COMESA

Onsando Osiemo

LONDON AND NEW YORK

First published 2017
by Routledge

2 Park Square, Milton Park, Abingdon, Oxfordshire OX14 4RN
711 Third Avenue, New York, NY 10017

Routledge is an imprint of the Taylor & Francis Group, an informa business

First issued in paperback 2018

Copyright © 2017 Onsando Osiemo

The right of Onsando Osiemo to be identified as author of this work has been asserted by him in accordance with sections 77 and 78 of the Copyright, Designs and Patents Act 1988.

All rights reserved. No part of this book may be reprinted or reproduced or utilised in any form or by any electronic, mechanical, or other means, now known or hereafter invented, including photocopying and recording, or in any information storage or retrieval system, without permission in writing from the publishers.

Notice:
Product or corporate names may be trademarks or registered trademarks, and are used only for identification and explanation without intent to infringe.

British Library Cataloguing in Publication Data
A catalogue record for this book is available from the British Library

Library of Congress Cataloging-in-Publication Data
Names: Osiemo, Onsando, author.
Title: Food safety standards in international trade : the case of the EU and the COMESA / Onsando Osiemo.
Description: Abingdon, Oxon ; New York, NY : Routledge, 2016. | Includes index. | Based on author's thesis (doctoral - Universiteit van Amsterdam, 2012) issued under title: Harmonization of sanitary and phytosanitary standards in international trade : the case of the EU and the COMESA.
Identifiers: LCCN 2016013505 (print) | LCCN 2016014012 (ebook) | ISBN 9781138694125 (hbk) | ISBN 9781315526614 (e-book) | ISBN 9781315526607 (Web PDF) | ISBN 9781315526591 (ePub) | ISBN 9781315526584 (Mobipocket)
Subjects: LCSH: Food law and legislation. | Foreign trade regulation. | Food law and legislation—European Union countries. | Food law and legislation—Africa. | Non-tariff trade barriers—Law and legislation—European Union countries. | European Union countries—Foreign economic relations—Africa. | Africa—Foreign economic relations—European Union countries. | European Union. | Common Market for Eastern and Southern Africa. | Agreement on the Application of Sanitary and Phytosanitary Measures (1995 January 1)
Classification: LCC K3626 .O839 2016 (print) | LCC K3626 (ebook) | DDC 344.04/232—dc23
LC record available at https://lccn.loc.gov/2016013505

ISBN: 978-1-138-69412-5 (hbk)
ISBN: 978-1-138-61612-7 (pbk)

Typeset in Galliard
by Apex CoVantage, LLC

 Printed in the United Kingdom
by Henry Ling Limited

Contents

Acknowledgements   vii
List of abbreviations   viii
Table of cases   xi

Introduction   1

    I.1 *Introduction* 1
    I.2 *Why SPS standards?* 4
    I.3 *Why the EU and the COMESA?* 6
    I.4 *Objectives and scope* 7
    I.5 *Plan of this book* 8

1 SPS standards under the WTO SPS Agreement   10

    1.1 *Introduction* 10
    1.2 *The significance of SPS standards* 17
    1.3 *The WTO SPS Agreement* 28
    1.4 *Harmonisation of SPS standards* 37
    1.5 *Provisions for developing countries under the SPS Agreement* 41
    1.6 *Chapter discussion and conclusions* 46

2 EU food safety standards   60

    2.1 *Introduction* 60
    2.2 *Regulation 178 of 2002* 63
    2.3 *The European Food Safety Authority (EFSA)* 65
    2.4 *A critical overview of the EU food safety policy and standards* 69
    2.5 *Global administrative and constitutional law perspectives* 94
    2.6 *Chapter discussion and conclusions* 96

3 COMESA food safety standards   101

    3.1 *Introduction* 101
    3.2 *An overview of the COMESA* 102

vi *Contents*

    3.3 SPS policies and regulations in the COMESA 111
    3.4 Chapter discussion and conclusions 122

4 Case studies in food safety standards in EU–COMESA trade   127

    4.1 Introduction 127
    4.2 The two schools of thought on the impact of food safety standards on trade 130
    4.3 COMESA trade concerns with EU food safety regulations in beef, fishery, and horticultural products 137
    4.4 Private voluntary standards (PVS) and EU food safety standards 151
    4.5 Chapter discussion and conclusions 163

5 Towards a model for co-operation in food safety standards in EU–COMESA trade   168

    5.1 Introduction 168
    5.2 Tools for upgrading COMESA national food safety control systems 171
    5.3 The COMESA food control system (CFCS) 196
    5.4 Towards an EU–COMESA food control system 206
    5.5 The EU–COMESA food control system (ECFCS) 212
    5.6 Chapter discussion and conclusions 214

6 Conclusions   218

    6.1 Introduction 218
    6.2 The SPS Agreement 219
    6.3 EU food safety standards 221
    6.4 COMESA food safety standards 223
    6.5 A food control system for EU–COMESA food products trade 225
    6.6 Final remarks 226

Index   229

Acknowledgements

I am greatly indebted to professors P J Kuijper and J H Mathis of the University of Amsterdam faculty of law for their support and input in writing this book.

I am most grateful to Alison Kirk, Routledge's Senior Commissioning Editor, for her support in bringing the book to life. My gratitude is also extended to the editor and anonymous reviewers of the book.

Abbreviations

AFSA	African Food Safety Authority
ALOP	appropriate level of protection
AMPRIP	Agricultural Marketing Promotion and Regional Integration Project
ARSO	African Organization for Standardization
ASEAN	Association of Southeast Asian Nations
AU	African Union
AU-IBAR	African Union Interafrican Bureau for Animal Resources
BRC	British Retail Consortium Global Standard for Food Safety
BSE	Bovine Spongiform Encephalopathy
CAADP	Comprehensive Africa Agricultural Development Programme
CARICOM	Caribbean Community
CBA	Cost Benefit Analysis
CFCS	COMESA Food Control System
CFSA	COMESA Food Safety Authority
CGP	COMESA Green Pass
CJ	Court of Justice of the EU
Codex	Codex Alimentarius Commission
COMESA	Common Market for Eastern and Southern Africa
CPA	Cotonou Partnership Agreement
CRO	common regulatory objectives
DG SANCO	Directorate-General on Consumer Policy and Consumer Health
DSB	Dispute Settlement Body
DSU	Understanding on Rules and Procedures Governing the Settlement of Disputes
EAC	East African Community
EBA	Everything But Arms
EC	European Community
ECFCS	EU–COMESA Food Control System
ECOWAS	Economic Community of West African States
EFSA	European Food Safety Authority
EFTA	European Free Trade Association

EPA	Economic Partnership Agreement
EU	European Union
EURL	EU reference laboratories
FAO	Food and Agriculture Organization of the United Nations
FAO	Food and Agriculture Organization
FMD	Foot-and-Mouth disease
FVO	food and veterinary office
GAL	Global Administration Law
GAP	good agriculture practices
GATT 47	General Agreements on Tariffs and Trade 1947
GATT 94	General Agreements on Tariffs and Trade 1994
GC	General Court of the EU
GDP	gross domestic product
GHP	good hygiene practices
GlobalGAP	Global Good Agricultural Practices
GMO	genetically modified organism
GMP	good manufacturing practices
HACCP	hazard analysis critical control point
IA	impact assessment
IEC	International Electro-technical Commission
IGAD	Intergovernmental Authority for Development
IILJ	Institute for International Law and Justice
IPPC	International Plant Protection Convention
IRPA	Institute for Research on Public Administration
ISO	International Standardization Organization
JFCC	Joint Food Control Committee
JSC	Joint Scientific Committee
LDC	Least Developed Countries
LOD	lower limit of determination
MEA	Multilateral Environmental Agreements
MERCOSUR	South American Regional Economic Organization
MRL	maximum residue level
NAFTA	North American Free Trade Agreement
NGOs	non-governmental organisations
NRL	national reference laboratories
nvCJD	new variant Creutzfeldt-Jakob Disease
OECD	Organization for Economic Co-operation and Development
OIE	World Organization for Animal Health
PCE	Phytosanitary Capacity Evaluation
PPPP	public-private partnerships Protection
PTA	preferential trade area
PVS	private voluntary standards
RASFF	Rapid Alert System for Food and Feed
RIA	regulatory impact assessment
RSP	reference to standards principle

RSPSRL	Regional SPS Reference Laboratories
RTA	regional trading agreement
SADC	Southern African Development Community
SCFCAH	Standing Committee on the Food Chain and Animal Health
SDT	Special and Differential Treatment
SPS Agreement	Agreement on the Application of Sanitary and Phytosanitary Measures
STDF	Standards and Trade Development Facility
TBT Agreement	Agreement on Technical Barriers to Trade
TFEU	Treaty on the Functioning of the European Union
UEMOA	West African Economic and Monetary Union
UNCTAD	United Nations Conference on Trade and Development
UNDP	United Nations Development Programme
UNECA	United Nations Economic Commission for Africa
UNIDO	United Nations Industrial Development Organization
US	United States of America
USTR	United States Trade Representative
VCLT	Vienna Convention on the Law of Treaties
WHO	World Health Organization
WTO	World Trade Organization

Table of cases

WTO panel reports

Panel Report, *United States – Measures Affecting the Importation of Animals, Meat and Other Animal Products from Argentina*, WT/DS447/R, adopted 24 July 2015.

Panel Report, *United States – Measures Affecting the Production and Sale of Clove Cigarettes*, WT/DS406/R, adopted 24 April 2012.

Panel Report, *Australia – Measures Affecting the Importation of Apples from New Zealand*, WT/DS367/R, adopted as modified by the Appellate Body, 17 December 2010.

Panel Report, *United States – Certain Measures Affecting Imports of Poultry from China*, WT/DS392/R, adopted 25 October 2010.

Panel Report, *Canada – Continued Suspension of Obligations in the EC Hormones Dispute*, WT/DS321/R, adopted as modified by the Appellate Body, 14 November 2008.

Panel Report, *United States – Continued Suspension of Obligations in the EC Hormones Dispute*, WT/DS320/R, adopted as modified by the Appellate Body, 14 November 2008.

Panel Reports, *European Communities – Measures Affecting the Approval and Marketing of Biotech Products*, complaint by the United States of America, WT/DS291/R; complaint by Argentina, WT/DS292/R; complaint by Canada, WT/DS293/R, adopted on 26 November 2006.

Panel Report, *European Communities – Conditions for the Granting of Tariff Preferences to Developing Countries*, WT/DS246/R, adopted as modified by the Appellate Body report, 20 April 2004.

Panel Report, *Japan – Measures Affecting the Importation of Apples*, WT/DS245/R, adopted as modified by the Appellate Body Report, 10 December 2003.

Compliance Panel Report, *Australia – Measures Affecting Importation of Salmon – Recourse to Article 21.5 by Canada*, WT/DS18/RW, adopted 20 March 2000.

Panel Report, *Australia – Measures Affecting Importation of Salmon*, WT/DS18/R, adopted as modified by the Appellate Body, 6 November 1998.

Panel Report, *Japan – Measures Affecting Consumer Photographic Film and Paper*, WT/DS44/R, 31 March 1998.

Panel Report, *European Communities – Measures Concerning Meat and Meat Products (Hormones)*, complaint by the United States of America, WT/DS26/R/USA; complaint by Canada, WT/DS48/R/CAN, adopted as modified by the Appellate Body, 13 February 1998.

Panel Report, *United States – Standards for Reformulated and Conventional Gasoline*, WT/DS2/R, adopted as modified by the Appellate Body Report, 20 May 1996.

WTO appellate body reports

Appellate Body Report, *United States – Measures affecting the Production and Sale of Clove Cigarettes*, WT/DS406/AB/R, adopted 24 April 2012.

Appellate Body Report, *Australia – Measures Affecting the Importation of Apples from New Zealand*, WT/DS367/AB/R, adopted 17 December 2010.

Appellate Body Report, *Canada – Continued Suspension of Obligations in the EC – Hormones Dispute*, WT/DS321/AB/R, adopted 14 November 2008.

Appellate Body Report, *United States – Continued Suspension of Obligations in the EC Hormones Dispute*, WT/DS320/AB/R, adopted Nov.14, 2008.

Appellate Body Report, *United States – Countervailing Duty Investigation on Dynamic Random Access Memory Semiconductors (DRAMS) from Korea*, WT/DS296/AB/R, adopted 20 July 2005.

Appellate Body Report, *European Communities – Conditions for the Granting of Tariff Preferences to Developing Countries*, WT/DS246/AB/R, adopted 20 April 2004.

Appellate Body Report, *Japan – Measures Affecting the Importation of Apples*, WT/DS245/AB/R, adopted 10 December 2003.

Appellate Body Report, *Korea – Measures Affecting Imports of Fresh, Chilled and Frozen Beef*, WT/DS161/AB/R, WT/DS169/AB/R, adopted 10 January 2001.

Appellate Body Report, *Canada – Certain Measures Affecting the Automotive Industry*, WT/DS139/ AB/R, WT/DS142/AB/R, adopted 19 June 2000.

Appellate Body Report, *Japan – Measures Affecting Agricultural Products*, WT/DS76/AB/R, adopted 19 March 1999.

Appellate Body Report, *Australia – Measures Affecting Importation of Salmon*, WT/DS18/AB/R, adopted 6 November 1998.

Appellate Body Report, *European Communities – Measures Concerning Meat and Meat Products (Hormones)*, WT/DS26/AB/R, WT/DS48/AB/R, adopted 13 February 1998.

Appellate Body Report, *European Communities – Regime for the Importation, Sale and Distribution of Bananas*, WT/DS27/ AB/R, adopted 25 September 1997.

EU judgments

Joined Cases C-402/05 P and C-415/05 P, *Yassin Abdullah Kadi and Al Barakaat International Foundation v. Council of the European Union and Commission of the European Communities* [2008] ECR I-06351.

Joined Cases C-439/05 P and C-454/05 P *Land Oberosterreich and the Republic of Austria v. Commission* [2007] I-7141.

Table of cases   xiii

Case T-229/04, *Sweden v. Commission (Paraquat)* [2007] ECR 2437.
Case T-19/01 *Chiquita Brands International, Inc. and Others v. Commission of the European Communities* [2005] ECR II-00315.
Case 236/01 *Monsanto Agricoltura Italiana SpA and Others v. Presidenza del Consiglio dei Ministri and Others* [2003] ECR I-8105.
Case 192/01 *Commission v. Denmark* [2003] ECR 9693.
Case C-93/02 P, *Biret International v. Council* [2003] ECR I-10497.
Joint cases: T-76/00, T-83/00, T-84/00, T-85/00, T-132/00, T-141/00 and T-144/00 *Artegodan GmbH and Others v. Commission* [2002] ECR 4945.
Case T-70/99 *Alpharma Inc. v. Council of the European Union* [2002] ECR II-O3495.
Case T-13/99, *Pfizer Animal Health SA v. Council of the European Union* [2002] ECR II-03305.
Case C-377/98 *Kingdom of Netherlands v. European Parliament and Council of the European Union* [2001] ECR I-07079.
Case C-1/00 *Commission v. France* [2001] ECR I-9989.
Case E-3/00 *EFTA Surveillance Authority v. Norway* [2001] EFTA Court Report 2000/2001.
Case C-120/97 *Upjohn Ltd v. The Licensing Authority established by the Medicines Act 1968 and others* [1999] ECR I-223.
Case C-149/96, *Portugal v. Council* [1999] ECR I-8395.
Case C-157/96 *The Queen v. the Minister for Agriculture, Fisheries and Food and the Secretary of State for Health, ex parte: National Farmers' Union and Others* [1998] ECR I-2211.
Case C-157/96 *The Queen v. the Minister for Agriculture, Fisheries and Food and the Secretary of State for Health, ex parte: National Farmers' Union and Others* [1998] ECR I-2211.
Case C-162/96 *Racke GmbH & Co. v. the Hauptzollamt Mainz* [1998] ECR I-3655.
Case C-180/96 *United Kingdom of Great Britain and Northern Ireland v. Commission of the European Communities* [1998] ECR I-2265.
Case C-341/95 *Gianni Bettati v. Safety Hi-Tech Srl* [1998] ECR I-04355.
Case T-115/94, *Opel Austria v. Council of the European Union* [1997] ECR II-39.
Joined Cases C-13/91 and C-113/91, *Criminal proceedings v. Michel Debus* [1992] ECR I-03617.
Case C-35/89 *Commission v. Italian Republic (nitrates)* [1992] ECR I-4545.
Case C-69/89, *Nakajima All Precision Co. Ltd v. Council* [1991] ECR I-2069.
Case C-331/88 *The Queen v. the Minister for Agriculture, Fisheries and Food and the Secretary of State for Health, ex parte: Fedesa and Others* [1990] ECR I-4023.
Case 70/87, *Federation de l'industrie de l'huilerie de la CEE (Fediol) v. Commission* [1989] ECR 1781.
Case 68/86 *United Kingdom of Great Britain and Northern Ireland v. Council of the European Communities* [1988] ECR 855.
Case 298/87 *Proceedings for compulsory reconstruction v. Smanor SA* [1988] ECR 4512.

Case 178/84, *Commission v. Germany (Rheinheitsgebot)* [1987] ECR 1227.
Case 304/84 *Ministere public v. Claude Muller and Others* [1986] ECR 1511.
Case 35/84 *Commission v. Italy (health checks on the imports of curds)* [1986] ECR 545.
Case 247/84 *Criminal Proceedings v. Leon Motte* [1985] ECR 3887.
Case 15/83 *Denkavit Nederland v. Hoofdproduktschap voor Akkerbouwprodukten* [1984] ECR 2171.
Case 174/82, *Criminal proceedings v. Sandoz BV* [1983] ECR 2445.
Case 53/80 *Officer van justitie v. Koninklijke Kaasfabriek Eyssen BV* [1981] ECR 409.
Case C-87/75 *Conceria Daniele Bresciani v. Amministrazione dellefinanzedello Stato* [1976] ECR I00129.

Introduction

Food safety is not simply a matter of concern to consumers, the food industry, and public administration. It is not just an interest worth protecting. Food safety is a fundamental right that is clearly derived from other fundamental rights such as the right to life, human dignity, the right to protection of health, and the right to consumers' protection.[1]

I.1 Introduction

In June in 2011 Europe woke up to the news of a widespread food-borne outbreak of *Escherichia coli* (E. Coli) caused by the consumption of fresh sprouted fenugreek seeds. The seeds were found to originate from Egypt. In its wake the outbreak, described as the biggest in Europe for decades, left over 3,000 cases of infection and 50 deaths. The outbreak led to the European Union (EU) banning imports of leguminous vegetables from Egypt, along with imports of certain types of seeds.[2] However, EU vegetable exports were also banned from its main markets, notably from the Russian Federation, causing a loss of over one billion Euros to EU farmers.[3]

In 2009 the United States of America (US) commenced legal proceedings against the EU at the World Trade Organization (WTO) in *EC – Poultry (US)*.[4]

---

1 Miguel A Recuerda, 'Food Safety: Science, Politics and the Law' (2006) 1 *European Food and Feed Law Review* 1.
2 European Commission Health and Consumers Directorate-General, 'Rapid Alert System for Food and Feed (RASFF): Annual Report 2011' 16–17 (RASFF Annual Report, 2011).
3 European Commission Health and Consumers Directorate-General, 'Lessons Learned from the 2011 Outbreak of Shiga Toxin-Producing Escherichia Coli (STEC) O104:H4 in Sprouted Seeds, SANCO/13004/2011, 2011' 11–12, <http://ec.europa.eu/food/food/biosafety/salmonella/docs/cswd_lessons_learned_en.pdf> accessed 10 January 2014.

For further analysis see Tim Knowles, Richard Moody and Morven G McEachern, 'European Food Scares and their Impact on EU Food Policy' (2007) 109 (1) *British Food Journal* 43–67.
4 WTO Dispute DS389 of 2009, '*European Communities – Certain Measures Affecting Poultry Meat and Poultry Meat Products from the United States*'. The panel was established on 19 November 2009 but not yet composed to date.

2   *Introduction*

The US alleged that since 2002 the EU had prohibited the import of poultry that had been processed with chemical treatments (pathogen reduction treatments or PRTs) designed to reduce the amount of microbes on the meat, effectively prohibiting the shipment of virtually all US poultry to the EC.[5] The EU has not lifted the ban on PRTs to date.

In September 2008 some popular Chinese brands of powdered milk formula were found to be contaminated by melamine, an industrial chemical used as a binding agent for plastics and glue. The incidence led to the death of 6 infants and the hospitalisation of 52,000, with a further 250,000 estimated to have suffered mild kidney and urinary problems.[6] The EU reacted to the scare by banning the importation of Chinese milk products into the EU.[7]

In 2013 there were 99 EU border detentions of horticultural exports from Africa. These products were found to contain pesticide residues above the prescribed maximum levels.[8] The EU acknowledged:

> The banning of many active substances in pesticide formulations in the EU has placed particularly developing countries in a difficult spot to comply with the new and strict legal requirements in the EU. The authorities face the problem of controlling compliance by the often small scale producers supplying produce that is exported to the EU.[9]

To the extent that each of the above incidents was perceived to be a threat to human health, the resultant remedial measures had serious impacts on international trade of agricultural products with attendant negative economic consequences. These incidents raise the dilemma of the balance between protecting human life while at the same time ensuring that such protection does not hinder international trade of agricultural products. Moreover, this raises the issue as to what international means are available to ensure that countries do not use such human health protection measures as a disguised means of protecting their own agricultural producers or to unnecessary hinder international trade in such products.

Furthermore, the above incidents pose questions as to the effect of these human health protection measures on developing countries' agricultural products exports to developed countries: Are developing countries able to meet developed

---

5   For background information and analysis of the facts of the dispute see Renee Johnson, *U.S. – EU Poultry Dispute on the Use of Pathogen Reduction Treatments (PRTs)* (Congressional Research, USA Congressional Research Service, CRS Report for Congress No. 7–5700, 2015).
6   Xiaofang Pei and others, 'The China Melamine Milk Scandal and Its Implications for Food Safety Regulation' (2011) 36 *Food Policy* 412.
7   Denis Coulombier and others, 'Melamine Contamination of Dairy Products in China – Public Health Impact on Citizens of the European Union' (2008) 13 *Euro Surveillance*.
8   European Commission Health and Consumers Directorate-General, 'Rapid Alert System for Food and Feed (RASFF): Annual Report 2013', 17–18 (RASFF Annual Report, 2013).
9   RASFF Annual Report 2013, 18.

countries' import requirements for agricultural products? What is the impact of these requirements on developing countries' agricultural products exports to developed countries?

The significance of the above incidents becomes apparent when it is noted that international trade in agricultural products constitutes about 10 per cent of world merchandise trade and about 28.6 per cent of world primary products trade. Exports of food products account for 83 per cent of this trade.[10] For many developing countries, particularly in Sub-Saharan Africa, agriculture is their main source of employment, gross domestic product (GDP), exports, and foreign exchange earnings.[11] With a degree of difference, up to 65 per cent of developing countries' rural populations are employed in agriculture and about 29 percent of their gross domestic product (GDP) is attributable to agriculture.[12] On the other hand, the EU is the world's leading importer and exporter of both agricultural and food products.[13]

To address the issues arising from situations such as illustrated by the above incidents, the World Trade Organization (WTO)[14] enacted the Agreement on the Application of Sanitary and Phytosanitary Measures (SPS Agreement).[15] The main objective of the SPS Agreement is to discipline WTO Members' Sanitary and Phytosanitary Measures (SPS standards), which may directly or indirectly affect international trade.

This book is about WTO Members' SPS standards, in particular their food safety standards, and their impact on international trade and the role of the WTO and the SPS Agreement in disciplining such standards. The book seeks to do this by way of a case study of the role of SPS standards in the food products trade between the EU and the Common Market for Eastern and Southern Africa (COMESA).[16]

---

10 WTO, 'International Trade Statistics 2013', 52, 61 and 64, <https://www.wto.org/english/res_e/statis_e/its2013_e/its13_toc_e.htm> accessed 4 October 2014.
11 Evdokia Moise, *Estimating the Constraints to Agricultural Trade of Developing Countries* (OECD Trade Policy Papers, COM/DCD/TAD (2012) 16/REV2, No. 142, OECD Publishing, 2012) 7–9.
12 The World Bank, *World Development Report 2008: Agriculture for Development* (The World Bank, Washington, DC, 2007) 3.
13 European Commission, 'Monitoring Agri-Trade Policy: Agricultural Trade in 2013: EU Gains in Commodity Exports, MAP 2014-1, 2014', <http://ec.europa.eu/agriculture/trade-analysis/map/2014-1_en.pdf> accessed 10 January 2014.
14 WTO, *The Marrakesh Agreement Establishing the World Trade Organization, The Legal Texts, The Results of the Uruguay Round of Multilateral Trade Negotiations* (Cambridge University Press, 2004) 4–14 (WTO Agreement).
15 Reprinted in Ibid 59–72 (SPS Agreement).
16 COMESA is composed of 19 Member states: Burundi, Comoros, Democratic Republic of Congo, Djibouti, Egypt, Eritrea, Ethiopia, Kenya, Libya, Madagascar, Malawi, Mauritius, Rwanda, Seychelles, Sudan, Swaziland, Uganda, Zambia and Zimbabwe. COMESA was initially established in 1981 as the Preferential Trade Area for Eastern and Southern Africa (PTA). The PTA was transformed into COMESA in 1994 and notified to the WTO, under the Enabling Clause, in 1995. COMESA achieved a Free Trade Area (FTA) in 2000 and became a Customs Union in June 2009.

I.2 Why SPS standards?

At the end of the Second World War, high tariffs were seen to be the main hindrance to international trade. Hence, the main objective of the General Agreement on Tariffs and Trade (GATT)[17] was the facilitation of trade among Members through the reduction of tariffs. Consequently, between January 1948, when it became applicable, and January 1995, when it was supplanted by the World Trade Organization (WTO Agreement),[18] the GATT 48 managed, through successive negotiating rounds, to reduce tariffs on industrial products from over 40 per cent, on average, to less than 4 per cent, on average.[19] As tariffs decreased with each negotiating round, so did their importance as barriers to trade. In their place non-tariff barriers to trade in the form of technical regulations and SPS standards assumed greater importance.

SPS standards affect international trade in three ways.[20] First, SPS standards may prohibit imports or exports by banning such imports or exports or by imposing temporary restrictions such as seasonal access or quarantine periods. Second, SPS standards may divert trade through discriminatory regulations that favour one supplier over others. Third, SPS standards may reduce trade by increasing costs or raising barriers for potential traders.[21]

Even where standards are neutral, they may impede trade due to differences in national standards: where a standard applies equally to both domestic and imported products, the costs of compliance by importers may be higher, and as a result of differences in conformity assessment procedures, an importer may be faced with multiple assessments and tests, in addition to domestic ones, thereby increasing compliance costs.[22]

There are differences in SPS standards between developed and developing countries: the former have stricter standards than the latter, which, more often than not, lack such standards.[23] As a result, developing countries incur higher costs in meeting the strict SPS standards of developed countries than they do

---

17 Reprinted in WTO (n 14) 423–492 (GATT).
18 The WTO Agreement.
19 Peter Van den Bossche, *The Law and Policy of the World Trade Organization* (Cambridge University Press, 2005) 81–82.
20 Spencer Henson and others, *Impact of Sanitary and Phytosanitary Measures on Developing Countries* (University of Reading, Department of Agricultural and Food Economics, 2000) 18–19.
21 For analysis see Timothy E Josling, Donna Roberts and David Orden, *Food Regulation and Trade: Towards a Safe and Open Global System* (Institute of International Economics, Washington, DC, 2004) 17–24.
22 Spencer Henson and Rupert Loader, 'Impact of Sanitary and Phytosanitary Standards on Developing Countries and the Role of the SPS Agreement' (1999) 15 *Agribusiness* 356, 358–360.
23 Jha Veena, 'Introduction' in V. Jha (ed) *Environmental Regulation and Food Safety: Studies of Protection and Protectionism* (Edward Elgar and IDRC, 2006) 1–12.

in meeting their own standards.²⁴ To the extent that developed countries' SPS standards are stricter than those of developing countries and impose higher compliance costs on developing countries, these standards amount to barriers on developing countries' exports. Moreover, developing countries perceive developed countries' standards as protectionist, serving as barriers to their food and agricultural trade, most particularly to the detriment of small producers.²⁵ Broadly, developing countries have three main concerns with regard to the SPS standards of developed countries: that these standards may be protectionist; that developing countries lack the technical and administrative capacities and resources to comply with these standards, or that compliance costs render their goods uncompetitive; and that poor and small countries and producers will be locked out of the developed countries' markets.²⁶

Moreover, the global significance and importance of SPS standards to international trade is demonstrated by the adoption of the WTO SPS Agreement; the creation of the Codex Alimentarius Commission (Codex), the International Office of Epizootics (OIE), and the International Plant Protection Convention (IPPC) as international organisations dedicated to the formulation of international standards; and the adoption of Codex, IPPC, and OIE standards as international SPS standards. The significance of SPS standards to developing countries' agricultural food exports is evidenced by the activities of international organisations such as the World Bank,²⁷ the United Nations Conference on Trade and Development (UNCTAD),²⁸ the Standards and Trade Development Facility (STDF),²⁹ the Food and Agriculture Organization of the United Nations (FAO),³⁰ and the World Health Organization (WHO).³¹

---

24 Miet Maertens and Johan F M Swinnen, *Transformations in Agricultural Markets: Standards and Their Implications* (Leuven Interdisciplinary Research Group on International Agreements and Development, Working Paper No. 11–2006) 10, <https://ghum.kuleuven.be/ggs/publications/working_papers/archive/wp11.pdf> accessed 12 February 2015.
25 Steven Jaffee (ed), *Food Safety and Agricultural Health Standards: Challenges and Opportunities for Developing Country Exports* (Poverty Reduction and Economic Management Unit and Agriculture and Rural Development Department, Report No. 31207, The World Bank, Washington, DC, 2005) 3–4.
26 Steven Jaffee and Spenser Henson, *Standards and Agro-Food Exports from Developing Countries: Rebalancing the Debate* (World Bank Policy Research Paper No. 3348, 2004) 2–3.
27 See, for example, the World Bank's research project: Challenges and Opportunities Associated with International Agro-Food Standards and the project report: Food Safety and Agricultural Health Standards: Challenges and Opportunities for Developing Country Exports. <http://go.worldbank.org> accessed 12 February 2015.
28 See, for example, UNCTAD's research on standards as reviewed in its Journal: Trade and Environment Review, 2006, >www.unctad.org> accessed 12 February 2015.
29 See, for example, STDF's research on Africa's SPS standards and its report: Regional Sanitary and Phytosanitary Frameworks and Strategies in Africa, <www.standardsfacility.org/> accessed 12 February 2015.
30 FAO website <www.fao.org/> accessed 12 February 2015.
31 WHO website <www.who.int/en/> accessed 12 February 2015.

6 *Introduction*

In light of the above, and given that agriculture and trade in its products plays a significant role in developing countries' economies, the understanding of the role of SPS standards in the trade of agricultural products from developing countries is crucial.

I.3 Why the EU and the COMESA?

By virtue of being the world's leading importer and exporter of agricultural products, the EU is also the world's largest importer and exporter of food and beverages.[32] Food and beverages constitute about 5 per cent of the EU total imports and exports,[33] and the food and beverages industry is an important contributor to the EU economy.[34]

The EU is the COMESA's biggest trading partner.[35] Agriculture and agricultural commodities are the backbone of the COMESA economy,[36] and food and agricultural products constitute an important share of EU–COMESA trade.[37] The stakes are high in the trade of African agricultural products as whole, according to the African Union:

> The potential for agriculture and agricultural trade to reduce poverty in Africa is enormous. This is only possible if producers are able to access markets for agricultural products. Without adequate and timely access to markets, many

---

32 Eurostat, 'Statistics Explained: International Trade in Goods', <http://ec.europa.eu/eurostat/statistics-explained/index.php/International_trade_in_goods> accessed 20 February 2015.
    Food and beverages are defined as consisting of live animals; meat; dairy products; fish; cereals; vegetables and fruit; sugar and honey; coffee, tea, cocoa, and spices; animal feeds; miscellaneous edible products; beverages; and tobacco.
33 Ibid. Fruits and vegetables constitute 26 per cent, fish 20 per cent and meat 6 per cent of the food and beverage trade.
34 FOODDRINK Europe, Annual Report 2014 (2015), <http://www.fooddrinkeurope.eu/> According to FOODDRINK Europe, the European food and drinks industry organisation, the food and beverages industry purchases and processes 70 per cent of EU agricultural production, contributes 14 per cent of EU manufacturing sector turnover, and generates 14 per cent of the total jobs in EU manufacturing.
35 COMESA, 'International Trade Statistics Bulletin No. 12, September 2013', 9–10. The EU accounts for 32 per cent of COMESA exports and 22 per cent of COMESA imports.
36 COMESA, 'COMESA Regional CAADP Compact, April 2010', 13–14, <http://www.fanrpan.org/documents/d00926/COMESA_Regional_Compact_April2010.pdf> accessed 20 February 2015. Agriculture accounts for more than 32 percent of GDP for COMESA, employs 70 percent of the region's labour force and provides a livelihood to over 80% of the region's population.
37 Eurostat, 'EU trade with the Common Market for Eastern and Southern Africa (COMESA)', (2015), <http://ec.europa.eu/eurostat/statisticsexplained/index.php/EU_trade_with_the_Common_Market_for_Eastern_and_Southern_Africa_(COMESA)> accessed 20 February 2015. In 2014 the biggest share of COMESA exports to the EU consisted of petroleum and petroleum products, at 62 per cent of total exports while agricultural and food products made up 12 per cent.

poor people cannot benefit from a growing global market. Access to international markets for agricultural products requires compliance with World Trade Organization (WTO) Sanitary and Phytosanitary (SPS) measures that are designed to promote fair trade and to protect human, animal or plant life or health. Many African countries are still confronted with constraints to fully comply with the SPS measures and so cannot take advantage of the preferential market access offered by the EU (. . .).[38]

Furthermore, with the COMESA food products enjoying a duty- and quota-free status in the EU market, SPS standards are, potentially, the only remaining barrier to market access.[39]

I.4 Objectives and scope

This book sets out to critically evaluate the EU food safety standards, as a case study of developed countries' SPS standards, and their interaction with food exports from the COMESA, as a case study of developing countries' SPS standards. More specifically this book has five objectives. First, to analyse the provisions of the WTO SPS Agreement, particularly its scientific requirements provisions, and to assess the Agreement's impact on developing countries. Second, to analyse the EU's food safety standards and to find out whether these standards are in conformity with the provisions of the SPS Agreement and international standards, especially the standards set by the Codex. Third, to examine the particular EU food safety standards applied to horticulture, fish, and beef products and their impact on imports of these products from COMESA countries. Fourth, to scrutinise food safety standards in COMESA countries and to ascertain whether these standards are in conformity with international and EU standards. Fifth, to propose a legal SPS framework to be applied to the EU-COMESA trade in agricultural products.

The scope of this book encompasses the WTO SPS Agreement, WTO and international SPS institutions, and WTO Appellate and Panel decisions touching on the SPS Agreement. The scope will include EU food safety standards and their development; decisions of the Court of Justice of the EU (CJ) and General Court (GC); and COMESA countries' food safety standards. However, other areas of WTO, EU, and COMESA law, save where such areas might be relevant, are excluded. In particular, technical standards and regulations under the WTO TBT Agreement are not covered. Moreover, the case study aspect is limited to

---

38 Rhoda P Tumusiime, Commissioner for Rural Economy and Agriculture at the African Union Commission, on the occasion of the opening ceremony of the meeting of the chief veterinary officers of the African Union Member states, 5th to 6th may 2009, Nairobi, Kenya. <www.africa-union.org/> accessed 12 February 2015.

39 UNCTAD, *Private-Sector Standards and National Schemes for Good Agricultural Practices: Implications for Exports of Fresh Fruit and Vegetables from Sub-Saharan Africa Experiences of Ghana, Kenya, and Uganda* (United Nations, New York and Geneva, 2008) 17.

8 *Introduction*

SPS standards as they apply to EU–COMESA trade in horticultural, fish, and beef products: these are the COMESA countries' main tradable products.

I.5   Plan of this book

This book proceeds as follows. Chapter 1 examines the SPS Agreement. The chapter begins with an examination of the scientific disciplines of the SPS Agreement. These disciplines include risk assessment; appropriate level of protection (ALOP); scientific evidence; provisional measures; and the precautionary principle. Developing countries are placed in the context of the SPS Agreement through its provisions for technical assistance and special and differential treatment. The chapter concludes by critiquing the SPS Agreement from the perspective of developing countries. Ultimately, the Agreement is found to be facing a number of challenges that must be overcome if it is to achieve its objectives.

Chapter 2 turns to the examination of food safety standards in the EU. The EU, like every other WTO Member, is entitled to set its own level of protection, however high. Furthermore, the EU has chosen a high level of protection for the health of its citizens, which is not negotiable. The chapter examines of the framework regulation, Regulation 178 of 2002, and the European Food Safety Authority (EFSA). It analyses the EFSA's pivotal role in the EU food safety regime, its institutional set up, and its relations with the European Commission, with the Codex, and with national governments. EU food safety standards tend to be more stringent than the SPS Agreement's sanctioned Codex standards. This has resulted in trade concerns being raised in the SPS Committee on EU SPS standards and led to the two SPS disputes against the EU in the DSB. The chapter maps out and discusses the main controversial aspects of the EU food safety policy. These aspects concern its consideration of other factors in its risk analysis policy and its application of the precautionary principle. The controversy revolves around the question as to whether they are conforming to the requirements of the SPS Agreement and the Codex, the chapter's main conclusion being that the EU food safety standards, regardless of their socio-political underpinning, or because of this, are contestable in view of the scientific disciplines of the SPS Agreement.

Chapter 3 delves into the state of COMESA countries' food safety control systems. More particularly, after finding that there is no regional COMESA food safety control system, the chapter examines whether those countries' food safety control systems conform to the requirements of the SPS Agreement and to the standards of the Codex. The chapter finds that a majority of COMESA countries lack food control systems, and for those countries with some form of food safety control system, they are faced with a number of major challenges. Based on this analysis, the chapter goes on to examine whether the COMESA countries' food safety control systems have the capacity to meet the requirements of EU food safety regulations, and finds that a majority of COMESA countries lack the capacity to do so. The chapter concludes with an examination of the COMESA SPS regulations. The regulations are COMESA's response to its SPS challenges. The regulations are largely tailored upon the SPS Agreement, on its objectives and principal provisions. Upon examination, the regulations are found to be deficient in key aspects, such as the lack of institutional provisions and failure to adapt the regulations to regional and national conditions.

Chapter 4 examines the EU food safety regulations at play in the EU–COMESA food trade in the horticultural, beef, and fisheries products trade. The chapter discusses COMESA trade concerns with EU regulations on the importation of these products and the impact the regulations have had on their importation. COMESA countries find the EU regulations to be stringent and burdensome. Even more grievous is the EU shifting of the burden of implementing the regulations to the food business operators who are thereby compelled to institute private voluntary standards (PVS) in order to ensure compliance. These PVS and their compliance costs are viewed by COMESA countries as onerous and barriers to their exports.

Chapter 5 proposes and examines a model food control system for EU–COMESA trade. The proposed EU–COMESA food control system is viewed as a bridge between the two divergent food safety regimes that will facilitate the food trade between the two regions. Given that there is no COMESA food control system, the chapter first proposes a model COMESA food control system. Then it proposes a joint EU–COMESA food control system as a solution to the standards divide between COMESA and the EU.

Chapter 6 summarises the book's arguments and draws conclusions from them.

1 SPS standards under the WTO SPS Agreement

The decades-long process of lowering trade barriers resembles the draining of a lake that reveals mountain peaks formerly concealed or (more pessimistically) the peeling of an onion that reveals innumerable layers of barriers.[1]

1.1 Introduction

One of the successes of the General Agreement on Tariffs and Trade of 1947 (GATT)[2] was that in each successive round of negotiations[3] there was a further reduction in tariffs.[4] Consequently, starting from the Kennedy Round (1964–1967), this led to a shift in focus, from reducing tariffs to tackling non-tariff barriers to trade. The concern was increasingly on trade barriers 'within the border', as opposed to 'barriers at the border'.[5] The most important of these non-tariff barriers are sanitary and phytosanitary standards (SPS standards) enacted for protecting human, animal, and plant health and safety, and the environment. SPS standards are aimed at addressing risks from microbial pathogens, pesticides, and

---

1 Kahler Miles, 'Trade and Domestic Differences' in Berger Suzanne and Ronald P Dore R (eds) *National Diversity and Global Capitalism* (Cornell University Press, 1996) 298, 299.
2 The General Agreement on Tariffs and Trade, reprinted in *The Legal Texts, The Results of the Uruguay Round of Multilateral Trade Negotiations* (Cambridge University Press, 2004) 423–492 (GATT).
3 GATT, *40th Anniversary: A 40 Years Chronology of Events and Achievements* (GATT/40/2, 30-10-1987).
4 Ibid. The first six rounds of negotiations were focused on tariff reductions, mainly in industrial goods. By the Kennedy round, there was an average reduction of 50 per cent in tariffs from their 1948 levels. By the Tokyo round the weighted average tariff on manufactured goods in the world's nine major industrial markets declined from 7 per cent to 4.7 per cent.
5 Michael J Trebilcock and Robert Howse, *The Regulation of International Trade* (3rd edn, Routledge, 2005) 201. According to the authors: 'The WTO and many other trading arrangements have been largely successful in reducing both levels of tariffs worldwide and the scale of other border measures such as quotas. This has revealed a new and more subtle category of measures which restrict trade – the numerous common-place regulations which governments enact to protect the health and safety of their citizens and the environment in which they live'.

veterinary pharmaceuticals; environmental contaminants, mycotoxins, and the spread of plant pests and animal diseases.

Where SPS standards are applied for the protection of human health and safety, they are deemed to be food safety standards. Food safety standards are an important species of SPS standards.

SPS standards are paradoxical. On the one hand, they are considered to be protective of human, animal, and plant health and safety. Yet on other hand, they are perceived to be potential or actual barriers to trade in food and agricultural products.[6] The latter position has so far given rise to several international trade disputes under the World Trade Organization (WTO) SPS Agreement: *EC – Hormones*;[7] *Australia – Salmon*;[8] *Japan – Agricultural Products*;[9] *Japan – Apples*;[10] *EC – Biotech*;[11] *US – Continued Suspension*;[12] *Canada – Continued*

---

6 Donna Roberts, 'Preliminary Assessment of the Effects of The WTO Agreement on Sanitary and Phytosanitary Trade Regulations' (1998) 1 *Journal of International Economic Law* 377.
7 Panel Report, *European Communities Measures Concerning Meat and Meat Products (EC-Hormones)*, complaint by the United States of America, WT/DS26/R/USA, adopted as modified by the Appellate Body, 13 February 1998 [*Panel Report, EC- Hormones (US)*]; Panel Report, European Communities Measures Concerning Meat and Meat Products (Hormones), complaint by Canada, WT/DS48/R/CAN, adopted as modified by the Appellate Body, 13 February 1998 [*Panel Report, EC- Hormones (Canada)*]; Appellate Body Report, European Communities – Measures Concerning Meat and Meat Products (Hormones) WT/DS26/AB/R, WT/DS48/AB/R, adopted 13 February 1998 (*Appellate Body Report, EC – Hormones*).
8 Panel Report, *Australia – Measures Affecting Importation of Salmon*, WT/DS18/R, adopted as modified by the Appellate Body, 6 November 1998 (*Panel Report, Australia – Salmon*); Appellate Body Report Australia – Measures Affecting Importation of Salmon, WT/DS18/AB/R, adopted 6 November 1998 (*Appellate Body Report, Australia – Salmon*).
9 Panel Report, *Japan – Measures Affecting Agricultural Products*, WT/DS76/R, adopted as modified by the Appellate Body Report, 19 March 1999 (*Panel Report Japan – Agricultural Products*); Appellate Body Report, *Japan – Measures Affecting Agricultural Products*, WT/DS76/AB/R, adopted 19 March 1999 (*Appellate Body Report, Japan – Agricultural Products*).
10 Panel Report, *Japan-Measures Affecting the Importation of Apples*, WT/DS245/R, adopted as modified by the Appellate Body Report, 10 December 2003 (*Panel Report, Japan – Apples*); Appellate Body Report, Japan – Measures Affecting the Importation of Apples, WT/DS245/AB/R, 26 November 2003 (*Appellate Body Report, Japan – Apples*).
11 Panel Reports, *European Communities-Measures Affecting the Approval and Marketing of Biotech Products*, Complaint by the United States of America, WT/DS291/R; Complaint by Argentina, WT/DS292/R; Complaint by Canada, WT/DS293/R, adopted 26 November 2006 (*Panel Reports – EC-Biotech*).
12 Panel Report, *United States – Continued Suspension of Obligations in the EC Hormones Dispute*, WT/DS320/R, adopted as modified by the Appellate Body, 14 November 2008 (*Panel Report, United States – Continued Suspension of Obligations in the EC Hormones Dispute*); Appellate Body Report, *United States – Continued Suspension of Obligations in the EC Hormones Dispute*, WT/DS320/AB/R, adopted 14 November 2008 (*Appellate Body Report, United States – Continued Suspension of Obligations in the EC Hormones Dispute*).

Suspension;[13] *EC – Poultry(US)*;[14] *US – Poultry (China)*;[15] *Australia – Apples*;[16] and *US – Animals*.[17]

In *EC – Hormones*, the EU, claiming that beef from cattle treated with growth hormones was harmful to human health, banned the use of growth hormones in livestock rearing and also banned beef imports produced from cattle that had received these hormones. The effect of the EU ban was a virtual ban on all beef imports from the complainants, United States of America (US) and Canada, because they produced most of their beef with the use of the banned growth hormones.[18]

In *Australia – Salmon*, Australia banned the importation of dead salmon unless it was treated in such a way as to prevent the introduction of contagious diseases or pests that would affect humans, plants, or animals. The complainant, Canada, could not export uncooked, wild, adult, ocean-caught Pacific salmon to Australia because of the ban. Australia justified the ban on the sanitary protection of its local fish stocks.[19]

In *Japan – Agricultural Products*, Japan, claiming to protect the health of its plants from certain pests, banned the importation of varieties of agricultural products (mainly fruits, and in particular apples) on which it claimed that a pest, the Codling Moth, might occur until such time as each variety had been separately quarantined and tested with respect to the efficacy of treatment with a chemical (methyl bromide) or treatment with the chemical and cold storage. For each agricultural product that required quarantine treatment, Japan banned

---

13 Panel Report, *Canada – Continued Suspension of Obligations in the EC Hormones Dispute*, WT/DS321/R, adopted as modified by the Appellate Body, 14 November 2008 (*Panel Report, Canada – Continued Suspension of Obligations in the EC Hormones Dispute*); Appellate Body Report, *Canada – Continued Suspension of Obligations in the EC Hormones Dispute*, WT/DS321/AB/R, adopted 14 November 2008 (*Appellate Body Report, Canada – Continued Suspension of Obligations in the EC Hormones Dispute*).
14 WTO Dispute: DS389 of 2009: *European Communities – Certain Measures Affecting Poultry Meat and Poultry Meat Products from the United States* [*EC – Poultry (US)*]. The panel was established on 19 November 2009 but has not yet been composed to date.
15 Panel Report, *United States – Certain Measures Affecting Imports of Poultry from China*, WT/DS392/R, adopted 25 October 2010 [*Panel Report, US–Poultry (China)*].
16 Panel Report, *Australia – Measures Affecting the Importation of Apples from New Zealand*, WT/DS367/R, adopted as modified by the Appellate Body, 17 December 2010 (*Panel Report, Australia – Measures Affecting the Importation of Apples from New Zealand*); Appellate Body Report, *Australia – Measures Affecting the Importation of Apples from New Zealand*, WT/DS367/AB/R, adopted 17 December 2010 (*Appellate Body Report, Australia – Measures Affecting the Importation of Apples from New Zealand*).
17 Panel Report, *United States – Measures Affecting the Importation of Animals, Meat and Other Animal Products from Argentina*, WT/DS447/R, adopted 24 July 2015.
18 For analysis of the dispute see Vern R Walker, 'Keeping the WTO from becoming the "World Trans-Science Organization": Scientific Uncertainty, Science Policy, and Fact Finding in the Growth Hormones Dispute' (1998) 31 *Cornell International Law Journal* 251.
19 For analysis of the dispute see Frank J Garcia, 'The Salmon Case: Evolution of Balancing Mechanisms for Non-Trade Values in WTO', in George A Bermann and Petros C Mavroidis (eds) *Trade and Human Healthand Safety* (Cambridge University Press, 2006).

the importation of each variety of that product until the quarantine treatment had been tested for that variety, even though the treatment had proven effective with respect to other varieties of the same product. This effectively banned the importation of most varieties of apples from the US, which was the complainant.[20]

In *Japan – Apples*, Japan applied quarantine restrictions on US apples imported into Japan to protect against the introduction of a plant disease known as Fire Blight. Japan prohibited the importation of US apples unless they were produced, harvested, and imported according to Japan's Fire Blight restrictions. It imposed nine requirements that had to be satisfied before imports of US apples could be permitted. The US complained that Japan could not restrict the importation of apples without scientific evidence that exported apples could transmit the disease.[21]

In *EC – Biotech*, the US, Argentina, and Canada complained against a general and individual products moratorium applied by the EU since October 1998 on the approval of biotech products that restricted imports of their agricultural and food products. Furthermore, the complainants claimed that some EU Member states had maintained national marketing and import bans on their biotech products even though those products had already been approved by the EU for import and marketing in the EU.[22]

In *EC – Poultry (US)*, the US complained about EU regulations on the importation of poultry meat and poultry meat products. EU defines 'poultry meat' as only 'poultry meat suitable for human consumption, which has not undergone any treatment other than cold treatment'. The EU prohibits the import of poultry meat and poultry meat products treated with any substance other than water unless that substance has been approved by the EU. However, the EU has not established the process for approving such substances. Furthermore, the EU prohibits the import and marketing of poultry meat and poultry meat products that have been processed with chemical treatments designed to reduce the amount of microbes on poultry meat. The US complained that these measures effectively ban the imports of US poultry meat and poultry meat products to the EU, since it uses chemical treatments to reduce the amount of microbes on poultry meat.[23]

In *US – Poultry (China)*, the US Congress restricted the ability of the United States Department of Agriculture and its agency, the Food Safety and Inspection

---

20 For analysis of the dispute see Joseph P Whitlock, 'Japan – Measures Affecting Agricultural Products: Lessons for Future SPS and Agricultural Trade Disputes' (2001) 33 *Law and Policy in International Business* 741.
21 For analysis of the dispute see Damien J Neven and Joseph H H Weiler, 'Japan – Measures Affecting the Importation of Apples (AB-2003-4): One Bad Apple? (DS245/AB/R): A Comment' (2006) 5 *World Trade Review* 280.
22 For analysis of the dispute see Robert Howse and Henrik Horn, 'European Communities – Measures Affecting the Approval and Marketing of Biotech Products' (2009) 8 *World Trade Review* 49.
23 For analysis of the dispute see Renee Johnson, *U.S.- EU Poultry Dispute on the Use of Pathogen Reduction Treatments (PRTs)* (Congressional Research, USA Congressional Research Service, CRS Report for Congress No. 7–5700, 2015).

Service, to use funds allocated by the US Congress for the purpose of establishing or implementing a rule permitting the importation of poultry products from China into the United States. China complained that this regulation effectively banned the importation of its poultry products.[24]

In *Australia – Apples*, Australia imposed 16 measures aimed at protecting its plants' health from the introduction of plant diseases through the importation of apples from New Zealand. New Zealand complained against the measures as being inconsistent with the requirements under the SPS Agreement.[25]

In *US – Continued Suspension* and *Canada – Continued Suspension*, the EU complained that the US and Canada had failed remove their retaliatory measures once the EU had removed the measures found to be WTO-inconsistent in *EC – Hormones*.[26]

In *US – Animals*, the United States maintained an import prohibition on all Foot-and-Mouth disease (FMD) susceptible animals and animal products from Argentina imposed following an outbreak of FMD in Northern Argentina in 2001. Argentina complained against the prohibition; the failure by the US to recognise certain areas of Argentina's territory as free of FMD; and the undue delays in recognizing the animal health status of an Argentinian region or in granting approval to export animals or animal products from that region.

The above disputes reveal another paradox. Although under Article 3.3 of the SPS Agreement, Members have a right to establish SPS standards that meet their chosen level of appropriate protection, and that right has been affirmed by the Appellate Body,[27] the complaints were largely upheld (except in *US – Continued Suspension* and *Canada – Continued Suspension*) by the dispute Panels and Appellate Body of the WTO. Hence, on the one hand Members are assured of their right to maintain SPS standards according to their own chosen level of protection. But on the other hand, whenever such standards have been challenged by

---

24 For analysis of the dispute see Christophe Charlier, 'Distrust and Barriers to International Trade in Food Products: An Analysis of the US–Poultry Dispute' GREDEG Working Paper No. 2012–02, University of Nice-Sophia Antipolis, <www.gredeg.cnrs.fr/working-papers/GREDEG-WP-2012–02.pdf> accessed 13 March 2015; Brendan McGivern, 'WTO Panel Report: United States – Poultry from China', 4 October 2010, <www.whitecase.com/files/Publication/76702638-6bd6-4da9-9a0ffefd971df892/Presentation/PublicationAttachment/bcb92415-b1fc-4cf7-b9e9-03cab1216b00/Article_WTO_Panel_Report_United_States_Poultry_from_China.pdf> accessed 13 March 2015.
25 For analysis of the dispute see Simon A B Schropp, 'Commentary on the Appellate Body Report in Australia–Apples (DS367): Judicial Review in the Face of Uncertainty' (2012) 11 *World Trade Review* 171.
26 For analysis of the dispute see Bernard Hoekman and Joel Trachtman, 'Continued Suspense: EC – Hormones and WTO Disciplines on Discrimination and Domestic Regulation Appellate Body Reports: Canada/United States – Continued Suspension of Obligations in the EC–Hormones Dispute, WT/DS320/AB/R, WT/DS321/AB/R, adopted 14 November 2008' (2010) 9 *World Trade Review* 151.
27 *Appellate Body Report, EC – Hormones*, para 172.

fellow Members, the dispute Panels and Appellate Body have found them wanting and their scientific underpinnings deficient.[28]

Several preliminary lessons may be gleaned from the disputes. First, SPS standards are sometimes perceived to be an impediment to international trade in food and agricultural products, even when they are apparently neutral, due to difficulties faced by exporters in navigating through the different national SPS standards. Second, national SPS standards differ not only in their formulation but also in their application and may therefore hinder trade either in their formulation or in their application. Third, each country enacts SPS standards reflecting such matters as its own food and agricultural practices and culture; its experiences with food safety issues; its capacity and willingness to control these risks; and its consumers' perceptions, preferences, and demands. This increases the possibility of conflicts between these differing standards. Fourth, developed countries, led by the EU, have, in comparison with developing countries, enacted more stringent and problematic SPS standards. Fifth, a majority of the disputes are between developed countries. This reflects the importance of agricultural trade in developed countries and also the fact that even developed countries are challenged by fellow developed countries' SPS standards. The absence of developing countries as parties in these disputes, save for China and Argentina, is notable. A ready explanation might be their lack of capacity to initiate complaints at the WTO.[29] These factors have resulted in differing SPS standards across the globe, with different requirements that have to be met by exporters.

A further consequence of the above differences is that food and agricultural products exporters face the immediate costs associated with meeting these different standards, going against economies of scale, and affecting the competitive environment in which they operate. As illustrated above, differences in SPS standards among countries can precipitate international trade disputes and interfere with international trade in food and agricultural products.[30]

---

28 Joan Scott, *The WTO Agreement on Sanitary and Phytosanitary Measures: A Commentary* (Oxford University Press, 2007) 3.
29 Gregory Shaffer, 'How to Make the WTO Dispute Settlement System Work for Developing Countries: Some Proactive Developing Country Strategies' (ICTSD Resource Paper No. 5, 2003) 15. For a comparative analysis see Gregory Shaffer and Ricardo Melendez-Ortiz R (eds) *Dispute Settlement at the WTO: The Developing Country Experience* (Cambridge University Press, 2014).
30 Jean C Buzby and Laurian Unnevehr, 'Introduction and Overview', in Jean C Buzby (ed) *International Trade and Food Safety: Economic Theory and Case Studies* (United States Department of Agriculture (USDA), Agricultural Economic Report No. 828, 2003) 1, 5. The authors argue that differences in SPS measures may lead to trade disputes arising from the following grounds. First, new or more stringent standards and rapidly changing food safety regulations. Second, the difficulty of separating the roles of food safety and non-science issues in regulation enactment. Third, difficulties in determining equivalence in process standards. Fourth, the role of consumer risk perceptions and preferences in risk regulations. Sixth, new or unfamiliar hazards. Seventh, new or less proven product sources.

16 SPS standards under WTO SPS Agreement

Since the GATT came into force, there has been a proliferation of SPS standards.[31] This has led, on the one hand, to a need for international disciplines to mediate the inherent conflict between international trade liberalisation in food and agricultural products, as part of global trade liberalisation and, on the other hand, to a need for states to protect the health of their citizens, animals, and plants from risks posed by imported food and agricultural products.[32]

Despite the enactment of the SPS Agreement, developing countries continue to be challenged by developed countries' SPS standards. The developing countries view developed countries' SPS standards as too stringent, inappropriate, not based on international standards, and of protectionist intent. Since it came into existence, achievement of the aim of the SPS Agreement – to discipline members' SPS measures – has had mixed results. The disputes under the SPS Agreement serve to illustrate the deep-rooted problems involving SPS standards. The SPS Agreement's reliance on scientific evidence as a basis for SPS measures has also proved controversial, not least because of the uncertainty of science itself.[33] It is clear that new solutions must be identified to address these negative developments. SPS standards continue to play a vital role in the international trade of food and agricultural products, with a significant impact on countries' economies.

This chapter offers a critical analysis of the SPS Agreement, in particular its scientific requirements provisions. It discusses the nature of the scientific disciplines of the SPS Agreement and their impact, particularly on developing countries.

The chapter begins by considering, in part 2, the significance, nature, and form of standards, and their impact on international trade. Part 3 discusses the WTO SPS Agreement and its scientific disciplines. The Agreement's scientific

---

31 Denise Prevost and Peter Van den Bossche, 'The Agreement on the Application of Sanitary and Phytosanitary Measures' in Arthur E Appleton and Michael G Plummer (eds), *The World Trade Organization: Legal, Economic and Political Analysis* (Springer, 2005) 231, 233. The authors attribute the proliferation of SPS measures to three factors:

> First, there has been an increase in the number and variety of potential risks contained in food and agricultural products due to both increasing use of new technologies in agriculture and food processing (such as pesticides, additives and genetic modification) and the growth in imports from developing countries whose domestic food-safety infrastructures are often inadequate. Second, rising consumer expectations and demands with regard to food standards in developed countries resulting from increased affluence and consumer awareness of food related risks and regulators responses to these concerns. Third, pressure from agriculture and food industry lobbies faced with increased competition due to agricultural trade liberalization forces regulators to enact more SPS measures. This results in the adoption of more and more SPS measures and market access for food and agricultural products is greatly reduced.

> Whereas the first two factors are legitimate, the third factor is illegitimate as it emanates from protectionist underpinnings. The problem arising from these factors is how to distinguish between SPS measures based on the first two legitimate factors from those that arise from the third protectionist factor.

32 Ibid.
33 Walker V R (n 18) 261–263.

disciplines include the concepts of risk assessment; the appropriate level of protection (ALOP); scientific evidence; provisional measures; and the precautionary principle. Part 4 discusses the all-important concepts of harmonisation and equivalence. The discussion encompasses the place of the SPS Agreement in international standardisation and the role of international organisations in the process. The examination of the SPS Agreement concludes, in part 5, with an analysis of the provisions in the SPS Agreement that concern developing countries. These include provisions for technical assistance and special and differential treatment. This is followed, in part 6, by a critique of the SPS Agreement and its main disciplines from the perspective of developing countries.

The chapter concludes by arguing that the Agreement faces many challenges that need to be overcome if it is to achieve its objectives. The major challenges are the slow harmonisation process, the problems faced by developing countries in meeting developed countries standards, and the persistence of SPS standards as non-tariff barriers.

1.2 The significance of SPS standards

International trade in food and agricultural products accounts for an average of 10 per cent of the world's trade in goods.[34] One notable characteristic of this trade is that it is not evenly spread out among countries and regions: some regions have a higher share than others.[35] In developing countries agriculture accounts for a large percentage of the gross domestic product (GDP) and employment: in Sub-Saharan Africa agriculture is on average 34 per cent of GDP and 64 per cent of the labour force; among Asian countries agriculture represents on average 20 per cent of GDP and 43 per cent of the labour force; and in Eastern Europe and Latin America agriculture comprises on average 8 per cent of GDP and 22 per cent of the labour force.[36] International trade in

---

34 WTO, 'International Trade Statistics 2013' 52, 61 and 64, <https://www.wto.org/english/res_e/statis_e/its2013_e/its13_toc_e.htm> accessed 4 October 2014.
35 Ibid. For example, the European Union constitutes the main export market for developing countries' agricultural products; for instance, importing 50 percent of Africa's agricultural products.
36 The World Bank, *World Development Report 2008: Agriculture for Development* (World Bank, Washington, DC, 2007) 27. See also, Merlinda D Ingco and John D Nash, 'What is at Stake? Developing-Country Interests in the Doha Development Round' in Merlinda D Ingco and John D Nash (eds) *Agriculture and the WTO: Creating a Trading System for Development* (The World Bank and Oxford University Press, 2004) 1–23, 4. The authors postulate:

> Agricultural growth is important for developing countries as it enhances overall economic growth, reduces poverty, improves food security and conserves natural resources. Furthermore, many of the world's poor depend on agriculture for their livelihoods and increased agricultural productivity provides cheaper food alleviating poverty further since food makes up a large share of expenditure of poor households. Also, a modernizing agriculture creates jobs in agricultural processing and marketing, and indirectly generates jobs for those leaving the farm. Agriculture thus contributes to economic

food and agricultural products also contributes significantly to the economies of developed countries.[37]

While it would appear that both developed and developing countries have a more or less equal interest in the liberalisation of international trade in food and agricultural products, the impact of this trade is greater on the latter than on the former. This is because developing countries' economies are predominantly, primarily, and directly dependent on food and agricultural products, while developed countries' economies are industrialised, and food and agricultural products serve as inputs for a section of their industries: the agro-processing industries. The situation is further complicated by developed countries' use of agricultural subsidies.[38] Subsidised farmers constitute a special interest group, lobbying governments to protect their markets, and they can exert pressure on domestic regulators to enact protectionist regulations, including SPS standards.

Some of the SPS standards enacted by developed countries have a potentially devastating effect on developing countries[39] and, where they diverge from international standards, may serve to block developing countries' food and

---

growth both directly, through greater production and exports, and indirectly, by raising demand in farm and rural communities for industrial goods and services.

37 See, for example, FOODDRINK Europe, 'Annual Report 2013', <www.fooddrinkeurope.eu/S=0/publication/fooddrinkeuropes-annual-report-2013/> accessed 4 October 2014.
According to FOODDRINK Europe, the food and beverages industry purchases and processes 70 per cent of EU agricultural production, contributes 14 per cent of EU manufacturing sector turnover, and generates 14 per cent of the total jobs in EU manufacturing.
38 OECD, *Agricultural Policy Monitoring and Evaluation 2011: OECD Countries and Emerging Economies* (OECD, Paris, 2011). According to the OECD New Zealand has the lowest level of government subsidies to agriculture in the OECD, at just 1 per cent of farm income, with some of the other countries faring as follows: Australia 3 per cent; Chile 4 per cent; USA 9 per cent; EU 22 per cent; South Korea 47 per cent; Iceland 48 per cent; Japan 49 per cent; Switzerland 56 per cent; and Norway 60 per cent. These subsidies serve to keep agricultural products' prices artificially high in the domestic market. Moreover the subsidies mainly benefit large farms. Furthermore the subsidies distort international trade and distort world prices of food and agricultural products.
39 For example, a World Bank study found that a 1998 European Union directive on Maximum Residue Levels for aflatoxin B1, a common contaminant in nuts and grains, would have cost African exporters US$700 million per year in lost nut and grain exports while reducing human health risks to 1.4 human lives per 1 billion. See Tsunehiro Otsuki, John S Wilson and Mirvat Sewadeh, *Saving Two in a Billion: A Case Study to Quantify the Trade Effect of European Food Safety Standards on African Exports* (The World Bank, Washington, DC, 2000) 18. Another study by the World Bank found that a 10 per cent increase in the regulatory stringency of the pesticide chlorpyrifos by 11 OECD countries led to a 1.48 per cent decrease in banana exports in 19 countries in Latin America, Asia, and Africa. Further, if the European Union level for pesticides were to be adopted, instead of the one set by Codex Alimentarius Commission, there would have been a loss of US$5.3 billion in world banana exports. See John S Wilson and Tsunehiro Otsuki, 'To Spray or not to Spray: Pesticides, Banana Exports, and Food Safety' (Policy Research Paper No. 2805, World Bank, Washington, DC, 2002) 21.

agricultural exports from entering the global market.[40] This would defeat the expansion principles of the production of, and trade in, goods and services, sustainable development, and the special and differential treatment for developing countries provided for in the WTO Agreement.[41] Of note is the recognition by WTO Members of the necessity for expansion of the production of and trade in goods and services. This underpins the other factors of increasing standards of living, full employment, incomes, and effective demand. Tariffs and other non-tariff barriers, including SPS standards, hinder the expansion of production of and trade in goods, and negate the principle. Furthermore, undermining the expansion principle with stringent or protectionist SPS standards weakens the principle of sustainable development, especially when these undermining standards are applied to developing countries, as they fail to take into account different levels of economic development.

Both developed and developing countries, being exporters as well as importers of food and agricultural products, have an interest in promoting fair SPS standards in the international trade of these products. As exporters, they both have an interest in SPS standards being no more stringent than necessary, and that these standards are not protectionist in their intent or application. As importers, they are both concerned that their SPS standards will ensure that imports of food and agricultural products do not pose unacceptable risks to the health and life of people, plants, or animals. Paradoxically, in as much as developing countries complain against developed countries' stringent SPS standards, developed countries also complain about developing countries' and other developed countries' SPS standards being barriers to their exports.[42]

---

40 John S Wilson and Victor O Abiola, 'Introduction' in John S Wilson and Victor O Abiola (eds) *Standards and Global Trade: A Voice for Africa* (The World Bank, Washington, DC, 2003) xxv, xxx.
41 WTO Agreement, paragraph 1 of the preamble provides:

> Recognizing that their relations in the field of trade and economic endeavor should be conducted with a view to raising standards of living, ensuring full employment and a large and steadily growing volume of real income and effective demand, and expanding the production of and trade in goods and services, while allowing for the optimal use of the world's resources in accordance with the objective of sustainable development, seeking both to protect and preserve the environment and to enhance the means for doing so in a manner consistent with their respective needs and concerns at different levels of economic development (. . .).

Further, paragraph 2 of the preamble provides: 'Recognizing further that there is need for positive efforts designed to ensure that developing countries, and especially the least developed among them, secure a share in the growth in international trade commensurate with the needs of their economic development (. . .)'.

Stringent or protectionist SPS standards violate the differential treatment principle enunciated in the second paragraph. These standards hinder developing countries' efforts to participate in international trade, which they need to do for their development.

42 See, for example, complaints by the EU and the US: European Commission, 'Market Access Database: Sanitary and Phytosanitary Issues', <http://madb.europa.eu/madb/sps_cross

1.2.1 The definition, nature, and form of SPS standards

SPS standards are enacted in the form of national regulations that govern the sale of food and agricultural products in a given national market. A standard may be broadly defined as 'a technical specification or set of specifications related to characteristics of a product or its manufacturing process'.[43] SPS standards are specifically defined under the WTO SPS Agreement Annex A (1) as follows:

Sanitary or phytosanitary measure – Any measure applied:

(a) to protect animal or plant life or health within the territory of the Member from risks arising from the entry, establishment or spread of pests, diseases, disease-carrying organisms or disease-causing organisms;
(b) to protect human or animal life or health within the territory of the Member from risks arising from additives, contaminants, toxins or disease-causing organisms in foods, beverages or feedstuffs;
(c) to protect human life or health within the territory of the Member from risks arising from diseases carried by animals, plants or products thereof, or from the entry, establishment or spread of pests; or
(d) to prevent or limit other damage within the territory of the Member from the entry, establishment or spread of pests.

Sanitary or phytosanitary measures include all relevant laws, decrees, regulations, requirements, and procedures including, *inter alia*, end product criteria; processes and production methods; testing, inspection, certification, and approval procedures; quarantine treatments including relevant requirements associated with the transport of animals or plants, or with the materials necessary for their survival during transport; provisions on relevant statistical methods, sampling procedures, and methods of risk assessment; and packaging and labelling requirements directly related to food safety.

SPS standards can be either voluntary (private) and set by private organisations (such as the Global Good Agricultural Practices [GlobalGAP] standard and the British Retail Consortium Global Standard for Food Safety [BRC standard]) or mandatory (public) and set by governments (these usually take the form of laws,

---

Tables.htm?table=countryproduct> accessed 10 April 2015; The Office of the United States Trade Representative (USTR), '2014 Report on Sanitary and Phytosanitary Measures', <www.ustr.gov/sites/default/files/FINAL-2014-SPS-Report-Compiled_0.pdf> accessed 10 April 2015.

43 Donna Roberts, Timothy E Josling and David Orden, *A Framework for Analyzing Technical Barriers in Agricultural Markets* (United States Department of Agriculture, Technical Bulletin No. 1876, March 1999) 3. The prima facie objective of such standard being: '(...) the correction of market inefficiencies stemming from externalities associated with the production, distribution, and consumption of these products', where an externality is defined as a direct and unintended side effect of an activity of one individual or firm on the welfare of other individuals or firms.

decrees, regulations, requirements, and procedures).[44] Mandatory standards may be classified by their implementing policy instrument, their scope of application, or their regulatory goals.[45] When markets function optimally, firms have incentive to supply products that are safe and of good quality, as this enhances their profitability because their reputations are critical for repeat sales. However, more often than not, markets fail, which leads to the supply of unsafe and bad quality products and consequential costs. This necessitates government intervention in the form of the enactment of mandatory standards.[46]

SPS standards are therefore potentially welfare enhancing because they may correct market failures stemming from externalities that arise from the importing of products that may be accompanied by pests or diseases, or from asymmetrically distributed product information.[47] However, not all government intervention is benign. Interest groups such as private businesses, consumer groups, and taxpayers often influence governments in the enactment of standards. Such regulatory capture aggravates existing market failures and leads to protectionism.[48] On the

---

44 Ibid. The authors, citing literature, opine that voluntary standards can effectively bar imports if they become standard business practice. This is more so where importers insist on compliance with voluntary standards as a precondition for accepting products. According to the World Bank, although mandatory standards continue to define trade and market access in food and agricultural products, private standards now rival the importance of these public standards. See also, Steven Jaffee (ed), *Food Safety and Agricultural Health Standards: Challenges and Opportunities for Developing Country Exports* (World Bank Report No. 31207, 2005) 4–5; Grace C Lee, *Private Food Standards and their Impacts on Developing Countries* (European Commission, DG Trade, Unit G2, Brussels, 2006) 6. The author further distinguishes between public (mandatory) and private (voluntary) standards in the European Union on the basis that the former prescribe 'equivalence of risk-outcome', where the characteristics of the finished product are specified and the producers and importers meet these, while the latter require 'equivalence of systems', where requirements are set for the entire system of production and supply to be met by producers.

45 Roberts D, Josling T E and Orden D (n 43) 6. According to the authors, policy instruments take the forms of the following:

> Bans, these may be total or partial; Mandatory technical specifications such as process or product standards; Informational remedies such as packaging standards and labeling requirements. The scope of the standard defines its application, either universal (applying to both domestic and imported products e.g. maximum pesticide residue levels) or specific (applying to imported products only e.g. bans imposed on importation of infected animals). The goal of the standard may be risk reduction, such as animal and plant health protection or food safety, or non-risk reduction such as quality attributes.

46 Lorraine Mitchell, 'Economic Theory and Conceptual Relationships between Food Safety and International Trade' in Jean C Buzby (ed) *International Trade and Food Safety: Economic Theory and Case Studies* (United States Department of Agriculture, Agricultural Economic Report No. 828, 2003) 10. The author points out that market failure occurs for two reasons: when consumers cannot determine how safe a product is before buying it; and when consumers become ill from consuming unsafe products – costs extend to the healthcare system, employers, and family members.

47 Roberts D (n 6) 378.
48 Jaffee S (ed.) (n 44) 9.

other hand, private standards are motivated by strategies geared towards meeting consumer demands, keeping and acquiring customers, economic efficiency, and gains among competing firms.[49]

1.2.2 The effect of SPS standards on international trade

SPS standards distort trade flows in three major ways: by imposing bans or prohibitive compliance costs; by their compliance costs acting to reduce trade flows; and by discriminating among producers.[50] Due to the pivotal role played by food and agricultural exports in developing countries, their economies are disproportionately affected by SPS standards relative to developed countries. Moreover, in the development of international SPS standards, developing countries – due to their limited participation and capacity in the standards-setting process – are 'standards takers', while developed countries, which dominate this process, are 'standards makers'.[51] As a result, developing countries perceive international and developed countries' SPS standards as marginalizing their food and agricultural trade, more particularly to the detriment of small producers.[52]

The complexity and lack of harmonisation of standards, even where they are apparently neutral, reinforces this view. A number of studies carried out appears to support this position.[53] Standards tend to increase developing countries'

---

49 Linda Fulponi, *Private Standard Schemes and Developing Country Access to Global Value Chains: Challenges and Opportunities Emerging from Four Case Studies* (OECD, AGR/CA/APM (2006) 20/FINAL, 3 August 2007).
50 Steven Henson and Rupert Loader, 'Impact of Sanitary and Phytosanitary Standards on Developing Countries and the Role of the SPS Agreement' (1999) 15 *Agribusiness* 355, 358–360. According to the authors, even where standards are neutral they may impede trade due to two standardisation factors: due to differences in national standards, where a standard applies equally to both domestic and imported products, the costs of compliance by importers may be higher; and as a result of differences in conformity assessment procedures, an importer may be faced with multiple assessments and tests, in addition to domestic ones, hence increasing compliance costs.
51 Sherry M Stephenson, *Standards and Conformity Assessment as Non-Tariff Barriers to Trade* (World Bank Policy Research Working Paper No.1826, 1997) 88. According to the author, though many developing countries are members of international standardisation bodies, they do not participate actively in their working committees. This is in contrast to developed countries, which actively participate in and dominate the activities of these bodies.
52 Jaffee S (ed.) (n 44) 3.
53 See, for example, David Orden and Euardo Romano, 'The Avocado Dispute and Other Technical Barriers to Agricultural Trade Under NAFTA' Conference on NAFTA and Agriculture: Is the Experiment Working, San Antonio, Texas, 18 November 1996, <http://agrinet.tamu.edu/trade/papers/orden.pdf> accessed 18 February 2015. The authors argue that the US longstanding ban of Mexican avocados was protectionist in intent and underpinned by the capture of the regulatory process by the California Avocado Commission, a trade body; Spencer Henson and Julie Caswell, 'Food Safety Regulation: An Overview of Contemporary Issues' (1999) 24 *Food Policy* 589, 599. The authors point out that standards are frequently inconsistent, are not based on science, but on consumer expectations and the fact that risk management decisions often vary between similar types of hazards; Stephenson

short-run production costs by requiring additional inputs of labour and capital.[54] Moreover, standards compliance costs are higher for developing countries than for developed countries.[55] This therefore reduces developing countries' comparative advantage in the production and trade of food and agricultural products, especially tropical products. Nevertheless, when standards are properly developed, operationalised, and enforced, they can play a role in overcoming market failures.[56]

S M (n 51) 87. The author cites the lack of infrastructure and human capital as factors contributing to developing countries poor performance in international standardisation; Veena Jha, 'Strengthening Developing Countries' Capacities to Respond to Health, Sanitary and Environmental Requirements: A Scoping Paper for South Asia' (UNCTAD, Geneva, April 2002) 33–34, <http://r0.unctad.org/trade_env/test1/meetings/standards/paper2.pdf> accessed 20 February 2015. The author argues that South Asia lacks the technology for testing and certification, personnel, and management skills required to meet developed countries' standards. There is also lack of clarity and transparency in the implementation of standards by developed countries, which frequently use standards for protectionist purposes and to bid down prices.

54 Xiaoyang Chen, Tsunehiro Otsuki and John S Wilson, 'Standards and Technical Regulations: Do They Matter to Export Success in Developing Countries?' (OECD workshop on: Standards and Conformity Assessment in Trade: Minimizing Barriers and Maximizing Benefits, Berlin, 21–22 November 2005) 80, <http://www2.chuo-u.ac.jp/office/econ/jeaf2005/program/docs/pm_18_5201c.pdf> accessed 20 February 2015. The authors find that testing procedures reduce export share by 9 per cent and the share increased to 16 per cent for domestically owned firms. They further find that testing procedures and lengthy inspection processes cause a larger adverse impact on agricultural firms, which produce highly perishable products. A significant finding of the research is that information barriers reduce firms' propensity to export by 18 per cent.

55 Miet Maertens and Johan F M Swinnen, 'Transformations in Agricultural Markets: Standards and Their Implications' (Leuven Working Paper No. 11–2006) 10, <https://ghum.kuleuven.be/ggs/publications/working_papers/archive/wp11.pdf> accessed 12 February 2015. According to the authors:

> Developing countries' compliance costs are higher because they generally have weak food safety capacities. They lack the institutional, technical and scientific capacity for food quality and safety management. There is generally a divergence between national food quality and safety norms and international standards. This standard divergence increases costs of compliance for developing countries. Lacking the financial means, some developing countries may find the compliance costs too high, undermining their competitive capacity.

This contrasts with developed countries, which have the capacities to set and apply standards.

56 Fernando H Casquet and Victor Abiola, 'The Role of Standards Under Kenya's Export Strategy' (Contribution to the Kenya Diagnostic Trade and Integration Study, The World Bank, Washington, DC, March 2005) 3–4, <http://siteresources.worldbank.org/INTEXPCOMNET/Resources/Kenya_Private_Sector-Lead_Change.pdf> accessed 30 March 2015. Standards are said to overcome market failures in various ways. First, by conveying information about products, such as safety and quality requirements, standards improve competition among producers and increase consumer capacity to choose between genuine and counterfeit products. Second, standards act as vehicles for the transfer of the technology embodied in them to developing countries. Third, standards promote the sustainable use and quality of environmental resources and improvement of living conditions. Fourth, standards

1.2.3 Comparing perspectives between developed and developing countries

Regulatory heterogeneity among states can, by itself, impede international trade. But determining when a domestic policy is benign and when it is protectionist is complex, given the apparent neutrality of some domestic policies. Such analysis may call for a normative standard of review for domestic policies within the overall framework of the international trade regime.

Among developed countries, there is concern that increased international disciplines of domestic regulations will lead to 'a race to the bottom' (where countries are forced to adopt laxer policies and regulations) – the so-called 'Delaware effect' – as opposed to 'a race to the top' (where countries are forced to adopt stricter or higher policies and regulations) – the so-called 'California effect'.[57] Free-trade advocates in the developed countries oppose the use of domestic regulations as barriers to trade, while consumers want to prevent free trade from limiting domestic regulation.[58] As a result of these competing forces, developed countries' standards and regulations have experienced the 'California effect'.[59] Developing countries, however, argue that the higher standards of the developed countries

---

help in the reduction of food-borne diseases by safeguarding public health. Fifth, standards facilitate developing countries to integrate into global supply chains. Developing countries enhance their capacities to meet developed countries' health and safety standards and by doing so create new forms of competitive advantages, new trade, new growth, and employment.

57 David Vogel, *Trading Up: Consumer and Environmental Regulation in a Global Economy* (Harvard University Press, 1997) 5–6. According to the author, 'Agreements and treaties to promote liberal trade policies have contributed to limiting the role of national regulations as trade barriers. And their authority over national regulatory standards is increasing. But trade liberalisation can just as easily be achieved by forcing nations with lower standards to raise them as by forcing nations with higher standards to lower them'. The former circumstances will lead to 'a race to the top' while the latter will lead to 'a race to the bottom'. The 'Delaware effect' is so named after the state of Delaware in the US. Delaware has the most liberal corporate chartering law among states in the US, and because states are required to recognise each other's charters, Delaware has been the most successful state in the issuance of charters. On the other hand, the 'California effect' refers to the state of California, the richest state in the US and the one with the most stringent environmental regulations, which has helped drive environmental regulations upwards in the US.

58 Ibid. See also Gunnar Trumbull, 'More Trade, Safer Products' (2000) 6 (2) *Swiss Political Science Review* 79, 89. The author argues that the growth of international trade tends to increase rather than decrease consumer protection in democratic societies; Bruce A Silverglade, 'The WTO Agreement on Sanitary and Phytosanitary Measures: Weakening Food Safety Regulations to Facilitate Trade?' (2000) 55 *Food and Drug Law Journal* 517, 520. The author points out that the international food safety standards are designed to facilitate trade and not protect public health and that a country only attracts sanctions for having higher standards, not low standards. Hence there is pressure to harmonise food safety regulations downwards.

59 See, for example, David Vogel and Robert A Kagan, *Dynamics of Regulatory Change: How Globalization Affects National Regulatory Policies* Vol 1 (University of California Press, 2004) 1–28. The authors find that there has been a 'California effect' in Europe as a result of the 'greener' countries forcing the European Union to harmonise product standards upwards to their levels.

are protectionist in intent because they are meant to protect their domestic producers from developing countries' more competitive products.[60]

Differences in domestic policies, regardless of protectionist intent, result in differences in competitiveness among the producers of different countries, and therefore distort trade.[61] The issue that arises is whether there are existing remedies and tools available to evaluate such non-tariff barriers.

1.2.4 Global administrative law perspectives

While SPS standards, as developed by national and regional governments and international organisations such as the Codex, IPPC, and OIE, are mainly

---

60 See, for example: Sungjoon Cho, 'Linkage of Free Trade and Social Regulation: Moving beyond the Entropic Dilemma' (2005) 5 *Chicago Journal of International Law* 625, 645. The author points out that under the principle of comparative advantage, producers in developed countries find it easier to comply with higher regulatory standards than developing countries producers since the former enjoy higher levels of technology. He further argues that cheap imports from developing countries are less a function of higher regulatory compliance costs for developed countries producers than of the lower labour costs of producers in developing countries; Jagdish Bhagwati, 'The Demands to Reduce Domestic Diversity among Trading Nations' in Jagdish Bhagwati and Robert E Hudec (eds) *Fair Trade and Harmonization: Prerequisites for Free Trade? Vol 1: Economic Analysis* (MIT Press, Cambridge, MA, 1996) 9, 10; Simonetta Zarrilli and Irene Musselli, 'The Sanitary and Phytosanitary Agreement, Food Safety Policies, and Product Attributes' in M D Ingco and J D Nash (eds) (n 36) 234, 215; Dale Andrew, Karim Dahau, and Ronald Steeenblik, 'Addressing Market Access Concerns of Developing Countries Arising from Environmental and Health Requirements: Lessons from National Experience' (OECD Trade Policy Paper, No.5, 2004) 5–6. The authors examine the trade concerns of developing countries in accessing OECD markets, which are as follows: lack of information on regulations; difficulties in meeting technical regulations and standards; difficulties in the procedures for developing standards and regulations; and mechanisms for implementation and periodic review of such measures; Spencer Henson and others, *Impact of Sanitary and Phytosanitary Measures on Developing Countries* (University of Reading, Department of Agricultural and Food Economics, 2000). The authors tabulate the main difficulties faced by African developing countries in exporting food products; among these are the prohibitive costs of compliance with the higher standards and regulations of developed countries; Jha Veena, 'Introduction' in V. Jha (ed) *Environmental Regulation and Food Safety: Studies of Protection and Protectionism* (Edward Elgar and IDRC, 2006) 10. The research project showed that in several cases exporters from developing countries perceive that standards and regulations applied in developed country markets are unjustified and are used for protectionist purposes for the following reasons. First, the severity of certain controls increases when prices in the domestic market of the importing country are low, and consequently imports are discouraged as they would further drag down the price. Second, scientific data for specific thresholds or limit values sometimes appear to be questionable. The fact that such threshold values vary widely between countries would seem to strengthen this point. Third, in some cases products that had earlier been refused were subsequently allowed into the domestic market at a lower price. Fourth, countries in the same region that share the same water or climatic conditions may be subject to differential degrees of standards.

61 Joel P Trachtman, 'International Regulatory Competition, Externalization, and Jurisdiction' (1993) 34 *Harvard International Law Journal* 47, 64–65. The author poses the question as to which of these regulatory differences GATT should discipline and how should it do so. In other words, where should the balance be struck between regulatory competition and cooperation.

concerned with international trade law, they also give rise to concerns on the process of their development and implementation: How legal, transparent, and accountable is the process? How participatory is the process? Does it involve all that are impacted by the standards, among them consumers, producers, governments, and their citizens (both in developed and developing countries)? Is the process subject to review? These concerns fall within the purview of global administration law (GAL).[62]

GAL has been defined as

> comprising the mechanisms, principles, practices, and supporting social understandings that promote or otherwise affect the accountability of global administrative bodies, in particular by ensuring they meet adequate standards of transparency, participation, reasoned decision, and legality, and by providing effective review of the rules and decisions they make.[63]

Under GAL the issue that arises is how and to what extent are these accountability concerns addressed in the WTO and the international standard-setting organisations. GAL thus provides necessary checks and balances on these organisations' operational procedures for conformity with its principles.[64] Moreover, these organisations strive to meet their obligations under GAL through such provisions as each Member state having one vote, decisions being taken by consensus or in case of default by majority vote,[65] and the due process procedures under the WTO Understanding on rules and procedures governing the settlement of disputes (DSU);[66] the IPPC dispute settlement procedures;[67] and the OIE informal

---

62 For an overview see Sabino Cassese and others (eds), *Global Administrative Law Cases, Materials, Issues* (2nd edn, Institute for Research on Public Administration (IRPA) and Institute for International Law and Justice (IILJ), 2008).
63 Benedict Kingsbury, Nico Krisch and Richard B Stewart, 'The Emergence of Global Administrative Law' (2005) 68 (15) *Law and Contemporary Problems*, 15, 17.
64 Andrew D Mitchell and Elizabeth Sheargold, 'Global Governance: The World Trade Organization's Contribution' (2009) 46 *Alberta Law Review* 1061, 6. See also Carol Harlow, 'Global Administrative Law: The Quest for Principles and Values' (2006) 17 *European Journal of International Law* 187.
65 WTO Agreement, art ix; Procedural Manual of the Codex Alimentarius Commission (22nd edn, FAO/WHO, Rome, 2014 (Codex Procedural Manual, 2014), Rules of Procedure, r viii; International Plant Protection Convention, Procedural Manual (IPPC Procedural Manual, 2011 Edition), art xi (9); Procedures used by the OIE to set Standards and Recommendations for International Trade, 2.
66 Reprinted in *The Legal Texts The Results of the Uruguay Round of Multilateral Trade Negotiations* (Cambridge University Press, 2004) 354–379. For analysis of the DSU see Claus D Ehlermann and Nicolas Lockhart, 'Standard of Review in WTO Law' (2004) 17 *Journal International Economic Law* 491; Michael M Du, 'Standard of Review under the SPS Agreement after EC-Hormones II' (2010) 59 *International and Comparative Law Quarterly* 441.
67 IPPC Convention (1997 Edition), art XIII and the IPPC Dispute settlement Manual, 25 June 2014.

mediation procedure.⁶⁸ The WTO SPS Agreement goes further to embrace GAL principles such as transparency,⁶⁹ and consultations and dispute settlement.⁷⁰

However, the WTO and the international standard-setting organisations have been criticised for being undemocratic and unaccountable to their members, for not adequately representing or reflecting the will of their members, and for suffering from the so called 'democratic deficit'.⁷¹ For example, the EU has expressed strong reservations on the mandate of the WTO thus:

> It is not the function of the WTO Agreement to allow one group of countries to impose its values on another group. Nor is it the purpose of the WTO Agreement to trump the other relevant rules of international law which permit – or even require – a prudent and precautionary approach (. . .).⁷²

The EU has similarly contested the legitimacy of the Codex procedures.⁷³ Indeed the notion that Codex standards have a binding force upon adoption is questionable.⁷⁴

Moreover, although most developing countries lack the financial and scientific capacity to participate effectively in the standards-setting processes of the Codex, IPPC, or OIE, they are bound by the standards that are approved.⁷⁵ Besides, where the standards are approved by a majority vote and not consensus and yet they are binding on all Member states, the ensuing standards suffer from a democratic and legitimacy deficit. Equally, developing countries were constrained under the single undertaking principle of the Uruguay round (every item of the

---

68 OIE Terrestrial Animal Health Code, 24th edn (2015), cha 5.3.8.
69 SPS Agreement, art 7 and Annex B.
70 SPS Agreement, art 11.
71 Alois Stutzer and Bruno S Frey, 'Making International Organizations More Democratic' (2005) 1 *Review of Law and Economics* 305, 306; Sanford Levinson, 'How the United States Constitution Contributes to the Democratic Deficit in America' (2007) 55 *Drake Law Review* 859, 860. For further analysis see also Daphne Barak-Erez and Oren Perez, 'Whose Administrative Law Is It Anyway? How Global Norms Reshape the Administrative State' (2013) 46 *Cornell International Law Journal* 455.
72 European Communities, 'First Written Submission in EC – Measures Affecting the Approval and Marketing of Biotech Products (17 May 2004)' para 10, <http://trade.ec.europa.eu/doclib/docs/2004/june/tradoc_117687.pdf.> accessed 30 February 2015. See also Robert Howse and Petros C Mavroidis, 'Europe's Evolving Regulatory Strategy for GMOs-the Issue of Consistency with WTO Law of Kine and Brine' (2000) 24 *Fordham International Law Journal* 317.
73 Marielle D M Matthee, *The Codex Alimentarius Commission and Its Standards* (T.M.C. Asser Press, The Hague, 2007) 202.
74 Ibid 205. For analysis see Filippo Fontanelli, 'ISO and CODEX Standards and International Trade Law: What gets Said is not What's Heard' (2011) 60 *International and Comparative Law Quarterly* 895, 905–915.
75 Ravi Afonso Pereira, 'Why Would International Administrative Activity Be Any Less Legitimate? – A Study of the Codex Alimentarius Commission' (2008) 9 *German Law Journal* 1693, 1709–1710.

negotiation was part of a whole and individual package and could not be agreed to separately) to consent to all the WTO agreements despite their well-known capacity deficits in the trade negotiations.[76] Furthermore, the large number of negative rulings against Member states' SPS standards in the WTO have raised issues of Member states' sovereignty versus the mandate of the WTO, particularly under the scientific requirements of its SPS and TBT Agreements.[77]

In as much as the WTO and the international standards-setting organisations are contributors to the principles and values of GAL, the standards emanating from them, including SPS standards, are subject to the disciplines of GAL. Hence, the procedures for the setting, enforcement, and adjudication of SPS standards need to conform to the principles of GAL. On the other hand, GAL itself is subject to criticism on a number of fronts particularly its Western lineage and its imposition of global values on developing countries which may not necessarily carry favour with their citizens or cultures and hence lead to them not being implemented.[78]

1.3 The WTO SPS Agreement

1.3.1 Overview

The SPS Agreement aims at balancing the liberalisation of international trade in food and agricultural products and the right of Members to protect human, animal, and plant life or health within their territories. It seeks to achieve this aim by ensuring that Members' SPS measures are not applied in a manner that would constitute a means of arbitrary or unjustifiable discrimination among Members where the same conditions prevail, or a disguised restriction on international trade.[79] It lays down norms for the adoption, maintenance, and application of SPS measures that elaborate on the provisions of Article XX (b) of the General Agreement on Tariffs and Trade of 1994 (GATT 1994),[80] particularly the introductory clause of Article XX.[81]

---

76 Mitchell A and Sheargold E (n 64) 16–17.
77 Alan O Sykes, 'Domestic Regulation, Sovereignty, and Scientific Evidence Requirements: A Pessimistic View' (2002) 3 *Chicago Journal of International Law* 353, 364.
78 Harlow C (n 64) 209–211.
79 SPS Agreement, preamble, para 1. Hence the SPS Agreement's main objective is positive harmonisation, as opposed to the negative harmonisation of the GATT. See also Veijo Heiskanen, 'The Regulatory Philosophy of International Trade Law' (2004) 38 (1) *Journal of World Trade* 1, 14. According to the author, 'This conceptual move represents a shift from a system based on the liberalisation of international trade, or trade between nations, to a system based on the establishment of a global marketplace. As a result of this conceptual shift in the underlying philosophy of the multilateral trading system, the need to regulate the emerging global marketplace arises almost by logical necessity'.
80 Reprinted in *The Legal Texts, The Results of the Uruguay Round of Multilateral Trade Negotiations* (Cambridge University Press, 2004) 17–30. GATT 1994 adopts the provisions of GATT 47 by its art 1 (a).
81 SPS Agreement, preamble, para 8. The preamble and para (b) of art xx GATT provides:

> Subject to the requirement that such measures are not applied in a manner which would constitute a means of arbitrary or unjustifiable discrimination between countries where the

The SPS Agreement is anchored on scientific-validity tests to a greater extent than its broader sister, the Agreement on Technical Barriers to Trade (TBT Agreement).[82] The substantive requirements of the SPS Agreement provide for a normative basis for SPS measures, while the procedural provisions facilitate the decentralised policing of such measures.[83] It requires the SPS measures to be based on science, and the science must be demonstrated in the form of risk assessment.[84] Members are further encouraged to harmonise their standards in accordance with international standards set by the Codex, the OIE, and the IPPC.[85] Where SPS measures conform to international standards, they are presumed to be consistent with the relevant provisions of the SPS Agreement and the GATT 1994,[86] but where they deviate from international standards, they must provide scientific justification in the form of risk assessment.[87] Members are required to accept other Members' SPS measures as the equivalent of their own as long as it is objectively demonstrated that they meet the importing Members' level of protection.[88] They must adapt their measures to the SPS characteristics of the relevant exporting and importing country or region and to recognise the concepts of pest- or disease-free areas and areas of low pest or disease prevalence.[89] Interested Members must be provided with notification of new or amended SPS measures and to provide reasonable periods for Members to adapt to them.[90] Members must also administer their control, inspection, and approval procedures so that they are no more burdensome, lengthy, or costly than is reasonable and

---

same conditions prevail, or a disguised restriction on international trade, nothing in this Agreement shall be construed to prevent the adoption or enforcement by any contracting party of measures: (. . .) (b) necessary to protect human, animal or plant life or health.

The SPS Agreement incorporates and elaborates these provisions under its provisions: under paragraph one of the preamble, the provisions are reiterated. Under art 2.2, SPS measures must be necessary to protect human, animal, and plant health or life. Under art 2.3, SPS discriminative SPS measures and measures that are applied so as to constitute disguised restriction on trade are prohibited. Under arts 5.4 and 5.6, SPS measures may not be more trade restrictive than required to achieve a chosen level of protection and must aim at minimizing negative trade effects. Under art 5.5, Members may not make arbitrary or unjustified distinctions in the levels of protection they deem appropriate in different but comparative situations. Under art 2.4, SPS measures that are in conformity with the provisions of the Agreement are presumed to be in accordance with art xx (b).

82 Reprinted in *The Legal Texts, The Results of the Uruguay Round of Multilateral Trade Negotiations* (Cambridge University Press, 2004) 121–142. See also, David A Wirth, 'The Role of Science in the Uruguay Round and NAFTA Trade Disciplines' (1994) 27 *Cornell International Law Journal* 817, 825.
83 Roberts D (n 6) 282.
84 SPS Agreement, arts 2.2 and 5.
85 Ibid, art 3.
86 Ibid, art 3.2.
87 Ibid, art 3.3.
88 Ibid, art 4.
89 Ibid, art 6.
90 Ibid, art 7 and Annex B.

necessary.[91] The Agreement also provides for technical assistance[92] and special and differential treatment for developing countries.[93]

1.3.2 The scientific disciplines of the SPS agreement

Scientific tests lie at the core of the SPS Agreement's disciplines.[94] Science constitutes a 'normative yardstick' for evaluating national SPS standards.[95] The SPS Agreement endeavours to use science to distinguish between legitimate and illegitimate SPS measures.[96] Under Article 2.2, Members are enjoined not to maintain SPS measures 'without sufficient scientific evidence (...)'. Under Article 5.1, Members are to ensure that their SPS measures are based on a risk assessment as defined under Annex A paragraph 4. Articles 5.2 and 5.3 set out the factors to be taken into consideration in a risk assessment. Article 5.7 provides for SPS measures where 'relevant scientific evidence is insufficient'. With a view to harmonisation, Article 3.1 provides that SPS measures are to be based on international standards, with particular exceptions.

Article 2.2 contains three elements to be fulfilled by an SPS measure: First, the measure must be applied only to the extent necessary to protect human, animal, or plant life or health. Second, the measure must be based on scientific principles. Third, the measure must not be maintained without sufficient scientific evidence, except as provided for under Article 5.7.

1.3.3 SPS measures to be applied only to the extent necessary to protect human, animal, or plant life or health

The necessity test under Article 2.2 may be understood, by way of analogy, to entail the following criteria: first, that no alternative measure consistent with the provisions of the SPS Agreement is reasonably available; and second, that the factors to be considered in determining necessity include the contribution made by the measure to the aim it pursues, the importance of the common interest of values protected by the measure, and the trade restrictive effect of the measure.

Further, the trade restrictive aspect of the necessity criteria is elaborated under Article 5.6 of the SPS Agreement, which provides: 'Members shall ensure that

---

91 Ibid, art 8 and Annex C.
92 Ibid, art 9.
93 Ibid, art 10.
94 Wirth D A (n 82) 825. For further analysis see Lukasz Gruszczynski, 'The Role of Science in Risk Regulation Under the SPS Agreement' (EUI Law Working Paper No. 2006/03), <http://ssrn.com/abstract=891114> accessed 30 April 2015; S R Subramanian, 'Science-Based Risk Regulation Under the SPS Agreement of the WTO: An Appraisal Post-US/Canada Continued Suspension of Obligations in the EC-Hormones Dispute' (2015) 24 (3) *European Energy and Environmental Law Review* 55.
95 Jacqueline Peel, 'Risk Regulation under the WTO SPS Agreement: Science as an International Normative Standard?' (NYU School of Law, Jean Monnet Working Paper No 2/2004) 96, <www.jeanmonnetprogram.org/archive/papers/04/040201.pdf> accessed 30 April 2015.
96 Walker V R (n 18) 256.

such measures are not more trade-restrictive than required to achieve their appropriate level of sanitary or phytosanitary protection, taking into account technical and economic feasibility'.

The Appellate Body in *Australia – Salmon* held that the footnote to Article 5.6, echoing the 'reasonably available alternative' criterion of the necessity test, lays down a three-pronged test for such an alternative measure: First, there is another measure, reasonably available, taking into account technical and economic feasibility. Second, such a measure achieves the Member's appropriate level of sanitary or phytosanitary protection. Third, the measure is significantly less restrictive to trade.[97]

1.3.4 SPS measures to be based on scientific principles and not to be maintained without sufficient scientific evidence

The evidence to be considered under Article 2.2 of the SPS Agreement is that gathered by scientific method.[98] It includes evidence that a particular risk may occur as well as evidence that a particular requirement may reduce or eliminate that risk.[99] In a dispute examining the SPS Agreement, the Panel in *Japan – Apples* determined that scientific evidence might be direct or indirect, the only consideration being its probative value.[100]

The Appellate Body in *Japan – Agricultural Products* held that there must be an adequate relationship between the scientific evidence and the SPS measure in order to fulfil the sufficiency requirement. This will necessarily include risk assessment under the SPS Agreement's Article 5.1. Further, there must be a rational or objective relationship between the measure and the scientific evidence.[101]

The Panel in *Japan – Apples* went further to point out that 'we should not leave aside the fact that scientific evidence relates to a risk and is supposed to confirm the existence of a given risk'.[102] Thus sufficient scientific evidence ought to indicate the existence of a risk. The Panel also added a *proportionality* criterion to the 'rational or objective relationship between an SPS measure and the scientific evidence' requirement found by the *Japan – Agricultural Products* Appellate Body.[103]

1.3.5 Risk assessment

The scientific disciplines of the SPS Agreement are anchored on risk assessment. Risk assessment is a scientific process aimed at establishing the scientific basis for

---

97 *Appellate Body Report, Australia – Salmon*, para 194.
98 *Panel Report, Japan – Apples*, para 8.92.
99 Ibid.
100 Ibid, para 8.98.
101 *Appellate Body Report, Japan – Agricultural Products*, paras 73–74 and 84.
102 *Panel Report, Japan – Apples*, para 8.104.
103 Ibid, para 8.198. This was confirmed by the Appellate Body, *Appellate Body Report, Japan – Apples*, Paras 164–5.

SPS measures.[104] It is a process characterised by systematic, disciplined, and objective enquiry and analysis.[105]

The SPS Agreement defines two types of risk assessment under Annex A paragraph 4: first, the evaluation of the likelihood of entry, establishment, or spread of a pest or disease within the territory of an importing Member according to the sanitary or phytosanitary measures which might be applied and an assessment of the associated potential biological and economic consequences; and second, the evaluation of the potential for adverse effects on human or animal health arising from the presence of additives, contaminants, toxins, or disease-causing organisms in food, beverages, or feedstuffs.

The first type of risk assessment relates to risks arising from the entry, establishment, or spread of pests or diseases, and concerns the health and life of humans, plants, and animals. The second type applies to risks arising from additives, contaminants, toxins, or diseases present in food, beverages, or feedstuff, and applies only to human and animal health or life. Furthermore, the Appellate Body in *US/Canada – Continued Suspension* held that it is the prerogative of the Member to perform the risk assessment, and not the Panel.[106]

1.3.6 Risks arising from the entry, establishment, or spread of pests or diseases

The Panel in *Australia – Salmon* further clarified the risks to be determined under the first type of risk assessment, by breaking it into two broad categories: (1) the risk of 'entry, establishment or spread' of a disease, and (2) the risk of the 'associated potential biological and economic consequences'.

The Panel further distilled three essential elements to be fulfilled by such an assessment by a Member. First, identification of the disease(s) whose 'entry, establishment or spread' within its territory it wants to prevent as well as the 'associated potential biological and economic consequences'. Second, an 'evaluation of the likelihood' of entry, establishment, or spread of these diseases and of the associated potential biological and economic consequences. Third, the evaluation of the likelihood of entry, establishment, or spread of these diseases need be conducted 'according to the sanitary (. . .) measures which might be applied'.[107]

Moreover, where there are several diseases, the risk assessment must be specific to each disease and not general for all diseases.[108]

The Appellate Body concurred with the Panel's definitions and clarified further that the risk assessment should evaluate the 'likelihood' and the 'probability', and

---

104 *Panel Report, EC- Hormones (US)*, para 8.107; *Panel Report, EC-Hormones (Canada)*, para 8.110.
105 *Appellate Body Report, EC – Hormones*, para 187.
106 *Appellate Body Report U.S./Canada Continued Suspension*, para 590.
107 *Panel Report, Australia – Salmon*, para 8.72.
108 Ibid, para 8.74.

not the 'possibility', of entry, establishment, or spread of these diseases, as well as the associated potential biological and economic consequences.[109]

1.3.7 Risks arising from additives, contaminants, toxins, or diseases present in food, beverages, or feedstuff

The Panel in *EC – Hormones* set a two-step analysis for the second type of risk assessment: '(i) identify the adverse effects on human health (if any) arising from the presence of the hormones at issue when used as growth promoters in meat or meat products, and (ii) if any such adverse effects exist, evaluate the potential or probability of occurrence of these effects'.[110]

According to this Panel's analysis, the adverse effects (harm) are to be identified first, and then the potential or probability of the occurrence of these effects is to be evaluated. The Appellate Body in *EC – Hormones* went further, to hold that there must be proof of actual, not theoretical, risk, and that risk is not quantifiable in terms of a minimum threshold. Moreover, all that needs to be proved is that a measure is sufficiently supported or reasonably warranted by a risk assessment.[111]

The Appellate Body in *Australia – Salmon* distinguished the two types of risk assessment in terms of 'likelihood' and 'potential' thus, 'while the second requires only the evaluation of the potential for adverse effects on human or animal health, the first type of risk assessment demands an evaluation of the likelihood of entry, establishment or spread of a disease, and of the associated potential biological and economic consequences'.[112]

1.3.8 Appropriate to the circumstances

Under Article 2.2, SPS measures are to be 'based on scientific principles' and must not be 'maintained without sufficient scientific evidence'. These basic scientific obligations are specifically applied under Article 5.1. Therefore Article 2.2 informs and imparts meaning to Article 5.1.[113]

Consequently, SPS measures have to be based on a risk assessment as defined under Annex A paragraph 4 of the SPS Agreement, as appropriate to their circumstances and taking into account risk assessment techniques developed by the relevant international organisations. The Panel in *Australia – Salmon* found that the reference 'as appropriate to the circumstances (. . .) relates, rather, to the way risk assessment has to be carried out'.[114]

---

109 *Appellate Body Report, Australia – Salmon*, paras 121 and 123. The Appellate Body went on to clarify that the likelihood may be expressed either quantitatively or qualitatively – para 124.
110 *Panel Report, EC- Hormones (US)*, para 8.98; *Panel Report, EC- Hormones (Canada)*, para 8.101.
111 *Appellate Body Report, EC – Hormones*, para 186.
112 *Appellate Body Report, Australia – Salmon*, fn 69.
113 *Appellate Body Report, EC – Hormones*, para 180.
114 *Panel Report, Australia – Salmon*, para 8.70.

Accordingly, for a risk assessment to be appropriate to the circumstances, it must take into account the source and subject of the risk and be carried out on case-by-case basis in terms of product, origin, and destination, including country-specific situations. It must also take the risk assessment techniques of international organisations into consideration, as well as opinions of scientific experts. Further, an SPS measure may be based on a risk assessment carried out by another WTO Member or an international organisation.[115]

1.3.9 Factors to be taken into account in risk assessment

The Appellate Body in *EC – Hormones* characterised the risk to be taken into consideration in risk assessment as not only risk ascertainable in a science laboratory, but also risk in 'the real world where people live and work and die'.[116]

Articles 5.2 and 5.3 of the SPS Agreement describe the scientific and economic factors to be taken into account in a risk assessment. Article 5.2 requires the consideration of a number of broad scientific, environmental, and ecological factors.

The Appellate Body in *EC – Hormones* further held that the list of factors set out in Article 5.2 is not closed[117] and may include risks arising from difficulties of control, inspection, and enforcement of the requirements of good veterinary practice.[118]

Article 5.3 of the SPS Agreement lists economic factors to be taken into account in risk assessments concerning plant and animal health or life.

Thus risk assessment is not purely a scientific exercise, but must also take into account these economic factors. However, when assessing risk to human life or health, there is no obligation to take into account economic factors.

1.3.10 The requirement to be 'based on' risk assessment

The Appellate Body in *EC – Hormones* characterised the requirement, in Article 5.1, for an SPS measure to be 'based on' a risk assessment as connoting an objective relationship between that measure and its underlying risk assessment.[119]

The Appellate Body found that the requirement that SPS measures be 'based on' a risk assessment is a substantive requirement and there must be a rational relationship between the measure and the risk assessment.[120] Furthermore, the Appellate Body concluded that a risk assessment need not only embody the prevailing views of 'mainstream' scientific opinion but could also include divergent scientific opinions.[121]

---

115 *Appellate Body Report, EC – Hormones*, para 130.
116 Ibid, para 187.
117 Ibid, paras 186–187.
118 Ibid, para 205.
119 Ibid, para 189.
120 Ibid, para 193.
121 Ibid, paras 193–194.

The Appellate Body in *U.S./Canada – Continued Suspension* held that 'the panel must determine whether the results of the risk assessment "sufficiently warrant" the SPS measure at issue'.[122]

Where a Member has chosen a level of protection that is higher than would be achieved by a measure based on an international standard, it may be required to carry out certain research as part of its risk assessment that is different from the parameters considered and the research carried out in the risk assessment underlying the international standard.[123]

The 'based on' risk assessment requirement applies to all SPS measures, regardless of the fact they may have been in place prior to the commencement of the SPS Agreement.[124] For SPS measures enacted before the commencement of the SPS Agreement, the risk assessment may be undertaken after their enactment. However, measures enacted after the commencement of the Agreement have to be preceded by a risk assessment, even though the risk assessment is published after enactment of the measure.[125]

1.3.11 *Where there is insufficient scientific evidence*

Article 5.7 of the SPS Agreement provides for situations where there is insufficient relevant scientific evidence. In such situations it allows for conditional provisional SPS measures.

The Appellate Body in *U.S./Canada – Continued Suspension* clarified that 'when determining whether such deficiencies exist, a Member must not exclude from consideration relevant scientific evidence from any qualified and respected source'.[126] The Appellate Body went on to hold that, 'moreover, where a Member adopts a higher level of protection than an international standard, the legal test that applies to the "insufficiency" of the evidence under Article 5.7 is not made stricter'.[127]

The Appellate Body in *Japan – Agricultural Products* clarified that 'Article 5.7 operates as a qualified exemption from the obligation under Article 2.2 not to maintain SPS measures without sufficient scientific evidence'.[128] However, the Panel in *EC – Biotech* went further, to find that Article 5.7 is an autonomous right and not an exception from Articles 2.2 and 5.1.[129]

1.3.12 *Conditions for the application of provisional measures*

The Appellate Body in *Japan – Agricultural Products* identified four cumulative conditions to be met in the application of provisional measures.[130] First,

---

122 *Appellate Body Report, U.S./Canada – Continued Suspension*, para 591.
123 Ibid, para 685.
124 *Panel Report, EC – Hormones (US)*, para 8.99; *Panel Report, EC- Hormones (Canada)*, para 8.102; *Panel Report, Australia – Salmon*, para 8.56.
125 *Compliance Panel Report, Australia – Salmon*, paras 7.76–7.77.
126 *Appellate Body Report, U.S./Canada – Continued Suspension*, para 677.
127 Ibid, para 708.
128 *Appellate Body Report, Japan – Agricultural Products*, para 80.
129 *Panel Reports, EC – Biotech*, para 7.3007.
130 *Appellate Body Report, Japan – Agricultural Products*, para 89.

the measure is imposed in respect of a situation where 'relevant scientific information' is insufficient. Second, the measure is adopted 'on the basis of available pertinent information'. Third, the Member seeks to obtain the additional information necessary for a more objective assessment of risk. Fourth, the Member reviews the measure accordingly within a reasonable period. If any one of these conditions is not met, the measure will be found to be inconsistent with Article 5.7.

1.3.13 Distinction between 'insufficient relevant scientific information' and 'without sufficient scientific evidence'

The Panel in *Japan – Apples* found that 'insufficient scientific evidence' refers to evidence in general on the SPS question at issue[131] and, furthermore, that Article 5.7 of the SPS Agreement is designed to be invoked where little or no reliable evidence was available on the subject matter at issue.[132] The Appellate Body in *Japan – Apples* found that relevant scientific evidence will be insufficient if it 'does not allow, in qualitative or quantitative terms, an adequate assessment of risks as required under Article 5.1'.[133] It further held that Article 5.7 'is triggered not by scientific uncertainty, but rather by the insufficiency of scientific evidence'.[134]

1.3.14 Additional information and reasonable period of time

Under the SPS Agreement's Article 5.7, a Member that maintains a provisional SPS measure is enjoined to 'seek to obtain the additional information necessary for a more objective assessment of risk (. . .)'. The Appellate Body in *Japan – Agricultural Products* elucidated this requirement, finding that the additional information must be germane to conducting a risk assessment.[135]

A further requirement of Article 5.7, second sentence, is that a Member maintaining a provisional SPS measure shall 'review the sanitary or phytosanitary measure accordingly within a reasonable period of time'. This requirement relates to the maintenance of a provisional measure and highlights the provisional nature of measures adopted pursuant to Article 5.7.[136] The Appellate Body in *Japan – Agricultural Products* characterised a 'reasonable period of time' as depending on the specific circumstances of each case, including the difficulty of obtaining the additional information necessary for the review and the characteristics of the provisional SPS measure.[137]

---

131 *Panel Report, Japan – Apples*, para 8.218.
132 Ibid, para 8.219.
133 *Appellate Body Report, Japan – Agricultural Products*, para 179.
134 Ibid, para 184.
135 Ibid, para 92.
136 *Appellate Body Report, Japan – Apples*, fn 318 to para 176.
137 Ibid, para 93.

1.3.15 The precautionary principle

In *EC – Hormones*, the EC invoked the precautionary principle[138] in defence of its impugned measures. The EC contended that the precautionary principle is a customary rule of international law or at least a general principle of law applicable to risk assessment principles under Article 5.1. The Appellate Body in that case, in dismissing the EC's defence, held that it was doubtful whether the precautionary principle had developed into a principle of general or customary international law.[139]

Further, the Appellate Body concurred with the Panel that the precautionary principle does not override the provisions of Articles 5.1 and 5.2 of the SPS Agreement and went on to note four elements concerning the relationship between the precautionary principle and the SPS Agreement.[140] First, the precautionary principle has not been written into the SPS Agreement as a ground for justifying SPS measures that are otherwise inconsistent with the provisions of the SPS Agreement. Second, the precautionary principle finds reflection in Article 5.7 of the SPS Agreement. Third, a panel should bear in mind that responsible, representative governments commonly act from perspectives of prudence and precaution where risks of irreversible life-terminating damage to human health are concerned. Fourth, the precautionary principle does not relieve a panel from applying the normal principles of treaty interpretation in reading the provisions of the SPS Agreement.

1.4 Harmonisation of SPS standards

The SPS Agreement does not aim at complete harmonisation. It allows for divergent SPS standards under the disciplines of Articles 3.3 and 5. The right of Members to set their own level of appropriate protection, different from the one that may be provided under international standards, is recognised under the preamble, paragraph 6, and provided for under Articles 3.3, 5.5, and 5.6 of the SPS Agreement. Furthermore, the Appellate Body affirmed this right in *Australia – Salmon*.[141]

1.4.1 Harmonisation under the SPS agreement

Harmonisation of SPS measures is one of the primary objectives of the SPS Agreement, as stated in the sixth paragraph of its preamble: 'Desiring to

---

138 The *Cartagena Protocol on Biosafety to the Convention on Biological Diversity* (2000), art 10(6), defines the precautionary principle as follows:

> Lack of scientific certainty due to insufficient relevant scientific information and knowledge regarding the extent of the potential adverse effects of a living modified organism on the conservation and sustainable use of biological diversity in the Party of import, taking also into account risk to human health, shall not prevent that Party from taking a decision, as appropriate, with regard to the import of the living modified organism in question (. . .) in order to avoid or minimise such potential adverse effects.

139 *Appellate Body Report, EC – Hormones*, para 123.
140 Ibid, paras 124–125.
141 *Appellate Body Report, Australia – Salmon*, para 199.

further the use of harmonised sanitary and phytosanitary measures between Members (...)'.

Harmonisation is also the objective of the Codex,[142] the OIE,[143] and the IPPC.[144] Harmonisation is defined in Annex A paragraph 2 of the SPS Agreement as 'the establishment, recognition and application of common sanitary and phytosanitary measures by different Members'. The objective of harmonisation is the increase of international trade through the reduction or elimination of trade barriers caused by divergent SPS standards, to be achieved without compromising Members' rights to choose their own level of sanitary and phytosanitary protection.[145] The Appellate Body in *EC – Hormones* explained the justification for harmonisation thus: 'The ultimate goal of the harmonization of SPS measures is to prevent the use of such measures for arbitrary or unjustifiable discrimination between Members or as a disguised restriction on international trade'.[146]

Thus, viewed broadly, harmonisation under the SPS Agreement seeks to eliminate the arbitrary or unjustifiable discriminatory usage of SPS measures among Members or the use of those measures as disguised restrictions on international trade. These objectives are to be achieved without curtailing Members' rights to set their own levels of appropriate protection, with a caveat that SPS measures must be necessary for the protection of human, animal, or plant life or health; be based on scientific principles; and not be maintained without sufficient scientific evidence. The SPS Agreement provides for two approaches towards the fulfilment of these objectives. First, the harmonisation of SPS measures through international standards is required under Article 3.1, by providing that SPS measures must be 'based on' international standards and, through the presumption in Article 3.2, that SPS measures that 'conform to international standards, guidelines or recommendations' are consistent with the provisions of the SPS Agreement and the GATT 1994. Second, the SPS

---

142 'The publication of the Codex Alimentarius is intended to guide and promote the elaboration and establishment of definitions and requirements for foods to assist in their harmonisation and in doing so to facilitate international trade'. Codex Procedural Manual, General Principles, para 1.

143 '(...) to maximize harmonization of the sanitary aspects of international trade, Veterinary Authorities of Member Countries should base their import requirements on the OIE standards, guidelines and recommendations'. OIE Terrestrial Animal Health Code, 24th edn (2015), General Obligations, art 1.2.1.1; '(...) to maximize harmonization of the aquatic animal health aspects of international trade, Competent Authorities of Member Countries should base their import requirements on the OIE standards, guidelines and recommendations'. The World Organization for Animal Health (OIE), Aquatic Animal Health Code, 14th edn, 2011, General Obligations, art 1.3.1.1.

144 'Desiring to provide a framework for the development and application of harmonized phytosanitary measures and the elaboration of international standards to that effect'. International Plant Protection Convention, 1997, Preamble, para 4.

145 *Appellate Body Report, EC- Hormones*, para 177.

146 Ibid.

Agreement contains substantive provisions against the use of SPS measures for arbitrary or unjustifiable discrimination among Members[147] or as a disguised restriction on international trade.[148] The SPS Agreement also provides an alternative to harmonisation in its provisions on equivalence under Article 4 of the Agreement.

1.4.2 The distinction between 'based on' and 'conform to' in relation to international standards

Regarding the obligation of WTO Members to base their SPS measures on international standards, the Panel in *EC – Hormones* noted that in making a finding on whether a Member has an obligation to base its sanitary measure on international standards the Panel needs to determine whether such international standards exist.[149]

The Appellate Body distinguished the terms 'based on' and 'conform to', as found in Articles 3.1 and 3.2, by their ordinary meanings: 'A measure that "conforms to" and incorporates a Codex standard is, of course, "based on" that standard. A measure, however, based on the same standard might not conform to that standard, as where only some, not all, of the elements of the standard are incorporated into the measure'.[150]

---

147 SPS Agreement, art 2.3, provides:

> Members shall ensure that their sanitary and phytosanitary measures do not arbitrarily or unjustifiably discriminate between Members where identical or similar conditions prevail, including between their own territory and that of other Members. Sanitary and phytosanitary measures shall not be applied in a manner which would constitute a disguised restriction on international trade.

The compliance Panel in *Australia – Salmon* found three elements, cumulative in nature, are required for a violation of the Article: (1) the measure discriminates between the territories of Members other than the Member imposing the measure, or between the territory of the Member imposing the measure and another Member; (2) the discrimination is arbitrary or unjustifiable; and (3) identical or similar conditions prevail in the territories of the Members compared. The Panel further found that discrimination in the sense of art 2.3, first sentence, may also include discrimination between different products. *Compliance Panel Report, Australia – Salmon,* paras 7.111–7.112.

148 SPS Agreement, art 2.3, second sentence. The Appellate Body in *Australia – Salmon* found that a finding of a violation of art 5.5 will necessarily imply a violation of art 2.3 first or second sentence. *Appellate Body Report, Australia – Salmon,* para 252. Furthermore, the Panel in *Australia – Salmon* found three warning signals that would indicate a measure is a restriction on international trade disguised as an SPS measure: First, the arbitrary character of the differences in levels of protection. Second, the rather substantial differences in levels of protection. Third, the absence of scientific justification. *Panel Report, Australia – Salmon,* paras 8.149–151.

149 *Panel Report, EC- Hormones (US),* para 8.69; *Panel Report, EC – Hormones (Canada),* para 8.72.

150 *Appellate Body Report, EC – Hormones,* para 163.

Moreover, an SPS measure that is 'based on' the existing relevant international standard, guideline, or recommendation, in the sense of having adopted some, but not all, of the international standard, does not benefit from the presumption of consistency under Article 3.2, unlike measures which 'conform to' such standards, which do benefit from the presumption of consistency with the SPS Agreement and the GATT 1994.[151] On the other hand, an SPS measure that 'conforms to' an international standard has to embody the international standard completely, thus converting it into a municipal standard.[152] It is, however, arguable that measures both 'based on' and 'conforming to' international standards are required to be based on the risk assessments of those standards. Furthermore, the goal of harmonisation is one to be realised in the future,[153] which allows Members some flexibility in utilizing those standards.

1.4.3 *Higher level of protection than in an international standard*

Members are entitled to set for themselves a level of protection higher than the one in an international standard, and to implement or embody that level of protection in a measure that is not 'based on' the international standard. Article 3.3 of the SPS Agreement provides for the right of a Member to enact SPS measures providing a higher level of protection than that of international standards. This is an autonomous right, and not an exception from the obligations of Article 3.1.[154]

However, a Member seeking a level of protection higher than the one in an international standard, must meet two conditions attached to this right. First, there must be scientific justification for the measure. Second, and alternatively, the measure must be the result of the higher level of protection chosen by the Member in accordance with Articles 5.1 to 5.8 of the SPS Agreement. Under both situations, the measure must be based on a risk assessment.[155]

The Appellate Body in *Japan – Agricultural Products* further emphasised the 'scientific justification' requirement: 'There is a "scientific justification" for an SPS measure, within the meaning of Article 3.3, if there is a rational relationship between the SPS measure at issue and the available scientific information'.[156]

---

151 Ibid, para 171.
152 Ibid, para 170.
153 Ibid, para 165.
154 Ibid, para 172.
155 Ibid, paras 175–176.
156 *Appellate Body Report, Japan – Agricultural Products*, para 79.

1.4.4 The use of international standards and harmonisation

The SPS Agreement seeks to achieve harmonisation in two ways. First, it encourages Members to base their SPS measures on international standards, and it rewards those that conform to such standards by granting them a presumption of consistency with the SPS Agreement and the GATT 1994. Second, it provides for a comprehensive harmonised system of principles with which Members' SPS measures are evaluated for consistency with the SPS Agreement's provisions.

Thus the SPS Agreement enables Members to retain their regulatory autonomy while disciplining their divergent regulations. Note that the SPS Agreement itself does not provide for any standards, and neither does the WTO set standards. The function of setting standards has been left to the Codex, the OIE, and the IPPC. This division of roles has several advantages: First, it provides the WTO with some insulation from the criticism that is now directed at these standard-setting organisations. Second, the procedure for setting and amending standards in these organisations is easier and simpler: while the WTO requires consensus in its decisions, the organisations provide for majority voting in case of failure of consensus. Third, with the interpretative and oversight function of the WTO dispute settlement mechanism, there is a possibility of overriding unsuitable standards set by these organisations. Fourth, the international organisations have professionalised the standards-setting process, hence attracting confidence and faith in the standards thus set.

These circumstances tend to lead the SPS Agreement to focus on process-oriented disciplines, rather than substantive disciplines involving international standards.[157] These process-oriented disciplines are resulting in the harmonisation of national SPS procedures, such as the requirement of risk assessment.

1.5 Provisions for developing countries under the SPS Agreement

The SPS Agreement recognises that developing countries are constrained when it comes to the implementation of importing Members' SPS measures.[158] This is stated in paragraph 7 of its preamble: 'Recognizing that developing country Members may encounter special difficulties in complying with the sanitary or phytosanitary measures of importing Members (...)'.

The SPS Agreement has specific provisions that cater to the constraints of a developing country. It provides for technical assistance (Article 9); special and differential treatment (Article 10); a reasonable adaptation period (paragraph 2

---

157 Cho S (n 60) 665.
158 For analysis of the provisions for developing countries in the SPS Agreement see Denise Prevost, *Balancing Trade and Health in the SPS Agreement: The Development Dimension* (Wolf Legal Publishers, 2009) 941–1023; Scott J (n 28) 280–311.

of Annex B); special notification requirements (paragraphs 8 and 9 of Annex B); and delayed implementation of the Agreement (Article 14).

1.5.1 Technical assistance

The objective of technical assistance for developing countries, as provided for under Article 9, is to enhance their capacities so that they may participate more effectively in international trade of their agricultural products. It encompasses assistance to improve their scientific and technological capacity to enable them to exercise their rights and obligations under the SPS Agreement and to meet the SPS requirements of importing countries. It includes training of personnel, construction of scientific infrastructure, and supply of scientific equipment.[159]

Such technical assistance is primarily geared towards enabling developing countries to achieve the appropriate level of SPS protection in their export markets. It would appear, therefore, that the technical assistance obligation lies with importing Member countries.

Where substantial investments are required in order for a developing country Member to meet the SPS standards of an importing Member, Article 9.2 obligates the importing Member to consider providing technical assistance to the developing country Member.

1.5.2 Technical assistance and international organisations

Technical assistance is a regular agenda item for the meetings of the SPS Committee, which regularly assesses the technical assistance needs of WTO Members, providing a basis for its technical-assistance programmes. Pursuant to this objective the WTO Secretariat undertook 288 SPS training activities from September 1994 to December 2013.[160]

The OIE and the IPPC have also developed training programmes, including conferences, seminars, and workshops, to enhance national capacities on WTO matters. In addition, the IPPC has developed a diagnostic tool, the Phytosanitary Capacity Evaluation (PCE), to help countries address their current capacity and identify where assistance is needed. Similar diagnostic tools have been developed by the FAO/WHO with respect to food safety, and by the OIE. The FAO and the WHO also provide technical assistance regarding food safety and food control; conferences, seminars, workshops, tools and training

---

159 WTO Committee on Sanitary and Phytosanitary Measures, 'Technical Assistance Typology – Note by the Secretariat' (G/SPS/GEN/206, 18 October 2000).
160 WTO Committee on Sanitary and Phytosanitary Measures, 'SPS Technical Assistance and Training Activities (1 September 1994 to 31 December 2013), Note by the Secretariat' (G/SPS/GEN/521/Rev. 9, 7 March 2014) (Committee on Sanitary and Phytosanitary Measures (2014)).

materials; and specific projects related to the Codex, at the global, regional, and country levels.[161]

In 2002, the WHO, the FAO, the WTO, the OIE, and the World Bank jointly established the Standards and Trade Development Facility (STDF). The objective of the STDF, which is administered by the WTO, is to enhance the standards capacity of developing countries through cooperation among relevant institutions in SPS-related activities, including through the development of joint institutional projects and the provision of STDF funding to projects in developing countries. The STDF maintains a database that provides information on SPS-related technical assistance and capacity-building projects.[162]

1.5.3 Special and differential treatment (SDT)

Under Article 10.1 of the SPS Agreement, Members are required to take into account the special needs of developing and least-developed countries in the preparation and application of their SPS measures. Article 10.1 provides that 'in the preparation and application of sanitary or phytosanitary measures, Members shall take account of the special needs of developing country Members, and in particular of the least-developed country Members'.

The use of the term 'take account' in Article 10.1 suggests that it is non-enforceable, that is it is soft law. The Panel in *EC – Biotech* examined the phrase 'take account' and held that it does not prescribe a specific result to be achieved.[163] The Panel further held that while a developed country Member must 'take account' of the interests of developing country Members in applying its approval legislation, it may at the same time take account of other legitimate interests, including those of its own consumers and its environment.[164] Moreover, the Panel proceeded to hold that it was 'incumbent on Argentina as the Complaining Party to adduce evidence and argument sufficient to raise a presumption that the European Communities has failed to take into account Argentina's special needs as a developing country Member'.[165] Hence, the burden of proof lies with a complaining developing country Member to show that a developed country Member has failed to 'take account' of its special needs in the preparation and application of its SPS measures. The Panel further held that it is not sufficient, for establishing a claim under Article 10.1, to point to the absence in an SPS law or regulation of a reference to the needs of developing

---

161 WTO Committee on Sanitary and Phytosanitary Measures, 'Review of the Operation and Implementation of the Agreement on the Application of Sanitary and Phytosanitary Measures' (G/SPS/W/273, 12 December 2013) (Committee on Sanitary and Phytosanitary Measures (2013)) 10–15.
162 STDF website: <http://stdfdb.wto.org>
163 *Panel Reports, EC-Biotech*, para 7.1620.
164 Ibid, para 7.1621.
165 Ibid, para 7.1622.

country Members.[166] Furthermore, the Panel held that Article 10.1 does not specifically require the importing Member to document how it has complied with that Article.[167]

In 2004, the SPS Committee adopted a decision on a procedure to enhance transparency of special and differential treatment in favour of developing country Members.[168] This procedure provides for the submission of specific addenda to notifications which indicate the special and differential treatment or technical assistance that has been requested. In the context of the notification of a new or modified SPS measure, it should specify what assistance was provided and, if it was not, the reasons why.

1.5.4 Phased introduction of measures and time limited exceptions

Under Article 10.2, the SPS Agreement provides for the phased introduction of new SPS measures. The phased introduction of SPS measures is conditional, depending on whether a Member's appropriate level of protection allows for a phased introduction of SPS measures. The longer time frames are non-obligatory, as they are dependent on a Member's determination of whether its SPS measures would accommodate such extensions of time for compliance. Developing countries will be accorded longer time frames for compliance where the importing Member's appropriate level of protection allows. The provision is intended to allow developing countries to maintain their export markets while adjusting to the new measures.

Article 10.3 of the SPS Agreement provides the SPS Committee with the ability to grant developing countries limited exceptions from their obligations. This provision is aimed at enabling developing countries to comply with the provisions of the SPS Agreement. The SPS Committee may grant certain developing countries exceptions from their obligations under the Agreement, recognizing their financial, trade, and development constraints. The exceptions are upon request, and must be specific and time limited. It is to be noted that whereas Article 10.2 provides for phased introduction of SPS measures by Members, Article 10.3 provides for time-limited exceptions in whole or in part from obligations under the SPS Agreement.

1.5.5 Participation in international organisations

WTO Members are required to encourage and facilitate the participation of developing countries in relevant international organisations, under Article 10.4

---

166 Ibid, para 7.1623.
167 Ibid.
168 WTO Committee on Sanitary and Phytosanitary Measures, 'Procedure to Enhance Transparency of Special and Differential Treatment in Favour of Developing Country Members' (G/SPS/33, 27 October 2004; G/SPS/33/Add.1, 6 February 2006).

of the SPS Agreement, which provides that 'members should encourage and facilitate the active participation of developing country Members in the relevant international organizations'. It is of note that by using the phrase 'should encourage and facilitate', this provision is hortatory and non-binding.

The relevant international organisations under Annex A paragraph 3 are the Codex, the OIE, and the IPPC. There is a consensus among Members that financial support is necessary to enhance the participation of developing country Members in these international organisations[169] and their committees, and also to improve developing countries' technical capabilities in the standards-setting process. In addition to the STDF,[170] the Codex, the OIE, and the IPPC have each established trust funds to encourage effective participation in their activities by developing countries.[171]

1.5.6 *Ministerial decision on special and differential treatment*

The Fourth Ministerial Conference of the WTO, held in 2001, adopted a decision on implementation and related issues (Ministerial Decision).[172] The decision instructed the Committee on Trade and Development to examine the special and differential provisions with a view to making them more effective.[173]

The Ministerial Decision specifies the 'longer time-frames for compliance' under Article 10.2 of the SPS Agreement to be a period of not less than six months, and further requires Members to enter into consultations where this is not possible.[174] Paragraph 2 of Annex B of the SPS Agreement provides:

> Except in urgent circumstances, Members shall allow a reasonable interval between the publication of a sanitary or phytosanitary regulation and its entry into force in order to allow time for producers in exporting Members, and particularly in developing country Members, to adapt their products and methods of production to the requirements of the importing Member.

The Ministerial Decision clarifies that a 'reasonable interval' shall be understood to mean a period of not less than 6 months. However, the entry into force of

---

169 WTO Committee on Sanitary and Phytosanitary Measures, 'Procedure to Enhance Transparency of Special and Differential Treatment in Favour of Developing Country Members' (G/SPS/33, 27 October 2004) 15.
170 STDF website: http:/stdfdb.wto.org.
171 For the Codex, see website: http://www.who.int/foodsafety/codex/trustfund/en/index.html; For the OIE, see website: http://www.oie.int/eng/en_index.htm; For the IPPC see website: http://www.ippc.int.
172 WTO Ministerial Conference, 'Implementation – Related Issues and Concerns, Decision of 14 November 2001' (WT/MIN (01)/17, 20 November 2001) (Ministerial Decision).
173 Ministerial Decision, para 12.1.
174 Ibid, para 3.1.

measures which contribute to the liberalisation of trade is not to be delayed unnecessarily.[175]

The Appellate Body in *US – Clove Cigarettes* held that 'paragraph 5.2 of the Doha Ministerial Decision constitutes a subsequent agreement between the parties, within the meaning of Article 31(3)(a) of the Vienna Convention, on the interpretation of the term 'reasonable interval' in Article 2.12 of the TBT Agreement'.[176] It may be inferred that a similar interpretation will apply to the 'reasonable interval' under paragraph 3.2 of the Ministerial Decision, thus confirming the reasonable interval under Paragraph 2 of Annex B of the SPS Agreement to mean a period of not less than 6 months.

The SPS Committee was mandated to come up with recommendations on special and differential treatment, as regards the SPS Agreement, for a decision by the General Council. However, despite receiving proposals from Members, the Committee has to date been unable to develop any such recommendations.[177]

1.6 Chapter discussion and conclusions

The SPS Agreement was intended as a solution to SPS measures acting as non-tariff barriers. WTO Members hoped that its disciplines would eliminate the discriminatory use of SPS measures as well as their misuse as disguised restriction on international trade. However, the application of the SPS Agreement has revealed a number of problems. These are mainly concerned with the interpretation and application of its key concepts, such as harmonisation and risk assessment. There are also questions as to whether the Agreement is fulfilling its objectives. Some of these problems are considered below.

One of the objectives of the SPS Agreement is the harmonisation of domestic regulations on the basis of international standards.[178] This function is promoted in the sixth paragraph of the preamble: 'Desiring to further the use of harmonised sanitary and phytosanitary measures between Members, on the basis of international standards, guidelines and recommendations developed by the relevant international organizations (. . .)' – the designated international organisations, under Annex A of the SPS Agreement, being the Codex, the OIE, and the IPPC. The function is to be achieved through the obligation found in Article 3.1 of the SPS Agreement, which requires that 'Members shall base their sanitary or

---

175 Ibid, para 3.2.
176 *United States – Measures Affecting the Production and Sale of Clove Cigarettes*, WT/DS406/AB/R, modifying *Panel Report, United States – Measures Affecting the Production and Sale of Clove Cigarettes*, WT/DS406/R, adopted 24 April 2012, para 268.
177 WTO Committee on Sanitary and Phytosanitary Measures, 'Report on Proposals for Special and Differential Treatment' (G/SPS/35, 7 July 2005) 10.
178 Heiskanen V (n 79) 16. For further analysis see Lukasz Gruszczynski, *Regulating Health and Environmental Risks Under WTO Law: A Critical Analysis of the SPS Agreement* (International Economic Law Series, Oxford University Press, 2010) 75–106; Prevost D (n 158) 603–632.

phytosanitary measures on international standards, guidelines or recommendations (...)'. Article 3.2 provides Members with an incentive to conform their SPS measures to international standards by granting to such measures a rebuttable presumption of consistency with the SPS Agreement and the GATT 1994.

Through this function, the three Annex A international organisations are thereby elevated to 'quasi-legislators' for the standards within their respective areas of competence, thus creating a system of applied subsidiarity that allows for national autonomy, subject to certain constraints as provided for in the SPS Agreement.[179]

Furthermore, the regulatory structure of the SPS Agreement is one that is underpinned by the scientific paradigm of risk assessment: either a Member conforms its SPS measures to international standards, or it bases them on risk assessments. Thus the SPS Agreement is remarkable in its conceptual framework in that it shifts from the traditional GATT negative harmonisation – the elimination of discrimination in international trade – to that of positive harmonisation – the creation of a uniform regulatory structure.[180] Hence, together with the development of substantive international SPS standards by the Codex, the SPS disciplines of the SPS Agreement have had a positive impact on national and regional SPS standards.

1.6.1 International SPS standards and harmonisation

The adoption and effectiveness of international SPS standards in the promotion of harmonisation is doubtful.[181] On the one hand, international standards reflect professional values because they are set by qualified experts; on the other hand, the domestic process of adopting such international standards is subject to influence by domestic political consideration, often leading to more stringent domestic standards. With consumer awareness and activism, especially in developed countries, consensus is hard to achieve among politicians, and even among

---

179 Gabrielle Z Marceau and Joel P Trachtman, 'A Map of the World Trade Organization Law of Domestic Regulation of Goods: The Technical Barriers to Trade Agreement, the Sanitary and Phytosanitary Measures Agreement, and the General Agreement on Tariffs and Trade' (2014) 48 *Journal of World Trade* 351, 388. Subsidiarity is the principle that action should not be taken at a higher vertical level of organisation if the goal can be accomplished satisfactorily at a lower level. The complex constraints of the SPS Agreement, combined with the international standards to which it refers, set up a system for scrutinizing certain types of state actions and supporting certain types of standard-setting at the international level.
180 Heiskanen V (n 79) 14. According to the author, 'While the traditional regulation of international trade based on the principle of non-discrimination merely seeks to open the borders between countries for international trade, in order to allow access for foreign goods to the various domestic markets, the philosophy of positive harmonization seeks to efface the borders in order to create a global, integrated marketplace' (fn 51).
181 Donna Roberts and Timothy Josling, Tracking the Implementation of Internationally Agreed Standards in Food and Agricultural Production, Background paper for conference on Non-Tariff Measures in Food and Agriculture: Which Road Ahead? IPC and the OECD, Paris, 13 September 2011, 4, <www.oecd.org/tad/ntm/48632912.pdf> accessed 30 April 2015.

the scientists setting the standards. This serves to undermine the effectiveness of international standards as benchmarks for national standards.

To date, international standards, guidelines, or recommendations are skewed towards establishing meta-standards that provide for common approaches to risk identification, assessment, and management rather than to specific international standards. This gives leeway to the development of divergent national standards.[182] For instance, although both the US and the EU have adopted the Codex General principles of Food Hygiene,[183] there are differences in their requirements for reduction of microbial risks leading to the EU ban on US chicken imports, which resulted in the *EC – Poultry (US)*[184] dispute. Perhaps as result of this, a high percentage of SPS measures notified under Article 7 and Annex B of the SPS Agreement by Members are not based on international standards, guidelines, or recommendations.[185] This serves to undermine harmonisation.

From a Global Administrative Law (GAL) perspective, the standards-setting international organisations fall short of meeting the participatory and democratic principles. Despite the setting up of trust funds to enhance the participation of developing countries in the activities of the international organisations, developing countries continue to have limited ability to actively participate in the development of international standards.[186] The developing countries are also concerned about the lack of a mechanism to take into account their economic and technical capacity to implement international standards.[187] The developing countries further lack effective technical infrastructures and human capabilities

---

182 Timothy Josling, Donna Roberts and David Orden, *Food Regulation and Trade: Towards a Safe and Open Global System* (Institute of International Economics, Washington, DC, March 2004) 45–46.
183 CAC/RCP 1–1969 (Adopted 1969. Amended 1999. Revised 1997 and 2003).
184 WTO Dispute DS389 of 2009: *European Communities – Certain Measures Affecting Poultry Meat and Poultry Meat Products from the United States (EC – Poultry [US])*. The panel was established on 19 November 2009 but has not yet been composed to date.
185 WTO Committee on Sanitary and Phytosanitary Measures (n 161) 9–10. See also: WTO Committee on Sanitary and Phytosanitary Measures, 'Procedure to Monitor the Process of International Harmonization, Fifteenth Annual Report, Adopted by the Committee on 28 June 2013' (G/SPS/60, 30 July 2013) 1. The report notes that Chile had noted that more than 57 per cent of the notified SPS measures did not indicate any international standards, even in cases where the standards existed; WTO Committee on Sanitary and Phytosanitary Measures, 'Monitoring the Use of International Standards: Background Note' (G/SPS/GEN/1086, 30 May 2011).
186 Gruszczynski L (n 178) 86–88; Prevost D (n 158) 987–989.
187 WTO Committee on Sanitary and Phytosanitary Measures, 'Review of the Operation and Implementation of the Agreement on the Application of Sanitary and Phytosanitary Measures, G/SPS/53, 3 May 2010', 9. See also, Brian Perry and others, *An Appropriate Level of Risk: Balancing the Need for Safe Livestock Products with Fair Market Access for the Poor* (International Livestock Research Institute and United Nations Food and Agricultural Organization, Pro-Poor Livestock Policy Initiative, PPLPI Working Paper No. 23, 2005) 49.

at the national level for the evaluation of draft standards and the formulation of positions in consultation with other interested Members.[188]

These factors have resulted in international standards that are inappropriate to the developing countries' situations and that require infrastructure not available in those countries. A further consequence is that standards which reflect the interests of developing countries are slow to develop.[189] Given the dominant role played by the developed countries in the international standards-setting process, in addition to their developed technology, international standards are similar to the standards of developed countries, and hence developed countries' costs of compliance are lower compared to those of developing countries, further marginalizing them.[190] These factors put into question the legitimacy of international standards in the eyes of developing countries.[191]

Furthermore, although the SPS Agreement encourages Members to use international standards, guidelines, or recommendations, there is no distinction between them in the SPS Agreement as to their relative normative value and status. There is also no specific procedure set out concerning how these standards, regulations, and recommendations are to be established. This renders the standards less effective.

The Panel in *EC – Hormones* held that it only needed to determine whether such international standards exist: 'We need not consider (i) whether the standards reflect levels of protection or sanitary measure or the type of sanitary measure they recommend, or (ii) whether these standards have been adopted by consensus or by a wide or narrow majority (. . .)'.[192] This holding creates ambiguities and confusion among Members and leads to the conclusion that in the WTO, the terms standards, regulations, and recommendations have the same meaning, while in the Codex they do not have the same meaning or normative significance. This ambiguity raises a further issue of effectiveness: if there is no difference between these terms, what is their import?

Critically, for the legitimacy of international standards, the process of international standards-setting has become increasingly politicised since the advent of the SPS Agreement, with its harmonisation provisions encouraging conformity with international standards. This has resulted in making the adoption of standards a more complex and time-consuming process, with implications that

---

188 UNCTAD, 'TNCD Training Module on the WTO Agreement on Sanitary and Phytosanitary Measures' (UNCTAD/DITC/ /2004/3, 2005) 28.
189 Michael F Jensen, 'Reviewing the SPS Agreement: A Developing Country Perspective' (The Royal Veterinary and Agricultural University, Copenhagen, Denmark, Paper No. FO1, 2002) 23.
190 Henson S and Loader R (n 30) 359–360; Otsuki T, Wilson J S and Sewadeh M (n 39) 503. These costs arise from two sources, the costs of compliance with importing country standards and the cost of conformity assessment procedures.
191 For further analysis see Michael A Livermore, 'Authority and Legitimacy in Global Governance: Deliberation, Institutional Differentiation and the Codex Alimentarius' (2006) 81 *New York University Law Review* 766, 783–784.
192 *Panel Report, EC- Hormones (US)*, para 8.69; *Panel Report, EC – Hormones (Canada)*, para 8.72.

non-scientific considerations could be playing a role in the process.[193] An example of this conundrum is the long and acrimonious process that led to the adoption of a maximum residue limit for ractopamine[194] by Codex.[195]

Furthermore, although the Codex standards are meant to be scientifically sound, the scientific expert system that sets these standards lacks transparency, does not conform to the scientific principles of independence and objectivity, and does not provide opportunities for debates among scientists on controversial issues.[196] Moreover, since the Codex does not provide information on how it manages scientific controversies, there is no avenue for assessing its conclusions concerning the extent to which they may be contested in a peer review, or how minority views among experts are dealt with.[197] The system lacks accountability and gives rise to a democratic deficit that jeopardises the legitimacy and credibility of the Codex.

A variety of ways to mitigate these factors could be explored. First, in addition to the ongoing efforts by the WTO and the international organisations to increase developing country capacities in standards,[198] developing countries should be further encouraged to coordinate efforts and resources at the regional or sub-regional level, with the aim of reducing their participation costs in the international organisations; to promote the development of standards in their common interest; and to invest in the necessary regional or sub-regional control, inspection, and accreditation bodies.[199]

Second, the international organisations and developed countries should transfer funds, expertise, and technology to developing countries' regional and sub-regional organisations to strengthen their standards coordination efforts.[200]

Simonetta Zarrilli, 'WTO Sanitary and Phytosanitary Agreement: Issues for Developing Countries' (T.R.A.D.E. Working Papers No.3, 1999) 16; Fontanelli P (n 74) 922–923 and foot note 129; Frode Veggeland and Svein O Borgen, 'Negotiating International Food Standards: The World Trade Organization's Impact on the Codex Alimentarius Commission' (2005) 18 *Governance* 675, 698. The authors argue that in the Codex, Members push for norms that are compatible with their national interests thereby creating rivalry and tensions between the different interest groups.

194 Ractopamine is a feed additive to promote leanness in animals raised for their meat.
195 WTO Committee on Sanitary and Phytosanitary Measures, 'Monitoring the use of International Standards: Thirteenth Annual Report (Revision)' (G/SPS/W/260/Rev.1, 19 July 2011) 2–4. For analysis see Alberto Alemanno and Giuseppe Capodieci, 'Testing the Limits of Global Food Governance: The Case of Ractopamine' (2012) 3 *European Journal of Risk Regulation* 400–407.
196 Urs P Thomas, 'The Codex Alimentarius and Environmental-Related Food Safety: The Functioning of the Global Standards' (2004) 2 *Economic Policy and Law* 15–16.
197 Ibid.
198 See pt 1.5.1–2.
199 UNCTAD (n 188) 28.
200 Para 8 of the preamble of the Standards Code recognised that 'the contribution which international standardization can make to the transfer of technology from developed to developing countries'.

Third, the SPS Committee should develop principles or guidelines for Members to aid the development of international standards, along the same lines as those established by the TBT Committee. The TBT principles set the following criteria: openness, impartiality, and consensus; effectiveness and relevance; coherence; and attention to the concerns of developing countries.[201] The SPS Committee should monitor the implementation of these principles or guidelines by the international bodies.[202]

1.6.2 Equivalence

Equivalence facilitates regulatory diversity while at the same time permitting market integration.[203] The recognition of equivalence can lead to the same results as harmonisation. Regulatory barriers are removed and products are accepted on the basis that they fulfil the regulatory objectives of the importing country. Equivalence makes it possible to maintain distinct regulatory measures, while at the same time removing the measures' trade restrictiveness. Equivalence is the best option when harmonisation of standards is not desirable or when international standards are lacking or are inappropriate. It is also easier to achieve in the framework of regional or sub-regional agreements.[204]

However, some developing countries have contended that developed countries require 'sameness' rather than equivalence of standards.[205] This denies developing countries the right to choose their own SPS standards to meet developed countries' appropriate level of protection (ALOP). And instead this restricts them to the use of the developed countries' standards. On the one hand, developed countries claim that the negotiation of equivalence agreements is too costly, too resource-intensive, and too time consuming relative to the anticipated trade benefits. On the other hand, developing countries are in favour of equivalence agreements as a means of gaining market access.[206] As a result, there are few equivalence agreements. Moreover, developing countries lack the necessary scientific resources to demonstrate equivalence. The international organisations and

---

201 WTO TBT Committee, 'Principles for the Development of International Standards, Guides and Recommendations with Relation to Articles 2, 5 and Annex 3 of the TBT Agreement' (G/TBT/9, July 2000).
202 In October 1997, the WTO SPS Committee adopted a provisional procedure to monitor the use of international standards under arts 3.5 and 12.4. This procedure was extended indefinitely in July 2006.
203 Scott J (n 28) 165, 162–179; Prevost D (n 158) 750–769.
204 Zarrilli S (n 193) 17.
205 Humberto Z Schroder, *Harmonization, Equivalence and Mutual Recognition of Standards in WTO Law* (Kluwer Law International Publishing, 2011) 119–120; UNCTAD (n 188) 30; Jensen M F (n 189) 24.
206 Frode Veggeland and Christel Elvestad, 'Equivalence and Mutual Recognition in Trade Arrangements: Relevance for the WTO and the Codex Alimentarius' (Norwegian Agricultural Economics Research Institute, NILF-Report 2004-9, 2005) 69. See also UNCTAD (n 188) 30.

developed countries should finance and supervise developing countries' regional and sub-regional laboratories, certification bodies, and accreditation institutions and then recognise conformity assessment certificates from these institutions. This would facilitate the recognition of equivalence for developing-country measures. This is important, as equivalence recognition makes ultimate harmonisation easier since the different regulatory systems are already in the process of converging.[207]

1.6.3 The scientific requirements

Science is a pillar of the disciplines of the SPS Agreement.[208] In *Japan – Apples*, the Appellate Body determined that Article 11 of the Understanding on Rules of Procedures Governing the Settlement of Disputes (DSU), which requires a panel to 'make an objective assessment of the matter before it', does not require panels, when assessing the 'rational or objective relationship' between an SPS measure and the scientific evidence,[209] to give precedence to the importing Member's evaluation of scientific evidence and risk.[210]

The Appellate Body in *U.S./Canada – Continued Suspension* created more flexibility for Members in their conduct of risk assessment. Members' risk assessments are required to derive from respected and qualified sources that can be considered 'legitimate science' according to the standards of the relevant scientific community; the reasoning of their risk assessors is required to be objective and coherent; and their conclusions should find sufficient support in the underlying scientific basis.[211] Moreover, a Member with a chosen level of protection that is higher than would be achieved by a measure based on an international standard may perform its risk assessment differently from the parameters considered and the research carried out in the risk assessment underlying the international standard.[212]

It is doubtful that panels are the optimal forums for determining scientific questions.[213] Neither does the use by the panels of science experts improve the

---

207 Veggeland F and Elvestad C (n 206) 69.
208 For further analysis see Jacqueline Peel, *Science and Risk Regulation in International Law* (Cambridge University Press, 2010) 171–263.
209 *Appellate Body Report, Japan – Agricultural Products*, paras 73–74.
210 *Appellate Body Report, Japan-Apples*, para 166.
211 *Appellate Body Report, U.S./Canada – Continued Suspension*, para 598.
212 Ibid, para 685.
213 Walker V R (n 18) 22–25. The author argues that since science is inherently uncertain, Panels should not step in to resolve such uncertainty, which should be left to scientists. Second, scientific determinations should not be second-guessed by Panels. Third, risk regulation incorporates various science policies; Panels, mostly consisting of lay persons, are not suited to inventory such policies. Fourth, Panels do not have the institutional capacity to decide among scientifically plausible alternatives. Panels are ad hoc and formed to decide a particular case. As such Panels lack the resources and the mandate to monitor and re-evaluate the evolving scientific debate. Fifth, Since the Appellate Body may not overturn a Panel's finding of fact, the Appellate Body may not overturn a Panel's finding on a scientific alternative.

situation.²¹⁴ It is therefore proposed that panels should confine themselves to a procedural rather than a substantive review.²¹⁵

The Panel in *EC – Hormones* interpreted the term 'based on' in Article 5.1 of the SPS Agreement as imposing both a procedural and substantive requirement on Members' risk assessments. The Panel found it a procedural requirement that a Member imposing an SPS measure must show that it took risk assessment into account when enacting or maintaining its SPS measure,²¹⁶ and a substantive requirement that the scientific conclusions of the risk assessment and those reflected in the SPS measure should be in conformity.²¹⁷ The Appellate Body overturned the Panel's 'procedural requirement' finding, but upheld its 'substantive requirement' finding.²¹⁸

As a result, Panels may make different and inconsistent scientific determinations. Sixth, the objective of fostering transparency does not itself justify Panels' fact-finding about the truth of a scientific issue, as contrasted with fact-finding about reasonableness. See also Andrew T Guzman, 'WTO Dispute Resolution in Health and Safety Cases' (UC Berkeley Public Law Research Paper no. 989371, 2007) 5–14. The author argues that the standard of review applied in SPS cases should be deferential to domestic decisions with reference to evaluation of science, the level of risk a state is prepared to tolerate, and the relationship between an SPS measure and the risk assessment. The Appellate Body and the Panel should decline to review these decisions. However, there should be review of transparency and procedural requirements.

214 Theophanis Christoforou, 'Settlement of Science-Based Trade Disputes in the WTO: A Critical Review of the Developing Case Law in the Face of Scientific Uncertainty' (2000) 8 *New York University Environmental Law Journal* 622, 638–640. The author faults the use of individual experts instead of expert review groups as contrary to the provisions of Article 13.2 of the DSU, which provides for 'expert review group' and Article 11.2 of the SPS Agreement, which provide for 'technical experts group'. There is a possibility of the individual experts submitting different and conflicting responses to all the written questions of the Panel. The Panel in such a situation may be incompetent to resolve the conflict. Furthermore, the Panel's quest for scientific advice, even when the evidence is clear and none of the parties to the dispute has requested it, and its selective use of such advise, may imply that Panels resort to scientific advice in order to solidify the legitimacy of its findings rather than out of a real need to solve the scientific issues underlying the legal dispute. Moreover, the Appellate Body's holding that the 'objective assessment of facts' criteria of Article 13.2 of the DSU is negated by 'willful distortion or misrepresentation of the evidence put before the Panel' (*Appellate Body Report, EC – Hormones*, para 133) is flawed since a Panel may make serious mistakes in evaluating scientific evidence, regardless of its intention or state of mind and may therefore need to be reviewed. See also Joost Pauwelyn, 'The Use of Experts in WTO Dispute Settlement' (2002) 51 *International and Comparative Law Quarterly* 325; Steven P Croley and John H Jackson, 'WTO Dispute Procedures, Standard of Review, and Deference to National Governments' (1996) 90 *American Journal of International Law* 193, 193–213.
215 Trebilcock M J and Howse R (n 5) 209; Walker V R (n 18) 25; Christoforou T (n 214) 635–636; Jan Bohanes, 'Risk Regulation in WTO Law: A Procedure-Based Approach' (2001) 40 *Columbia Journal of Transnational Law* 323, 371.
216 *Panel Report, EC – Hormones (US)*, para 8.113; *Panel Report, EC – Hormones (Canada)*, para 8.116.
217 *Panel Report, EC – Hormones (US)*, para 8.119; *Panel Report, EC – Hormones (Canada)*, para 8.119.
218 *Appellate Body Report, EC – Hormones*, paras 189–193.

Ultimately, with the goal of harmonisation in mind, the Panel's procedural interpretation appears more compelling. Members taking SPS measures for similar SPS risks will, when required to take risk assessment into account, prefer to use similar risk assessments in order to withstand scrutiny. This promotes harmonisation. On the other hand, the substantive requirement would shield Members whose measures are non-conforming, as they would only need to show conformity if their measures were challenged, if at all.[219]

The Panel in *EC – Hormones* further distinguished risk assessment from risk management on the basis that the former is a scientific examination of data and factual studies, while the latter is a policy exercise involving social value judgements made by political bodies. Thus the Panel concluded that risk management or policy issues should be excluded from risk assessment decisions.[220] The Appellate Body rejected the Panel's distinction on the grounds that it was not supported by the text of the SPS Agreement.[221]

While the text of the SPS Agreement does not explicitly refer to risk management, it does so indirectly under the provisions of Articles 5.4 and 5.5. The Panel merely took issue with the factors of these provisions being brought under risk assessment. By so doing, the Panel restricted the scope of risk assessment, and its finding would have prevented the abusive use of risk assessment by the inclusion of non-scientific factors.[222]

However, there is a school of thought that views risk assessment not as a purely scientific exercise, but as one that it is contingent on social values and policy judgements and, furthermore, dependent on political, social, and regulatory contexts.[223]

1.6.4 Special and differential treatment

The developing countries lack the capacity to comply with and benefit from the provisions of the SPS Agreement.[224] The provisions on special and differential treatment (SDT) are therefore intended to enable developing countries to comply with and benefit from the disciplines under that Agreement.[225] The need for SDT

---

219 David R Hurst, Hormones, 'European Communities-Measures Affecting Meat and Meat Products' (1998) 9 (1) *European Journal of International Law* 16.
220 *Panel Report, EC – Hormones (US)*, paras 8.94–95; *Panel Report, EC – Hormones (Canada)*, paras 8.97–98.
221 *Appellate Body Report, EC – Hormones*, para 181.
222 In the context of the Codex, the issue of whether non-scientific factors should be included in risk assessment is a highly contested one. The US and the Cairns group of countries advocate for the exclusion of non-scientific factors in risk assessment, claiming these factors will legitimise disguised restrictions, while the EU and other European countries advocate for the inclusion of these factors. See Thomas U P (n 196) 15; Veggeland F and Borgen S O (n 193) 697.
223 David Winickoff and others, 'Adjudicating the GM Food Wars: Science, Risk and Democracy in World Trade Law' (2005) 30 *Yale Journal of International Law* 81, 94–99.
224 SPS Agreement, preamble para 7.
225 For analysis see Scott J (n 28) 284–296; Prevost D (n 158) 946–977.

arises in two main areas. First, the developing countries' lack of resources makes compliance with the obligations of the SPS Agreement difficult. This is exacerbated by their lack of capacity to enforce their rights under the Agreement. Second, developing countries suffer limitations in their abilities to meet the SPS requirements of their trading partners, particularly developed countries, even when these are consistent with the provisions of the SPS Agreement.[226]

The WTO has classified SDT provisions into six categories: provisions aimed at increasing the trade opportunities of developing countries; provisions under which Members should safeguard the interests of developing country Members; flexibility of commitments, of action, and of use of policy instruments; transitional time periods; technical assistance; and provisions relating to least-developed country Members.[227] These provisions contain no binding obligations and are 'remarkably vague and aspirational in approach'.[228] Furthermore, they are mostly unenforceable, as they are expressed in imprecise and hortatory language.[229] Even where these provisions are couched in mandatory terms, this may not be sufficient to make them enforceable.[230]

The status of SDT provisions renders developing countries even more vulnerable in the WTO rule-based system, since provisions intended to enable them to integrate into the system are unenforceable. This has the effect of increasing legal inequality between developed and developing countries and creates an imbalance in a rule-based system.[231] Moreover, it is contended by developing countries that even in the dispute settlement system, the development aspect is rarely taken into account:

> A careful reading of the accumulated jurisprudence of the [dispute settlement] system thus far reveals that the interests and perceptions of developing countries have not been adequately taken into account. The panels and the Appellate Body have displayed an excessively sanitized concern with

---

[226] Denise Prevost, 'Operationalising Special and Differential Treatment of Developing Countries under the SPS Agreement' (2005) 30 *South Africa Yearbook of International Law* 7. For analysis pertaining to the EU and ACP trade, see Denis Prevost, 'Sanitary, Phytosanitary and Technical Barriers to Trade in the Economic Partnership Agreements between the European Union and the ACP Countries' (International Centre for Trade and Sustainable Development (ICTSD), Geneva, Switzerland, 2009), <http://papers.ssrn.com/sol3/papers.cfm?abstract_id=1692634>

[227] WTO Secretariat, 'Note on Implementation of Special and Differential Treatment Provisions in WTO Agreements and Decisions' (WT/COMDT/W/77, 25 October 2000) 3.

[228] John H Jackson, *The World Trading System* (2nd edn MIT Press, Cambridge, Massachusetts, 1997) 319.

[229] Edwini Kessie, 'Enforceability of the Legal Provisions Relating to Special and Differential Treatment Under the WTO Agreements' (2000) 3 *The Journal of World Intellectual Property* 955, 964–974.

[230] Prevost D (2005) (n 226) 13. See also *Panel Reports, EC – Biotech*, paras 7.1620–7.1625.

[231] Gustavo Olivares, 'The Case of Giving Effectiveness to GATT/WTO Rules on Developing Countries and LDCs' (2001) 35 *Journal of World Trade* 545, 550.

legalisms, often to the detriment of the evolution of a development-friendly jurisprudence.[232]

The Doha Ministerial Decision addressed the problem of making SDT provisions more precise, effective, and operational by recommending that they be analysed with a view to converting them into mandatory provisions.[233] There have been a few proposals by Members to the SPS Committee towards converting SDT provisions into mandatory provisions, but these have not resulted in any recommendations to the General Council because of their far-reaching implications on the other obligations under the WTO Agreements.[234] In effect, the proposal to make the SDT provisions mandatory is impractical. Mandatory SDT provisions could create a conflict with the right of Members to achieve their chosen level of protection under Article 3.3 of the SPS Agreement. Furthermore, since SPS measures are primarily aimed at protecting the health and life of domestic consumers, plants, and animals, it might be impractical to expect Members to effectively take into account developing country constraints, which are many and varied, in their domestic regulations.

At the level of implementation, technical assistance is often characterised as supply driven, and may be determined to a greater extent by the policy interests of the donors rather than the specific needs of the recipients. Members have expressed concern that in the absence of more targeted, specific, trade-assistance goals, addressing timelines and sustainability in an efficient manner may be difficult.[235] Although the non-mandatory nature of technical assistance provisions is blamed for their lack of effectiveness in generating support for developing countries, the more cogent reason might be lack of efficient articulation between trade-related assistance and reforms undertaken pursuant to such assistance. The assistance may not always correspond to the recipient's priorities and demands in the context of its development strategy.[236] This calls for technical cooperation between the developed and developing countries and among regional trade organisations that would entail targeted research into assessing trade-related needs; assistance in upgrading scientific infrastructure such as laboratories,

---

232 Asif H Qureshi, *Interpreting WTO Agreements: Problems and Perspectives* (Cambridge University Press, 2006) 114–159 (fn 3) quoting Zambia, on behalf of the LDC Group, in proposals for amending the WTO DSU (TN/DS/W/17, 9 October 2002). The author concludes that although there is a need for a development-friendly interpretation of the WTO Agreements, there is no coherent and expressly articulated development-friendly approach to that effect.
233 Ministerial Decision, para 12.1.
234 WTO Committee on Sanitary and Phytosanitary Measures, 'Report on Proposals for Special and Differential Treatment' (G/SPS/35, 7 July 2005) 3–6.
235 Ibid 6.
236 OECD, 'Special and Differential Treatment in the Area of Trade Facilitation' (OECD Trade Policy Working Paper No. 32, TD/TC/WP (2006) 9/FINAL, 28 March 2006) 4.

certification bodies, and accreditation institutions; and financial assistance to meet SPS obligations.[237]

The Panel in *EC – Biotech*, while considering Article 10.1 of the SPS Agreement, which requires Members to 'take account' of the special needs of developing countries, noted that the Article does not prescribe 'a specific result to be achieved', and that the SDT factor is just one among several to be considered.[238] Even though the Article is couched in mandatory language, it is difficult to enforce because a Member only has to show that it took account of the special needs of developing countries, not that it took any action in that regard. Perhaps under the procedure to enhance the transparency of the SDT of developing countries there will be sufficient evidence to show whether or not a developing Member's needs were taken into account in a contested measure.

Members' proposals for amendments to Articles 9.2 and 10.1 of the SPS Agreement are to the effect that where the importing Member is unable to provide assistance, it should withdraw the measure or compensate the developing countries for loss resulting from the measure.[239] This may not be practical, as it will amount to a tax on importing countries that are unable to accommodate the special needs of developing countries.

Article 10.2 of the SPS Agreement provides for longer compliance periods to be accorded to developing countries in cases where an SPS measure allows for phased introduction. The operative word in the provision is 'should' but, unlike Article 10.1, it does provide for specific actions to give effect to the provision. The Ministerial Decision further concretised the provision by providing for the longer time to be a period not less than six months and, if this is not possible, Members are required to enter into consultation. However, with the noted disadvantages faced by developing countries, it is arguable whether what is needed is the extension of compliance periods or the encouragement of alternative ways of meeting the requirements of SPS measures. For instance, while developed countries have the technological ability to devise and meet standards, it should also be recognised that such standards might be fulfilled by other means not utilizing such technology.

1.6.5 Conclusion

Since the enactment of the Standards Code and its successor, the SPS Agreement, there has been some hope that the disciplining of SPS measures will eliminate or at least minimise SPS measures as non-tariff barriers. The emphasis on

---

237 Michael F Jensen 'Special and Differential Treatment and Differentiation between Developing Countries in the WTO' (Danish Institute for International Studies, A Policy Study Commissioned by the Danish Ministry of Foreign Affairs, 5 July 2005) 17, <http://forskning.ku.dk/find-en-forsker/?pure=files%2F8065189%2FSDTpolicystudy.pdf>
238 *Panel Reports EC-Biotech*, paras 7.1620–7.1621.
239 WTO Committee on Sanitary and Phytosanitary Measures, 'Report on Proposals for Special and Differential Treatment' (G/SPS/35, 7 July 2005) 5.

harmonisation was viewed as a means of removing trade distorting differences in SPS measures among countries. However, experience with the application of the SPS Agreement has shown that differences in SPS measures among countries still persist. This may be attributable to the Appellate Body's interpretation, in *EC – Hormones*, that strict harmonisation is not a requirement of the SPS Agreement and its granting greater flexibility to Members in setting their own levels of appropriate protection. The Appellate Body has further loosened the strictness of the SPS Agreement with its lax interpretation of risk assessment and the introduction of the rational relationship test, under which a risk assessment may pass muster with a tenuous connection to science.

Developing countries still continue to face hurdles posed by developed countries' SPS measures. Developed countries have continued in their policy of maintaining stringent SPS standards. The solution offered to developing countries – that of enhancing their capacities to meet these stringent standards – faces many limitations, including the inadequacy of such capacity-building exercises. This has led to a situation where, particularly for exports to the European Union, developing countries have the choice of either adopting the developed country standards in order to gain access to their markets, or trading in primary commodities and live animals, which face fewer SPS requirements than processed products.[240] This confines developing countries to their traditional role as exporters of low value raw materials and importers of high value finished goods. In turn, this exacerbates the poverty of developing countries, thus defeating the sustainable development objectives of the WTO Agreement.

Given the problems of interpretation faced by Panels and the Appellate Body in defining risk assessment and harmonisation, the SPS Committee should clearly define these terms in order to make them more effective and in particular provide for the factors, scientific and non-scientific, to be taken into account in a risk assessment. Where there are no international standards, it may be difficult to contest a Member's risk assessment in the absence of recognised benchmarks and set criteria. Furthermore, it appears that there is a conflict between the objective of harmonisation and the right of Members to set their own level of appropriate protection. The latter necessarily diminishes the former. The Committee should further clarify Article 11 paragraph 2 of the Agreement by providing a procedure for the establishment of the advisory technical experts group when required to do so by the Panel.[241]

---

240 See Spencer Henson and Steven Jaffee, 'Agro-Food Exports from Developing Countries: The Challenges Posed by Standards' in M A Aksoy and J C Beghin (eds) *Global Agricultural Trade and Developing Countries* (The World Bank, Washington, DC, 2005) 91, 103–105.

241 The WTO Dispute Settlement Body (DSB) was mandated, by the Fourth Ministerial Conference. See Doha Ministerial Declaration, WT/MIN (01)/DEC/1, 20 November 2001, para 30 – to open formal negotiations on amendments to the DSU. However, to date no clear recommendations have been forwarded to the General Council for a decision. See Special Session of the Dispute Settlement Body: Report by the Chairman, Ambassador Ronald Saborio Soto, to the General Council (TN/DS/11 September 2006).

The challenges faced by developing countries in the implementation of the SPS Agreement may eventually be overcome if these countries become standards setters instead of standards takers. This will be achieved when developing countries' technical capacities regarding SPS issues have advanced to the level of developing countries. This will enable their effective participation in the standards-setting process in the relevant international organisations. With their enhanced capacity, developing countries will be able to determine standards that will be suitable to their conditions and to justify these whenever challenged to do so. Developing countries will also be able to participate in and contribute to the setting of international standards in the international organisations.

2 EU food safety standards

In matters relating to the health of the consumer, scientific evidence is of the utmost importance at all stages of the drawing up of new legislation and for the execution and management of existing legislation.[1]

EU food safety standards are not negotiable.[2]

2.1 Introduction

In 1996, hard on the heels of the enactment of the SPS Agreement, there was a food safety crisis in the EU. This was the 1996 Bovine Spongiform Encephalopathy (BSE) epidemic.[3] BSE is a degenerative brain disease that affects cattle and is transmissible to other animals and to humans. BSE occurred for the first time in the United Kingdom in 1984, and grew into a European epidemic by 1996.[4] The disease caused panic and fear among Europeans with the announcement by the United Kingdom, in March 1996, of the potential link between BSE and the new variant human disease Creutzfeldt-Jakob Disease (nvCJD).[5]

---

1 European Commission, 'Communication on Consumer Health and Food Safety' (COM (1997) 183 final).
2 David Byrne, EU Commissioner for Health and Consumer Protection, European Commission (Press Release (2001), Round table on food and agriculture in Copenhagen: Strategic re-thinking of food production in terms of quality, safety and costs, IP/01/1724, Copenhagen, 3 December 2001), <http://europa.eu/rapid/press-release_IP-01-1724_en.htm> accessed 10 April 2015.
3 Ellen Vos, 'EU Food Safety Regulation in the Aftermath of the BSE Crisis' (2000) 23 *Journal of Consumer Policy* 227, 233–234. The author points out that the Commission moved away from an approach emphasizing food security to an approach emphasizing food safety, linked to the protection of consumers.
4 For details see the OIE web page <www.oie.int/eng/ressources/en_BSE_Disease_Card.pdf> accessed 10 April 2015.
5 For an analysis of the BSE crisis see Keith Vincent, '"Mad Cows" and Eurocrats-Community Responses to the BSE Crisis' (2004) 10 *European Law Journal* 499. For an analysis of the impact of food safety scares on EU food policy, see Tim Knowles, Richard Moody and Morven G McEachern, 'European Food Scares and Their Impact on EU Food Policy' (2007) 109 (1) *British Food Journal* 43. The authors conclude that there is evidence of evolution from a product-focused food policy to a risk-based policy, which has developed into a tentative EU consumer-based food policy.

The BSE crisis brought to the fore all the shortcomings that had hitherto bedevilled the EU's food safety policy and institutions.[6] As a consequence of the BSE crisis, the EU developed a new policy on food safety based upon a comprehensive, integrated approach that took into account traceability of feed and food, and their ingredients; risk analysis; and the precautionary principle and other legitimate factors. Henceforth, under the Treaty on the Functioning of the European Union (TFEU), EU food safety policy and regulations would be anchored on scientific justification[7] and would aim at a high level of protection of human health.[8] Moreover, scientific justification would be a necessary requirement for Commission proposals, decisions, and policy relating to consumer health.[9] The new policy orientation led to the enactment of Regulation 178 of 2002,[10] the EU general food law,[11] whose main objective is the assurance of a high level of protection of human health and consumers' interests while ensuring the effective functioning of the internal market.[12]

There is no specific provision in the TFEU that deals with Members' SPS regulations.[13] The EU SPS regulations are a result of the harmonisation of national SPS regulations designed to facilitate the free movement of foodstuffs, alongside other goods, and to prevent anti-competitive behaviour in the establishment of the single market.[14] National SPS regulations constitute barriers to the free

---

6 For analysis of the development of the EU food safety regulation, see Alberto Alemanno, *Trade in Food: Regulatory and Judicial Approaches in the EC and the WTO* (Cameron May, London, 2008) 31–72. For an overview of EU food law, see Bernhard M J V Meulen (ed), *EU Food Law Handbook* (European Institute for Food Law, Wageningen Academic Publishers, Wageningen, The Netherlands, 2014).
7 Consolidated version of the Treaty on the Functioning of the European Union [2008] OJ C 115/47 of 9 May 2008 TFEU, art 9.
8 TFEU, art 114 (3).
9 Commission Decision (EC) 2008/721/EC of 5 August 2008, setting up an advisory structure of Scientific Committees and experts in the field of consumer safety, public health, and the environment and repealing Decision 2004/210/EC [2008] OJ L 241/21 of 10.9.2008, preamble, para 6.
10 Regulation (EC) 178 of 2002 of the European Parliament and of the Council of 28 January 2002, laying down the general principles and requirements of food law, establishing the European Food Safety Authority, and laying down procedures in matters of food safety [2002] OJ L 031/1 of 1. 2. 2002 (Regulation 178 of 2002).
11 Damian Chalmers, '"Food for Thought": Reconciling European Risks and Traditional Ways of Life' (2003) 66 *The Modern Law Review* 532, 534. The author argues that food safety risks were no longer matters of national concern but of European political concern. Henceforth, risks were to be measured by the Commission in terms of European norms of safety.
12 Regulation 178 of 2002, art 1(1).
13 Marco M Slotboom, *Do Different Treaty Purposes Matter for Treaty Interpretation? A Comparison of WTO and EC Law* (Cameron May, Brussels, 2005) 130.
14 Alberto Alemanno, 'Food Safety and the Single European Market' in Christopher Ansell and David Vogel (eds) *What's the Beef? The Contested Governance of European Food Safety* (MIT Press, Cambridge, MA, 2006) 237, 239. The author postulates that EU food legislation has mainly been prompted by the desire to eliminate trade obstacles within the internal market and so food legislation has been designed to create uniformity and to have community-wide effect.

movement of goods, and hence trade.[15] As such, they may infringe on Article 34 of the TFEU, which provides that 'quantitative restrictions on imports and all measures having equivalent effect shall be prohibited between Member States'. Such national regulations may be justified under the exceptions of Article 36 TFEU, which provides that 'the provisions of Articles 34–35 shall not preclude prohibitions or restrictions on imports, exports or goods in transit justified on grounds of (. . .) the protection of health and life of humans, animals or plants. (. . .) Such prohibitions or restrictions shall not, however, constitute a means of arbitrary discrimination or a disguised restriction on trade between Member States'. Hence, EU SPS regulations have to reconcile the principle of free movement of goods within the internal market with the need for protection of human health.[16]

Having examined the general SPS disciplines as laid down in the SPS Agreement in chapter one, this chapter will examine the EU food safety legal framework regulation and its main food safety policies. This will serve as an illustration of the application of the principles of the SPS Agreement in developed countries. It will also seek to determine to what extent the EU food safety regime is in line with the SPS Agreement and the jurisprudence of the WTO dispute panels and Appellate Body.

The chapter proceeds as follows. Section 2 will be an overview of the EU general food law under Regulation 178 of 2002. Section 3 will analyse the European Food Safety Authority (EFSA). This will be followed in section 4 with a critical analysis of the EU food safety policy and regulation. The section will analyse the role of science in EU food safety risk analysis vis-à-vis the international SPS standards. The analysis will encompass the jurisprudence of the CJ and GC and WTO panels and Appellate Body. The roles of 'other legitimate factors' and the precautionary principle in EU risk analysis are contrasted with the roles that these factors and principle play in international standards-setting organizations. Section 5 will examine the Global Administrative and constitutional law perspectives of

---

15 Ellen Vos and Frank Wendler, 'Food Safety Regulations in the EU Level' in E Vos and F Wendler (eds) *Food Safety Regulations in Europe: A Comparative Institutional Analysis* (Intersentia, Antwerpen-Oxford, 2006) 65, 67. The authors argue that EU SPS regulations were developed to eliminate national SPS regulations as barriers to intra EU trade.
16 Anna Szajkowska, 'Ensuring Food Safety in the Internal Market: Legislative Dynamics in EU Food Law' (Law and Governance Workshop, Wageningen University, 14 December 2006) 1, <www.researchgate.net/publication/40108730_Ensuring_Food_Safety_in_the_Internal_Market_Legislative_Dynamics_in_EU_Food_Law>. The author characterises food safety law as an example of risk regulation, understood as, 'governmental interference with market or social processes to control potential adverse consequences to health' (citation omitted). The author argues that the EU shares competence with Members in food safety law: Members have competence unless there is a harmonising regulation at the EU level. Consequently, there are two types of SPS regulations in the EU: national non-harmonised regulations and EU-wide harmonised regulations.

2.2 Regulation 178 of 2002

Regulation 178 of 2002[17] lays down the general principles governing food and feed in general, and food and feed safety in particular, at the EU and national levels, and applies to all stages of production, processing, and distribution of food and feed.[18] The Regulation defines food as 'any substance or product, whether processed, partially processed or unprocessed, intended to be, or reasonably expected to be ingested by humans'.[19]

Regulation 178 has three objectives: the protection of human life and health and the protection of consumers' interests, with due regard for the protection of animal health and welfare, plant health, and the environment; the free movement of human food and animal feed in the internal market; and that international standards are taken into consideration in the development or adaptation of food law.[20]

Regulation 178 seeks to achieve its objectives by providing for a comprehensive EU food policy that applies at national and community levels and to food imports, in four ways. First, it provides for general principles for ensuring food safety.[21] Second, it provides for obligations and requirements of the EU food law.[22] Third, it provides for some procedures relating to matters of food safety.[23] Fourth, it provides for the establishment of the European Food Safety Authority (EFSA).[24]

Risk analysis is defined under the Regulation as a process consisting of the three components of risk assessment, risk management, and risk communication. Risk assessment is defined as 'a scientifically based process consisting of four steps: hazard identification, hazard characterisation, exposure assessment and risk characterisation', while risk management is defined as 'the process, distinct from risk assessment, of weighing policy alternatives in consultation with interested parties,

---

17 The Regulation is founded on arts 43, 114, 207, and 168 (4) (b) TFEU. For an in-depth analysis of the Regulation see Alemanno A (n 6) 73–160. See also Morten P Broberg, 'Transforming the European Community's Regulation of Food Safety' (Swedish Institute for European Policy Studies, Report No. 5, April/2008) 62–80.
18 Regulation 178 of 2002, art 1(1) (2).
19 Ibid, art 2.
20 Ibid, art 5.
21 Ibid, arts 5–10.
22 Ibid, arts 10–21.
23 Ibid, arts 50–57.
24 Ibid, arts 21–49.

considering risk assessment and other legitimate factors, and, if need be, selecting appropriate prevention and control options'.[25]

Moreover, and significantly, under Regulation 178, food law is to be based on risk analysis, except where this is not appropriate to the circumstances or the nature of the measure.[26] Where there is scientific uncertainty after a risk assessment, precautionary measures may be taken pending further information and a more comprehensive assessment.[27] Furthermore, the traceability of food, food-producing animals, and any other substance intended to be, or expected to be, incorporated into a food must be established at all stages of production, processing, and distribution.[28]

Food business operators are responsible for the fulfilment of the requirements of the Regulation at all stages of production, processing, and distribution. National governments are responsible for enforcing the Regulation and for the monitoring and verification of the fulfilment of its requirements by food business operators.[29]

Regulation 178/2000 was reinforced by several implementing regulations and directives.[30] Furthermore, the Regulation establishes the European Food Safety Authority (EFSA) as the centre of EU food safety scientific basis.

---

25 Ibid, art 3 (11) (12).
26 Ibid, art 6. Para 19 of the Regulation's preamble provides that, in risk management, other factors should be taken into account, including societal, economic, traditional, ethical, and environmental factors and the feasibility of controls.
27 Ibid, art 7. See also European Commission, 'Communication from the Commission on the Precautionary Principle' (COM (2000) 1 final).
28 Ibid, art 18. See also Christophe Charlier and Egizio Valceschini, 'Coordination for Traceability in the Food Chain: A Critical Appraisal of European Regulation' (2008) 25 *European Journal of Law and Economics* 1, 2. The authors argue that 'complete traceability through the entire food chain is useless if the sanitary risk emanates from the distribution stage and not the extraction of the raw materials. To be efficient, traceability must be able to be adjusted to the data. With "universal" mandatory traceability, such as that required by European Regulation 178 of 2002, this kind of adjustment is impossible'.
29 Ibid, art 17.
30 The main implementing regulations and Directives are: Regulation (EC) no 852/2004 of the European Parliament and of the Council on the hygiene of foodstuffs [2004] OJ L 226/3, 29 April 2004; Regulation (EC) no 853/2004 of the European Parliament and of the Council, laying down specific hygiene rules for food of animal origin, [2004] OJ L 226/22, 29 April 2004; Regulation (EC) no 854/2004 of the European Parliament and of the Council, laying down specific rules for the organization of official controls on products of animal origin intended for human consumption, [2004] OJ L 226/83, 29 April 2004; Directive (EC) 2004/41/EC, repealing certain Directives concerning food hygiene and health conditions for the production and placing on the market of certain products of animal origin intended for human consumption and amending Council Directives 89/662/EEC and 92/118/EEC and Council Decision 95/408/EC, [2004] OJ L157/33, 21 April 2004; Regulation (EC) no 882/2004 of the European Parliament and of the Council on official controls performed to ensure the verification of compliance with feed and food law, animal health, and animal welfare rules, [2004] OJ L 191/1, 29 April 2004; Council Directive (EC) 2002/99/EC, laying down the animal health rules governing the production, processing, distribution, and introduction of products of animal origin for human consumption, OJ L 18/11, 16 December 2002.

2.3 The European Food Safety Authority (EFSA)

The establishment of EFSA[31] was the final step in re-establishing EU credibility in food regulation.[32] The EFSA is a normative agency:[33] it provides scientific advice and scientific and technical support for the EU legislation on food safety.[34] The EFSA has a dual objective: to protect public health and secure food safety, and to ensure the operation of the internal market.[35]

Article 1 of Regulation 178 sets the assurance of high levels of protection of public health and consumer interest and the effective functioning of the internal market as the basic aims of the Regulation. Article 5 of the Regulation, which sets out the general principles of food law, puts the protection of a high level of public health and consumer protection, together with the free movement of food and feed, as some of the objectives of food law. Article 8 of the Regulation emphasises the aim of food law as the protection of consumer interests and provides the basis upon which consumers will make informed choices concerning the food they consume, also aiming to prevent 'fraudulent or deceptive practices; the adulteration of food; and any other practices which may mislead the consumer'. Under Article 22 of the Regulation, which establishes the EFSA, the scientific work of the EFSA will be carried out 'in the context of the internal market'. Moreover, under paragraph 3 of the Regulation's preamble, the objectives of the protection of public health and the consumer are seen as enhancing the free movement of food within the internal market. Furthermore, the EFSA is to 'provide scientific advice and scientific and technical support for EU legislation (. . .)'[36] and to 'serve

---

31 For an in-depth analysis of EFSA, see Alberto Alemanno and Simone Gabbi (eds), *Foundations of EU Food Law and Policy – Ten Years of European Food Safety Authority* (Ashgate Publishing, London, 2014).
32 Klara Kanska, 'Wolves in the Clothing of Sheep? The Case of the European Food Safety Authority' (2004) 29 *European Law Review* 711. According to the author, the reforms necessary to accomplish credibility consisted of ultimately replacing the scientific committees that were controlled by the Commission with the more transparent and independent EFSA. See also Susana Borras, Charalampos Koutalakis and Frank Wendler, 'European Agencies and Input Legitimacy: EFSA, EMeA and EPO in the Post-Delegation Phase' (2007) 29 *Journal of European Integration* 583, 589–590. The authors argue that among agencies, the issue of trust and credibility is particularly essential in the case of EFSA.
33 Chalmers D (n 11) 533. The author views EFSA as a transnational governance regime whose norms influence and determine food law in the European Union. Arguably these norms may be in the form of 'Soft Law'. See also Frank Wendler, 'The European Food Safety Authority as a Source of "Soft Law": Towards more Effective and Legitimate EU Food Safety Governance?' (Paper presented at the CONNEX Workshop: Soft Governance and the Private Sector: The EU and Global Experience, Darmstadt, 1–3 November 2005) 5–7, <http://www.mzes.uni-mannheim.de/projekte/typo3/site/fileadmin/research%20groups/6/Papers_Soft%20Mode/Wendler.pdf> accessed 1 May 2015.
34 Regulation 178 of 2002, art 22 (2).
35 Lise Hellebo, 'Food Safety at Stake: The Establishment of Food Agencies' (Stein Rokkan Centre for Social Studies, Working Paper No. 14, 2004) 23, <http://hdl.handle.net/1956/1351> accessed 1 May 2015.
36 Regulation 178 of 2002, art 22 (2).

as a point of reference (. . .)'[37] for the same. Ultimately, the aims of the Regulation and the EFSA are to enhance EU integration through the harmonisation of EU food law.[38]

Through the EFSA, Regulation 178 seeks to restore consumer confidence and regain the credibility of EU food legislation and institutions.[39] To begin with, the Regulation states that it shall apply to all stages of food production, processing, and distribution.[40] In effect, all aspects of food are to be regulated to ensure safety and public health. A high level of protection is sought under Article 5, and henceforth food law is to be based on risk analysis and, where appropriate, the precautionary principle will be applied. Article 8 ensures consumers of their protection. Under Article 9, the public is to be involved during the preparation, evaluation, and revision of food law. Where there is suspicion that a food may present a risk for human health, Article 10 mandates that the public shall be informed of the risk, and the remedial measures to be taken. Article 13 ensures that while the EU food laws are benchmarked with international standards, the EU higher level of protection is maintained. Misleading labels, advertisements, and presentations of food are prohibited under Article 16. The EFSA's Scientific Committee and permanent Scientific Panels, which are said to be independent from the Commission, conduct independent studies and issue opinions which are taken into account in formulating food law.[41] Overall, the EFSA's principles of independence,[42] transparency,[43] and confidentiality,[44] and its duties to ensure communication of its risk decisions,[45] access to its documents,[46] and to develop effective contacts with consumers and other stakeholders,[47] may all be viewed in the light of developing confidence and regaining credibility in EU food safety law.

The main mission of the EFSA is the provision of scientific advice and scientific and technical support for the EU's legislation and policies in all fields which have a direct or indirect impact on food and feed safety.[48] This includes the provision of scientific advice about and scientific and technical support for human nutrition in relation to EU legislation and also of scientific opinions on products other than food and feed relating to genetically modified organisms.[49]

Although the EFSA has no risk management functions (that is, legislative and enforcement powers), it has normative authority, and its opinions structure

---

37 Ibid, art 22 (7).
38 Hellebo L (n 35) 23.
39 Regulation 178 of 2002, preamble paras 9, 22, 23, 35 and 40.
40 Regulation 178 of 2002, art 1 (3).
41 Ibid, arts 28, 29 and 32.
42 Ibid, art 37.
43 Ibid, art 38.
44 Ibid, art 39.
45 Ibid, art 40.
46 Ibid, art 41.
47 Ibid, art 42.
48 Ibid, art 22 (2).
49 Ibid, art 22 (5).

institutional and individual choices on food safety within the EU.[50] To fulfil its mandated mission, the Regulation assigns the EFSA the following main tasks:[51] (a) the promotion and coordination of the development of uniform risk assessment methodologies in the fields falling within its mission; (b) the provision of scientific and technical support for the Commission in the areas within its mission and, when so requested, in the interpretation and consideration of risk assessment opinions; (c) the commissioning of scientific studies necessary for the accomplishment of its mission;[52] (d) the search for, collection, collation, analysis, and summary of scientific and technical data in the fields within its mission;[53] (e) the identification and characterisation of emerging risks in the fields within its mission;[54] (f) the establishment of a system of networks of organisations operating in the fields within its mission and responsibility for their operation;[55] (g) the provision of scientific and technical assistance, when requested by the Commission, in the crisis management procedures implemented by the Commission with regard to the safety of food and feed; (h) the provision of scientific and technical assistance, when requested by the Commission, with a view to improving cooperation among the EU, applicant countries, international organisations, and third countries, in the fields within its mission; (i) ensuring that the public and interested parties receive rapid, reliable, objective, and comprehensible information in the fields within its mission;[56] (j) the expression of its independent conclusions and orientations on matters within its mission; and (k) the provision of scientific opinions to the EU institutions and the Member states.[57] The EFSA's scientific functions may therefore be characterised as providing scientific opinions, guidance, and advice as well as risk assessment; monitoring specific risk factors and diseases as well as identifying and characterising emerging risks; and developing, promoting, and applying new and harmonised scientific approaches for hazard and risk assessment of food and feed.[58]

50 Chalmers D (n 11) 540. The author argues that EFSA's opinions have a legal effect in that EU institutions and national institutions are bound to take them into account in their food legislation. Private food operators are also bound to place only safe food in the market; this entails risk analysis. See also Kanska K (n 32) 712. The author argues that since food law is mainly science based, EFSA's scientific risk assessment mandate gives it power similar to regulatory power; Wendler F (n 33) 7. The author points out to the various provisions of the Regulation laying down the functions of EFSA and asserts that these provisions allow EFSA to exercise various elements of 'soft governance' in principle.
51 Regulation 178 of 2002, art 23. See generally Marco Silano and Vittorio Silano, 'The Fifth Anniversary of the European Food Safety Authority (EFSA): Mission, Organization, Functioning and Main Results' (2008) 79 *Fitoterapia* 149.
52 Regulation 178 of 2002, art 32.
53 Ibid, art 33.
54 Ibid, art 34.
55 Ibid, art 36.
56 Ibid, arts 9–10.
57 Ibid, art 29.
58 Alberto Alemanno, 'The European Food Safety Authority at Five' (2008) 1 *European Food and Feed Law Review* 6.

To carry out its tasks, the EFSA is composed of a Management Board, an Executive Director with staff, an Advisory Forum, a Scientific Committee, and Scientific Panels.[59] The Management Board is composed of 14 members, appointed for a renewable period of four years by the Council in consultation with the European Parliament from a list drawn up by the Commission, plus a representative of the Commission. Four of the members have backgrounds in organisations representing consumers and other interests in the food chain. The Management Board ensures that the EFSA carries out its mission and performs the tasks assigned to it. It does this by adopting the EFSA's annual budget and its programme of work for the coming year together with a revisable multi-annual programme and the general report on the EFSA's activities for the previous year.[60] Of note is that the Board members are not state representatives but are independent, save for the four consumers' and stakeholders' representatives.

The Executive Director is appointed by the Management Board from a list proposed by the Commission, for a renewable period of five years, and may be removed from office by a majority of the Management Board. The Executive Director is the legal representative of the EFSA and is mainly responsible for (a) overseeing the day-to-day administration of EFSA; (b) drawing up a proposal for the EFSA's work programmes in consultation with the Commission; (c) implementing the work programmes and the decisions adopted by the Management Board; (d) ensuring the provision of appropriate scientific, technical, and administrative support for the Scientific Committee and the Scientific Panels; (e) ensuring that the EFSA carries out its tasks in accordance with the requirements of its users, in particular with regard to the adequacy of the services provided and the time taken; (f) preparing the statement of revenue and expenditure and executing the EFSA's budget; (g) preparing the statement of revenue and expenditure and executing the budget of the Authority; (h) developing and maintaining contact with the European Parliament, and ensuring a regular dialogue with its relevant committees; and (i) annually submitting to the Management Board for approval, (1) a draft of a general report covering all the activities of the Authority in the previous year; (2) a draft of programmes of work; (3) a draft of the annual accounts for the previous year; and (4) a draft of the budget for the coming year.[61]

The Advisory Forum is composed of representatives from national European food safety authorities, on the basis of one representative per Member state. It advises the Executive Director in the performance of his or her duties, particularly in drawing up the proposal for the Authority's work programme. It constitutes a mechanism for the exchange of information about potential risks and the pooling of knowledge, and ensures close cooperation between the EFSA and the competent bodies in the Member states.[62]

59 Regulation 178 of 2002, art 24.
60 Ibid, art 25.
61 Ibid, art 26.
62 Ibid, art 27.

The Scientific Committee is composed of the Chairs of the Scientific Panels and six independent scientific experts who do not belong to any of the Scientific Panels. The members of the Scientific Committee are appointed by the Management Board, acting upon a proposal from the Executive Director, for a renewable three-year term. The Scientific Committee is responsible for the general coordination necessary to ensure the consistency of the scientific opinion procedure, especially with regard to the adoption of working procedures and the harmonisation of working methods. It also provides opinions on multi-sectoral issues falling within the competence of more than one Scientific Panel, and on issues which do not fall within the competence of any of the Scientific Panels.[63]

Scientific Panels are composed of independent scientists appointed by the Management Board, acting upon a proposal from the Executive Director, for a renewable three-year term. The main task of the Scientific Panels is the issuance of scientific opinions based on risk assessment in their spheres of competence.[64]

Having examined the EU general food law and EFSA, the following sections will critically examine the EU general food law in the light of the provisions of the SPS Agreement and the Codex Alimentarius Commission (the Codex) in light of the jurisprudence of the WTO panels and Appellate Body decisions and the judgements of the Court of Justice of the EU (the CJ) and the General Court (GC).

2.4 A critical overview of the EU food safety policy and standards

Both the SPS Agreement and the EU require scientific justification for food safety standards. However, tension between the two regulatory regimes arises from their divergent underpinnings. On the one hand, the primary justification of the SPS Agreement is the elimination of protectionist food safety standards and also genuine food safety standards which are more trade restrictive than necessary. On the other hand, the EU food safety standards are justified under the common market imperative of free movement of goods and also the protection of consumer health.[65] Hence, the EU's food safety objectives go further, to include the

---

63 Ibid, art 28.
64 Ibid. There are currently 10 Scientific Panels: Panel on food additives and nutrient sources added to food (ANS); Panel on additives, flavourings, processing aids, and materials in contact with food (AFC); Panel on animal health and welfare (AHAW); Panel on biological hazards (BIOHAZ); Panel on contaminants in the food chain (CONTAM); Panel on additives and products or substances used in animal feed (FEEDAP); Panel on Genetically Modified Organisms (GMO); Panel on dietetic products, nutrition, and allergies (NDA); Panel on plant protection products and their residues (PPR); Panel on plant health (PLH) (added by Commission Regulation [EC] No 575/2006, amending Regulation [EC] No 178 of 2002 of the European Parliament and of the Council as regards the number and names of the permanent Scientific Panels of the European Food Safety Authority [2006] OJ L100/3, 7 April 2006). See EFSA Website: www.efsa.europa.eu.
65 Alemanno A (n 6) 313.

protection of consumers' interests; fair practices in food trade; the protection of animal health and welfare; and health of plants and the environment.⁶⁶ The EU's food safety objectives are also intended to achieve the EU's general objective of free movement of food and feed.⁶⁷

Moreover, although WTO Members are required to base their SPS standards on the standards set by the Codex,⁶⁸ and there is a safe harbour rebuttable presumption of conformity for Members that conform their SPS standards to the Codex standards,⁶⁹ the EU is a selective policy recipient of Codex standards. These standards are taken into account in the adoption of EU food safety standards so long as they are compatible with the EU's food safety objectives.⁷⁰

As a result of these differences in policy orientation, a number of the EU's food safety standards have been contested in the SPS Committee.⁷¹ Some of these standards have also been the subject of trade concerns by WTO Members in the SPS Committee⁷² and resulted in two WTO disputes: *EC – Hormones* and *EC – Biotech*.

Broadly, the main EU food safety policies and regulations that are controversial and of concern to international trade in food products are the policy of considering 'other legitimate factors' in its risk analysis; the policy of the precautionary principle; regulations on Maximum Residue Limits (MRLs) of contaminants, additives, and pesticides; and regulations on genetically modified organisms (GMOs).

The EU's risk analysis policy, by incorporating 'other legitimate factors' apart from science, has generated controversy in the Codex standardisation process.⁷³ The EU's policy on the precautionary principle is, in light of the WTO's Panels and Appellate Body findings on the principle, likely to be in conflict with the provisions of the SPS Agreement.⁷⁴ Moreover, the principle is contentious within the Codex.⁷⁵ The EUMRL's regulations are also contested, in particular its pes-

---

66 Regulation 178 of 2002, art 5.1.
67 Ibid, art 5.2.
68 SPS Agreement, art 3(1).
69 Ibid, art 3(2).
70 Sara Poli, 'The European Community and the Adoption of International Food Standards within the Codex Alimentarius Commission' (2004) 10 *European Law Journal* 613, 616.
71 Marco M Slotboom, 'Do Public Health Measures Receive Similar Treatment in European Community and World Trade Organization Law?' (2003) 37 *Journal of World Trade* 553, 553. See also Alasdair R Young and Peter Holmes, 'Protection or Protectionism? EU Food Safety and the WTO' in D Vogel and C Ansell (eds) *What's the Beef? The Contested Governance of European Food Safety* (MIT Press, Cambridge, MA, 2006) 281, 286.
72 WTO Committee on Sanitary and Phytosanitary Measures, 'Specific Trade Concerns, Note by the Secretariat, Revision' (G/SPS/GEN/204/Rev.14, 4 March 2014) 8–26 and 41–51.
73 Frode Veggeland and Svein O Borgen, 'Negotiating International Food Standards: The World Trade Organization's Impact on the Codex Alimentarius Commission' (2005) 18 *Governance* 675, 698. See also Alemanno A (n 6) 403; Marielle D M Matthee, *The Codex Alimentarius Commission and Its Standards* (T.M.C. Asser Press, The Hague, 2007) 72–73.
74 *Appellate Body Report, EC – Hormones*, para 123.
75 See Veggeland F and Borgen S O (n 73) 695–697. See also Urs P Thomas, 'The Codex Alimentarius and Environmental-Related Food Safety: The Functioning of the Global Standards' (2004) 2 *Economic Policy and Law* 15–17.

ticides[76] and contaminants regulations, with arguments that the regulations are not science based and are inconsistent with Codex standards.[77] The EU's GMO regulations are controversial and have been challenged in the SPS Committee, and gave rise to the *EC – Biotech* dispute.[78]

The following sections will analyse the EU food safety policies and regulations vis-à-vis the provisions of the SPS Agreement and international food safety standards as provided for under the Codex Alimentarius Commission (the Codex).[79] The analysis will incorporate the jurisprudence of the CJ and GC, and the WTO Panels and Appellate Body.

2.4.1   EU food safety standards and international standards

Historically, both the EU and the GATT had as their primary objective, in their food safety standards, the free movement of foodstuffs, and allowed public health measures as exceptions to the rule.[80] However, the protection of human health and consumer safety has become an autonomous additional objective of the EU food safety standards and under the SPS Agreement.[81]

The WTO food safety standards are delegated, through the SPS Agreement, to the Codex. WTO Members are encouraged to harmonise their SPS standards with those of the Codex.[82] Although the EU is a Member of the WTO, and thus bound by WTO norms and Codex standards, unless there is a risk assessment–justified divergence,[83] its food safety standards further other public policies,

---

76 Ellen Pay, 'Overview of the Sanitary and Phytosanitary Measures in QUAD Countries on Tropical Fruits and Vegetables Imported from Developing Countries' (T.R.A.D.E. papers, South Center, 2005) 32. The author argues that the EU's MRLs are usually lower or equal to Codex's but rarely higher. However, where there are no Codex MRLs, such as for tropical fruits and vegetables, EU sets MRLs at the lower limit of determination (LOD), effectively close to zero.
77 WTO Committee on Sanitary and Phytosanitary Measures (n 72) 8–26.
78 Ibid. Concerns raised by Canada, US, and Argentina ultimately led to the *EC – Biotech* dispute.
79 SPS Agreement, Annex A, para 3 (a). For animal health, the designated organization is the International Office Epizootics (OIE), and for plant health it is the International Plant Protection Convention (IPPC).
80 Alemanno A (n 6) 377. The EU allowed public health measures as exceptions under art 36 TFEU, while the GATT 47 did so through art XX (b).
81 Regulation 178 of 2002, art 1 and SPS Agreement, art 2 (1).
82 Jacqueline Peel, *Science and Risk Regulation in International Law* (Cambridge University Press, 2010) 266. Under the sixth paragraph of the Preamble of the SPS Agreement, harmonisation of Members' SPS measures is expressed to be an objective of the Agreement. This is sought to be effectuated under art 3 (1), where Members are urged to base their measures on international standards and under art 3 (2), where Members' measures that conform to international standards are presumed to be consistent with the provisions of the Agreement.
83 Richard J Dawson, 'The Role of the Codex Alimentarius Commission' (1995) 6 *Food Control* 261, 264. According to the author, although the Codex standards may or may not be accepted as such, they act as a 'benchmark' or 'yardstick' of national requirements. WTO members are required to submit scientific justification for food import restrictions based on national regulations that are stricter than Codex standards.

whereas Codex standards have as their objective the protection of the consumer and the facilitation of international trade.[84]

2.4.2 Risk analysis in the Codex and the EU

The Codex did not have principles related to risk assessment and risk management prior to the coming into force of the SPS Agreement.[85] In 1995, the 21st Session of the Codex adopted the 'Statements of Principle Concerning the Role of Science in the Codex Decision-Making Process and the Extent to Which Other Factors are Taken into Account'.[86] These Statements, together with the Working Principles for Risk Analysis for Application in the Framework of the Codex Alimentarius[87] and the Definitions of Risk Analysis Terms Related to Food Safety,[88] constitute the risk analysis principles of the Codex.

However, significantly the Codex does not conduct its own risk analysis. The actual risk assessment is carried out by independent experts who are appointed by the FAO and the WHO, and who are not part of the staff of the Codex, the FAO, or the WHO. The findings and conclusions of these experts represent the foundation of the Codex standards.

The Codex receives expert advice from individual scientists, laboratories, institutes, universities, national governments, NGOs, the Joint FAO/WHO Expert Committee on Food Additives (JECFA), the Joint FAO/WHO Meetings on Pesticide Residues (JMPR), the Joint FAO/WHO Meetings on Microbiological Risk Assessment (JEMRA), the FAO/WHO Food Safety Assessments of Foods Derived from Modern Biotechnology, and the FAO/WHO ad hoc Expert Consultations.[89]

2.4.3 EU reference to Codex standards

The EU took Codex standards into account in its early legislative process, in particular its secondary legislation. But with the completion of the internal market, the influence of Codex standards on EU legislation has diminished.[90]

---

84 Alemanno A (n 6) 382–383.
85 David Victor, 'The Sanitary and Phytosanitary Agreement of the World Trade Organization: An Assessment After Five Years' (2000) 32 *International Law and Politics* 865, 930. The author notes that before the conclusion of the SPS Agreement, the Codex had no principles or definitions related to the application of risk assessment and risk management.
86 Matthee M D M (n 73) 72. The statements are an appendix of Procedural Manual of the Codex Alimentarius Commission, 22nd edn (2014), FAO and WHO, Rome, 2014 (Procedural Manual of the Codex (2014)) 209.
87 Procedural Manual of the Codex (2014), s IV, 109.
88 Ibid, s IV, 116.
89 Thomas U P (n 75) 12. According to the author, the Codex is by no means a scientific body carrying out risk evaluations in the various food categories. Instead, it can be considered as a multilateral regulatory agency that commissions such evaluations. See also Matthee M D M (n 73) 34–47.
90 Matthee M D M (n 73) 102–108. The author notes that in the early phase of the EU food safety regulation harmonisation, the European Commission hoped to use Codex standards as

References to Codex standards in EU standards are mainly related to the promotion of uniformity in the Member states' provisions on compliance or verification procedures that give effect to EU law.[91]

The CJ and GC have from time to time referred to the Codex standards. In *Commission v. Germany (Rheinheitsgebot)*,[92] the CJ ruled that a Member state could not prohibit the use of food additives, the use of which had been approved by the Scientific Committee for Food (SCF) and the Codex.[93] In *Debus*,[94] the CJ held that a Member state could not prohibit the additive sulphur dioxide in beer when the additive's maximum daily dose was within the parameters set by the Codex.[95] In *Smanor*,[96] the CJ referred to the Codex's definition of 'yoghurt' in order to determine whether 'deep-frozen yoghurt' was substantially different from 'yoghurt'.[97] In *Pfizer*,[98] the GC defined the terms 'hazard' and 'risk assessment' by reference to Codex definitions.[99] In *Monsanto*,[100] the CJ analysed the concept of 'substantial equivalence', found in Regulation 258/97, in the context of the Codex.[101]

The role of Codex standards is formally incorporated in EU food law under Article 5 (3) of Regulation 178 of 2002. The provision signifies that the EU now systematically takes into account international standards, unlike in the past when such standards were taken into account on an ad hoc basis. Moreover, the provision enables EU and national regulations to be challenged before the CJ and

---

   a harmonisation instrument. However, neither the Council nor the Member states attached much importance to the Codex standards and as a result the EU had accepted only four Codex standards by 1977. Although the EU was not enthusiastic in the acceptance of the Codex standards, it took these into account in its legislation. The author explains that in the 1970s and 1980s Codex standards had an impact on EU legislation and gives three illustrations: Directive 79/112/EEC, which was largely based upon the General Standard for labeling of pre-packaged foods (CAC/RS 1–1969); the European Commission relied on the work of JECFA and JMPR to assemble scientific conclusions to be used as a basis for EU food standards; reports of the Scientific Committee for Food (SCF) show that JECFFA's ADIs were taken into account during its risk assessments.
91 Ibid. See also Poli S (n 70) 616, fn 18.
92 Case 178/84, *Commission v. Germany (Rheinheitsgebot)* [1987] ECR 1227 (*Commission v. Germany (Rheinheitsgebot)*).
93 *Commission v. Germany (Rheinheitsgebot)*, para 44.
94 Joined Cases C-13/91 and C-113/91, *Criminal proceedings v. Michel Debus* [1992] ECR I-03617 (*Debus*).
95 Debus, para 24.
96 Case 298/87 *Proceedings for Compulsory Reconstruction v. Smanor SA* [1988] ECR 4512 (*Smanor*).
97 *Smanor*, paras 22–23.
98 Case T-13/99, *Pfizer Animal Health SA v. Council of the European Union* [2002] ECR II-03305 (*Pfizer*).
99 *Pfizer*, paras 147 and 156.
100 *Monsanto Agricoltura Italia SpA and Others v Presidenzadel Consigliodei Ministri and Others* [2003] ECR I-8105 (*Monsanto*).
101 *Monsanto*, paras 78–79.

74 *EU food safety standards*

GC, as it is an implementation of Articles 3.1 and 3.3 of the SPS Agreement.[102] However, the provision only applies to standards, thereby excluding guidelines and recommendations as provided for under the SPS Agreement.

Significantly, the provision only creates an obligation to 'take into consideration' international standards, while Article 3.1 of the SPS Agreement obliges Members to 'base' their regulations on international standards. Hence the provision only creates a procedural requirement, whereas the SPS Agreement's provision creates a substantive obligation.[103]

To the extent that the CJ and GC have contributed towards affirming the requirement for a scientific basis for EU food safety regulations and the need for a risk analysis basis for such measures, they have in effect contributed to the ultimate recognition of Codex standards in EU food safety regulations.

2.4.4 EU jurisprudence on scientific evidence

Just as the GATT and the Codex did not originally have risk analysis requirements, the original EC Treaty did not have evidentiary scientific requirements for Members' or the EU's food legislation.[104] However, because Member states were submitting scientific evidence in support of their health measures under Article 36 of the TFEU, the CJ resorted to requiring scientific justifications for such measures.

In *Sandoz*,[105] the CJ, after evaluating the scientific evidence, held:

> In view of the uncertainties inherent in the scientific assessment, national rules prohibiting, without prior authorization, the marketing of foodstuffs to which vitamins have been added, are justified on principle within the meaning of article 36 of the treaty on grounds of the protection of human health.[106]

In *Motte*,[107] the CJ first confirmed that it is for Member states to decide what degree of protection of the health and life of humans they intend to assure, but stated that they 'must take into account the results of international scientific research and, in particular, the work of the EU scientific committee for food'.[108] The CJ proceeded to examine the scientific evidence advanced by the parties and found that 'that problem was dealt with by the scientific committee for food in

---

102 See Matthee M D M (n 73) 122.
103 Ibid.
104 Alberto Alemanno, 'EU Risk Regulation and Science: The Role of Experts in Decision-Making and Judicial Review' in Ellen Vos (ed) *European Risk Governance Its Science, Its Inclusiveness and Its Effectiveness* (CONNEX Report Series No. 6, 2008) 37, 38.
105 Case 174/82, *Criminal Proceedings v. Sandoz BV* [1983] ECR 2445 (*Sandoz*).
106 *Sandoz*, para 17.
107 Case 247/84 *Criminal Proceedings v. Leon Motte* [1985] ECR 3887 (*Motte*).
108 *Motte*, para 20.

its report of 22 February 1980 which was the subject of the commission recommendation of 11 November 1980 addressed to the Member states concerning tests relating to the safety evaluation of food additives'.[109] The CJ concluded that 'EU law (. . .) does not preclude (. . .) a scientific evaluation of the risk (. . .) to human health'.[110]

In *Commission v. Germany (Rheinheitsgebot)*, the CJ held that where a product is authorised in a Member state based on the findings on international scientific research, and where it does not present a risk to public health, it must be authorised for importation into other Member states.[111]

Thus, though not provided for in the TFEU, references to 'international scientific research', the FAO, the WHO, and the Codex permeated the CJ's jurisprudence under Articles 34 and 36 of the TFEU.[112] Consequently, there was a de facto requirement that Member states justify their measures under Article 36 of the TFEU, or those derogating from harmonised measures under Article 114(4) of the TFEU, on the basis of scientific evidence.

The Treaty of Amsterdam (ToA) introduced the 'scientific requirement'.[113] Hence Member states and EU institutions are required not only to base their food regulations on a 'high level of protection', but also to take into account 'any new development based on scientific facts'.[114] In *Pfizer* the GC held risk analysis, as defined by the Codex, to be an essential element in the enactment of EU food safety measures,[115] hence bringing the scientific requirements of EU food safety standards in line with the SPS Agreement and the Codex. Furthermore, Article 3.1 of Regulation 178 of 2002 formally provides for a risk analysis in EU food law.

2.4.5 Risk analysis in EU food safety standards

While Article 5(1) of the SPS Agreement requires Members to base their SPS measures on risk assessment and provides for the factors to be taken into account,[116] the Agreement does not provide for a detailed risk management regime. All the Agreement requires towards risk management is that Members'

---

109 *Motte*, para 21.
110 *Motte*, para 22.
111 *Commission v. Germany (Rheinheitsgebot)*, para 44.
112 See also Case 53/80 *Officer van justitie v. Koninklijke Kaasfabriek Eyssen BV* [1981] ECR 409, para 13; Case 304/84 *Ministere public v. Claude Muller and Others* [1986] ECR 1511, para 25; Case 35/84 *Commission v. Italy (health checks on the imports of curds)* [1986] ECR 545, para 11; Case C-35/89 *Commission v. Italian Republic (nitrates)* [1992] ECR I-4545, para 19.
113 TFEU, art 114 (3).
114 European Commission (Decision) to set up Scientific Committees in the Fields of Consumer Safety, Public Health and the Environment, [2004] Decision 2004/210/EC, 3 March 2004, OJ L 66/45, preamble para 6.
115 *Pfizer*, paras 156–157.
116 For analysis see Peel J (n 82) 80–110.

SPS measures take into account the objective of minimizing negative trade effects when determining their appropriate level of protection[117] and when establishing or maintaining measures to achieve their chosen level of protection.[118] Instead, the Agreement refers Members to 'risk assessment techniques developed by the relevant international organizations'.[119] Moreover, the Appellate Body has expressly rejected the risk assessment–risk management dichotomy read into the Agreement by the Panel in *EC–Hormones* by holding that such an interpretation was not founded on the Agreement's text.[120] The SPS Agreement's risk management regime results in the centralisation of risk assessment; its brevity distinguishes it from the EU's risk assessment and risk management regime, with its strict and detailed procedural requirements.[121]

The objectives of EU food law – a high level of protection, free movement, and the use of international standards[122] – are to be achieved through basing food regulations (both harmonising and national regulations) on risk[123] analysis.[124] Risk analysis itself is composed of three processes: risk assessment, risk management, and risk communication.[125] The EU defines risk assessment as a 'scientifically based process consisting of four steps: hazard identification, hazard characterization, exposure assessment and risk characterization'.[126] The EU goes

---

117 SPS Agreement, art 5 (4).
118 Ibid, art 5 (6). The establishment or maintenance of a measure is in fact risk management.
119 Ibid, art 5 (1). For analysis see Joan Scott, *The WTO Agreement on Sanitary and Phytosanitary Measures: A Commentary* (Oxford University Press, 2007) 91–110.
120 *Appellate Body Report, EC – Hormones*, para 181.
121 Alemanno A (n 6) 390. See also Joseph H H Weiler, 'Epilogue: "Comitology" as Revolution – Infranationalism, Constitutionalism and Democracy' in Christian Joerges and Ellen Vos (eds) *EU Committees: Social Regulation, Law and Politics* (Hart Publishing, Oxford, 1999) 339, 345. The author disagrees with the division between risk analysis and risk management and attributes it to judicial policy-making beginning with Article 36 TFEU jurisprudence and the exercise of the proportionality test.
122 Regulation 178 of 2002, art 5.
123 Risk has been defined as 'the possibility that human actions or events lead to consequences that harm aspects of things that human beings value. (. . .) Therefore risk is both analytical and a normative concept'. See Andreas Klinke and Ortwin Renn, 'A New Approach to Risk Evaluation and Management: Risk-Based, Precaution-Based, and Discourse-Based' (2002) 22 *Risk Analysis* 1071. Codex defines risk as 'a function of the probability of an adverse health effect and the severity of that effect, consequential to a hazard(s) in food'. Procedural Manual of the Codex (2014) 116. The WTO SPS Committee has defined risk thus: 'Risk in the context of the SPS Agreement refers to the likelihood that an adverse event (pest or disease) will occur and the magnitude of the associated consequences on plant or animal life or health of the adverse event'. WTO SPS Committee, 'Guidelines to Further the Practical Implementation of Article 5.5' (G/SPS/15, 18 July 2000) paras A4 and B2.
124 Regulation 178 of 2002, art 6 and preamble paras 4 and 5.
125 Ibid, art 3 (10). This composition is in accordance with the Codex definition. However, the SPS Agreement has not provided for it.
126 Ibid, art 3(11). The SPS Agreement defines risk assessment, at Annex A para 4, as follows:

> The evaluation of the likelihood of entry, establishment or spread of a pest or disease within the territory of an importing Member according to the sanitary or phytosanitary

further to define risk management as 'the process, distinct from risk assessment, of weighing policy alternatives in consultation with interested parties, considering risk assessment and other legitimate factors, and, if need be, selecting appropriate prevention and control options'.¹²⁷ The 'other legitimate factors' include societal, economic, traditional, ethical, and environmental factors, and the feasibility of controls.¹²⁸ Moreover, subject to conditions laid down in Article 7 of the Regulation, the precautionary principle is also considered in risk management.¹²⁹

These EU provisions are in contrast with the SPS Agreement, which does not specify the extent to which 'other factors' may be taken into account in Members' national regulations.¹³⁰ The EU provisions are also in contrast with the Codex Statements of Principle Concerning the Role of Science in the Codex Decision-Making Process and the Extent to Which Other Factors are Taken into Account, which does not enumerate such factors, only providing that such factors be acceptable worldwide or regionally and that they should not affect the scientific basis of risk analysis.¹³¹

2.4.6 EU risk analysis and 'other legitimate factors'

The cultural, social, and economic issues underlying national risk management policies are not universally shared by WTO Members. If these issues are to play a substantive role in risk management decisions, it may defeat the harmonisation objective of the SPS Agreement and the consequential reduction of the trade impacts of Members' SPS measures.¹³² Consequently, science and risk assessment

---

   measures which might be applied, and of the associated potential biological and economic consequences; or the evaluation of the potential for adverse effects on human or animal health arising from the presence of additives, contaminants, toxins or disease-causing organisms in food, beverages or feedstuffs.

   The SPS Agreement therefore bifurcates risk assessment: the first part of the definition pertains to quarantine risks, while the second part relates to risks arising from the presence of substances in food, beverages, and feedstuffs.
127 Ibid, art 3 (12). Codex defines risk management thus: 'The process, distinct from risk assessment, of weighing policy alternatives, in consultation with all interested parties, considering risk assessment and other factors relevant for the health protection of consumers and for the promotion of fair trade practices, and, if needed, selecting appropriate prevention and control options'. See Procedural Manual of the Codex (2014) 116.
128 Ibid, preamble para 19.
129 Ibid, art 6 (3) and preamble paras 20–21.
130 Alemanno A (n 6) 396.
131 Procedural Manual of the Codex (2014) 209.
132 Jacqueline Peel, 'Risk Regulation under the WTO SPS Agreement: Science as an International Normative Standard?' (NYU School of Law, Jean Monnet Working Paper No 2/2004, 2004) 63, <www.jeanmonnetprogram.org/archive/papers/04/040201.pdf> accessed 30 April 2015. The author argues that the Appellate Body by ruling, in *EC – Hormones*, that a rational relationship between a risk assessment and a Member's SPS measure is required, without indicating that science will determine the relationship, left open the question of the role and scope of risk management policies under the SPS Agreement.

were enshrined as the principal requirements of the SPS Agreement.[133] Therefore non-scientific factors are not clearly provided for in the SPS Agreement's risk analysis.[134] The question then arises as to whether 'an EU food safety measure taking into account 'other factors' could still be considered as 'based on' risk assessment within the meaning of the SPS Agreement'.[135]

The Appellate Body in *EC – Hormones* held that a risk assessment may be quantitative or qualitative,[136] that a risk assessment does not require the establishment of a 'minimum magnitude of risk'[137] and, moreover, that a risk assessment may be based on a minority scientific opinion.[138] These rulings by the Appellate Body appear to indicate that Members may take 'other factors' into consideration in their risk management. However, a re-examination of the provisions of the SPS Agreement and the Appellate Body jurisprudence indicates that Members may not have much leeway in considering 'other factors'.

Article 5.1 of the SPS Agreement provides for a review of Members' SPS measures on their scientific basis and not on 'other factors' that arise at the risk management stage.[139] Since such factors are not enumerated anywhere in the Agreement, there is no basis on which they can be taken into account in a judicial review. Moreover, as such factors are not universal, they vary among Members depending on culture, consumption habits, level of technology, consumer awareness, etc. This makes it difficult to determine when the use of such factors is legitimate. Furthermore, '"based on" is appropriately taken to refer to a certain *objective relationship* between two elements; that is to say, to *an objective situation* that *persists* and *is observable* between an SPS measure and a risk assessment'.[140]

Risk assessment assesses 'ascertainable' risk, and not 'uncertainty' about risk.[141] 'Therefore, in practice, whether a risk is determined to be purely a matter of "theoretical uncertainty" or a serious cause for concern will depend upon how demanding reviewing courts are in asking for risk regulatory measures to have scientific support'.[142] Consequently, it may not be possible to determine the role of 'other factors' in risk management, and so these factors become non-justiciable.

---

133 Doaa A Motaal, 'The Multilateral Scientific Consensus and the World Trade Organization' (2004) 38 *Journal of World Trade* 855, 856.
134 Alemanno A (n 6) 396. The author argues that the SPS Agreement focuses on risk assessment and by implication therefore risk management 'should focus solely on the rational, science-driven data stemming from risk assessment, by thus ruling out all 'other factors' from consideration'.
135 Ibid 397.
136 *Appellate Body Report, EC – Hormones*, para 187.
137 Ibid, para 186; *Appellate Body Report, Australia – Salmon*, para 125.
138 Ibid, para 194.
139 Alemanno A (n 6) 397. The author queries whether WTO judicial bodies can review Members reliance on 'other factors' and the extent to which such factors can be recognised as having a legitimate role in decision making.
140 *Appellate Body Report, EC – Hormones*, para 189.
141 Ibid, para 186.
142 Peel J (n 132) 70. The author argues the ruling that risk is about ascertainable risk and not uncertainty about risk 'reflects the concern that Members might maintain SPS measures in

EU food safety standards 79

A high degree of specificity is required in a risk assessment.¹⁴³ This entails a rigorous approach to the scientific evidence that is to be considered in risk assessment. In *EC – Hormones*, the EU submitted general studies that showed a general risk of cancer. The Appellate Body held that 'those general studies are in other words, relevant but do not appear to be sufficiently specific to the case at hand. Furthermore, a risk assessment has to identify risk on a disease on a specific basis (. . .)'.¹⁴⁴

The 'specific' requirement for risk assessment restricts Members' use of minority scientific opinions in risk assessment. There are two main reasons for this:

> Oftentimes, a 'divergent' scientific viewpoint is held only by a minority of scientists because it is based on the kind of suggestive but not definitive scientific evidence that qualifies as 'general' (or 'indirect') scientific evidence in the scheme of WTO decision-makers. (. . .) The high standard of proof required under the scientific method, as well as the operation of peer review processes in science, may place significant limitations on the ability of a minority viewpoint to attract greater support within the scientific community.¹⁴⁵

WTO Panels, in contrast to the EU's judicial practice,¹⁴⁶ do not adopt a deferential stance in reviewing Members' SPS measures.¹⁴⁷ Instead of Panels deferring

---

respect of *de minimis* risks – risks not supported by available scientific evidence but which, given the limitations of the scientific method, cannot be ruled out by science'.
143 Prevost D and Van den Bossche P (n 31) 75. The authors point out that a risk assessment has 'to focus and address the particular kind of risk at stake from the product at issue (. . .)' and 'it must assess the risk for each type of disease or harmful substance at issue separately (. . .)'.
144 *Appellate Body Report, EC – Hormones*, para 200.
145 Peel J (n 132) 71–72.
146 The CJ's deferential position as regards EU SPS measures is exemplified in its ruling that

> since the Commission enjoys a wide measure of discretion, particularly as to the nature and extent of the measures which it adopts, the Community judicature must, when reviewing such measures, restrict itself to examining whether the exercise of such discretion is vitiated by a manifest error or a misuse of powers or whether the Commission did not clearly exceed the bounds of its discretion'.

Case C-157/96 *The Queen v The Minister for Agriculture, Fisheries and Food and the Secretary of State for Health, ex parte: National Farmers' Union and Others* [1998] ECR I-2211, para 39. See also Case C-331/88 *The Queen v The Minister for Agriculture, Fisheries and Food and the Secretary of State for Health, ex parte: Fedesa and Others* [1990] ECR I-4023, para 14; Case C-120/97 *Upjohn Ltd v The Licensing Authority established by the Medicines Act 1968 and Others* [1999] ECR I-223, para 34; Case T-13/99, *Pfizer Animal Health SA v. Council of the European Union* [2002] ECR II-03305, paras 168–169.
147 Appellate Body Report, *EC – Hormones*, para 117. The Appellate Body held that in SPS disputes, the standard of review, 'is neither de novo review as such, nor "total deference"', but rather the 'objective assessment of the facts'. See also Vern R Walker, 'Keeping the

to Members' interpretation of their scientific evidence, Panels choose to rely on appointed scientific experts to assess scientific evidence tendered in disputes.[148] The Appellate Body has held that deference to Members' appreciation of scientific evidence will not ensure 'an objective assessment of facts'.[149] Ultimately, 'the result is that a Member adopting risk regulatory measures generally needs to be able to demonstrate scientific evidence supporting the alleged SPS risk which is sufficiently well-developed to amount to more than an "interesting hypothesis" and is specific to the risk at issue'.[150]

Paradoxically, while on the one hand the Appellate Body in *US/Canada – Continued Suspension* appears to allow some flexibility in Members' risk assessments,

> the review power of a panel is not to determine whether the risk assessment undertaken by a WTO Member is correct, but rather to determine whether that risk assessment is supported by coherent reasoning and respectable scientific evidence and is, in this sense, objectively justifiable.[151]

On the other hand, the EU courts appear to have developed a hardened stance on the scientific evidence requirement. Whereas in *Pfizer* the GC held that a precautionary measure may be based on 'inconclusive evidence',[152] in a later case the GC held that such a measure may be based on 'solid evidence' which raises doubts as to the safety of a substance.[153] Moreover, the EU courts appear to be unwilling to re-evaluate the scientific opinions of the EFSA. The CJ dismissed an appeal by Austria of a judgement of the GC on the grounds that the Commission had taken account of an EFSA opinion which the GC affirmed.[154]

Furthermore, the EU, through its Members, had argued for the inclusion of 'other factors' in the Codex standards-setting process.[155] 'Other factors' were

---

WTO from becoming the "World Trans-Science Organization": Scientific Uncertainty, Science Policy, and Fact Finding in the Growth Hormones Dispute' (1998) 31 *Cornell International Law Journal* 280. According to the author: 'A WTO panel cannot merely defer in its fact finding to any member that cries "science"'.
148 See Theophanis Christoforou, 'Settlement of Science-Based Trade Disputes in the WTO: A Critical Review of the Developing Case Law in the Face of Scientific Uncertainty' (2000) 8 *New York University Environmental Law Journal* 622, 642–643. See also Joost Pauwelyn, 'The Use of Experts in WTO Dispute Settlement' (2002) 51 *International and Comparative Law Quarterly* 325, 358.
149 *Appellate Body Report, Japan – Apples*, para 165.
150 Peel J (n 132) 75.
151 *Appellate Body Report U.S./Canada Continued Suspension*, para 590.
152 *Pfizer*, para 144.
153 Case T-229/04, *Sweden v Commission* [2007] ECR 2437, para 161.
154 Joined Cases C-439/05 P and C-454/05 P *Land Oberösterreich and the Republic of Austria v Commission* [2007] I-7141, para 64.
155 Veggeland F and Borgen S O (n 73) 697. Sweden, on behalf of EU Members, argued that the inclusion of 'other factors' would secure legitimacy among consumers. The EU as an organisation joined Codex in 2003; see Matthee M D M (n 73) 131. The author notes that

included in the second statement of the Codex's 'Statements of Principle Concerning the Role of Science in the Codex Decision-Making Process and the Extent to Which Other Factors are Taken into Account', which was adopted in 1995. The second statement provides as follows: 'When elaborating and deciding upon food standards Codex Alimentarius will have regard, where appropriate, to other legitimate factors relevant for the health protection of consumers and for the promotion of fair practices in food trade'.

However, in 2001, the Codex adopted the Criteria for Consideration of the Other Factors referred to in the Second Statement of Principle.[156] Criterion number three provides, in the relevant part, 'consideration of other factors should not affect the scientific basis of risk analysis (. . .)', while criterion number five provides that 'only those other factors which can be accepted on a worldwide basis, or on a regional basis in the case of regional standards and related texts, should be taken into account in the framework of Codex'. Hence, 'other factors' may not be in conflict with the scientific evidence supporting a measure, and these factors should be acceptable worldwide or on a regional basis, in the case of regional standards. These two criteria render the application of 'other factors' impossible. First, it is precisely because the EU wishes to go 'beyond science' in its risk management that it invokes these 'other factors'. If these factors are to be compliant with the scientific evidence, they are rendered superfluous. Second, since other Members of the WTO object to these factors, they cannot receive worldwide acceptance. Further, it may also prove to be difficult to obtain acceptance among the regional 28 Member states of the EU, given their past disagreements on food safety standards, as evidenced by CJ jurisprudence.[157]

Taking into consideration 'other factors' may accentuate divisions among EU Member states in the assessment of their appropriate levels of protection and put the EU food regulations in conflict with the SPS Agreement.[158] Moreover, these 'other factors' are nowhere defined or enumerated in the Codex working principles and Criteria. This renders the legitimacy of 'other factors' tenuous.

---

the influence and impact of Codex standards on EU food safety regulations has reduced considerably with increasing EU scientific competence.
156 Codex Decision of the 24th Session of the Commission, 2001. The Decision forms the second part of the Statements annexed to the Procedural Manual of the Codex (2014) 209.
157 See, for example, Case 68/86 *United Kingdom of Great Britain and Northern Ireland v Council of the European Communities* [1988] ECR 855, paras 34–36. The UK and Northern Ireland strongly objected to the banning of hormones for beef fattening purposes. This hormone ban eventually led to *EC – Hormones*; Case C-180/96 *United Kingdom of Great Britain and Northern Ireland v Commission of the European Communities* [1998] ECR I-2265. The UK and Northern Ireland challenged the Commission ban on the export of their beef due to the BSE crisis; Case C-1/00 *Commission v. France* [2001] ECR I-9989. France refused to lift its ban on British beef despite the Commission's Directive that lifted the ban.
158 Alemanno A (n 6) 91. According to the author, under the SPS Agreement scientific evidence is the only criterion upon which an SPS measure may be based.

2.4.7 The precautionary principle and SPS standards

The precautionary principle[159] may be regarded as a general principle of customary international environmental law.[160] The principle is referred to in various multilateral environmental agreements (MEAs)[161] and is defined in one MEA as follows:

> In order to protect the environment, the precautionary approach should be widely applied by States according to their capabilities. Where there are threats of serious and irreversible damage, lack of full scientific certainty shall not be used as a reason for postponing cost-effective measures to prevent environmental degradation.[162]

Thus the precautionary principle is triggered by threats of serious and irreversible damage to the environment. However, the application of the principle is

---

159 For an analysis of the issues pertaining to the principle, see Giandomenico Majone, 'What Price Safety? The Precautionary Principle and Its Policy Implications' (2002) 40 (1) *Journal of Common Market Studies* (2006) 89; Jonathan B Wiener, 'Whose Precaution Afterall? A Comment on the Comparison and Evolution of Risk Regulatory Systems' (2003) 13 *Duke Journal of Comparative and International Law* 207; Gary E Marchant and Kenneth L Mossman, *Arbitrary and Capricious: The Precautionary Principle in the European Union Courts* (American Enterprise Institute Press, Washington, DC, 2004); Jose L C Vilaça, 'The Precautionary Principle in EC Law' (2004) 10 *European Public Law* 369; Sabrina Shaw and Risa Schwartz, 'Trading Precaution: The Precautionary Principle and the WTO' (United Nations University, Institute of Advanced Studies (UNU-IAS) Report, 2005); Diahanna L Post, 'The Precautionary Principle and Risk Assessment in International Food Safety: How the World Trade Organization Influences Standards' (2006) 26 *Risk Analysis* 1259; Eadaoin N Chaoimh, 'Trading in Precaution: A Comparative Study of the Precautionary Jurisprudence of the European Court and the WTO's Adjudicating Body' (2006) 33 *Legal Issues of Economic Integration* 139; Nicolas D Sadeleer, 'The Precautionary Principle in EC Health and Environmental Law' (2006) 12 *European Law Journal* 139; Llona Cheyne, 'Risk and Precaution in World Trade Organization Law' 40 *Journal of World Trade* 837; Rene V Schomberg, 'The Precautionary Principle and Its normative Challenges' in E Fisher, J Jones and R V Schomberg (eds) *Implementing the Precautionary Principle: Perspectives and Prospects* (Edward Elgar, Cheltenham, UK, 2006) 19; Marjolein B A V Asselt and Ellen Vos, 'The Precautionary Principle and the Uncertainty Paradox' (2006) 9 *Journal of Risk Research* 313; Arie Trouwborst, 'The Precautionary Principle in General International Law: Combating the Babylonian Confusion' (2007) 16 *Review of European Community and International Environmental Law* 185; Anna Szajkowska, *Regulating Food Law: Risk Analysis and the Precautionary Principle as General Principles of EU Food Law* (Wageningen Academic Publishers, European Institute for Food Law series, 2012).
160 *Appellate Body Report, EC – Hormones*, para 123.
161 For example: art 3.3 of the 1992 United Nations Framework Convention on Climate Change; art 15 of the 1992 United Nations Environment Programme (UNEP) Conference on the Environment and Development (UNCED) Rio de Janeiro (Rio Declaration); the preamble of the 1992 Convention on Biological Diversity; art 10.6 of the 2000 Cartagena Protocol on Biosafety to the Convention on Biological Diversity; art 1 and 8.9 and Annex C part V (B) of the 2001 United Nations Environment Programme (UNEP) Stockholm Convention on Persistent Organic Pollutants.
162 Rio Declaration, art 15.

conditioned on two factors: that there is a state of scientific uncertainty and that the precautionary measure is to be cost-effective. Moreover, the application of the principle is dependent on states' capabilities and this, together with the fact that the definition is couched in non-mandatory terms, implies that the principle is discretionary. The precautionary principle pertains to uncertain risks.[163] The uncertainty relates to scientific uncertainty as to the relationship between a particular hazard and a particular harm.[164] The evidential value of scientific knowledge as a basis for regulatory policy is contested.[165] The contestation arises due to the *ex-ante* nature of standard-setting and risk appraisal, the use of regulatory science, and the fact that science has methodological and epistemological problems in relation to risk analysis.[166] Moreover, scientific uncertainty is inherent in each element of the four elements of risk assessment.[167] This uncertainty, which is essentially a reflection of limited scientific knowledge, compels risk assessors to take into account factors other than science in risk assessment.[168]

It may therefore be concluded that the application of precaution in risk analysis is a valid scientific exercise in situations of scientific uncertainty.[169] The problem

---

163 Asselt M B A V and Vos E (n 159) 313, 316–317. The authors argue that these risks are not fully calculable and controllable because the probability of occurrence or the effects of the damage cannot be estimated. This leads to the uncertainty paradox: while it is acknowledged that science may not provide evidence on uncertain risks, it is increasingly resorted to for that very evidence.
164 Michael D Rogers, 'Risk Analysis under Uncertainty, the Precautionary Principle, and the New EU Chemicals Strategy' (2003) 37 *Regulatory Toxicology and Pharmacology* 370. According to the author, there are three categories of uncertainty in relation to risk assessment: uncertainty in effect, uncertainty in cause, and uncertainty in the relationship between a hypothesised cause and effect. The Precautionary Principle relates to the third type of uncertainty. See also Vern R Walker, 'The Myth of Science as a "Neutral Arbiter" for Triggering Precautions' (2003) 26 *Boston College International and Comparative Law Review* 197, 205. According to the author, scientific evidence leading to a finding of risk involves at least five types of scientific uncertainty: conceptual uncertainty, measurement uncertainty, sampling uncertainty, modelling uncertainty, and causal uncertainty. Further, uncertainty of each type is to be found in scientific proof of each scientific finding.
165 See Michelle Everson and Ellen Vos, 'European Risk Governance in a Global Context' in E Vos (ed) *European Risk Governance; Its Science, Its Inclusiveness and Its Effectiveness* (CONNEX Report Series No. 06, 2008) 7, 16.
166 See Elizabeth Fisher, 'Opening Pandora's Box: Contextualising the Precautionary Principle in the European Union' in M Everson and E Vos (eds) *Uncertain Risks Regulated* (Routledge-Cavendish, New York, 2009) 21, 24. The author posits that the precautionary principle highlights the lack of ontological security in risk analysis and, in particular, the provisional nature of scientific knowledge.
167 Walker V R (n 147) 259.
168 Ibid. The author terms as science policy the considerations underlying risk assessment, both scientific and non-scientific. Science policy dictates to risk assessors their selection of alternative models and inputs in the performance of risk assessment.
169 Gavin Goh, 'Precaution, Science and Sovereignty Protecting Life and Health under the WTO Agreements' (2003) 6 *Journal of World Intellectual Property* 441, 450. According to the author, precaution may be applied in both qualitative and quantitative risk assessments since uncertainty is inherent in all risk assessments. Furthermore, precaution may be

84 *EU food safety standards*

with the precautionary principle is not in its formulation per se, but in its application.[170] The determination of the triggering risk, its magnitude and probability; what constitutes scientific uncertainty; what factors are to be taken into account in a cost-benefit analysis; and the discretionary nature of the precautionary principle application are problematic issues in the application of the principle. These problems underlie much of the controversy surrounding the principle.

Following is an examination of the precautionary principle in EU food safety regulations and policies contrasted with the treatment of the principle under the SPS Agreement and the Codex together with the relevant jurisprudence.

2.4.7.1   *Precautionary principle and the SPS Agreement*

There is no provision for the precautionary principle in the SPS Agreement.[171] However, the principle finds 'reflection' in its Articles 3.3 and 5.7 and in the sixth paragraph of its preamble.[172] Moreover 'responsible, representative governments commonly act from perspective of prudence and precaution (. . .)'.[173] Despite its reflection in these provisions, the principle does not relieve Members of their duty to base their measures on risk assessment.[174] Hence, regardless of the principle,

---

applied in selecting risk management measures on the basis of risk assessment and in case of divergent or conflicting risk opinion.

170   Theophanis Christoforou, 'The Precautionary Principle in European Community Law and Science' in Joel A Tickner (ed) *Environmental Science and Preventive Public Policy* (Island Press, Washington, DC, 2003) 241. According to the author, the precautionary principle deals with what actions are to be taken to protect health and the environment in the face of scientific uncertainty. Differences in the understanding of the principle arise as to the nature or extent of risk identified or the need to conduct a risk assessment or cost benefit analysis which do not affect the core and basic rationale of the principle.

171   *Appellate Body Report, EC – Hormones,* para 124. The Appellate Body held that the precautionary principle had not been written into the SPS Agreement as a ground for justifying measures that are otherwise inconsistent with the provisions of the Agreement.

172   Ibid. The Appellate Body found that the right of Members to maintain their own higher, hence more cautious, levels of protection as provided for under the sixth paragraph of the preamble, and Article 3.3 was a reflection of the precautionary principle. Article 5.7 may be said to reflect the principle in its conditional authorisation of provisional measures where relevant scientific evidence is insufficient. See also Prevost D and Van den Bossche P (n 143) 299. The authors argue that the provisions of the sixth paragraph and Article 3.3 do not reflect the precautionary principle. Instead these provisions reflect the situation where a Member is able to carry out a risk assessment in order to determine a chosen level of protection, whereas the precautionary principle comes into play where the scientific evidence is insufficient to conduct a risk assessment. The authors posit that the Appellate Body confused the precautionary principle with its forerunner the protective principle, which obligated governments to act on risks that had been scientifically proven.

173   Appellate Body Report, *EC – Hormones,* para 124.

174   Ibid para 125. The Appellate Body confirmed the panel's finding that the precautionary principle does not override the provisions of the Agreement. This may be due to the fact that the Appellate Body was doubtful whether the principle was widely accepted by Members as a principle of general or customary international law. If it had been such a principle, the Appellate Body would have been obligated to use the principle in interpreting the

Members are obligated to base their SPS measures on a risk assessment subject to the provisions of Article 5.7. Under Article 5.7, a provisional SPS measure has to meet four conditions. It must be imposed in respect of a situation where 'relevant scientific information is insufficient' and adopted 'on the basis of available pertinent information'. The measure may not be maintained unless the Member seeks to 'obtain the additional information necessary for a more objective assessment of risk' and reviews the measure accordingly 'within a reasonable period of time'.[175] The four requirements were held to be cumulative, and preconditioned the application of Article 5.7.

Furthermore, the Appellate Body in *Japan – Apples* held that Article 5.7 is triggered by the insufficiency of scientific evidence and not scientific uncertainty.[176] The insufficiency pertained only to situations where little or no reliable scientific evidence was available to carry out a risk assessment. Hence scientific uncertainty was ruled out as a factor in the application of Article 5.7. The Appellate Body's holding is in diametrical opposition to the EU's position of authorizing precautionary measures based on scientific uncertainty as provided for in its Communication on the precautionary principle[177] and Regulation 178 of 2002.[178]

2.4.7.2 *The precautionary principle and the Codex*

The precautionary principle has a controversial history within the Codex.[179] Despite the controversy, in 2003 the Codex adopted the Working Principles for Risk Analysis for Application in the Framework of the Codex Alimentarius.[180] Paragraph 10 of the Principles provides as follows:

> When there is evidence that a risk to human health exists but scientific data are insufficient or incomplete, the Codex Alimentarius Commission should

---

Agreement. See also Panel Report *EC – Biotech*, para 7.89. According to the Panel there has been no authoritative decision by an international court or tribunal which recognises the precautionary principle as a principle general or customary international law.
175 *Appellate Body Report Japan – Agricultural Products*, para 89; *Appellate Body Report Japan – Apples*, para 176.
176 *Appellate Body Report Japan – Apples*, para 184.
177 European Commission, 'Communication from the Commission on the Precautionary Principle' (COM (2000) 1) para 5.1.2. The communication provides for the application of the precautionary principle where 'scientific information is insufficient, inconclusive or uncertain (. . .).'
178 Regulation 178 of 2002, art 7. Under the Article, application of the precautionary principle is authorised in situations of 'scientific uncertainty'.
179 Veggeland F and Borgen S O (n 73) 695–697. The authors state that the issue of the inclusion of the precautionary principle in Codex standards was heavily debated in the Codex from 1995 onwards. The Cairns Group and the US were against the inclusion while the EU Members were for its inclusion. See also Poli S (n 70) 619–622. The author also notes that the principle generated a heated debate before finally a loose version of the principle was adopted in 2003.
180 Procedural Manual of the Codex (2014), s IV, 109.

not proceed to elaborate a standard but should consider elaborating a related text, such as a code of practice, provided that such a text would be supported by the available scientific evidence.

The provision means that, in a condition of scientific uncertainty, the Codex should not make standards. At best, under such conditions, the Codex may adopt a code of practice.[181] The provision therefore effectively negates the precautionary principle. Paragraph 11 of the Working Principles provides:

> Precaution is an inherent element of risk analysis. Many sources of uncertainty exist in the process of risk assessment and risk management of food related hazards to human health. The degree of uncertainty and variability in the available scientific information should be explicitly considered in the risk analysis. Where there is sufficient scientific evidence to allow Codex to proceed to elaborate a standard or related text, the assumptions used for the risk assessment and the risk management options selected should reflect the degree of uncertainty and the characteristics of the hazard.

The provision does not define what precaution is, and offers no guidelines on when and how to use it. Therefore the paragraph offers no illumination on the role of the principle in the Codex.[182] Moreover, in 2007, the Codex adopted the Working Principles for Risk Analysis for Food Safety for Application by Governments.[183] The Principles had been expected to provide guidance to governments and the WTO judiciary on the problematic and controversial areas of 'other factors' and the precautionary principle.[184] However, they merely reproduced,

---

181 Alemanno A (n 6) 416. The author sees this provision as reflecting the US vision of risk analysis favouring a risk management policy where only scientific evidence is taken into account.
182 Poli S (n 70) 622. The author argues that since the paragraph already envisages a situation where there is sufficient scientific evidence, it offers no guidelines on situations of scientific uncertainty. Moreover, since the precautionary principle is being evoked in a situation where there is sufficient scientific evidence, the paragraph appears to equate the principle with the proportionality principle. The author concludes that the precautionary principle as envisaged by the EU is yet to find a place amongst the principles underlying the Codex decision making process. See also Post D L (n 159) 1259, 1264–1270. The author cites three cases in the Codex where the precautionary principle was rejected: Working Principles for Risk Analysis for Application in the Framework of the Codex Alimentarius; Principles of Microbiological Risk Assessment and Risk Management; and Maximum Residue Limits for Aflatoxins. Christiane Gerstetter and Matthias L Maier, 'Risk Regulation, Trade and International Law: Debating the Precautionary Principle in and around the WTO' (Bremen University, TranState Working Papers No. 18, 2005) 20–27, <http://econstor.eu/bitstream/10419/28268/1/497822245.pdf> accessed 10 May 2015. The authors analyse the factors underlying the controversy generated by the precautionary principle in the Codex in respect of the Working Principles in the years 1997–2003.
183 CAC/GL 62-2007.
184 Alemanno A (n 6) 423.

as they pertain to the precautionary principle, at paragraph 12, the provisions of paragraph 11 of the 'Working Principles for Risk Analysis for Application in the Framework' of the Codex.

By adopting the 'Working Principles for Risk Analysis for Food Safety for Application by Governments', and in particular paragraph 12 thereof, the Codex has shown that it is unable to formulate guidelines for the application of the precautionary principle, and that the problem of the principle is not yet resolved within the Codex.

2.4.7.3 The precautionary principle and the EU food safety standards

The precautionary principle formally entered into EU legislation, as an environmental policy principle,[185] through Article 191(2) of the TFEU, which provides:

> EU policy on the environment shall aim at a high level of protection taking into account the diversity of situations in the various regions of the EU. It shall be based on the precautionary principle and on the principles that preventive action should be taken, that environmental damage should as a priority be rectified at source and that the polluter should pay (. . .).

The principle has since been extended to public health and consumer protection by virtue of the interpretation of Articles 11 and 12 of the TFEU.[186]

In *Artegodan*,[187] the GC interpreted the scope of the principle as follows:

> Therefore, although the precautionary principle is mentioned in the Treaty only in connection with environmental policy, it is broader in scope. It is intended to be applied in order to ensure a high level of protection of health, consumer safety and the environment in all the EU spheres of activity.[188]

In its Communication on Consumer Health and Food Safety, the Commission had asserted its right to use the precautionary principle in circumstances where scientific evidence was insufficient or uncertain.[189] The Commission reiterated its

---

185 The EU environmental policy is provided for under TFEU, arts 191–193.
186 Majone G (n 159) 89, 94.
187 Joined Cases: T-76/00, T-83/00, T-84/00, T-85/00, T-132/00, T-141/00 and T-144/00 *Artegodan GmbH and Others v. Commission* [2002] ECR 4945 (*Artegodan*).
188 *Artegodan*, para 183. The courts had earlier applied the principle to human health in the BSE cases: Case C-157/96 *The Queen v The Minister for Agriculture, Fisheries and Food and the Secretary of State for Health, ex parte: National Farmers' Union and Others* [1998] ECR I-2211 and Case C-180/96 *United Kingdom of Great Britain and Northern Ireland v Commission of the European Communities* [1998] ECR I-2265.
189 COM (97) 183 final, 20.

88 EU food safety standards

position in its Green Paper on the General Principles of Food Law.[190] In its Communication on the Precautionary Principle, the Commission elevates the precautionary principle to a 'full-fledged and general principle of international law' and 'an essential plank' of EU policy.[191] The principle is now an autonomous general principle of EU law.[192] However, neither the TFEU nor any of these instruments legally defined the principle.[193]

Article 7(1) of Regulation 178 of 2002 defines the precautionary principle as follows:

> In specific circumstances where, following an assessment of available information, the possibility of harmful effects on health is identified but scientific uncertainty persists, provisional risk management measures necessary to ensure the high level of health protection chosen in the EU may be adopted, pending further scientific information for a more comprehensive risk assessment.

Hence the application of the principle is to be preceded by a risk assessment, or at least an appraisal of the scientific data available.[194] The risk assessment should identify a possibility of a health hazard, but with persisting scientific uncertainty.[195] The chosen measure to address the risk should be necessary and proportional to the health objective[196] being pursued, depending on the cho-

---

190 COM (97) 176 final, 11.
191 COM (2000) 1, 10–12. For a critical analysis of the Communication see Natalie McNelis, 'EU Communication on the Precautionary Principle' (2000) 3 *Journal of International Economic Law* 545; Majone G (n 186).
192 *Artegodan*, para 184. See also Case T-70/99 *Alpharma Inc. v. Council of the European Union* [2002] ECR II-O3495, at para 135.
193 Majone G (n 186) 93.
194 *Pfizer*, paras 143–144. As regards the scientific evidence required, the GC held as follows:

> A preventive measure cannot properly be based on a purely hypothetical approach to the risk, founded on mere conjecture which has not been scientifically proven (. . .). Rather, it follows from the Community Courts' interpretation of the precautionary principle that a preventive measure may be taken only if the risk, although the reality and extent thereof have not been 'fully' demonstrated by conclusive scientific evidence, appears nevertheless to be adequately backed up by the scientific data available at the time when the measure was taken.

In *Monsanto* the requirement is for 'a risk assessment which is as complete as possible in the particular circumstances of an individual case'. *Monsanto*, para 107. For a comment on the Monsanto judgment, see Patrycja Dąbrowska, 'Risk, Precaution and the Internal Market: Who Won the Day in the Recent Monsanto Judgment of the European Court of Justice on GM Foods?' (2004) 5 *German Law Journal* 152.
195 The CJ has characterised the nature of this risk assessment as 'a comprehensive assessment of the risk to health based on the most reliable scientific data available and the most recent results of international research'. Case 192/01 *Commission v Denmark* [2003] ECR 9693, para 51.
196 *Sandoz*, para 18; *Pfizer*, para 163.

sen level of protection.[197] Article 7(2) goes on to provide for the provisional, proportional, and least trade-restrictive conditions under which the principle is to be applied:

> Measures adopted on the basis of paragraph 1 shall be proportionate and no more restrictive of trade than is required to achieve the high level of health protection chosen in the EU, regard being had to technical and economic feasibility and other factors regarded as legitimate in the matter under consideration. The measures shall be reviewed within a reasonable period of time, depending on the nature of the risk to life or health identified and the type of scientific information needed to clarify the scientific uncertainty and to conduct a more comprehensive risk assessment.

These conditions for the application of the principle are built upon the Communication on the Precautionary Principle[198] and the jurisprudence of the EFTA Court, which was subsequently confirmed and developed by the case law of the EU courts.[199]

2.4.7.4 Discussion

Although it may be regarded as a general principle of customary international environmental law, the precautionary principle's application in SPS matters is contested. The Appellate Body has rejected its status as a principle of general or customary international law.[200] This rejection means that a WTO Member may not rely on it unilaterally and that any such reliance is bound to be in violation of the SPS Agreement. Moreover, even the TFEU confines the principle to the environment title under Article 191 of the TFEU, and does not refer to it in

---

197 The EU institutions enjoy a broad discretion in determining their chosen level of protection: *Pfizer*, para 163. For an analytical review of the Pfizer judgment, see Karl H Ladeur, 'The Introduction of the Precautionary Principle into EU Law: A Pyrrhic Victory for Environmental and Public Health Law? Decision-making under Conditions of Complexity in Multi-Level Political Systems' (2003) 40 *Common Market Law Review* 14559; Olivier Segnana, 'The Precautionary Principle: New Developments in the Case Law of the Court of First Instance' (2002) 3 *German Law Journal* 5; Caoimhin MacMaolain, 'Using the Precautionary Principle to Protect Human Health: Pfizer v Council' (2003) 28 *European Law Review* 723.
198 COM (2000) 1, 3.
199 For example, in *EFTA v Norway*, the EFTA Court held that precautionary measures taken 'must be based on scientific evidence; they must be proportionate; non-discriminatory, transparent and consistent with similar measures already taken'. Case E-3/00 *EFTA Surveillance Authority v Norway* [2001] EFTA Court Report 2000/2001, 73, para 26. This was followed in Case C-192/01 *Commission v Denmark* [2003] ECR 9693; Case C-24/00 *Commission v France* [2004] ECR I-1277, para 52 and C-41/02 *Commission v Denmark* [2004] ECR I-11375, para 46.
200 *Appellate Body Report, EC – Hormones*, para 123.

the health provisions of Articles 168 and 169 of the TFEU. The extension of the application of the principle to matters of human, plant, and animal health is based on the misinterpretation of the principle and its scope, as well as equating it with the notion of precaution.[201] The widening of the scope of the principle, in *Artegodan*, to cover human health would appear to be tenuous and unsupported by the texts of the TFEU, and to be politically motivated.[202]

Scientific uncertainty is the core principle of the precautionary principle.[203] However, scientific uncertainty was rejected by the Appellate Body, in *Japan – Apples*, as a trigger for precautionary action.[204] Moreover, Regulation 178 of 2002 does not establish who will determine that scientific uncertainty exists: Should it be the EFSA, or national authorities? And in the event of divergences in these bodies' opinions, whose opinion will prevail?[205] Further, the principle

201 Trouwborst A (n 159) 185, 189–191. The author distinguishes the precautionary principle from the exercise of precaution. While the former is limited to matters environmental, the latter extends beyond environmental matters and is based on the customary principle 'to err on the safe side', which has formed part of the health law and policy of states. Indeed the pre-2000 CJ cases may be viewed as enunciating precaution and not the principle. The protection of human health is encompassed within the principle to the extent that it benefits from environmental protection. Food safety falls outside this scope. Moreover, most MEA do not mention the protection of human health. Notable exceptions, that maybe said to prove the rule, are the Cartagena protocol and the Stockholm Convention. Besides, even in these two Agreements reference to human health is with the objective of affording protection from environmental pollution. See also Sadeleer N D (n 159) 139, 140. The author makes a pointed distinction between health and food safety cases and environmental cases:

> One needs to draw a line between, on the one hand the health and food safety cases, where scientific knowledge is far more advanced than in the environmental sector, and on the other hand genuine environmental cases (waste management, nature conservation) where the uncertainties are far more important, given the difficulties of predicting the reactions of ecosystems to ecological risks (e.g. climate change).

202 Chaoimh E N (n 159) 139, 158–159. The author posits that the CJ, as part of a constitutional structure consisting of the European Parliament, the Council, the Commission and the Member states, does not wish to interfere with politically sensitive and complex issues which are better handled by the political authorities. The author suggests

> that this factor influenced the European Courts when adjudicating in Fedesa, in Pfizer, in BSE and in the myriad of cases looking at national measures, for it was seen that the Court generally refrained from interfering, unless in cases of blatant abuse, and its review of process was not such as to fetter the discretion to decide whether to regulate.

203 Asselt M B A V and Vos E (n 163) 339.
204 *Appellate Body Report Japan – Apples*, para 184.
205 Alemanno A (n 6) 128. The author points out that as there is no hierarchy between EFAS's scientific committees, EU scientific bodies, and national scientific authorities (Article 30 [3] and [4] of Regulation 178 of 2002). Article 30 does not provide a solution; it merely provides for consultations between the diverging bodies, and in the event of disagreement, the publication of a joint document that indicates the contentious issues.

EU food safety standards 91

suffers from vagueness in its definition and scope,[206] leading to its arbitrary and capricious application.[207]

Moreover, the precautionary principle's reliance on scientific uncertainty gives rise to a paradox: whereas the principle is predicated on scientific uncertainty, at the same time it seeks to rely on scientific evidence to prove the uncertainty.[208] Under Article 5.7 of the SPS Agreement, after adopting provisional measures, Members are required to seek additional information for a more objective assessment of risk and to review the measure accordingly within a reasonable period of time; under Article 7(2) of the Regulation 178 of 2002, the review of the measure is conditional, depending upon the nature of the risk to life or health identified and the type of scientific information needed to clarify the scientific uncertainty and to conduct a more comprehensive risk assessment. Hence, whereas under Article 5.7 of the SPS Agreement provisional measures are to be reviewed within a reasonable time, under Article 7(2) of Regulation 178 of 2002 the review is not so bound, and the precautionary measure may be taken in situations of lasting uncertainty.[209] It may therefore be argued that, strictly speaking, the precautionary

---

206 Ibid 144. The author argues that the definition of the principle in the Regulation still leaves the balance between science and political discretion to be contentious. The scope of the principle remains textually vague, leaving the EU courts to flesh it out on a case-by-case basis, thereby creating uncertainty on the scope and application of the principle. This creates possibilities for states to invoke the principle to adopt protectionist measures. See also Ladeur K H (n 197). According to the author, the case-by-case approach has its drawbacks in that it is difficult to make use of comparisons or take into consideration constraints created by patterns of decisions made in the past. The author illustrates his argument by citing the *Artegodan* and *EFTA v Norway* cases. In *Artegodan*, a Council Regulation had excluded from a prohibition the use of certain hormones in stock farming, whereas the Commission had at the same time delayed a decision on the inclusion of progesterone in a procedure for the establishment of maximum residue limits of veterinary medicinal products in food stuffs. In the *EFTA v Norway*, Norway had prohibited the sale of cornflakes fortified with iron while at the same time accepting this kind of treatment for cheese.
207 Marchant G E and Mossman K L (n 159) 46–54. The authors argue that the precautionary principle is inherently ambiguous and arbitrary. There is no consensus definition or formulation of the precautionary principle or agreed on guidelines or criteria for its application. There is also ambiguity within and between different formulations of the precautionary principle as to when it applies and what it requires when it does apply. They cite the GC judgements in *Pfizer* and *Alpharma*, where the court upheld the contested ban of the antibiotics in question despite a negative scientific risk assessment in the former and in the absence of a risk assessment in the latter.
208 Asselt M B A V and Vos E (n 163) 317. The authors term as 'uncertainty paradox' the circumstances where, 'on the one hand, it is increasingly recognised that science cannot provide decisive evidence on uncertain risks, while on the other hand policy-makers and authorities increasingly resort to science for more certainty and conclusive evidence'.
209 Alemanno A (n 6) 409. More to the point, the Communication on Precautionary Principle provides: 'The measures, although provisional, shall be maintained as long as the scientific data remain incomplete, imprecise or inconclusive and as long as the risk is considered too high to be imposed on society'. See also Asselt M B A V and Vos E (n 163) 330. The authors note that the antibiotic ban in Pfizer was meant to be a

principle as applied in the EU is not the equivalent of the provisional measure envisaged under Article 5.7 of the SPS Agreement, and it cannot therefore be expected to meet the requirements of the SPS Agreement. From such a perspective, Regulation 178 of 2002 is in essence non-conforming with the SPS Agreement.

The EU institutions have a wide discretion[210] in risk management, and the GC has restricted judicial review of such discretion to manifest errors or misuse of powers or whether such powers have been exceeded.[211] The discretion extends to disregarding scientific opinion (on the ground of protecting human health) and on the basis of their democratic legitimacy and political responsibilities.[212] This discretion constitutes a degree of unpredictability for international trade that may amount to a disguised restriction on international trade, contrary to Article 2.3 of the SPS Agreement. Moreover, 'other factors', such as restoration of consumer confidence, are admitted to be legitimate objectives of risk management.[213] Besides, the risk assessment to be relied upon does not have to be specific to the particular risk being managed,[214] which is contrary to the jurisprudence of the Appellate Body.[215] It may therefore be argued that, even in its jurisprudence, the EU is non-conforming to WTO jurisprudence on the criteria for the invocation of Article 5.7 of the SPS Agreement, in that it does not conform to the four requirements of the Article.[216]

---

temporary measure, according to the Council. However, the ban was only reviewed in 2001, when the original council position was confirmed and amendments were passed to ban all antibiotics use as growth promoters by January 2006. Hence the ban was not temporary at all.

210 In other words, the GC's and CJ's strong deferential attitude when reviewing EU institutions' interpretation of scientific evidence and their determination of scientific uncertainty. However, the courts are less deferential when it comes to Member states measures, demanding that such measures be based on the most reliable scientific data available and the most recent results of international research. See *Commission v Denmark*, para 51. See also Peel J (n 132) 39–50.

211 *Pfizer*, para 406.

212 *Pfizer*, paras 199–201. The Communication on the Precautionary Principle asserts that 'the appropriate response in a given situation is thus the result of an eminently political decision (. . .)'. COM (2000) 1, 15.

213 *Pfizer*, para 462.

214 *Alpharma*, para 240. The Council and the Commission had not asked the Scientific Committee on Animal Nutrition (SCAN) for an opinion before instituting the impugned measure. But the GC held that the Council and the Commission could themselves assess the risk 'on the basis of information contained in the SCAN opinions relating to the other antibiotics whose authorisation was withdrawn by the contested regulation and in the reports of the various international, Community and national bodies'.

215 The Appellate Body has held that risk assessment is required to be specific: *Appellate Body Report, EC – Hormones*, para 200; *Appellate Body Report, Australia – Salmon*, para 124; *Appellate Body Report, Japan – Apples*, para 203.

216 *Appellate Body Report, Japan – Agricultural Products*, para 89; *Appellate Body Report, Japan – Apples*, para 176.

More generally, the precautionary principle is criticised for not taking into account the opportunity costs of precautionary measures.[217] The principle is also said to lead to risk–risk trade-offs, with a result that managed risks lead to other hazardous risks.[218]

217 Frank B Cross, 'Paradoxical Perils of the Precautionary Principle' (1996) 53 *Washington and Lee Law Review* 851, 864–890. According to the author, insofar as the precautionary principle diverts action from problem A to problem B, the principle is counterproductive whenever the risk from A is greater in magnitude than that from B. Yet, by its very terms, the precautionary principle ignores this loss in its single-minded focus on eliminating any risk from the problem under attention. This approach fails to account for the inevitable trade-off between the 'depth' and the 'breadth' of government action. Regulating any one substance more strictly or deeply requires additional resources that will unintentionally preclude more widespread regulation of a greater number of risks. This leads to a trade-off of over-regulation and under-regulation. See also Majone G (n 186) 101. According to the author, the resources used in attempts to control poorly understood low-level risks could be more effectively used in the control of well-known large-scale risks. Moreover, precautionary measures taken on an ad hoc basis, often in response to political pressures, may distort priorities and compromise the consistency of regulatory policies.
218 Louis A Cox and Paolo F Ricci, 'Causal Regulations vs. Political Will: Why Human Zoonotic Infections Increase Despite Precautionary Bans on Animal Antibiotics' (2007) 34 (4) *Environment International* 8–14. The authors conducted a regulatory analysis of precautionary legal requirements of the 1998 EU ban on animal antibiotics used as growth promoters and to prevent illnesses and used Quantitative Risk Assessment (QRA) to assess a set of policy outcomes. They found several antibiotic resistance rates in isolates from human campylobacteriosis patients increased significantly. One possible explanation is that reduced animal antibiotic use increases human illnesses (for example, due to increased microbial loads in fresh meat products), leading to increased resistance in human isolates (for example, due to increased use of human antibiotics to treat illnesses). See also Cross F B (n 217) 864–890. According to the author, supply is as a result of demand. Where a product or activity is banned, the consumers and suppliers will shift to another product or activity. If the alternative is more hazardous than the original, then the precautionary action will cause more harm than it cures. The author illustrates the issue with the case of artificial sweeteners in the US. A family of sweeteners called Cyclamates was removed from the market in the late 1960s, due to their potential carcinogenicity. Suppliers and consumers turned to Saccharin to meet the market demand for artificial sweetening. The FDA then proposed to ban Saccharin because of evidence of carcinogenicity. Congress overturned the ban. Saccharin may be riskier than Cyclamates. Some suppliers and consumers turned to Aspartame, which has its own health concerns. Moreover, restricting artificial sweeteners increases the consumption of sugar, which is risky for diabetics; Per Sandin and others, 'Five Charges Against the Precautionary Principle' (2002) 5 *Journal of Risk Research* 287; Cass R Sunstein, 'Beyond the Precautionary Principle' (2003) 151 *University of Pennsylvania Law Review* 1003. According to the author, the principle threatens to be paralyzing, forbidding regulation, inaction, and every step in between. The principle turns a blind eye to many aspects of risk-related situations and focuses on a narrow subset of what is at stake; Cass R Sunstein, 'Irreversible and Catastrophic' (2005) 91 *Cornell Law Review* 841. For a contra view see: Marko Ahteensuu, 'Defending the Precautionary Principle Against Three Criticisms' (2007) 11 *Trames* 366; Steffen F Hansen, Martin K V Krauss and Joel A Tickner, 'The Precautionary Principle and Risk-Risk Tradeoffs' (2008) 11 *Journal of Risk Research* 464.

94 *EU food safety standards*

It may therefore be concluded that the EU application of the precautionary principle in its risk management policies and regulations is non-conforming to the 'normative yardstick of science'[219] of the SPS Agreement.

2.5 Global administrative and constitutional law perspectives

Generally the EU has a mixed relationship with international law. The EU may be said to be broadly receptive of customary international law norms. In *Opel Austria*,[220] the Court of First Instance held:

> The Court holds in this connection, first, that the principle of good faith is a rule of customary international law whose existence is recognized by the International Court of Justice (. . .) and is therefore binding on the Community.[221]

The court went further to hold in *Racke*:[222]

> [The] European Community must respect international law in the exercise of its powers. It is therefore required to comply with the rules of customary international law when adopting a regulation suspending the trade concessions granted by, or by virtue of, an agreement which it has concluded with a non-member country.[223]

Furthermore, the Court has held that rules based on international agreements undertaken by the EU which become part of the Community legal order under Article 218 TFEU have a direct effect in the EU under the similar conditions required for EU rules.[224] Moreover, where the EU incurs obligations under an international agreement not founded on the principle of mutual convenience, such obligations are a legitimacy benchmark for acts adopted by the EU, regardless of whether they have a direct effect.[225]

---

219 Peel J (n 132) 99. The author argues that by placing science in the role of an arbiter in the SPS context, it is constituted as a normative yardstick against which national risk regulations are judged, notwithstanding its own lack of normative content. See also Peter W B Phillips and William A Kerr, 'Alternative Paradigms: The WTO Versus the Biosafety Protocol for Trade in Genetically Modified Organisms' (2000) 34 (4) *Journal of World Trade* 63, 72. The authors argue that the approach to trade barriers under the SPS Agreement is the scientific question: Why? While the precautionary principle approach is the unscientific: Why not? Thus creating an irreconcilable difference.
220 Case T-115/94, *Opel Austria v. Council of the European Union* [1997] ECR II-39 (*Opel Austria*).
221 *Opel Austria*, para 90.
222 Case C-162/96 *Racke GmbH & Co. vis the Hauptzollamt Mainz*, 1998 ECR, I-3655(*Racke*).
223 *Racke*, para 45.
224 Case C-87/75 *Conceria Daniele Bresciani v. Amministrazione delle finanzedello Stato* [1976] ECR I00129, para 25.
225 Case C-377/98 *Kingdom of Netherlands v. European Parliament and Council of the European Union* [2001] ECR I-07079, paras 53–54.

In *Kadi*[226] the Court reiterated that the EU must respect international law in the exercise of its powers and that a measure adopted by virtue of those powers must be interpreted, and its scope limited, in the light of the relevant rules of international law. Further, in the sphere of cooperation and development the EU must exercise its legislative powers in observance of the undertakings given in the context of the United Nations and other international organisations.[227] By annulling the impugned regulation that was intended to implement a United Nations Security Council resolution on grounds of breaching EU fundamental rights, the Court in effect adopted a dualist approach by holding that international norms are subject to EU fundamental rights.[228]

On the other hand, when it comes to international trade law, the EU courts have been much more assertive of the supremacy of EU law over GATT and WTO law. It begun with *Portugal v Council*,[229] where the court held that the WTO Agreements are not in principle among the rules in the light of which the Court is to review the legality of measures adopted by the Community institutions, thus denying the agreement's direct effect.[230] However, *Portugal v Council* has two exceptions. In *Fediol*[231] direct effect is recognised where the community measure refers expressly to precise provisions of the GATT and WTO Agreements.[232] Further, in *Nakajima*[233] direct effect is recognised where the community intended to implement a particular obligation assumed under the GATT and WTO Agreements.[234] In *Biret*[235] the Court had opportunity to reconsider *Portugal v Council*, upon the opinion the Advocate General Alber,[236] but it failed to so and upheld the decision of the CFI though on different grounds. Ultimately

---

226 Joined Cases C-402/05 P and C-415/05 P, *Yassin Abdullah Kadi and Al Barakaat International Foundation v. Council of the European Union and Commission of the European Communities* [2008] ECR I-06351 (*Kadi*).
227 *Kadi*, paras 291–292.
228 Albert Posch, 'The Kadi Case: Rethinking the Relationship between EU Law and International Law?' (2009) 15 *Columbia Journal of European Law Online* 1, 4. For further analysis of the case see Juliane Kokott and Christoph Sobotta, 'The Kadi Case – Constitutional Core Values and International Law – Finding the Balance?' (2012) 23 *European Journal of International Law* 1015.
229 Case C-149/96, *Portugal v. Council* [1999] ECR I-8395 (*Portugal v. Council*).
230 *Portugal v. Council*, para 47. The Court provided for exceptions as follows (para 49):

> It is only where the Community intended to implement a particular obligation assumed in the context of the WTO, or where the Community measure refers expressly to the precise provisions of the WTO Agreements, that it is for the Court to review the legality of the Community measure in question.

231 Case 70/87, *Federation de l'industrie de l'huilerie de la CEE (Fediol) v. Commission* [1989] ECR 1781(*Fediol*).
232 *Fediol*, paras 19–22.
233 Case C-69/89, *Nakajima All Precision Co. Ltd v. Council* [1991] ECR I-2069 (*Nakajima*).
234 *Nakajima*, para 31.
235 Case C-93/02 P, *Biret International v. Council* [2003] ECR I-10497 (*Biret*).
236 Opinion of Advocate General Alber, delivered on 15 May 2003, in Case C-93/02 P, *Biret International v. Council* [2003] ECR I-10497.

96 EU food safety standards

the Court largely reaffirmed its decision in *Portugal v Council* in subsequent cases such as *Chiquita*[237] and, to some degree, in *Van Parys*.[238]

However, it is important to note that the EU position on the applicability of international trade law is not unique. Other major regional integration organisations such as the Caribbean Community (CARICOM), the Economic Community of West African States (ECOWAS), the South American regional economic organisation (MERCOSUR), and the Association of Southeast Asian Nations (ASEAN) have also not provided for the direct effect of international norms in their legal regimes.[239] Indeed major trading members of the WTO such as US, Canada, and China, which together with the EU constitute about 75 per cent of world trade, also deny direct effect to the WTO Agreements.[240] Nevertheless, the EU reluctance in the implementation of the WTO DSB rulings in *EC – Bananas*,[241] *EC – Hormones*, and *EC–Biotech* point to a disconnect with the Global Administrative Law core principle of accountability. Furthermore, the EU stance on WTO law serves to deny individuals within the EU the right to hold the EU and its national governments accountable for their international law infringements.[242]

2.6 Chapter discussion and conclusions

According to Bernd van der Meulen, 'The BSE crisis in the late 1990s caused an earthquake in the legal and regulatory landscape of Europe (. . .) and has been a catalyst for the recent developments in the field of EU food legislation'.[243]

---

237 Case T-19/01 *Chiquita Brands International, Inc. and Others v Commission of the European Communities* [2005] ECR II-00315.
238 Case C-377/02, *Léon van Parys NV v. BelgischeInterventie- en Restitutiebureau (BIRB)* [2005] ECR I-01465. For analysis see: Delphine De Mey and Pablo I Colomo, 'Recent Developments on the Invocability of WTO Law in the EC: A Wave of Mutilation' (2006) 11 *European Foreign Affairs Review* 63; Fabrizio D Gianni and Renato Antonini, 'DSB Decisions and Direct Effect of WTO Law: Should the EC Courts be More Flexible when the Flexibility of the WTO System has Come to an End?' (2006) 40 *Journal of World Trade* 777.
239 Andre Nollkaemper, 'The Duality of Direct Effect of International Law' (2014) 25 *European Journal of International Law* 105, 123.
240 Hellene R Fabri, 'Is There a Case – Legally and Politically – for Direct Effect of WTO Obligations?' (2014) 25 *European Journal of International Law* 151, 155.
241 *Appellate Body Report, European Communities – Regime for the Importation, Sale and Distribution of Bananas ('EC-Bananas III')*, WT/DS27/AB/R, adopted 25 Sep. 1997.
242 For a discussion see: Sebastiaan Princen, 'EC Compliance with WTO Law: The Interplay of Law and Politics' (2004) 15 *European Journal of International Law* 555; Antonello Tancredi, 'EC Practice in the WTO: How Wide is the "Scope for Manoeuvre"?' (2004) 15 *The European Journal of International Law* 933; Eva Steinberger, 'The WTO Treaty as a Mixed Agreement: Problems with the EC's and the EC Member states' Membership of the WTO' (2006) 17 *The European Journal of International Law* 837.
243 Bernd V D Meulen, 'The EU Regulatory Approach to GM Foods' (2007) 16 *Kansas Journal of Law and Public Policy* 286, 290. The crisis led to a parliamentary inquiry, the resultant Medina report and the White Paper on Food Safety upon which EU food safety regulations are based.

Moreover, the crisis came when the EU was already on a path of adopting very high levels of protection in its legislation.[244] The political environment was further compounded by pro-environmental NGOs, such as Greenpeace and Friends of the Earth, and Green parties mobilised sections of the population leading to mass protests against lax regulations on food safety, particularly GMO foods.[245] These factors and the charged climate they spawned led to, as well as informed, the incorporation of 'other legitimate factors' and the precautionary principle into EU risk management and the impugned EU de facto moratorium on approvals of GMO products.[246]

The GC and CJ, enveloped in the reigning political atmosphere, were sympathetic and deferential to EU food safety measures, and went further to endorse the application of the precautionary principle to the EU food safety regulatory regime. The courts' sympathy was first manifested in *Fedesa*, where the CJ upheld EU measures banning beef treated with hormones despite scientific evidence that it was safe and the hormones harmless, and culminated in *Pfizer*, where the GC held that EU institutions may disregard scientific evidence in their legislative measures, since 'scientific legitimacy is not a sufficient basis for the exercise of public authority'.[247]

Regardless of its socio-political underpinnings, or because of these, the EU food safety regulations regime flies in the face of the WTO scientific disciplines. The Appellate Body, in *EC-Hormones*, found the EU measures to be in violation of scientific requirements and found the EU's invocation of the precautionary principle untenable under the SPS Agreement. The Panel in *EC-Biotech* reiterated the

---

244 Theophanis Christoforou, 'The Regulation of Genetically Modified Organisms in the European Union: The Interplay of Science, Law and Politics' (2004) 41 *Common Market Law Review* 685. The author notes that the Single European Act (SEA) introduced qualified majority voting and the aim of 'high level of protection' in EU regulation of risk. However, Member states were allowed to apply even higher levels of protection under certain conditions. In order to discourage and to pre-empt Member states from applying disparate national standards that might undermine the internal market, EU legislation tended to choose very high levels of protection. Moreover, the TFEU and the ToA embedded a 'high level of health protection' in several Articles of the EC Treaty, as one of the objectives of the EU. The author further notes that two additional reasons have recently contributed to the stringency of EU health regulations: the discounting of the positivist view of science, as a powerful and neutral tool of risk assessment; and the finding that risk assessment methodologies are inherently biased in favour of avoiding over-inclusive regulatory measures for fear of imposing undue costs on technological progress, industry, and society. Besides, consumers, dissatisfied with the way in which the market and regulatory authorities have balanced risks and benefits, have influenced the Commission to take into account their concerns.
245 Christopher Ansell, Rahsaan Maxwell and Daniela Sicurelli, 'Protesting Food: NGOs and Political Mobilization in Europe' in C Ansell and D Vogel (eds) *What's the Beef? The Contested Governance of European Food Safety* (MIT Press, Cambridge, MA, 2006) 97.
246 *Panel Reports EC–Biotech*, paras 7. 1271-7. 1272. The Panel found that the moratorium was in effect from June 1999 to August 2003.
247 *Pfizer*, paras 200-201.

Appellate Body's finding on the precautionary principle. Furthermore, in *EC – Biotech*, the EU sought to defend its impugned GMO regulations under the Cartagena Protocol. The Panel rejected this reliance on the Protocol.

The EU agreed to resolve *EC – Hormones* after a long struggle,[248] and has only partly resolved *EC – Biotech*.[249] Arguably, the general de facto moratorium ended with the enforcement of the new regulations in April 2004, but national safeguard measures persist and the slow approval process is impugnable.[250] Moreover, the EU finally bowed down to Members' demands and allowed Member states to restrict or prohibit the cultivation of GMOs that had been authorised at EU level.[251]

The EU's intransigence may be understood as an outcome of its recent past turbulent experience with food safety policy and regulation. In addition, the multi-sectoral nature of food policy, encompassing various policy areas such as the internal market, the environment, and food safety and consumer concerns, renders coordination across these sectors difficult and uncertain. Besides, the multi-level governance structure of food safety has given rise to contention between the Commission, on the one hand, and the European Parliament, the Council, and Member states, on the other.[252] This has made it difficult to develop and implement common policy and regulations. As a result, when faced with its international obligations under the WTO, and in particular the SPS Agreement, the EU has found it difficult to justify its regulations. The Commission, which exercises the exclusive EU competence on external trade relations, is captive to the national and consumer interests which it is mandated to advance. Where these are in conflict with international obligations, the Commission is placed in a dilemma.

---

248 WTO, 'European Communities – Measures Concerning Meat and Meat Products (Hormones): Joint Communication from the European Communities and the United States' (WT/DS26/28, 30 September 2009); WTO, 'European Communities – Measures Concerning Meat and Meat Products (Hormones) – Joint Communication from the European Union and Canada' (WT/DS48/26, 22 March 2011).
249 The EU has resolved the dispute with Argentina and Canada, but not with the US. See WTO, 'European Communities – Measures Affecting the Approval and Marketing of Biotech Products: Status Report by the European Union: Addendum' (WT/DS291/37/Add 45, 14/10/2011).
250 European Commission, 'Questions and Answers on EU's Policies on Cultivation and Imports of GMOs' (MEMO/13/952, Brussels, 6 November 2013). Eight Member states, Austria, Bulgaria, Greece, Germany, Hungary, Italy, Luxembourg, and Poland, adopted safeguard measures and prohibited the cultivation of the GM maize MON810 in their territories.
251 Directive (EU) 2015/412 of the European Parliament and of the Council of 11 March 2015 amending Directive 2001/18/EC as regards the possibility for the Member states to restrict or prohibit the cultivation of genetically modified organisms (GMOs) in their territories, OJL 68/1 of 13.3.2015.
252 Thomas Bernauer and Ladina Caduff, 'Food Safety and the Structure of the European Food Industry' in C Ansell and D Vogel (eds) *What's the Beef? The Contested Governance of European Food Safety* (MIT Press, Cambridge, MA, 2006) 81, 84.

The SPS Agreement is a trade agreement, not a health agreement.[253] To the extent that the EU regulations seek to achieve a high level of protection for the health of its nationals through its food safety regulations, they are unassailable. However, to the extent that these regulations impinge on international trade, they are subject to scientific scrutiny and contestation. Given that the main objective of the SPS Agreement is the promotion of regulatory harmonisation with a view to trade liberalisation, national measures that derogate from these objectives are subject to stringent disciplines.

From the foregoing it may be concluded that the EU's food safety regulatory regime may be viewed as detracting from international harmonisation objectives and, as a consequence, curtailing international trade on the following grounds:

1   The objectives of the EU food safety regulations are wider than those of the SPS Agreement and the Codex, and such objectives are not universally shared among WTO Members.
2   The EU risk assessment and risk management regime, with its strict and detailed procedural requirements and its consideration of 'other legitimate factors' and the precautionary principle, is more stringent than necessary for purposes of international trade.
3   By taking into consideration 'other legitimate factors' in its risk management decisions, the EU goes against the Codex provisions on 'criteria for consideration of the other factors (...)'. Furthermore, the EU consideration of 'other legitimate factors' in its risk management goes against Appellate Body jurisprudence.
4   The EU application of the precautionary principle in its risk management policies is non-conforming with the requirements of Article 5.7 of the SPS Agreement.

The wide objectives of the EU food safety regulations; the stringency of the regulations; EU adoption of other legitimate factors, including consumer concerns, in risk management; and EU espousal of the precautionary principle are aspects of EU food safety regulations that are arguably antithetical to international harmonisation and trade liberalisation. Hypothetically, the effects of the application of these concepts on international trade may be contemplated in a situation where all states adopt the concepts in their food safety regulatory regimes. The result might not be tenable, as harmonisation and liberalisation may be rendered impossible.

---

253 Steve Charnovitz, 'The Supervision of Health and Biosafety Regulation by World Trade Rules' (2000) 13 *Tulane Environmental Law Journal* 271, 276. The author notes that although the preamble to the SPS Agreement, at paragraph 2, has the desire to improve human and animal health, there are no disciplines for low national SPS standards or lack of such standards. The SPS Agreement only disciplines overuse or misuse of SPS standards.

Perhaps even more so within the EU, its food safety regulations are also contested.[254] The contestation is between national measures and EU harmonising measures. The national measures are apparently taken under Article 36 and 114(4)–(7) of the TFEU. The case law attests to this contention. Invariably, it is the EU's overarching rationale – the internal market, particularly its free movement of goods principle – which is contested. Ultimately, the EU is forever struggling to maintain the delicate balance between national and supranational demands on food safety policy and regulations.

---

254 Marjolein V M B Asselt, Ellen Vos and Bram Rooijackers, 'Science, Knowledge and Uncertainty in EU Risk Regulation' in M Everson and E Vos (eds) *Uncertain Risks Regulated in National, European and International Context* (Routledge-Cavendish, 2008) 35. The authors note that Member states strongly disagree with EFSA's opinions on various grounds. See also Marion Dreyer and others, 'Institutional Re-Arrangements in European Food Safety Governance: A Comparative Analysis' in E Vos and F Wendler (eds) *Food Safety Regulation in Europe: A Comparative Institutional Analysis* (Intersentia, Antwerpen-Oxford, 2006) 9–64. The impetus for the institutional rearrangements of EU food safety regulations derives from the desire for harmonisation in order to minimise differences in various national authorities and EFSA.

3 COMESA food safety standards

Unfortunately, the food safety systems in most countries of the region (Africa) are generally weak, fragmented and not well coordinated; and thus are not effective enough to adequately protect the health of consumers and to enhance the competitiveness of food exports.[1]

3.1 Introduction

While the EU updated its food safety standards in the aftermath of the BSE crisis, African countries are still mired in a crisis of a paucity of food safety standards. African countries continue to lag behind in food safety standards, with devastating consequences. For instance, the World Health Organization Regional Office for Africa reports:

> The year 2008 recorded an unprecedented incidence of food borne diseases in the African Region including: anthrax in Zimbabwe; typhoid fever in Uganda; chemical poisoning due to consumption of seed beans and maize in Nigeria and Kenya; cholera from several countries e.g. Mozambique, Nigeria, Congo, Zambia, DRC, Kenya, Tanzania, South Africa, Zimbabwe; pesticide poisoning from cabbage and other vegetables in Senegal; fish mouse in Mauritius; mushroom poisoning in Algeria; Botulism and Hepatitis A in Uganda (. . .).[2]
>
> [In Africa] Vibrio cholerae, the bacterium that causes cholera, caused 55,812 illnesses and 709 deaths in 13 countries from January to May 2015 (. . .) Salmonella enterica serovar Typhi (S. Typhi) caused 19,824 illnesses and 9 deaths in 4 countries from January to May 2015.[3]

---

1 FAO/WHO, 'Final Report on: Regional Conference on Food Safety for Africa Harare, Zimbabwe, 3–6 October 2005' 47, <www.fao.org/docrep/meeting/010/a0215e/A0215E00.htm> accessed 10 January 2015.
2 WHO Africa Region website <www.afro.who.int/en/clusters-a-programmes/hpr/food-safety-and-nutrition-fan/overview.html> accessed 10 January 2015.
3 WHO Regional office for Africa, 'Food Safety Newsletter, Vol. 2, Issue no. 2, July 2015', <www.afro.who.int/en/clusters-a-programmes/hpr/food-safety-and-nutrition-fan.html> accessed 2 January 2016.

African countries, including members of the COMESA, are faced with major challenges in their food safety systems. These challenges include limited information, education, health promotion, and training programmes on food safety; and due to multiple food control agencies, there is no coordination among the agencies, leading to confusion over jurisdiction. They have inadequate enabling policies and outdated legislation and regulations. They also suffer from insufficient and inadequate resources and capacities regarding food safety.[4]

Consequently, trade in food products between African countries, and in particular the COMESA members, and the EU is faced by the challenge of navigating the gap between the high food safety standards in the EU and the low or non-existent standards in the COMESA. This imbalance poses a challenge for food products exporters from the COMESA: How do they navigate between the two regimes so as to gain and maintain access into the EU market?

After examining the EU food safety system in chapter two, this chapter will in turn examine the COMESA food safety system in light of the SPS Agreement provisions, Codex standards, and the guidelines set by the Food and Agricultural Organization of the United Nations (FAO).

The chapter proceeds as follows. Part two will examine the COMESA as a Regional Trading Agreement (RTA), its institutional set-up and socioeconomic aspects. Part three will examine the food safety layout in the COMESA and in particular its regulatory, management, inspection, laboratory, and enforcement aspects. The chapter closes with part four, which is a critical analysis of the COMESA food safety regime as analysed in the chapter.

3.2 An overview of the COMESA

The Common Market for Eastern and Southern Africa (COMESA)[5] was initially established in 1981 as the Preferential Trade Area for Eastern and Southern Africa (PTA). The PTA Treaty was signed on 21 December 1981, in Lusaka, Zambia, and came into force on 30 September 1982, after it had been ratified by more than seven signatory states as provided for in Article 50 of the Treaty.[6]

---

4 Mwamakamba L and others, 'Developing and Maintaining National Food Safety Control Systems: Experiences from the WHO African Region' (2012) 12 *African Journal of Food, Agriculture, Nutrition and Development* 6291; Mohammad A Jabbar and Delia Grace, 'Regulations for Safety of Animal Source Foods in Selected Sub-Saharan African Countries: Current Status and Their Implications' (Paper prepared for the Safe Food, Fair Food Project, International Livestock Research Institute, Nairobi, Kenya, January 2012), <http://ageconsearch.umn.edu/bitstream/181867/2/2012Food%20safety%20Synthesis%20Final%20ILRI%20%2030Jan2012.pdf> accessed 10 January 2015.
5 There are Nineteen COMESA Member states: Burundi, Comoros, Democratic Republic of Congo, Djibouti, Egypt, Eritrea, Ethiopia, Kenya, Libya, Madagascar, Malawi, Mauritius, Rwanda, Seychelles, Sudan, Swaziland, Uganda, Zambia and Zimbabwe.
6 Siteke G Mwale, 'An Historical Background to the Formation of COMESA' in Victor Murinde (ed) *The Free Trade Area of the Common Market for Eastern and Southern Africa* (Ashgate Publishing Ltd, Aldershot, 2001) 31, 35. For an analysis of COMESA development policy,

The PTA Treaty envisaged the transformation of the Preferential Trade Area into a Common Market and, in conformity with this, the Treaty establishing COMESA was signed on 5 November 1993 in Kampala, Uganda, and was ratified a year later in Lilongwe, Malawi, on 8 December 1994 (COMESA Treaty).[7] COMESA was notified to the WTO, under the Enabling Clause, in 1995.[8] COMESA achieved a Free Trade Area (FTA) in 2000 and launched its Customs Union in June 2009.[9]

The objectives of COMESA are expressed in the COMESA Treaty to be as follows: to attain sustainable growth and development of the Member states; to promote joint development in all fields of economic activity and the joint adoption of macroeconomic policies and programmes; to cooperate in the creation of an enabling environment for foreign, cross border, and domestic investment; to cooperate in the promotion of peace, security, and stability among the Member states; to cooperate in strengthening the relations between the Common Market and the rest of the world; and to contribute towards the establishment, progress, and realisation of the objectives of the African Economic Community.[10] The main institutions of COMESA are the COMESA Authority, the Council of Ministers, the Secretariat, and the Court of Justice.

3.2.1 *The institutional framework of the COMESA*

At the head of the institutional framework of COMESA is the COMESA Authority, composed of the Heads of State and Government of Member states, which is the supreme policy organ of COMESA. The Authority meets once in a year and controls the executive functions of COMESA, in addition to ensuring that its aims and objectives are achieved. Its decisions and directives are arrived at by

---

see Roselyn K Akombe, 'Regional Integration and the Challenge of Economic Development: The Case of the Common Market for Eastern and Southern Africa (COMESA)' (PhD thesis, Rutgers, The State University of New Jersey, 2005) 102–211. For an analysis of the COMESA Treaty, see Henry K Mutai, *Compliance with International Trade Obligations: The Common Market for Eastern and Southern Africa* (Kluwer Law International, The Netherlands, 2007) 97–126.

7 History of COMESA <http://about.comesa.int/lang-en/overview/history-of-comesa>; COMESA Treaty <http://about.comesa.int/attachments/comesa_treaty_en.pdf> accessed 15 February 2015.

8 GATT Document, 'Differential and More Favourable Treatment, Reciprocity and Fuller Participation of Developing Countries, (Decision of 28 November 1979, L/4903) (Enabling Clause). For an analysis of the Enabling Clause see *Panel Report, European Communities – Conditions for the Granting of Tariff Preferences to Developing Countries*, WT/DS246/R, adopted as modified by the Appellate Body report on 20 April 2004; *Appellate Body Report, European Communities – Conditions for the Granting of Tariff Preferences to Developing Countries*, WT/DS246/AB/R, adopted 20 April 2004.

9 COMESA Achievements <http://about.comesa.int/lang-en/overview> accessed 11 March 2015. The FTA currently consists of 15 Member states.

10 COMESA Treaty, art 3.

consensus and are binding on Member states and COMESA organs, other than the COMESA Court of Justice.[11]

The Council of Ministers, composed of Ministers designated by Member states, is the second highest institution in COMESA.[12] The Council meets once in a year and its main function is to ensure the proper functioning of COMESA in accordance with the COMESA Treaty. The Council makes decisions by consensus, and in the event that doesn't take place, decisions are made by a two-thirds majority. Any dissenting Member may lodge an objection to such a decision, and it will be referred to the Authority for a final decision.[13] The Council has the duty to monitor, review, and ensure the proper functioning of COMESA.[14] It carries out this mandate through the making of regulations, directives, decisions, recommendations, and opinions.[15] Regulations are binding on all Members in their entirety; directives are binding on each of the Member states to which they are addressed with regard to the result to be achieved but not the means to achieving it; decisions are only binding for those Members to whom they are addressed; and recommendations and opinions are not binding.[16]

The COMESA Secretariat, headed by a Secretary General (assisted by two Assistant Secretaries General, who are appointed by the COMESA Authority), is in charge of the operations of COMESA.[17] The Secretary General functions as the CEO of COMESA and personifies its legal personality.[18] In his or her role of monitoring the functioning of COMESA and ensuring compliance with the objectives of COMESA by Member states, the Secretary General has a more comprehensive mandate and more powers than the Council of Ministers.[19] In his or her functions, the Secretary General embodies the Secretariat and is elevated to a position of a COMESA organ, like the Authority and the Council of Ministers.

The COMESA Court of Justice, consisting of a First Instance Division and an Appellate Division,[20] is mandated to resolve disputes referred to it by Member states against one another, by the Council of Ministers, or by the Secretary General, or by corporations and natural persons, concerning the infringement of provisions of the Treaty or non-performance of obligations under the Treaty by a Member state.[21] The Court of Justice can also hear a reference from a Member state, or any corporation and natural person resident in a Member state, concerning

---

11 Ibid, art 8.
12 Ibid, art (1).
13 Ibid, arts 9 (6) and (7).
14 Ibid, art 9 (2) (a).
15 Ibid, arts 9 (2) and 10 (1).
16 Ibid, art 10 (1) – (5).
17 Ibid, art 17 (1) – (7).
18 Ibid, art 17 (8).
19 Mutai H K (n 6) 142.
20 COMESA Treaty, art 19 (2).
21 Ibid, arts 23–26.

the legality of any act, regulation, directive, or decision of the COMESA Council. The Court of Justice also has jurisdiction to determine arbitrations and special agreements where COMESA or any of its organs is a party.[22] Moreover, the Court of Justice has jurisdiction over disputes concerning COMESA employees and third parties against COMESA or its institutions and can act as an arbitral tribunal on any matter arising from a contract to which COMESA or any of its institutions is a party.

3.2.2 Discussion

Despite being designated as the final authority in COMESA, the COMESA Authority, meeting only once in year, lacks the time and capacity to carry out its mandate effectively. Moreover, as its decisions are made by consensus, the authority may be unable to take any meaningful decisions for fear of lack of consensus. Ultimately the Authority's usefulness will be its political role of harnessing political support for COMESA and its programmes.[23]

Like the Authority, the Council of Ministers meets once a year and is similarly constrained by time, which hampers the execution of its mandate, especially given its executive and supervisory authority. The Council often resorts to political persuasion, rather than legal enforcement, in its decisions, as exemplified in its decision on all Members becoming members of the FTA, which was couched in exhortatory language, and which did not meet the legal requirements of the Treaty.[24] This is exacerbated by the lack of an enforcement mechanism in the Treaty. Hence the Council's role in reality has more of a political nature than the legal one envisaged by the Treaty. Furthermore, the requirement that the Council's decisions be made by consensus or, in default, by a two-thirds challengeable majority, renders the decision-making process too long, tortuous, and uncertain, since ultimately it may be the Authority that will make the final decision on appeal. However, to date, such a situation has not arisen. Ultimately, the slow decision-making process may slow down the economic integration process of COMESA.

Although the Secretariat is entrusted with tasks that are meant to ensure the attainment of COMESA objectives, it is relegated to a subsidiary role, after that of the Authority and the Council of Ministers. This constrains the performance of the Secretariat and inhibits the performance of its mandate to the detriment of COMESA and the achievement of its goals. Moreover, the Secretariat may find it difficult to ensure compliance since the implementation of COMESA programmes is left to the Member states, in addition to the lack of a rule-based system and monitoring system.[25] Moreover, the Secretary General is overburdened

22 Ibid, art 28.
23 Mutai H K (n 6) 138.
24 Ibid.
25 Akombe R K (n 6) 196–199.

with political and technical functions and lacks the capacity, both in terms of the number of support staff and expertise, to carry out all the stipulated functions.[26]

The Court of Justice became operational in 1998 and was located within the COMESA Secretariat in Lusaka until June 2014 when it relocated to its permanent seat in Khartoum, Sudan.[27] However, due to lack of funding, the Court is unable to fully implement its programmes and is behind schedule in deciding cases brought before it.[28] These administrative and logistical constraints have led to poor performance of the Court in carrying out its mandate.

Furthermore, the Treaty does not provide for precedence or hierarchy where trade disputes are concerned. A trade dispute between COMESA Members may be adjudicated by the Court or by the WTO Dispute Settlement Body (DSB): the Treaty does not decide which body takes precedence.[29] This may facilitate forum shopping, create legal uncertainty, and cause a threat of incoherent jurisprudence that may ultimately lead to conflicting decisions being pronounced.[30]

It appears that while COMESA has clear objectives, its institutional framework is not set up to deliver on these objectives. The institutional framework is weak, the decision-making procedures are slow and inefficient, and there is a lack of capacity to deliver on core mandates by all institutions. There is evident need for structural reforms to address these shortcomings. There is also a strong need to review COMESA objectives in order to streamline them with the socio-political realities of the Member states. This is because one of the reasons for the institutional weaknesses of COMESA is the Members' reluctance to give up some of their state sovereignty to the COMESA institutions.[31]

3.2.3 Socioeconomic aspects of the COMESA

There is great heterogeneity among the 19 Member countries of COMESA in terms of land area, economic size and performance, and dependence on trade. COMESA Member states, in terms of physical area, range from small islands like Seychelles, Comoros, and Mauritius to large countries like Sudan, Libya, and the Democratic Republic of Congo. Moreover, regional per capita income varies

---

26 Ibid.
27 COMESA Court of Justice website <http://comesacourt.org/en/> accessed 10 April 2015.
28 COMESA Regional Investment Agency, 'News and Events, 15th March 2011: COMESA Court of Justice Open 2011 Sittings in Lusaka', <www.comesaria.org/site/en/news_details.php?chaine=comesa-court-of-justice-open-2011-sittings-in-lusaka&id_news=6&id_article=119> accessed 10 April 2015.
29 Felix Maonera, 'Dispute Settlement under COMESA' (Tralac Working Paper No. 7, October 2005) 20, <www.givengain.com/unique/tralac/pdf/20051206_felix_comesa.pdf> accessed 10 April 2015.
30 Pieter J Kuijper, 'Conflicting Rules and Clashing Courts: The Case of Multilateral Environmental Agreements, Free Trade Agreements and the WTO' (Issue Paper No. 10, ICTSD's Programme on Dispute Settlement and Legal Aspects of International Trade, International Centre for Trade and Sustainable Development, Geneva, 2010).
31 Mutai H K (n 6) 143; Akombe R K (n 6) 198.

widely, ranging from US$593 in Burundi to US$4,329 in Seychelles in 2005. Furthermore, while some countries in the region, such as Djibouti, Mauritius, Seychelles, Swaziland, and Zimbabwe, rely rather heavily on trade, trade constitutes a much smaller part of the economies of Burundi, Comoros, Rwanda, Uganda, and Zambia.[32] Some 12 of the COMESA Members are classified as Least Developed Countries (LDCs),[33] of which 6 are land-locked (LLDCs).[34] These factors have hindered economic growth and constrained the region's trade performance. Although there is significant diversity in performance across countries, overall, Sub-Saharan Africa's (which includes COMESA countries) long-term growth has been slow relative to other developing countries, experiencing less than half of the average growth and about half of average investment efficiency levels obtained in other developing regions.[35]

The inability of COMESA to positively harness the diversity of its Member states has had debilitating consequences on the region's economy, particularly its agricultural sector.[36] According to UNCTAD, the contribution of agriculture to total output in Sub-Saharan Africa has generally stagnated since 1980. The sector's contribution to Gross Domestic Product (GDP) in 2006, at about 19 per cent, was no higher than in 1980. Moreover, in the period of 2002 to 2005, just three countries accounted for about 56 per cent of total Sub-Saharan African

---

32 Betina Dimaranan and Simon Mevel, 'The COMESA Customs Union: A Quantitative Assessment' (Helsinki, GTAP Conference, 2008) 3, <http://gtap.agecon.purdue.edu> accessed 11 April 2015.
33 UNCTAD, 'The Least Developed Countries Report 2014: The Potential Role of South-South Cooperation for Inclusive and Sustainable Development' (United Nations, New York and Geneva, 2014).
  The LDCs in COMESA are Burundi, Comoros, the Democratic Republic of Congo, Djibouti, Eritrea, Ethiopia, Madagascar, Malawi, Rwanda, Sudan, Uganda, and Zambia. According to UNCTAD, LDCs are classified as such by the United Nations Organization and are a category of low-income states that are deemed structurally disadvantaged in their development process and facing more than other countries the risk of failing to come out of poverty. As such, LDCs are considered in need of the highest degree of attention on the part of the international community.
34 United Nations, 'Landlocked Developing Countries (LLDC's), Fact Sheet 2013' (Office of the High Representative for the Least Developed Countries, Landlocked Developing Countries and Small Island Developing States (UN-OHRLLS)). See also UNCTAD, 'Structurally Weak, Vulnerable and Small Economies: Who Are They? What Can UNCTAD Do for Them?' (TD/B/54/CRP.4, 2007). The LLDCs in COMESA are Burundi, Ethiopia, Malawi, Rwanda, Uganda, and Zambia.
35 Benno J Ndulu, 'Infrastructure, Regional Integration and Growth in Sub-Saharan Africa: Dealing with the Disadvantages of Geography and Sovereign Fragmentation' (2006) 15 (2) *Journal of African Economies* 212, 213.
36 COMESA, 'Agricultural Marketing Promotion and Regional Integration Project, Newsletter, Issue No. 4, April 2007' 1. In COMESA, among Member states whose mainstay is agriculture, agriculture accounts for 31 per cent of GDP, employs 75 per cent of the labour force, and provides 50 per cent of raw materials for the domestic industries.

agricultural exports.[37] According to the FAO, Africa's agricultural exports in 2005 were around 20 per cent of its total exports, the same level they were at in 1980. The value of Africa's agricultural exports, which amounted to some US$21 billion annually from 2002 to 2005, is growing extremely slowly, at 2.3 per cent annually since 1996. The share of Africa in world agricultural exports has dropped steadily, from 8 per cent in the 1970s to 1.3 per cent in 2006. Africa's failure to produce enough domestically has contributed to progressive growth in food imports, with Africa spending an estimated US$23 billion on food annually from 2002 to 2005, equal to 23 per cent of its total merchandise imports, significantly more than the value of exports.[38]

Furthermore, intra-COMESA trade is low as a percentage of the region's overall trade. While intra-COMESA trade amounts to about 7 per cent,[39] in the European Union it is about 67 per cent;[40] in Mercosur it is about 15 per cent;[41] and in ASEAN it is about 25 per cent.[42]

Moreover, intra-COMESA trade is dominated by a few countries,[43] while primary commodities dominate extra-COMESA trade exports. According to UNCTAD,

---

37 UNCTAD, 'Economic Development in Africa 2008: Export Performance Following Trade Liberalization: Some Patterns and Policy Perspectives' (UNCTAD/ALDC/AFRICA/2008, 2008) 29–30.
38 FAO, 'Intra-Africa Trade: Issues, Challenges and Implementations for Food Security and Poverty Alleviation' (Conference Background Paper, FAO Twenty-fifth Regional Conference for Africa, Nairobi, Kenya, 16–20 June 2008, ARC/08/5) 2–3. See also African Union, 'Boosting Intra-African Trade' (Issue Paper, Preparations for the 7th AU Trade Ministers Conference and the 18th Ordinary Session of the AU Assembly of Heads of State and Government, January/February 2012). For an analysis of COMESA trade performance and indexes, see COMESA, 'International Trade Statistics Bulletin No. 12, September 2013'.
39 COMESA, 'Report of the Thirty Second Meeting of the Council of Ministers, held at Kinshasa, Democratic Republic of Congo, 22–24 February 2014' para 57. For the eight African RTAs recognised by the African Union, during the period 2007–2011, their intra-trade as a percentage of total trade was as follows: COMESA at 6.7 per cent; SADC at 12.9 per cent: EAC at 12 per cent; and ECOWAS at 9.4 per cent. For analysis, see Alemayehu Geda and Haile Kebret, 'Regional Economic Integration in Africa: A Review of Problems and Prospects with a Case Study of COMESA' (2007) 17 *Journal of African Economies* 357.
40 Eurostat, '2015 Intra-EU Trade in Goods – Recent Trends', <http://ec.europa.eu/eurostat/statistics-explained/index.php?title=Intra-EU_trade_in_goods_-_recent_trends&oldid=218347>
41 UNCTAD, 'South – South Monitor, No. 2, July 2013' 6, <http://unctad.org/en/PublicationsLibrary/webditctab2013d1_en.pdf>
42 Association of Southeast Asian Nations (ASEAN) and the World Bank, 'ASEAN Integration Monitoring Report: A Joint Report by the ASEAN Secretariat and the World Bank' (ASEAN Jakarta and the WORLD Bank Washington, DC, World Bank Group, Report No. 83914, 2013) para 15. For analysis see Jane Korinek and Mark Melatos, 'Trade Impacts of Selected Regional Trade Agreements in Agriculture' (OECD Trade Policy Working Papers No. 87, 2009), <www.oecd.org/trade/benefitlib/42770785.pdf> accessed 10 March 2015.
43 COMESA (n 36) 1. COMESA notes that the top five leading exporters of agricultural commodities are Kenya (25.68 per cent); Zambia (21.10 per cent); Uganda (13.54 per cent); Malawi (10.15 per cent); and Egypt (6.13 per cent). According to UNCTAD (n 36), the low level of intra-COMESA trade is attributable to several factors: tariff cuts, which reduce the

primary commodities dominate Sub-Saharan exports: in terms of value as percentages of total exports, coffee, cotton, tobacco, and tea were the top exports in the year 2000, while cocoa, cotton, sugar, and wine were the top exports in the year 2005.[44] These commodities have in the past been characterised by high price volatility and generally falling prices. Globally, however, commodity prices have been on an upward trend in the recent past.[45] Moreover, the high dependence on traditional commodity exports reflects the region's inability to tap fully into the international trade in more profitable commodities, such as horticulture and processed foods. Kenya, Ethiopia, and Zambia have in recent years increased their exports of horticulture and processed foods, but their volumes are relatively small in comparison to traditional commodities, and account for less than 1 per cent of the global trade.[46] These factors undermine the stated objectives of COMESA, particularly the establishment of a fully integrated market that is internationally competitive and provides for a common market.[47]

The low intra-regional trade derogates from the perceived advantages of intra-regional trade. According to the United Nations Economic Commission for Africa (UNECA), intra-regional trade has three major advantages: enlarged regional markets provide incentives for private cross-border investments and foreign direct investment; expanded intra-regional trade generates faster growth and income convergence in regional economic communities; and, as production structures are diversified away from production and trade of primary commodities,

---

preference margins given to other African countries and therefore reduce the incentives for intra-regional trade; the products that African countries export tend to be similar in nature, thereby limiting the complementarity of exports; the infrastructure for intra-African trade is often poor, which leads to high transaction costs; regional agreements, such as COMESA, are generally slow to be implemented and there is little private sector involvement in them as compared with their equivalents in Europe, Latin America, or Asia.

44 UNCTAD (n 38) 30.
45 Lester Brown, 'The Great Food Crisis of 2011' (2011) 10 *Foreign Policy* 1–5. According to the author:

Whereas in years past, it's been weather that has caused a spike in commodities prices, now it's trends on both sides of the food supply/demand equation that are driving up prices. On the demand side, the culprits are population growth, rising affluence, and the use of grain to fuel cars. On the supply side: soil erosion, aquifer depletion, the loss of cropland to non-farm uses, the diversion of irrigation water to cities, the plateauing of crop yields in agriculturally advanced countries, and – due to climate change – crop-withering heat waves and melting mountain glaciers and ice sheets. These climate-related trends seem destined to take a far greater toll in the future.

46 UNCTAD (n 37) 30–33. See also Mauro Gioe, 'Can Horticultural Production Help African Smallholders to Escape Dependence on Export of Tropical Agricultural Commodities?' (2006) 6 (2) *Crossroads* 16, 24. According to the author, from 1980 to 2000, world prices for 18 major export commodities fell by more than 25 per cent in real terms. The decline was especially steep for cotton (47 per cent), coffee (64 per cent), rice (61 per cent), cocoa (71 per cent), and sugar (77 per cent).
47 COMESA Treaty, arts 3–4.

the long-term dependence of African countries on developed market economies for manufactures should weaken.[48]

The predominance of primary commodities in the region's exports negates the region's industrialisation policy,[49] while confining it to its colonial production pattern as an exporter of raw materials and importer of manufactured goods.[50] COMESA's poor agricultural trade indicators are a challenge to its poverty reduction objectives,[51] the attainment of the millennium development goals in the region,[52] and the region's economic development as a whole.

According to the World Bank,[53] agriculture continues to be a fundamental instrument for sustainable development and poverty reduction. The Bank provides two arguments in support of agriculture as a lead sector in the development of agriculture-based countries, as are most COMESA countries. First, since most agricultural production is non-tradable, agricultural productivity determines the price of food, which in turn determines wage costs and competitiveness of the tradable sectors. Second, comparative advantage in the tradable sub-sectors will still lie in agriculture and agro-processing for many years because of resource endowments and the difficult investment climate for manufactures. Moreover,

---

48 United Nations Economic Commission for Africa (UNECA), 'Assessing Regional Integration in Africa' (UNECA Policy Research Report, 2004) 83. See also: Padamja Khandelwa, 'COMESA and SADC: Prospects and Challenges for Regional Trade Integration' (IMF Working Paper, WP/04/227, 2004) 34. The author concludes that prospects for expansion of intra-regional trade might be limited due to the low levels of intra-regional trade and product complementarities. The author notes that exports of Eastern and Southern African countries are concentrated in a few primary commodities; Anna M Mayda and Chad Steinberg, 'Do South-South Trade Agreements Increase Trade? Commodity-Level Evidence from COMESA' (2009) 42 *Canadian Journal of Economics* 1361. In a study of the static effects of COMESA on Uganda's trade, the authors find minimal trade creation and trade diversion effects. The authors surmise that South-South PTAs, because member countries are not natural trading partners, are unlikely to produce substantial increases in trade volumes.
49 COMESA Treaty, arts 99–105.
50 Colin McCarthy, 'Is African Economic Integration in Need of a Paradigm Change? Thinking out of the Box on African Integration' in Anton Bosl and others (eds) *Monitoring the Process of Regional Integration in Southern Africa Yearbook* (Trade Law Centre for Southern Africa (Tralac), Vol. 7, 2007) 6, 16–18. The author argues that the typical African integration community does not meet the requirements of the static welfare effect of trade creation: 'A group of neighbouring commodity-producing economies and limited industrial capacity to produce tradable goods hardly meets the conditions for realizing the welfare benefits of trade creation'. However, the author goes on to argue that seeking static welfare effects has never been part of the post-colonial African regional integration agenda. Instead, the rationale has exclusively been to achieve the dynamic advantages of integration: economies of scale, resulting in competition among producers and inward investment flows, both internal and external. The sole aim of integration was to catch up with the developed world.
51 COMESA Treaty, art 3 (a) (b).
52 United Nations, 'United Nations Millennium Declaration' (General Assembly, 8th Plenary Meeting, 8 September 2000, A/RES/55/2). The declaration resolved to halve poverty by the year 2015, among other goals.
53 The World Bank, 'World Development Report 2008: Agriculture for Development' (The World Bank, Washington, DC, 2007) 1–26.

growth in both the non-tradable and tradable sectors of agriculture also induces strong growth in other sectors of the economy through multiplier effects.[54]

3.3 SPS policies and regulations in the COMESA

The COMESA Treaty enjoins Members to harmonise their SPS policies and regulations in order to enhance exports of their agricultural commodities: 'Member States shall (. . .) harmonise their policies and regulations relating to phytosanitary and sanitary measures without impeding the export of crops, plants, seeds, livestock, livestock products, fish and fish products'.[55] Under Article 50 of the COMESA Treaty, Members are permitted to introduce or continue with SPS measures. Under Article 113, Members are urged to adopt African regional standards and where these are unavailable, to adopt suitable international standards for products traded in the Common Market. Under Article 132 (d), Members are urged to harmonise their SPS regulations without impeding trade in agricultural products.

Unlike the EU, the COMESA has no comprehensive SPS policy; neither does it have a food safety policy.[56] There are COMESA SPS Regulations,[57] but these do not specifically address food safety and neither do they provide for a food control system. The Regulations provide for the SPS legal framework for COMESA, which is similar in form to the SPS Agreement but differ in substance by providing for a number of implementing measures. There are provisions for a COMESA Green Pass, which is a commodity-specific SPS certification scheme and authority for movement of food and agricultural products within COMESA, issued by Member states' SPS authorities.[58] Regional accreditation bodies are also provided for; these are designated national SPS-related institutions whose main function is to carry out audits, inspections, and accreditations of any recognised national SPS-related institution or process.[59] There are provisions for SPS regional reference laboratories, which are designated national SPS-related laboratories whose main function is to monitor compliance with regional disease and pest requirements and oversee the appropriate certification process.[60] Regional SPS satellite

---

54 For further analysis, see World Trade Organization (WTO), 'World Trade Report 2014: Trade and Development: Recent Trends and the Role of the WTO' (WTO Geneva, Switzerland, 2015) 135–145.
55 COMESA Treaty, art 132 (d).
56 COMESA appears to be pursuing its SPS issues under the umbrella of promoting agricultural marketing. Food safety is seen as a component of this wider strategy and not an independent issue. See COMESA Agricultural Marketing Promotion and Regional Integration Project (AMPRIP), <http://famis.comesa.int/index.php?option=articles&task=viewarticle&sid=4> accessed 10 March 2015.
57 COMESA Regulations on the Application of Sanitary and Phytosanitary Measures, COMESA Legal Notice No. 310 of 2009 (COMESA SPS Regulations). The regulations mostly reiterate the main provisions of the SPS Agreement.
58 COMESA SPS Regulations, regs 7–13.
59 Ibid, reg 15.
60 Ibid, reg 16.

laboratories are also provided for; these are designated national SPS-related laboratories that specialise in a specific area of competence whose main function is to process selected samples of commodities for the purpose of maintaining a databank of disease-causing agents and pests relevant to international trade.[61] The Regulations are in line with similar regulations in other African regional trade agreements (RTAs).[62]

The following is an in-depth analysis of food control systems in COMESA countries. The systems will be examined in light of the provisions of the SPS Agreement and the standards, guidelines, and recommendations established by the Codex. To a large extent, the success of COMESA countries' international food trade is dependent on their ability to meet international food safety standards as well as those of their export markets, in particular the EU. Hence, an examination of the status of the COMESA countries' food safety systems, in order to determine their strengths and weaknesses and compliance with international and EU standards, is critical to the development of their food exports.

3.3.1 Typology of food control systems in the COMESA

Food[63] control may be defined as

> a mandatory regulatory activity of enforcement by national or local authorities to provide consumer protection and ensure that all foods during production, handling, storage, processing, and distribution are safe, wholesome and fit for human consumption; conform to safety and quality requirements; and are honestly and accurately labelled as prescribed by law.[64]

---

61 Ibid, reg 17.
62 See, for example, East African Community (EAC), 'Protocol on Sanitary and Phytosanitary Measures for the East African Community – Annex III, May 2009; Southern African Development Community (SADC)' 'Sanitary and Phytosanitary (SPS) Annex to the SADC Protocol on Trade, 12 July 2008; West African Economic and Monetary Union (UEMOA) Regulations Nos. 7 of 2007, and 4 and 7 of 2009 on Sanitary and Phytosanitary Measures; Economic Community of Western African States (ECOWAS), 'Regulation C/REG . . . 06/09 on the Harmonization of the Structural Framework and Operational Rules Pertaining to the Health and Safety of Plant, Animals and Foods in the ECOWAS Region'.
63 CODEX defines food as 'any substance, whether processed, semi-processed or raw, which is intended for human consumption, and includes drink, chewing gum and any substance which has been used in the manufacture, preparation or treatment of "food" but does not include cosmetics or tobacco or substances used only as drugs'. See the Procedural Manual of the Codex Alimentarius Commission, 22nd edn, FAO and WHO, Rome, 2014 (Codex Procedural Manual 2014) 22. For a legal analysis of the definition of food, including a European perspective, see Alberto Alemanno, *Trade in Food: Regulatory and Judicial Approaches in the EC and the WTO* (Cameron May, London, 2007) 73–76.
64 FAO/WHO, *Assuring Food Safety and Quality: Guidelines for Strengthening National Food Systems* (FAO Food and Nutrition Paper No. 76, Rome, 2003) 3–6. See also EDES/COLEACP, *Handbook on Guidelines for Strengthening National Food Control Systems* (EDES/COLEACP, Brussels, September 2012).

Food control may therefore be seen as another term for food law or legislation. Food law may be defined as the legislation which regulates the production, trade, and handling of food. It encompasses specific food safety laws as well as consumer protection or fraud deterrence laws, laws on weights and measures, customs laws, import and export rules, meat inspection laws, fish products inspection rules, laws on pesticide and veterinary drug residues, and laws controlling fertilizers and animal feeds, and would include food security as well as implementation of the right to food.[65] When food control incorporates preventive and educational strategies that protect the whole food chain, it is deemed to be a food control system.[66] The Codex Principles and Guidelines for National Food Control Systems defines food control systems as follows:

> Official food control systems includes measures administered by the competent authority which ensure that foods, and their production systems, meet requirements for achieving the appropriate level of protection in order to protect the health of consumers.[67]

Hence, by definition, a food control system is an SPS regime, either national, when confined to an individual country, or regional, when applied within a specified region. As such, many or most elements of a food control system fall under the disciplines of the SPS Agreement.[68] Good examples of national food safety control systems abound among the EU Member states such Germany, France, and the United Kingdom. The EU food safety regime based on the concept of

---

65 Jessica Vapnek and Melvin Spreij, *Perspectives and Guidelines on Food Legislation, with a New Model Food Law* (FAO Legislative Study No. 87, FAO, Rome, 2005) 13–14. See also, Timothy Josling, Donna Roberts and David Orden, *Food Regulation and Trade: Toward a Safe and Open Global System* (Institute for International Economics, Washington, DC, 2004) 17–21. For purposes of gauging the impacts of regulatory decisions on international trade, the authors classify food regulations along four basic dimensions: Based on goals, risk-reducing regulations, which ensure an acceptable level of animal, plant, or human health safety; and quality regulations, which provide differentiation of goods based on content and process attributes not directly related to health or safety. Based on attribute focus, with content attributes regulations that target material aspects of the product; and process attributes regulations, which target the process by which a product is produced, processed, handled, or distributed. Based on breadth: vertical regulations, which are specific to a single product or closely related products in one or more stages of the marketing chain; and horizontal regulations, which are applied across products that are not necessarily closely related. Based on scope: uniform regulations, which apply equally to products of domestic and foreign origin; and specific regulations, which apply only to imported products, often of certain origins.
66 FAO/WHO (n 64). According to FAO/WHO, an ideal food control system should include effective enforcement of mandatory requirements, along with training and education, community outreach programmes, and promotion of voluntary compliance.
67 Codex Principles and Guidelines for National Food Control Systems (CAC/GL 82–2013).
68 Ibid, principle 6. The objectives and scope of a food control system fall under the scope of the SPS Agreement.

'food safety from farm to fork' established under Regulation 178 of 2002 and its implementing regulations and directives are examples of regional food control systems.[69]

In Africa generally, there is a paucity of food control systems, either nationally or regionally. For example, both Benin[70] and Mali[71] have set up food safety agencies. The few existing food control systems are lacking in various vital components and do not meet international standards. For example, various components of the Ugandan food control system were checked for compliance with international standards on a scale of 0 to 5, where 0 denotes none and 5 denotes full compliance, and earned a combined score 2.2, indicating practical non-compliance.[72] Even the South African food control system, which is reputed to be the most advanced in Africa, has been found to be fragmented and uncoordinated, among other challenges.[73]

According to the FAO, there are five core pillars in food control systems: food legislation; food control management; food inspection; official food control laboratories; and food safety and quality information, education, and communication.[74] The FAO has further developed tools to assist countries to assess their capacity in the core elements of their national food control systems and identify their related capacity building needs.[75]

The following sections will analyse the SPS capacities of the COMESA Member states based on some of the pillars, using the tools developed by the FAO.

---

69 For analysis of the EU and its Members' food safety systems see: Alemanno A (n 63); Ellen Vos and Frank Wendler (eds), *Food Safety Regulations in Europe: A Comparative Institutional Analysis* (Intersentia, Antwerpen-Oxford, 2006); Christopher Ansell and David Vogel (eds), *What's the Beef? The Contested Governance of European Food Safety* (MIT Press, Cambridge, MA, 2006).
70 Belgium Development Agency, 'Installation of the Benin Food Safety Agency (ABSSA)', <www.btcctb.org/en/casestudy/installation-benin-food-safety-agency-abssa> accessed 15 March 2015.
71 Mwamakamba L and others (n 4) 6295.
72 Ananias Bagumire and others, 'National Food Safety Control Systems in Sub-Saharan Africa: Does Uganda's Aquaculture Control System Meet International Requirements' (2009) 34 *Food Policy* 458.
73 R R Chanda, R J Fincham and P Venter, 'A Review of the South African Food Control System: Challenges of Fragmentation' (2010) 21 *Food Control* 816. For further analysis of the South African food control system, see United States Department of Agriculture and Foreign Agricultural Services, 'South Africa: Food and Agricultural Import Regulations and Standards' (USDA/FAS FAIRS Country Report, 31 December 2014).
74 WTO Committee on Sanitary and Phytosanitary Measures, 'FAO Capacity Evaluation Tools for Food Safety, Biosecurity and Plant Protection: Submission by the Food and Agriculture Organization of the United Nations (FAO)' (G/SPS/GEN/831, 25 March 2008) 3. See also FAO/WHO (n 63) 6–9.
75 Marlynne Hopper and Boutrif Ezzeddine, 'Strengthening National Food Control Systems: Guidelines to Assess Capacity Building Needs' (FAO, Rome, 2006); Marlynne Hopper and Boutrif Ezzeddine, 'Strengthening National Food Control Systems: A Quick Guide to Assess Capacity Building Needs' (FAO, Rome, 2007).

3.3.2 Food legislation or regulation

Food legislation consists of the legal framework that directly or indirectly governs the production, import, export, distribution, handling, and sale of food in a given country. Food legislation also includes food standards.[76] In the EU food legislation would encompass Regulation 178 of 2002 and its various implementing regulations and directives together with the specific regulations and directives that constitute EU food safety standards.

Among the COMESA Member countries, the legislation tends to be outdated and incomplete,[77] in some instances even dating back to colonial times.[78] The legislation does not adequately tackle current and emerging food safety problems in relation to pesticide residues, food additives, contaminants, and biotoxins.[79] Moreover, the legislation is often scattered over several uncoordinated statutes[80] and without implementation strategies, leading to high levels of default in implementation.[81]

Furthermore, the majority of food safety standards relate to product specifications. Only a limited number of standards cover sampling and testing methods, labelling, or other matters that are of more relevance to trade. Even where standards have been harmonised regionally, few are adopted nationally, thus limiting their effectiveness.[82]

---

76 Vapnek J and Spreij M (n 65) 149–190.
77 WTO Committee on Sanitary and Phytosanitary Measures, 'Overview of SPS Needs and Assistance in Eight Least Developed Countries: Note by the Secretariat' (G/SPS/GEN/900, 4 February 2009) 21. This is certainly the case among the 12 COMESA Members who are LDCs.
78 For example, Malawi's Public Health Act dates back to 1948. See FAO (n 1), 'Conference Room Document, No. 32, Situation Analysis of Food Safety Systems in Malawi' 2.
79 See, for example, European Commission, 'Final Report of a Mission Carried out in Uganda from 31 July to 8 August 2006, In Order to Assess the Public Health Controls and the Conditions of Production of Fishery Products, (DG (SANCO)/8240/2006 – MR Final) 3. The report finds the Ugandan standards inadequate in their provisions of contaminants and microbiological limits; FAO (n 1), 'Conference Room Document, No. 6, Situational Analysis of Food Safety Systems in Zimbabwe' 3. Zimbabwe admits that because of limited capacity, not much work has been done to base its standards and regulations on sound scientific evidence of risk analysis.
80 See for example, Mulat Abegaz, 'Assessment of the Capacity of Food Safety and Quality in Zambia' (Working Paper Prepared for the World Bank, June 2006) 9, <http://siteresources.worldbank.org/INTRANETTRADE/Resources/Topics/Standards/Zambia_Annex3.pdf> accessed 10 November 2014. The author notes that Zambia seems to have adequate food safety legislation; however, due to lack of enforcement, monitoring, and follow-up mechanisms and capacities, the existing food laws, policies, and strategies were not effectively implemented.
81 See, for example, FAO (n 1), 'Conference Room Document 1, Situation Analysis of Food Safety Systems in Ethiopia' 4. Ethiopia notes that lack of enforcement mechanisms for its food safety regulations is a challenge.
82 Standards and Trade Development Facility (STDF), 'Report on Workshop: Mobilizing Aid for Trade for SPS-Related Technical Cooperation in East Africa' (Standards and Trade Development Facility, Kampala, Uganda, 28–29 May 2008) 22.

Most of the standards are based on Codex standards, which are often not appropriate to some national circumstances. Some countries experience difficulty in adapting Codex standards to meet national needs due to lack of technical expertise. Furthermore, although some countries have standards based on Codex, they have difficulty in monitoring the implementation of these standards or lack laboratory facilities to verify compliance of food samples with relevant standards.[83]

Overall, most food safety legislation does not provide for a coherent food control structure that is anchored on a high level of health protection, based on scientific advice, and policed by a food safety authority. Hence it may be concluded that the food legislation in the COMESA region does not meet the Codex requirement of legislation:

> Legislation should provide authority to carry out controls at all stages of production, manufacture, importation, processing, storage, transportation, distribution and trade. It may also include provisions as appropriate for the registration of establishments or listing of certified processing plants, establishment approval, licensing or registration of traders, equipment design approval, penalties in the event of non-compliance, coding requirements and charging of fees.[84]

3.3.3 Food control management or risk management

Food control management refers to the necessary national and regional policy and operational coordination of a food control system.[85] Food safety legislation would provide for such management and, in particular, for the administrative structures and functions, including a leadership role.[86] The legislation would further provide

---

83 FAO/WHO, 'Report of the Seventeenth Session of the FAO/WHO Coordinating Committee for Africa, Rabat, Morocco, 23–26 January 2007' (ALINORM 07/30/28, 2007) paras 52–56. See also Michael F Jensen and John C Keyser, 'Non-Tariff Measures on Goods Trade in the East African Community – Assessment of Regional Dairy Trade' (The World Bank, Washington, DC, 2010) 40–46.

84 Codex Guidelines for the Design, Operation, Assessment and Accreditation of Food Import and Export Inspection and Certification Systems (CAC/GL 26–1997) paras 21–22.

85 FAO/WHO (n 64) 7. FAO has further defined food control management as follows:

> Food control management is the continuous process of planning, organizing, monitoring, coordinating and communicating, in an integrated way, a broad range of risk-based decisions and actions to ensure the safety and quality of domestically produced, imported and exported food for national consumers and export markets as appropriate. Food control management covers the various policy and operational responsibilities of competent government authorities responsible for food control. These include the development and implementation of food control policies, strategies and plans that reflect the government's commitment to food safety and quality and provide a sound framework for food control activities.

86 Codex Principles and Guidelines for National Food Control Systems (CAC/GL 82–2013) para 8.

for the development and implementation of an integrated national food control strategy; the operation of a national food control programme; securing funds and allocating resources; setting standards and regulations; participation in international food control related activities; developing emergency response procedures; and carrying out risk analysis. Major functions would include the establishment of regulatory measures, monitoring system performance, facilitating continuous improvement, and providing overall policy guidance.[87]

In the EU food control management is undertaken by the EU Commission under the Directorate General for Health and Consumers (DG SANCO) in consultation with the Standing Committee on the Food Chain and Animal Health (SCFCAH).[88]

A clear food safety policy is a necessary foundation for an effective food control management system. However, such policies are generally lacking in most COMESA countries, leading to a paucity of coordinated and sustainable food control management systems. Moreover, most countries in the region do not appreciate the major public health and economic implications of food safety, and as a consequence food safety remains a low priority in national policy-making.[89] As a result, essential elements of food control management are inadequate, or non-existent.[90]

For illustration, a study of SPS capacity in East Africa noted that both Kenya and Tanzania lack food safety policies, while Uganda's food safety strategic plan has yet to be implemented. This has led to weak food control management. However, food safety capacity within major export sectors, mostly horticultural products and fish and fishery products, have achieved compliance with SPS standards internationally.[91]

A similar situation exists among countries in the Economic Community of West African States (ECOWAS): each country has some capacity to meet SPS and food

---

87 Ibid. See also: Vapnek J and Spreij M (n 65) 207–264. The authors analyse three different types of model food laws that provide for differing administrative structures; Safe Food International, 'Guidelines for Consumer Organizations to Promote National Food Safety Systems', <www.safefoodinternational.org> accessed 12 April 2015.
88 For analysis of the EU food safety institutions see Ellen Vos and Frank Wendler, 'Food Safety Regulations in the EU Level' in E Vos and F Wendler (eds) *Food Safety Regulations in Europe: A Comparative Institutional Analysis* (Intersentia, Antwerpen-Oxford, 2006) 65.
89 FAO (n 1) 48.
90 For example, most LDCs have no functional food control management system. See WTO Committee on Sanitary and Phytosanitary Measures, 'Effects of SPS-Related Private Standards – Compilation of Replies: Note by the Secretariat, Revision' (G/SPS/GEN/932/Rev.1, 10 December 2009) 20. The WTO Secretariat notes that the absence of a coherent and modern food control system is of major concern in all the LDCs that were under consideration in the review.
91 Spencer Henson, 'Review of Case Studies and Evaluations of Sanitary and Phytosanitary Capacity: Kenya, Tanzania and Uganda' (Report presented at an STDF Aid for Trade Workshop on 30 September 2007 in Dar es Salaam, Tanzania) 22–24, <www.uneca.org/eca_programmes/trade_and_regional_integration/events/aidfortrade/docs/Synthesis-SPSevaluations%20_Henson.pdf> accessed 30 March 2015.

safety norms. But within a country, the ability to meet these norms varies greatly. The ability to meet international norms is dependent upon whether a product is exported internationally or sold only domestically; SPS capacity is higher for exported products than for products destined for domestic consumption.[92]

This has led to a dual economy phenomenon (an advanced production system catering for the export market with a less advanced system of production catering for the domestic market),[93] whereby a three-tier food control management system has emerged in most Sub-Saharan countries, including COMESA Members: one geared towards the local market (which is weak and dysfunctional); one geared towards the local supermarkets (which is relatively better than for the local markets); and another geared towards the export market (which is up to the export market's standards).

Thus COMESA Members' food control management systems clearly fall short of Codex guidelines in most aspects, but more particularly in the Codex criteria for the role of the competent authority, performance, enforcement, and infrastructure.[94]

3.3.4 Food inspection or compliance enforcement

According to Codex,

> inspection is the examination of food or systems for control of food, raw materials, processing, and distribution including in-process and finished product testing, in order to verify that they conform to requirements.[95]

The administration and implementation of the food control system requires an efficient food inspection service.[96] The food inspector administers the food law and supervises its implementation on a daily basis, and hence is in touch with the

---

92 T Deeb and K Humado, 'SPS Synthesis Report Summary of SPS and Food Safety Performance of Non-UEMOA Countries in West Africa' (WATH/Accra Technical Report No. 20, 2007) 18, <www.watradehub.com> accessed 12 April 2015.
93 For an analysis of the phenomenon, see Dale W Jorgenson, 'Surplus Agricultural Labour and the Development of a Dual Economy' (1967) 19 *Oxford Economic Papers* 288, 290. See also: Jerry M Silverman, 'Dual Economy Theory Revisited: Governance and the Role of the Informal Sector' (Presentation at Fourth Annual International Conference of the Society for the Advancement of Socio-Economics (SASE), Irvine, California, 27–29 March 1992), <http://internationaldevelopmentshould.files.wordpress.com/2011/09/dual-economy-theory-revisited.pdf> accessed 15 March 2015; Daron Acemoglue and James A Robinson, 'Why Is Africa Poor' (2010) 25 (1) *Economic History of Developing Regions* 21.
94 Codex Principles and Guidelines for National Food Control Systems (CAC/GL 82–2013) paras 17–33.
95 Codex Principles for Food Import and Export Inspection and Certification (CAC/GL 20–1995) s 2.
96 FAO/WHO (n 63) 7. The international standard for inspection is ISO/IEC 17020, entitled 'General Criteria for the Operation of Various Types of Bodies Performing Inspection'.

key players in the system, such as the producers, the consumers, and the traders. In order to be effective, the food inspector must be trained in food science and technology and also in food law, among other skills necessary to carry out the functions of the inspection services.[97]

Key functions of the inspection service include the following: inspecting premises and processes; evaluating HACCP plans; sampling food during harvest, processing, storage, transport, or sale; recognizing spoiled and hazardous food, food that is otherwise unfit for human consumption, or food that is sold or presented to consumers so as to deceive them regarding its safety or quality or origin, etc.; recognizing, collecting, and transmitting evidence; encouraging the use of voluntary quality assurance systems; conducting inspection, sampling, and certification of food for import/export purposes; conducting risk-based audits of food establishments with HACCP or other safety assurance programmes; and recommending formal action, including prosecution, where food safety lapses could endanger public health.[98]

In the EU, the Food and Veterinary Office (FVO), a department in DG SANCO, is mandated through its audits, inspections, and related activities to check on compliance with the requirements of EU food safety and quality, animal health and welfare, and plant health legislation within the European Union and on compliance with EU import requirements in third countries exporting to the EU.[99]

Most food inspection services in COMESA are underfunded, while the food inspectors are poorly trained, poorly paid, and tasked with additional functions over their core functions. According to the FAO,[100] food inspectors in Africa suffer generally from a low professional status, which is not commensurate with their responsibilities, and a lack of logistical support to carry out the inspections and the cumulative tasks often requested from them, such as price control, inspection of non-food consumer items, weights and measures, and environmental hygiene. Moreover, national food inspection services are often located in the capitals and

---

97 Ibid.
98 Safe Food International (n 87) 7. The international standard for Certification Systems is the European product certification standard EN 45011 or ISO/IEC Guide 65 (General requirements for bodies operating product certification systems)
99 Regulation (EC) no 882/2004 of the European Parliament and of the Council on official controls performed to ensure the verification of compliance with feed and food law, animal health and animal welfare rules, [2004] OJ L 191/1, 29 April 2004 (Regulation 882/2004) art 46.
100 FAO (n 1) 49–50. See also, for further illustration, European Commission, 'Final Report of a Mission Carried out in Eritrea from 25 February to 5 March 2008, In Order to Evaluate the Controls in place Governing the Production of Fishery and Aquaculture Products Intended for Export to the European Union' (DG (SANCO) /2008–7637– MR FINAL); European Commission, 'Final Report of a Mission Carried out in Swaziland, From 21 to 28 November 2007, In Order to Evaluate Animal Health Controls in Place, in Particular Over Foot and Mouth Disease, Public Health Control Systems and Certification Procedures' (DG (SANCO)/2007–7396 – MR FINAL).

major cities, with little if any control exercised in small towns and rural areas. Furthermore, contrary to Codex guidelines on requirements for official certification of food products,[101] few countries in the region have efficient national import/export inspection and certification systems.

Consequently, most food inspection services in COMESA are not as effective as required. This affects the effectiveness of the relevant food control systems and has negative consequences for food exports. For instance, Uganda's fish products were banned by the EU in 1997 and 1999, due to lack of standards. The SPS legislation was up to date, but the inspection service did not have clear guidelines and standard operating practices, particularly with regard to inspecting batches of fish being landed, hygiene conditions at landing sites, sampling procedure records of their own activities, and documents required for traceability of origin and transportation of fish.[102] Kenya's fish products were also banned by the EU in 1999 due to shortfalls in standards. The main fault was cited as weakness in the implementation and enforcement of existing regulatory requirements. The number of inspectors and other personnel was inadequate to inspect and monitor compliance on landing beaches and industrial fish processing plants. Whilst inspectors were generally well trained, their training was in need of updating; for example, in the principles of HACCP, and in some cases they lacked access to basic infrastructure and equipment.[103]

Hence, ineffective inspection services render SPS regulations and standards inoperative, as products cannot therefore be certified, and as a result they earn countries negative reputations in export markets, thus affecting their exports.[104]

3.3.5 Official food control laboratories

Laboratories enable the examination of food for chemical and microbiological hazards that are not apparent through physical examination. Laboratories serve

---

101 Codex Guidelines for the Design, Operation, Assessment and Accreditation of Food Import and Export Inspection and Certification Systems (CAC/GL 26–1997) ss 4, 6 and 7.
102 WTO Committee on Sanitary and Phytosanitary Measures, 'Fish Export from Lake Victoria – From Import Ban to Cash Earner, Communication from Uganda' (G/SPS/GEN/685, 6 April 2006) 5.
103 Spencer Henson and Winnie Mitullah, 'Kenyan Exports of Nile Perch: The Impact of Food Safety Standards on an Export-Oriented Supply Chain' (World Bank Policy Research Working Paper No. 3349, June 2004) 27.
104 Martin Doherty and others, 'Diagnostic Impact Study of the New European Regulation 882/2004 "Official Feed and Food Controls" and Recommendations, Phase One, Final Report' (COLEACP/PIP, March 2005) 20. According to the authors, the determination of the equivalence of third country SPS regulations, under Article 46 of Regulation 882/2004, is essentially a subjective exercise as there are no objective assessments to be made. Equivalence is made upon not only on the legislation, but its implementation and enforcement. Moreover, the frequency of inspections is determined by the perceived compliance with SPS regulations, among other factors.

to identify contaminated foods; identify sources of outbreaks of food poisoning; allow regulators to bring enforcement actions against adulterated and unsafe food; confirm the safety of food products; assist in the regulatory decision-making process; and evaluate the effectiveness of risk management interventions. Laboratories are thus an indispensable component of a food control system.[105]

According to Codex, laboratories involved in the import and export control of foods should adopt a strict quality criteria.[106] Food control systems are required to utilise laboratories that are evaluated and accredited under officially recognised programmes to ensure that adequate quality controls are in place to provide for the reliability of test results.[107] Moreover, laboratories are required to apply the principles of internationally accepted quality assurance techniques to ensure the reliability of analytical results.[108]

The EU has set up EU Reference Laboratories (EURLs) that aim to ensure high quality, uniform testing in the EU and to carry out support activities on risk management and risk assessment in the area of laboratory analysis. The EURLs also provide National Reference Laboratories (NRLs) in Member states with analytical methods and diagnostic techniques, and coordinate their application and also train NRL staff and experts from developing countries.[109]

Unfortunately, laboratories in COMESA are weak and fail to meet the above Codex criteria: most do not have the capacity to test for chemical contaminants and biotoxins.[110] Many laboratories are not accredited; for example, Ethiopia, Malawi, Sudan, Swaziland, and Zambia have no accredited laboratories.[111] This

---

105 FAO/WHO (n 64) 8. According to FAO/WHO, laboratories are expensive to build, maintain, and operate. For further analysis, see EDES/COLEACP, 'Handbook on Role of Laboratories in Food Safety System' (EDES/COLEACP, Brussels, 2012).
106 Codex Guidelines for the Assessment of the Competence of Testing Laboratories Involved in the Import and Export Control of Foods (CAC/GL 27–1997). The international standard for testing and calibration laboratories is the ISO/IEC 17025: 2005: General requirements for the competence of testing and calibration laboratories. Regulatory authorities and accreditation bodies may also use it in confirming or recognizing the competence of laboratories.
107 Accreditation is granted in accordance with the quality, administrative, and technical requirements of ISO/IEC 17025: 2005.
108 Codex Principles and Guidelines for National Food Control Systems (CAC/GL 82–2013) para 29; Codex Guidelines for the Assessment of the Competence of Testing Laboratories Involved in the Import and Export Control of Foods (CAC/GL 27–1997) paras 41–42.
109 Regulation 882/2004, arts 32–33.
110 FAO (n 1) 50. FAO identifies three causative factors: inadequate resources in terms of funding, equipment, and personnel; lack of recurrent expenditure to enable the repair of equipment and to maintain adequate supplies of chemicals and materials needed for analyses; and inadequate quality assurance procedures.
111 Ibid. Accreditation is the procedure by which a government agency having jurisdiction formally recognises the competence of an inspection and/or certification body to provide inspection and certification services.

has forced a number of countries to send their food samples to third countries for analysis.[112]

3.4 Chapter discussion and conclusions

COMESA has published several hundred harmonised standards, mainly on agricultural and food products, which have been adopted from international standards.[113] Most COMESA harmonised standards relate to specifications and compositional requirements of various products, with a few harmonised standards covering testing, sampling methods, and labelling.[114] As such, these standards, being vertical (prescribing specific composition requirements for products) and sectoral (confining themselves to particular types of products, such as milk or maize), are limited in their harmonisation impact.

Moreover, food safety concerns are not adequately addressed in COMESA Members' policies. According to the World Health Organization (WHO), data from all Member states in the WHO African Region indicated that 45 countries had proposed food control legislation, but only 13 had enacted any laws. In a survey, data from 36 respondent countries showed that 29 had national standards authorities that established food standards based on Codex guides. A few countries had legislation on pesticide residues, food additives and contaminants, biotoxins, and genetically modified foods. Of the 26 countries that provided data, 21 had import/export inspection and certification systems, but most of these controlled export products.[115]

As a consequence, coordinated and sustainable approaches to the holistic management of food safety are not implemented. According to the FAO, African countries are faced with myriad food safety problems. Their food legislation is outdated, inadequate, and fragmented, and is scattered through various statutes and codes, creating an inevitable confusion among food control enforcement agents, producers, and distributors. Except in a few countries, the bodies mandated to formulate and enforce standards, standards authorities or bureaus, are not well established and are not actively engaged in the development of national

---

112 For instance, most Southern African countries use South African laboratories for their analysis's accreditation.
113 COMESA-EAC-SADC, 'Tripartite Meeting Report of COMESA-EAC-SADC Tripartite Quality Infrastructure (QI) Meeting Held at Taj Pamodzi Hotel, Lusaka, Zambia, 25 to 28 October 2011' 8, <www.intraafrac.com/pdfs/EXECUTIVE%20SUMMARY%20-%20COMESA-EAC-SADC%20QI%20Meeting%2025–28%20Oct%202011-%20First%20Draft.pdf> accessed 3 April 2014.
114 See, for example, the draft COMESA maize and dairy products standards, available at <www.ratescenter.org/dairy.asp> accessed 9 April 2014. See also the Members' SPS requirements at the COMESA website <http://famis.comesa.int/index> accessed 9 April 2014.
115 WHO Food Safety and Health, 'A Strategy for the WHO African Region, Report of the Regional Director, Regional Committee for Africa, Fifty-Seventh Session, Brazzaville, Republic of Congo, 27–31 August 2007' (AFR/RC57/4, 25 June 2007) 3.

food standards. There is lack of expertise and difficulty in collecting toxicological and exposure assessment data to conduct risk assessments, and most countries of the region do not have adequate resources to effectively conduct the needed risk assessments at a national level.

Food inspectors in the region suffer generally from a low professional status which is not commensurate with their responsibilities and a lack of logistical support to carry out the inspections (transport, inspection equipment, etc.) and the cumulative tasks often requested from them (price control, inspection of non-food consumer items, weights and measures, environmental hygiene, etc.). Food control laboratories in the region are generally very weak; the majority of public health laboratories do not have the capacity to test for chemical contaminants and naturally occurring toxins. Only a few of the testing laboratories are accredited for specific tests in accordance with the quality, administrative, and technical requirements of ISO 17025, the international standard that provides general requirements for the competence of testing and calibration laboratories.[116]

Furthermore, the COMESA region lacks infrastructure for structured and regular acquisition and dissemination of relevant information to the public on food safety problems and corresponding measures taken to resolve them. No single country in the region has established ongoing educational programmes for government food control officials, food industry officials, and consumers. The training that does exist is sporadic, unfocused, and not based on actual and/or possible food safety problems.

This is the prevalent situation across the majority of RTAs in Africa,[117] except among Member countries of the West African Economic and Monetary Union (UEMOA), which has a regional standards body with the objective of harmonising standards, in particular food safety standards, in the Union.[118]

Moreover, there are no SPS management and enforcement institutions at the regional level in COMESA. According to the COMESA Secretariat, the failure to effectively implement SPS measures in most COMESA Member states, and hence the region, stems from constraints that include outdated legislation and regulations on SPS measures; insufficiently specified SPS procedures; limited knowledge of modern control procedures (inspection, identification and diagnosis of pests and diseases, pest risk analysis and surveillance, epidemiology, and quarantine) by SPS experts and lack of equipment; limited information on SPS, coupled

---

116 FAO (n 1) 48–52.
117 Sarah A H Olembo, 'Assessment of Capacity and Characterization of Resources for Risk Analysis in Africa' (International Conference on Risk Assessment Methodologies (ICRAM): Sharpening the Tool Box, Shoreham Hotel, Washington, DC, 9–11 August 2005) 9–10. The author notes that SPS incapacities are similar across Africa's RTAs and notes that SPS legislation is a key requirement for SPS risk analysis. See also WHO Food Safety and Health, 'Situation Analysis and Perspectives, Report of the Regional Director, Regional Committee for Africa, Fifty-Third Session, Johannesburg, South Africa, 1–5 September 2003' (AFR/RC53/12 Rev.1, 19 June 2003).
118 FAO/WHO (n 75) 8, para 59.

with poor networking to facilitate information exchange and notification; and inadequate regional cooperation and coordination on disease/pest outbreaks.[119]

COMESA initiated two programmes to ameliorate the situation. The Comprehensive Africa Agricultural Development Programme (CAADP),[120] under pillar II, aims at the strengthening of SPS capacity in the region. The Agricultural Marketing Promotion and Regional Integration Project (AMPRIP) had, as one of its objectives, the strengthening of the SPS institutional capacities in the region.[121]

The lack of SPS management and enforcement institutions at the regional level in COMESA may be attributable to the poor economic climate prevailing across most of Africa,[122] and to the problems inherent in the process of regional integration in Africa.[123] This lack of SPS capacity may also be due to constraints of regional harmonisation of SPS requirements. A World Bank study of the role of standards in Kenya's exports[124] noted that standards were a common issue

---

119 Moses Simemba, 'Sanitary and Phytosanitary Measures-The COMESA Experience', <http://famis.comesa.int/index.php?option=sps&task=analysis&analysis_id=5&lang=eng> accessed 9 April 2014. See also COMESA CAADP Regional Validation and Rwanda Roundtable Meeting: Statement by Mr. Sindiso Ngwenya, COMESA Assistant Secretary General, Serena Hotel, Kigali, Rwanda, 29 March, 2007, <http://famis.comesa.int/index> accessed 9 April 2014.
120 CAADP was established by the African Union's New Partnership for Africa's Development (AU/NEPAD) in July 2003. The overall goal of CAADP is to 'help African countries reach a higher path of economic growth through agriculture-led development, which eliminates hunger, reduces poverty and food insecurity, and enables expansion of exports'.
121 AMPRIP's main objective was to enhance safe intra- and extra-COMESA agricultural marketing. Among its main proposed outputs were the improvement and harmonisation of sanitary and phytosanitary measures and food safety standards and the strengthening of sanitary and phytosanitary institutions. AMPRIP wound up on 31 December 2010.
122 This may be related to Members' inability to meet costs of setting up modern SPS infrastructure.
123 Kenneth P Kiplagat, 'Legal Status of Integration Treaties and the Enforcement of Treaty Obligations: A Look at the COMESA Process' (1995) 23 *Denver Journal of International Law and Policy* 259, 283–284. The author argues that the COMESA Treaty does not create enforceable norms; it instead espouses political ambition and therefore is only good for political remedies. Furthermore, the author argues that the different judicial traditions (common law, Anglo-Dutch, civil law, Islamic law, and Amharic law systems) in COMESA and the linguistic diversity within the region make harmonisation of laws a daunting task. See also James T Gathii, *African Regional Trade Agreements as Flexible Legal Regimes* (Cambridge University Press, 2011). The author argues that African Regional Trade Agreements are best understood as flexible legal regimes, particularly given their commitment to variable geometry and multiple memberships.
124 Fernando H Casquet and Victor Abiola, 'The Role of Standards under Kenya's Export Strategy' (Contribution to the Kenya Diagnostic Trade and Integration Study, The World Bank, Washington, DC, March 2005) 23–25, <http://siteresources.worldbank.org/INTEXPCOMNET/Resources/Kenya_Private_Sector-Lead_Change.pdf> accessed 30 March 2015. See also William Hargraves, 'Survey of Existing and Planned SPS/Food Safety Standards Activities in the COMESA Region' (Submitted to USAID's East and Central Africa Global Competitiveness Trade Hub, 2005). The survey notes several gaps in the SPS regime in COMESA, including lack of SPS institutional capacity, lack of a regional SPS legal framework, and the paucity of accredited laboratories.

affecting exports from the East African Community (EAC) countries, which are members of COMESA, except Tanzania. However, as a region, there were constraints in harmonisation of standards that included the following: the harmonisation process was largely directed by high-level technicians, mainly from the standards bureaus, with limited involvement of political leaders; there was limited awareness among the private sector and civil society on standards and quality-related issues; there was no legal structure to effectuate harmonisation of standards and mutual recognition in order to make them effective for trade; and there were differences in SPS-related capacities between the EAC members.

For instance, Kenya had far greater capacities and better infrastructure than Tanzania and Uganda. In 2002, for example, Kenya had 17 accredited laboratories, and Uganda and Tanzania had none. During that year, metrology laboratories in Kenya performed 3,820 calibrations, compared to 68 in Tanzania and none in Uganda. There were conflicting national and regional interests; countries competed directly in international markets and had different interests; countries were not always ready to give up the setting of infrastructure or the developing of capacities within their countries; and there were conflicting regulatory and trade interests: some risk management measures unduly restricted trade, while at the same time, some institutional sustainability considerations took precedence over the objectives of trade facilitation and provision of public goods – for instance, the charging of fees for the registration of imports. National SPS regimes play a dominant role under these circumstances.

The COMESA Members' SPS regimes are weak and fall short of international standards. These regimes are largely incapable of meeting the scientific disciplines laid down in the SPS Agreement, particularly the requirement for risk analysis under Article 5. The regimes are also unable, to a large extent, to meet the requirements for the elements of a food control system as laid down in the Codex guidelines on food control systems.

COMESA Members' SPS regimes do not measure up to the SPS regimes of their trading partners, in particular the EU. The net effect of the inadequate SPS status is the reduction of COMESA's global competitiveness in agricultural trade.[125] As a result of their inadequate SPS regimes, COMESA Members, like the rest of Africa, are standards takers and not setters.[126] They have to strive to

---

125 Steven Jaffee (ed), *Food Safety and Agricultural Health Standards: Challenges and Opportunities for Developing Country Exports* (Report No. 31207, World Bank, 10 January 2005) 33. The report considers an effective SPS regime to be a core competence in competitiveness. Countries that achieve such SPS effectiveness are preferred suppliers in the global chain market and have thus a competitive edge over non-preferred countries, which are forced to trade under less favourable terms.
126 John S Wilson, 'Standards and Developing Country Exports: A Quick Review of Selected Studies and Suggestions for New Research' (Paper presented at the Summer Symposium of the International Agricultural Trade Research Consortium (IATRC): Food Regulation and Trade: Institutional Framework, Concepts of Analysis and Empirical Evidence, Bonn, Germany, 28–30 May 2006) 4. According to the author, developing countries are typically 'standards takers' rather than 'standards makers', since, at the national level, developing

achieve the SPS standards set by their export markets, especially the EU, in order to attain and maintain market access, standing to lose these markets if they fail. This not only applies to extra-COMESA trade, but also to intra-COMESA trade.[127]

The weak SPS regimes among COMESA Members are also one of the reasons for the low utilisation of preferences under the Cotonou Agreement and Everything But Arms (EBA), particularly regarding their beef exports to the EU.[128]

Having so far examined both the EU's and COMESA's food control systems, the next part further examines the two systems from the point of view of COMESA countries' concerns with the EU system. The examination is premised on the fact that EU regulations impact COMESA exports to a greater extent than COMESA regulations impact EU exports. A further premise is that the complexity and stringency of the EU regulations negatively impact COMESA exports to the EU because of the weak SPS capacities within COMESA. The part, by way of illustration, examines the impact of EU regulations on COMESA fish, beef, and horticultural exports to the EU.

---

their own standards tends to be more costly than adopting those of the major markets. Further, complying with differing standards in major export markets, such as the European Union, can add costs and limit export competitiveness.

127 See, for instance, The East African Magazine, 16 January 2009, 'Uganda Now Lifts Ban on Kenyan Semen, Beef Still off the Menu', <www.theeastafrican.co.ke/news>. The article highlights a trade war between Kenya and Uganda; Uganda had banned Kenyan bull semen and beef, while Kenya had banned Ugandan chicks; *The East African Magazine*, 11 August 2008, 'Nairobi Rules Souring Our Milk – Dar', <http://www.theeastafrican.co.ke/news/-/2558/454164/-/s343uez/-/index.html>. The article highlights complaints by Uganda and Tanzania against Kenya's complex animal products import regulations, which had the effect of locking out dairy imports from Tanzania and Uganda – thereby defeating the spirit of the East African Customs Union.

128 Atsushi Iimi, 'Infrastructure and Trade Preferences for the Livestock Sector: Empirical Evidence from the Beef Industry in Africa' (World Bank Policy Research Working Paper No. 4201, April 2007) 9–16. According to the author, the utilisation of these preferences has been low, at less than 50 per cent on the average. There are four main reasons for the under-utilisation of beef preferences: accelerated diversification of livestock products in the region to other products; the shocks associated with outbreaks of the foot-and-mouth disease and the Bovine Spongiform Encephalopathy (BSE) disease crisis in the 1990s led to stringent SPS beef standards with prohibitive compliance costs, particularly for small country producers like Swaziland and Botswana; Sub-Saharan Africa repeatedly suffering from periodic occurrence of severe droughts over the past decades, which have led beef exporters to reduce cattle processing; and lack of adequate processing, transport, and telecommunications infrastructure, which has undermined the beef export performance of the region. See also Brian Perry and others, 'An Appropriate Level of Risk: Balancing the Need for Safe Livestock Products with Fair Market Access for the Poor' (International Livestock Research Institute (ILRI), PPLPI Working Paper No. 5, 2005) 3–14.

4 Case studies in food safety standards in EU–COMESA trade

Consumer concerns in rich countries, increased technological detection capacity and so on, have created SPS standards that are now major barriers to African exports. It is not unwillingness to meet these standards that is the problem, nor disagreement with their rationale. The problem is that poor countries in Africa are not equipped to meet these demands.[1]

One of the biggest challenges faced by ACP farmers is the need to comply with not only the EU's non-negotiable standards but also with private standards which come on top of already high standards.[2]

4.1 Introduction

The central issue in EU–COMESA trade is how to enable COMESA exports to the EU without lowering the EU non-negotiable high food safety standards. The EU is the biggest trading partner of COMESA.[3] However, trade with COMESA represents a small percentage of total EU exports.[4] Trade between

---

1 Blair Commission for Africa, 'Our Common Interest: Report of the Commission for Africa' (March 2005) 286, <www.commissionforafrica.info/wp-content/uploads/2005-report/11-03-05_cr_report.pdf> accessed 13 April 2014.
2 Brussels Development Briefing No. 11, 'Meeting Food Safety Standards: Implications for ACP Agricultural Exports, Brussels, 11th May 2009' 6, <http://brusselsbriefings.net/> accessed 13 April 2014.
3 COMESA, 'International Trade Statistics Bulletin No. 12, September 2013' Statistics Unit Division of Trade, COMESA Secretariat, Lusaka, Zambia.
4 Eurostat, 'EU-Africa Summit: A deficit of 15 Billion Euro in EU28 Trade in Goods with Africa in 2013' (Eurostat News Release, STAT/14/50, 28 March 2014). According to Eurostat, in 2013, Africa as a whole accounted for 10 per cent of the EU imports and 9 per cent of its exports. Machinery and vehicles account for about half of EU exports to Africa, while energy accounts for about half of EU imports from Africa. For a detailed analysis, see European Commission, 'The European Union and the African Union – A Statistical Portrait' (Publications Office of the European Union, Luxembourg, 2013) 14–17.

the EU and COMESA is conducted under the Cotonou Agreement[5] and its trade protocol successor, the Economic Partnership Agreements (EPAs),[6] and, for Least Developed Countries (LDCs), the Everything But Arms (EBA) preference regime.[7]

However, there are no preferences for food safety standards, since these are qualitative and not quantitative.[8] Hence, while COMESA countries' economic and geographical constraints, in their trade with the EU, are sought to be alleviated through preferential trade agreements, these preferences are not extended to their sanitary and phytosanitary constraints. Apart from allowing longer time frames for compliance, preferential treatment of food safety standards may turn out to be counterproductive, as consumers will likely identify beneficiary products with low food safety standards. Moreover, even the special and differential treatment for developing countries under the SPS Agreement has not been operationalised and remains merely hortatory and unenforceable.[9]

---

5 The Partnership Agreement among the Members of the African, Caribbean, and Pacific Group of States, of the One Part, and the European Community and Its Member states, of the Other Part, signed in Cotonou, Benin on 23 June 2000, which was concluded for a period of 20 years (Cotonou Agreement). For a discussion of the Cotonou Agreement, see Manuel De la Rocha, 'The Cotonou Agreement and Its Implications for the Regional Trade Agenda in Eastern and Southern Africa' (World Bank Policy Research Working Paper No. 3090, June 2003).

6 For a discussion of EPAs see: Melaku G Desta, 'EC-ACP Economic Partnership Agreements and WTO Compatibility: An Experiment in North-South Inter-Regional Agreements?' (2006) 43 *Common Market Law Review* 1343; Alice N Sindzingre, 'The European Union Economic Partnership Agreements with Sub-Saharan Africa' (United Nations University, Comparative Regional Integration Studies, UNU-CRIS Working Papers, W-2008/5); Ruth Kelly, 'WTO Compatibility and the Legal Form of EPAs: A Case Study of Eastern and Southern Africa' (Society of International Economic Law (SIEL) Inaugural Conference, 2008); Lionel Fontagne, David Laborde and Cristina Mitaritonna, 'An Impact Study of the Economic Partnership Agreements in the Six ACP Regions' (2011) 20 *Journal of African Economies* 179.

7 Council Regulation (EC) 980/2005 of 27 June 2005, Applying a Scheme of Generalised Tariff Preferences [2005] OJ L 169/1, 30.6.2005. For a discussion of the Everything But Arms preference regime, see Paul Brenton, 'Integrating the Least Developed Countries into the World Trading System: The Current Impact of EU Preferences under Everything but Arms' (World Bank Policy Research Working Paper No. 3018, April 2003).

8 Bettina Rudoloff and Johannes Simons, 'Comparing EU Free Trade Agreements: Sanitary and Phytosanitary Standards' (InBrief, No. 6B, July 2004) 1, <www.ecdpm.org> accessed 1 May 2014. The authors argue that since SPS standards are qualitative in character, their aim being to provide a certain level of food safety; no preferences can be provided in the form of easier or softer requirements.

9 See the discussion by Denise Prevost, '"Operationalising" Special and Differential Treatment of Developing Countries under the SPS Agreement' (2005) 30 *South Africa Yearbook of International Law* 1. According to the author, developing countries are not only challenged by the SPS standards of developed countries, but even by the provisions of the SPS Agreement itself.

Agricultural and food products constitute a significant part of the EU–COMESA trade.¹⁰ Fruits and vegetables (horticulture)¹¹ and fish and fishery products (fishery products)¹² are the main COMESA food exports to the EU. Beef exports have great potential, but are currently under-exploited.¹³ Horticulture and fishery products are seen as diversifying agricultural production from the traditional commodities that are susceptible to price volatility and fluctuations; horticulture and fishery products are highly income-elastic, with lower rates of protection in industrialised and large developing countries.¹⁴

The main fruit exports to the EU are grapes, citrus fruit, apples and pears, bananas, pineapples, avocados, mangoes, papayas, and passion fruit; the most important vegetable exports are beans, peas, baby corn, mixed vegetables, and onions.¹⁵ Fish exports consist mainly of frozen white fish fillets, crustaceans, and canned tuna.¹⁶ Beef exports consist of beef and veal.¹⁷

Having so far examined both the EU's and COMESA's food control systems in chapters 2 and 3, this chapter further examines the two systems and their impact on COMESA exports to the EU. The examination is premised on the fact that EU regulations impact COMESA exports to a greater extent than COMESA regulations impact EU exports. A further premise is that the complexity and

---

10 European Commission (n 4) 14–17.
11 Ulrich Hoffmann and Renee Vossenaar (eds), *Private-Sector Standards and National Schemes for Good Agricultural Practices: Implications for Exports of Fresh Fruit and Vegetables from Sub-Saharan Africa, Experiences of Ghana, Kenya, and Uganda* (UNCTAD/DITC/TED/2007/13, 2008) 12–13.
    Fruit represents about 70 per cent of COMESA fruit and vegetables exports. Bananas and Pineapples represent about 80 per cent of EU fruit imports, while fresh beans and peas represent almost 70 per cent of EU vegetable imports. Of note is the fact that over 60 per cent of EU vegetables imports (in value terms) comes from Kenya. There has been very slow growth in volume terms, at 4.7 per cent per annum, compared to other developing countries, at 39.4 per cent per annum, with a decline since 2003. The value of the exports has also been growing at a slower pace than other developing countries, at 16.5 per cent per annum, compared to 48.2 per cent for all developing countries.
12 Stefano Ponte, Jesper Raakjær and Liam Campling, 'Swimming Upstream: Market Access for African Fish Exports in the Context of WTO and EU Negotiations and Regulation' (2007) 25 *Development Policy Review* 113, 115–116. In 2003, fish and fish products exports constituted about 38 per cent of Seychelles' total exports and about 30 per cent of its GNP, while for Madagascar the figure was about 5 per cent for each of the indicators.
13 Atsushi Iimi, 'Infrastructure and Trade Preferences for the Livestock Sector: Empirical Evidence from the Beef Industry in Africa' (World Bank Policy Research Working Paper No. 4201, April 2007) 13.
14 UNCTAD (n 11) 31.
15 Ibid 7.
16 Agritrade, 'Executive Brief Update 2013: ACP–EU fisheries: Market access and trade, December 2013', <http://agritrade.cta.int/en/Fisheries/Topics/Market-access/Executive-Brief-Update-2013-ACP-EU-fisheries-Market-access-and-trade> accessed 1 May 2014.
17 Agritrade, 'Executive Brief Update 2013: Beef sector, December 2013', <http://agritrade.cta.int/Agriculture/Commodities/Beef/Executive-Brief-Update-2013-Beef-sector> accessed 1 May 2014.

stringency of the EU regulations may negatively impact COMESA exports to the EU because of the weak SPS capacities within COMESA.

The examination proceeds by way of case studies of the EU regulations and their impact on COMESA countries' exports in horticulture, fish, and beef. The chapter starts with a caveat: the impact of food safety standards on trade is controversial. Hence, any perceived impact that the stringent EU food safety standards might have on the EU–COMESA trade is debatable as to whether its impact on food trade is positive or negative.

The chapter begins, in part two, with an examination of the conundrum posed by food safety standards: Are food safety standards a positive or negative force on international trade, and more particularly, on developing countries' exports? Part three goes on to examine specific COMESA trade concerns with EU food safety regulations in beef, fishery, and horticultural products. Part four examines the role and impact of private voluntary standards (PVS) in the EU–COMESA trade. The chapter concludes in part five with a discussion and the conclusions to be drawn from the chapter discussions.

4.2 The two schools of thought on the impact of food safety standards on trade

Although it is generally accepted that food safety standards do impact international trade in food products, the economic impact of individual standards, how they compare with other trade distorting measures, and their net effects are controversial. According to Jaffee and Henson:

> Testing the empirical impact of such standards on trade is enormously difficult. First, it requires assumptions about how the broad array of measures is actually enforced and how enforcement deters or encourages potential export suppliers, depending on whether suppliers need to make major or modest adjustments. This variable cannot be aggregated and differs across countries and industries. Second, food safety and agricultural health standards may have secondary effects, for example, leading to shifts in sourcing, the production of complementary and competitive goods, and the spread of regulations and restrictions to other countries. Third, a specific measure may not be a dominant or even important determinant of observed trade flows. There is a risk of ascribing agro-food standards to shifts in trade that are driven by other economic or technical factors. Fourth, there are problems in defining the counterfactual. Without the measure, would trade have been unimpeded, or would distributors and consumers have sought the product from other suppliers instead? In the absence of a (trade-restricting) measure, might overall demand have declined for a product for which certain problems were identified? Finally, many food safety and agricultural health measures will affect domestic

suppliers as well, with varied outcomes in terms of shifts in the relative competitiveness and market share of the different players.[18]

There are two schools of thought on the economic impact[19] of food safety standards on developing countries' food exports. The first is the World Bank's 'standards as catalysts' school, which views food safety standards as catalysts for trade, growth, and poverty reduction in developing countries. The second is the 'standards as a barrier' school, which holds these standards as barriers to the trade of developing countries, more so for small producers from these countries.

4.2.1 Food safety standards as a catalyst

According to the World Bank school,[20] high food safety standards can have important positive effects on the well-being of small farmers in developing countries. High food safety standards provide incentives for developing countries to upgrade their export capacity and to gain and maintain access to high-value food markets. Standards provide a bridge between producers in developing countries and consumer preferences in high-income markets, and could be used as catalysts for the upgrading and modernisation of developing countries' food supply systems and the improvement of their competitive capacity, thus providing a basis for long-term export growth.[21]

According to proponents of this school, high food safety standards lead to increased vertical coordination in supply chains that is realised by the emergence of extensive contracting between processing companies and farmers. Far from leading to the exclusion of poorer farmers, the rise of contracting is argued as improving access to credit, technology, and quality inputs for poor, small farmers who heretofore were faced with binding credit and information constraints due to poorly developed input markets.[22]

---

18 Steven Jaffee and Spencer Henson, 'Agro-Food Exports from Developing Countries: The Challenges Posed by Standards' in M A Aksoy and J C Beghin (eds) *Global Agricultural Trade and Developing Countries* (World Bank Publications, Washington, DC, 2004) 100.
19 For a review of the impact quantification methods and techniques, both in terms of a general overview and as concrete case studies, see Wyne Jones and Peter Walkenhorst, *The Impact of Regulations on Agro-Food Trade: The Technical Barriers to Trade (TBT) and Sanitary and Phytosanitary Measures (SPS) Agreements* (OECD Publishing, Paris, 2003); Jane Korinek, Mark Melatos and Marie L Rau, 'A Review of Methods for Quantifying the Trade Effects of Standards in the Agri-Food Sector' (OECD Trade Policy Working Paper No. 79, OECD publishing, Paris, 2008).
20 Steven Jaffee (ed), *Food Safety and Agricultural Health Standards: Challenges and Opportunities for Developing Country Exports* (World Bank Report No. 31207, 10 January 2005).
21 Ibid 71–74.
22 Liesbeth Dries, Thomas Reardon and Johan F M Swinnen, 'The Rapid Rise of Supermarkets in Central and Eastern Europe: Implications for the Agrifood Sector and Rural Development' (2004) 22 *Development Policy Review* 525.

Moreover, small farmers who participate in retail chain contracts, which typically espouse stringent food safety standards, have higher welfare, more income stability, and shorter lean periods. There are also significant effects on improved technology adoption, better resource management, and spill-overs on the productivity of the staple crops in the value chain.[23]

Furthermore, studies have shown that small farmer's exports grow despite increasing standards, resulting in important income gains and poverty reduction. For instance, empirical research done in Senegal showed that poverty in Senegal was 14 per cent points lower due to vegetable exports. On the other hand, stringent food safety standards induced a shift from smallholder contract-based farming to large-scale integrated estate production, altering the mechanism through which poor households benefited: through labour markets instead of product markets.[24]

4.2.2 Food safety standards as a barrier

On the other hand, the food safety standards as a barrier school holds that high food safety standards exclude poor farmers and fishermen from high-value supply chains, while the rents in the chain are extracted by multinational companies and developing country elite. For example, the failure of supermarkets in Southern Africa to tap into small producers who were, as a result, almost completely excluded from the dynamic urban markets due to quality and safety standards.[25] Even though the cost of compliance with standards is low as a percentage of the total export value in particular sectors, it is high relative to the means of small producers. This results in the small producers exiting the profitable food export market. For example, in Cote d'Ivoire, small producers were excluded from the export of fruits and vegetables, to the extent that almost all of the fruit and vegetables being produced for exports were being cultivated on large industrial estates.[26] A similar situation was found to exist in Kenya,[27] where the number of small holders in the export trade of horticultural products fell by 60 per cent between 1999 and 2006 due to strict standards.[28]

---

23 Bart Minten, Lalaina Randrianarison and Johan F M Swinnen, 'Global Retail Chains and Poor Farmers: Evidence from Madagascar' (2009) 37 *World Development* 1728.
24 Miet Maertens and Johan F M Swinnen, 'Trade, Standards and Poverty: Evidence from Senegal' (2009) 37 *World Development* 161.
25 Dave D Weatherspoon and Thomas Reardon, 'The Rise of Supermarkets in Africa: Implications for Agrifood Systems and the Rural Poor' (2003) 21 *Development Policy Review* 333.
26 Nicholas Minot and Margaret Ngigi, 'Are Horticultural Exports a Replicable Success Story? Evidence from Kenya and Cote d' Ivoire' (EPTD/MTID discussion paper, IFPRI, Washington, DC, 2004).
27 John Humphrey, Neil McCulloch and Masako Ota, 'The Impact of European Market Changes on Employment in the Kenyan Horticulture Sector' (2004) 16 (1) *Journal of International Development* 63.
28 Andrew Graffham, Esther Karehu and James MacGregor, 'Impact of EurepGAP on Small-scale Vegetable Growers in Kenya' (IIED, Fresh Insights 6, Agrifood standards and pro-poor growth in Africa, 2007).

According to the standards as a barrier school, the rising stringency and complexity of food safety standards in developed countries, and the lack of harmonisation among developing countries, undermines the expansion of some developing countries' exports of food products, while posing insurmountable barriers to new market entrants within the developing world.

Furthermore, according to the school, many developing countries lack the administrative, technical, and scientific capacities to comply with stringent non-conforming food safety standards, and are thus effectively barred from developed countries' food markets. Moreover, the recurrent and non-recurrent costs needed for compliance with these stringent non-conforming food safety standards weaken the competitiveness of developing countries and lower the profitability of their food exports.

Ultimately, these stringent non-conforming food safety standards may serve to marginalise developing countries and in particular their small producers. Although there is evidence of exclusion of small producers from the EU market, there is no consensus on its interpretation. It has been argued that the export of horticultural products is not a suitable activity for small producers and as such should not be encouraged.[29] Furthermore, it is argued that although small may be side-lined by stringent food safety standards, they are better off because they become employed in agro-food farms and industries that export food products.[30]

---

29 Patrick Labaste (ed), *The European Horticulture Market Opportunities for Sub-Saharan African Exporters* (World Bank Working Paper No. 63, Washington, DC, 2005) 87.
   The author suggests that it may be counterproductive to encourage smallholders, in an uncontrolled way, to venture into horticulture farming for exports and advocates entrepreneurship instead. See also, The World Bank, 'Challenges and Opportunities for African Agro-Food Trade, Standards and Trade: Challenges and Opportunities for African Agro-Food Trade, May 14– June 15, 2007' (Final Report of a Course Organized by The World Bank Institute in collaboration with the Agricultural and Rural Development Department, The World Bank, Washington, DC) 34. The report notes: 'It is also important to recognise that most small farmers will be unable to participate in export-oriented chains (e.g. the costs of upgrading their product supply might be too high, and the institutional efforts significant), thus the importance of looking for opportunities in regional and domestic markets'.
30 Maertens M and Swinnen J F M (n 24) 18. According to the authors:

> An important – and much overlooked – argument in the debate on the shift from smallholder contract-based production to large-scale integrated estate production is that the exclusion of small suppliers, if it happens, is only a partial outcome. One needs to take into account the new employment opportunities brought about by increased estate production. Rather than decreasing overall participation of small farmers, the induced shift to high-standards estate farming may primarily change the status of household participation in the supply chain from (contracted) farmers to (salaried) farm workers. Furthermore, if high-standards contract-based production is indeed biased to relatively larger farmers, it might well be that a shift from smallholder contract-based production to estate production improves the participation of poorer households as farm workers on agro-industrial estates.

4.2.3 The compliance costs of EU food safety standards

Compliance with food safety standards, both internationally (under the SPS Agreement) and under the EU food safety regulations, requires setting up food safety control systems (for those countries with none) or the reinforcement of the current systems (for those countries with weak systems, such as COMESA countries).[31] Setting up or reinforcing food safety control systems in order to comply with international or EU standards entails costs, which are known as compliance costs.[32] Compliance costs are divided into non-recurring and recurring costs.[33]

---

31 UNCTAD, 'Costs of Agri-Food Safety and SPS Compliance: United Republic of Tanzania, Mozambique and Guinea: Tropical Fruits' (UNCTAD/DITC/COM/2005/2, 2005) 8–11. The required changes to the food safety control systems will vary from country to country and involve changes to the food legislation; food control management; food inspection; official food control laboratories; and food safety information, education, and communication. For further analysis, see UNCTAD, 'SPS Compliance and Costs of Agri-Food Safety and Quality Standards in Selected Least Developed Countries in the Pacific Region: Samoa, Solomon Islands and Vanuatu' (UNCTAD/DITC/COM/2007/3, 2007).

32 Jaffee S (ed) (n 20) 67–68. According to the author:

> In the context of trade, compliance costs are defined as the additional costs necessarily incurred by government and/or private enterprises in meeting the requirements to comply with a given standard in a given external market. (. . .) There are two key elements to this definition. First, it covers the costs that are 'additional' to those which would have otherwise been incurred by government and/or the private sector in the absence of the standard. Second, it refers to those costs that are 'necessarily' incurred in complying with the standard (. . .).

See also Shafaeddin Mehdi, 'Who Does Bear the Costs of Compliance with Sanitary and Phytosanitary Measures in Poor Countries?' (MPRA Paper No. 6646, Munich Personal RePEc Archive) 14. According to the author:

> The cost of compliance is the sum of all expenses which accrues to the public as well as the private sector i.e. farmers and enterprises involved in the supply chain. Accordingly, it includes the cost of adjusting (not reorganizing) various components of the supply chain in order to conform to the SPS Agreement and SPS measures imposed by importing government and enterprises, the administrative cost of control, inspection, testing and certification. One could also add the cost of delays in exportation (e.g. interest charges) caused by the procedures necessary for the compliance. When the compliance may result in the reduction of exports, the loss of export earnings should also be taken into account. If exports are reduced, there will be secondary costs in terms of the loss of income at the country, farm and firm levels, as well as the loss of employment and household consumption.

33 Jaffee S (ed) (n 20) 68. Non-recurring costs are a one-off investments made to be able to achieve compliance. These include the upgrading of laboratory infrastructure and processing facilities, training of new personnel, and costs of designing new management systems such as the HACCP. Recurring costs are borne over time and include the costs of maintaining regular surveillance and laboratory testing.

Ultimately, compliance costs are akin to export taxes and transaction costs,[34] which do not add value to traded products.[35] Because of the divergence in food safety standards between COMESA countries and the EU (with the former having lower or non-existent standards, while the latter has high standards), the compliance costs are likely to be higher for COMESA countries compared to EU countries. According to Maertens and Swinnen:

> The compliance cost is likely to be higher for developing countries because they generally have a weakness in food safety capacity. Developing countries lack the institutional, technical and scientific capacity for food quality and safety management. Hence adherence to high standards imposed by high-income countries might require substantial investment – from the public sector as well as from the private sector – to realize that capacity. In addition, there is generally a divergence between national food quality and safety norms in a particular country and international standards. This 'standards diverge' increases the cost of compliance and is likely to be higher for developing countries. In general, consumers in less-developed countries are less demanding in terms of food quality and safety and have norms that are below international norms. For poor countries, lacking the financial means, the cost of compliance with food standards might be too high and undermine their competitive capacity. Hence, standards could act as barriers to trade for developing countries facing particular weaknesses in food safety capacity.[36]

---

34 Mehdi S (n 32) 15. According to the author, however, 'Unlike the case of export tax which creates revenues for the government, the cost of compliance is borne by the government and the private sector; and to individual producers and the firms involved, compliance costs are similar to transaction costs, which it may not be possible to pass on to importers'.

35 It may be argued that compliance costs do add value; they are very important for the trust put by the consumer in the product. If non-complying products could be sold next to complying products, only differentiated by labelling, the consumer would demand an enormous discount for the non-complying products, if they were bought at all. However, according to Henson and Humphrey, 'Food safety has largely become a non-competiveness issue. In the limited cases where individual firms promulgate standards that encompass food safety (for example Tesco's Nature's Choice), the food safety element is not presented to the consumer as basis for differentiation'. See Spencer Henson and John Humphrey, 'The Impacts of Private Food Safety Standards on the Food Chain and on Public Standard-Setting Processes' (Paper prepared for FAO/WHO, ALINORM 09/32/9D-Part II, May 2009) 15. Moreover, there is no price premium earned for compliance with standards; see Hoffmann U and Vossenaar R (eds) (n 11) 23.

36 Miet Maertens and Johan F M Swinnen, 'Transformations in Agricultural Markets: Standards and Their Implications' (LIRGIAD Working Paper No. 11–2006, Katholieke Universiteit Leuven, 2003), <https://ghum.kuleuven.be/ggs/publications/working_papers/archive/wp11.pdf> accessed 15 October 2015. However, the authors go on to argue that the compliance costs constitute a relatively low percentage of the total costs of exports.

Compliance costs are also higher for small producers compared to large producers. According to Jaffee and Henson:

> A particular concern is that smaller players can be disadvantaged where there are economies of scale or scope in the implementation of particular technologies or administrative systems. Studies of compliance with labour and environmental standards in the United States suggest that costs are proportionately higher for smaller firms (Crain and Johnson 2001). In some cases the necessary investments have elements of lumpiness, for example, laboratory equipment and cold-storage facilities, which are economically viable only for large-scale operations or require collective action. Likewise, smaller firms may find it more difficult to hire certain types of skilled personnel. More generally, smaller firms can be overwhelmed by the sheer number of changes needed to comply with new food safety requirements, even when the cash investments required are not substantial. Sometimes certifying that the standards have been met is more difficult for small producers than complying with food safety and agricultural health requirements.[37]

Therefore, the likely impact of compliance with the high EU food safety standards for COMESA food producers is increased costs and limited export competitiveness.[38]

4.2.4 Discussion

Compliance costs affect developing countries, hence COMESA countries, disproportionately relative to their resources. Developed countries have resources to meet these costs, but developing countries may not have such resources.

---

37 Jaffee S and Henson S (n 18) 99.
38 John S Wilson, 'Standards and Developing Country Exports: A Quick Review of Selected Studies and Suggestions for New Research' (Summer Symposium of the International Agricultural Trade Research Consortium (IATRC), Food Regulation and Trade: Institutional Framework, Concepts of Analysis and Empirical Evidence, 28–30 May 2006, Bonn, Germany) 4. The author notes:

> Developing countries are typically 'standards takers' rather than 'standards makers' since, at the national level, developing their own standards tends to be more costly than adopting those of the major markets. At the firm level, complying with differing standards in such major export markets as the European Union (EU), the United States, and Japan can add costs and limit export competitiveness. These costs associated with foreign standards and technical regulations may be borne publicly and privately. But developing countries typically have neither the public resources required to provide national laboratories for testing and certification nor the capability for collective action to raise their standards. As a result, a significant portion of meeting the costs of standards may be borne by individual firms (. . .).

For an assessment of the various methodologies for measuring non-tariff trade barriers in the agricultural and food sectors, see John C Beghin and Jean C Bureau, 'Measurement of Sanitary, Phytosanitary and Technical Barriers to Trade' (A consultants' Report Prepared for the Food, Agriculture and Fisheries Directorate, OECD, Paris, 17–18 September 2001), <www.oecd.org/tad/agricultural-trade/1816774.pdf> accessed 15 October 2015.

Compliance costs accentuate the lack of capacities of the developing countries. Whereas developed countries are able to set food safety standards which they are able to meet, these standards are passed on to developing countries without taking into account their abilities to meet the costs of compliance. Even where non-recurrent costs, such as infrastructure, have been met, the recurrent costs, such as chemicals in laboratories, might prove to be difficult to meet.

Hence although the impact of compliance costs may not be precisely determined, it is a justified fear that they may be detrimental to developing countries' exports. Since a majority of developing countries' producers are small, their marginalisation may in the end serve to exacerbate their poverty levels. This defeats the objective of using trade as a development tool. As such, compliance costs are effectively acting as barriers to COMESA countries' trade and may need to be reviewed.

4.3 COMESA trade concerns with EU food safety regulations in beef, fishery, and horticultural products

There is a 'regulatory gap' in EU–COMESA trade.[39] The regulatory gap is due to the evident differences in the SPS regimes of the two trading partners and to the fact that one is developed and the other a developing regime. This regulatory gap may impose extra compliance costs on COMESA exporters, over and above those incurred by EU suppliers. This 'gap' is a reflection of 'the feasibility of implementing alternative mechanisms of control, which itself is influenced by legal and industry structures as well as available technical, scientific, administrative and financial resources'.[40]

The disparities in food safety standards and food control systems between the EU and COMESA have led to fears that the EU standards may amount to a trade barrier to COMESA exports, particularly for its small producers and agro-enterprises. Furthermore, COMESA countries' demonstrated incapacities in food control, together with the costs of compliance, translate into non-compliance with EU standards, except for a few among them.[41]

---

39 Spencer Henson and Rupert Loader, 'Impact of Sanitary and Phytosanitary Standards on Developing Countries and the Role of the SPS Agreement' (1999) 15 *Agribusiness* 355, 359.
40 Spencer Henson and Steven Jaffee, 'Understanding Developing Country Strategic Responses to the Enhancement of Food Safety Standards' (2008) 31 *The World Economy* 548, 549. Differences in standards are attributable to distinct tastes, diets, income levels, perceptions, tolerance of populations towards the potential risks associated with food risks, differences in climate, and the application of production and process technologies.
41 Jaffee S (ed) (n 20) 3. Exceptions include countries like Kenya and Egypt. However, even in these two countries compliance with EU standards has been attributed to private enterprise. See also European Commission, 'Final Report on a Mission Carried Out in Egypt from 22 to 31 January 2007 Concerning Controls of Pesticides in Food of Plant Origin intended for Export to the European Union' (DG (SANCO) 2007-7183 – MR Final) 17. The report concludes:

> There is a very weak official control in place for pesticide residues in food of plant origin intended for export to the EU. Voluntary controls are applied by some exporters

There are five main food safety regulations in the EU. The framework Regulation 178 of 2002;[42] the hygiene regulations: 852/2004,[43] 853/2004,[44] and 854/2004;[45] and the official controls Regulation 882/2004.[46] These regulations apply to all foodstuffs categorised as food of non-animal origin (such as horticultural products and cereals); food of animal origin (food derived from animals and animal products, including fish and beef); and food containing both processed ingredients of animal origin and ingredients of plant origin. These regulations provide the bedrock of the EU 'farm to fork' food safety policy, which is underpinned by the concepts of the precautionary principle[47] and traceability.[48] In addition to hygiene requirements, other food safety regulations relate to

---

to meet the demands of their customers and may provide some assurance that foodstuffs of plant origin being exported to the EU will comply with EU legislation.

See also Steven Henson, 'Review of Case Studies and Evaluations of Sanitary and Phytosanitary Capacity: Kenya, Tanzania and Uganda' (Research Work for the Standards Development Trade Facility, 2007) 12, <www.uneca.org/eca_programmes/trade_and_regional_integration/events/aidfortrade/docs/Synthesis-SPSevaluations%20_Henson.pdf>. The author notes:

Ironically, the success of the Kenyan fresh vegetable and flower sectors has occurred not because of a strong national base of SPS management capacity, but in spite of the generally weak capacity. To the extent possible, these firms take active measures to by-pass limitations in public oversight and SPS management, either on an individual or a collective basis. Thus, much of the oversight of food safety controls in the horticultural supply chain comes through private systems of certification, for example the BRC Global Standard and EUREPGAP.

42 Regulation (EC) 178 of 2002 of the European Parliament and of the Council of 28th January 2002, Laying down the Principles and Requirements of Food Law, Establishing the European Food Safety Authority and Laying down Procedures in matters of Food Safety [2002] OJ L 31/1, 1.2.2002. See also Guidance on the implementation of articles 11, 12, 14, 17, 18, 19 and 20 of Regulation (EC) 178 of 2002 on general food law, 26 January 2010.
43 Regulation (EC) 852/2004 of the European Parliament and of the Council of 29th April 2004 on the Hygiene of Foodstuffs [2004] OJ L 226/3. 25.6.2004. See also European Commission, 'Guidance Document on the Implementation of Certain Provisions of Regulation (EC) No 852/2004 On the Hygiene of Foodstuffs, Brussels, Brussels, 16 February 2009'.
44 Regulation (EC) 853/2004 of the European Parliament and of the Council of 29th April 2004 Laying Down Specific Hygiene Rules for Food of Animal Origin [2004] OJL 226/22, 25.6.2004. See also European Commission, 'Guidance Document on the Implementation of Certain Provisions of Regulation (EC) No 853/2004 on the Hygiene of Food of Animal Origin, Brussels, (2014) SANCO/10098/2009 Rev. 2, POOL/G4/2009/10098/10098R2-EN.doc'.
45 Regulation (EC) 854/2004 of the European Parliament and of the Council of 29th April 2004 Laying Down Specific Rules for the Organisation of Official Controls on Products of Animal Origin Intended for Human Consumption [2004] OJ L 22683, 25.6.2004.
46 Regulation (EC) 882/2004 of the European Parliament and of the Council of 29 April 2004 on official controls performed to ensure the verification of compliance with feed and food law, animal health and animal welfare, [2004] OJ L 191/1, 28.5.2004. See also European Commission (2005) Guidance document: On official controls, under Regulation (EC) No 882/2004, concerning microbiological sampling and testing of foodstuffs, Brussels, 13 November 2006.
47 Treaty on the Functioning of the European Union (TFEU), art 191 (2); regulation 178 of 2002, art 7; European Commission (2000) Communication from the Commission on the precautionary principle, Brussels, 2 February 2000 (COM (2000) 1 final).
48 Regulation 178 of 2002, art 18.

contaminants, maximum residue limits for pesticides, the use of food additives, and materials and articles in contact with foodstuffs.[49]

Food business operators are charged with the responsibility for ensuring food safety, while governments are responsible for enforcement, monitoring, and verifying the application of the regulations by food business operators at all stages of production, processing, and distribution.[50]

The EU regulations apply equally to domestic food and imported food. Food imports into the EU are required to comply with the relevant regulations or conditions deemed to be equivalent. The EU food safety legal regime is premised on the concept of equivalence[51] of food safety regimes.[52] Imports are only allowed of food that complies with the relevant food safety regulations or from countries deemed to have equivalent food control systems. EU food importers must comply with EU food law, its specific and general hygiene requirements, official controls, registration, and approval and implement of the Hazard Analysis Critical Control Point (HACCP) principles[53] or their equivalent.

The food business operator, such as a supermarket food retailer or food processor, is required to ensure the safety of foods imported by the business by ensuring that they comply with EU regulations and is also required to withdraw from the market all non-conforming food.

The predicament of the COMESA countries arising from the stringency of EU food safety standards is illustrated by and manifested in the beef, fishery, and horticultural products trade. These will be discussed in the following sections.

---

49 See generally European Commission, 'Guidance Document: Key Questions Related to Import Requirements and the EU Rules on Food Hygiene and on Official Food Controls, Brussels, 2013' (draft SANCO/1446/2005 Rev.2014(PLSPV/2005/1446/1446R4-EN.doc).
50 Regulation 178 of 2002, art 17.
51 For elaboration on the application of equivalence, see WTO Committee on Sanitary and Phytosanitary Measures, 'Decision on the Implementation of Article 4 of the Agreement on the Application of Sanitary and Phytosanitary Measures' (G/SPS/19, 24 October 2001 and G/SPS/19/Rev. 2, 23 July 2004). See also Codex Alimentarius Commission: Guidelines on Equivalence: Guidelines for the Design, Operation, Assessment and Accreditation of Food Import and Export Inspection and Certification Systems (CAC/GL/26–1997); Guidelines for the Development of Equivalence Agreements Regarding Food Imports and Export Inspection and Certification Systems (CAC/GL/34–1999); Guidelines on the Judgement of Equivalence of Sanitary Measures associated with Food Inspection and Certification Systems (CAC/GL 53–2003 (Rev. 2008).
52 Regulation 178 of 2002, art 11. The Article provides:

> Food and feed imported into the Community for placing on the market within the Community shall comply with the relevant requirements of food law or conditions recognised by the Community to be at least equivalent thereto or, where a specific agreement exists between the Community and the exporting country, with requirements contained therein.

53 See European Commission, 'Guidance Document on the Implementation of Procedures Based on the HACCP Principles and on the Facilitation of the Implementation of the HACCP Principles in Certain Food Businesses' (Brussels, 16 November 2005). The Guidance document is based on Codex Alimentarius Commission, 'Annex on Hazard Analysis and Critical Control Point (HACCP) System and Guidelines for its Application in Recommended International Code of Practice General Principles of Food Hygiene' (CAC/RCP 1-1969, Rev. 4 (2003) 31–44. HACCP is a science-based, systematic tool that identifies specific hazards and measures for their control to ensure the safety of food.

4.3.1 The case of the EU–COMESA beef trade

Historically, the EU–COMESA beef trade has been conducted under the preferential trade rules of the Lome Convention,[54] the Cotonou Agreement (and its successor, the Economic Partnership Agreements [EPAs]),[55] and the beef and veal protocol under Lome IV, which gave special import quotas to five African countries – namely, Botswana (18,916 tonnes), Kenya (142 tonnes), Madagascar (7,579 tonnes), Swaziland (3,363 tonnes), and Zimbabwe (9,100 tonnes). Under the Contonou Agreement, the EU had removed ad valorem tariffs on all ACP beef imports. Under the Everything But Arms (EBA) initiative, LDCs were allowed duty-free and quota-free access into the EU market, including livestock products.[56] These benefits have been retained under the EPAs.[57]

In addition to the general food safety requirements for products of animal origin, there are specific provisions for beef.[58] These relate to requirements for approval of establishments,[59] hygiene criteria,[60] microbiological criteria,[61] chemical contaminants,[62] and veterinary residues.[63]

---

54 The Courier (1975) 'The Lome Dossier' (Special Issue No. 31, March 1975), <www.acp.int/content/lome-i-dossier-courier-magazine-n-31-march-1975>.
55 ACP-EC Partnership Agreement (Cotonou Agreement).
56 Melaku G Desta, 'EU Sanitary Standards and Sub-Saharan African Agricultural Exports: A Case Study of the Livestock Sector in East Africa' (2008) 1 *The Law and Development Review* 97, 103–109.
57 European Commission Trade policy-ACP Region <http://ec.europa.eu/trade/policy/countries-and-regions/regions/africa-caribbean-pacific/> accessed 1 June 2014.
58 For analysis of the EU meat import requirements, see United States Department of Agriculture (USDA), Food Safety and Inspection Service (FSIS): Export Requirements for the European Union, EU-206 (May 12, 2016) <http://www.fsis.usda.gov/wps/portal/fsis/topics/international-affairs/exporting-products/export-library-requirements-by-country/European-Union> accessed 5 June 2016.
59 Regulation 853/2004, Annex II, s III; Annex III, s I, chs II and III; Annex III, s V, Ch I; Annex III, s I, chs I and VII; Council Directive 93/119/EC of 22 December 1993 on the protection of animals at the time of slaughter or killing, OJ L 340/21, 31/12/1993; Council Regulation 1/2005 of 22 December 2004 on the protection of animals during transport and related operations and amending Directives 64/432/EEC and 93/119/EC and Regulation, (EC) No 1255/97, OJ L 3/1, 05.01.2005.
60 Regulation 852/2004, Annex I, pt A; Regulation 853/2004, Annex II and III; and Regulation 854/2004, art 5 and Annex I; Council Directive 2002/99/EC of 16 December 2002, laying down the animal health rules governing the production, processing, distribution, and introduction of products of animal origin for human consumption, OJ L 18, /11, 23.1.2003; Council Directive 96/93/EC of 17 December 1996 on the certification of animals and animal products, OJ L 013/28, 16/01/1997; Council Directive 97/78/EC of 18 December 1997, laying down the principles governing the organisation of veterinary checks on products entering the Community from third countries, OJ No L 24/9, 30.01.98.
61 Regulation 2073/2005, Annex I, chs 1.4 and 1.6–1.8; chs 2.1.1 and 2.1.3. and 2.1.6–2.1.8.
62 Commission Regulation (EC) No 1881/2006 of 19 December 2006, setting maximum levels for certain contaminants in foodstuffs, OJ L 364/5, 20.12.2006; Council Directive 96/22/EC, concerning the prohibition on the use in stock farming of certain substances having a hormonal or thyrostatic action and of ß-agonists, OJ L 125/3, 23.5.1996.
63 Council Directive 96/23/EC on measures to monitor certain substances and residues thereof in live animals and animal products and repealing Directives 85/358/EEC and 86/469/EEC and Decisions 89/187/EEC and 91/664/EEC, OJ L 125/10, 23.5.1996.

The EU regulations on foot and mouth disease (FMD)[64] are perceived as more stringent than provided for under the OIE Terrestrial Code[65] and are regarded as the main barrier for COMESA beef exports to the EU:

> There is increasingly a perception that the stringent standards applied to southern African exporters by the EU, above and beyond OIE standards, amount to non-tariff barriers. Particularly contentious is the stipulation that meat exported to the EU must be deboned even when it comes from areas with OIE FMD-free status. There is also justifiable confusion as to why – on top of quarantining and routine inspections of vaccinated animals prior to slaughter – a timed process of beef maturation with controlled pH and temperature, alongside deboning and removal of lymph nodes, should not be recognised as adequate for FMD deactivation (. . .).[66]

Despite their preferential trading terms, COMESA beef exports to the EU have been dismal.[67] Swaziland and Zimbabwe are the only COMESA countries on the establishment list of authorised beef processing plants which are permitted under Articles 11 and 12 of Regulation 854/2004.[68] However, even though they are on the list, Swaziland and Zimbabwe last exported beef to the EU in 2002, and Kenya last exported beef to the EU in 1992, while Madagascar last did so in 1998. This is mainly attributable to the rising costs of compliance with EU food safety regulations.[69] Indeed, it has been reported that, of all ACP countries, Namibia and Botswana are the only countries that have been able to meet the EU's strict food safety standards, but they have been unable to fill their quotas.[70] As of 2013 only Namibia, among ACP countries, still exports beef to the EU.[71]

---

64 Council Directive 2003/85/EC, of 29 September 2003, on Community measures for the control of foot-and-mouth disease repealing Directive 85/511/EEC and Decisions 89/531/EEC and 91/665/EEC and amending Directive 92/46/EEC.
65 World Organization for Animal Health (OIE), 'Terrestrial Animal Health Code', 224th edn (2015) ch 8.8 < http://www.oie.int/en/international-standard-setting/terrestrial-code/access-online/> accessed 6 June 2016.
66 Ian Scoones and William Wolmer, *Foot-and-Mouth Disease and Market Access: Challenges for the Beef Industry in Southern Africa* (Institute of Development Studies, Brighton, University of Sussex, 2008) 10–11.
67 Iimi A (n 12) 9–16.
68 The list is available at <http://ec.europa.eu/food/food/biosafety/establishments/third_country/index_en.htm.> accessed 15 June 2015. The other African countries on the list are Botswana, Namibia, and South Africa. Of note, from the lists, is that no African country is permitted to export milk or milk products and poultry or poultry products to the EU.
69 Agritrade, 'Executive Brief, Beef: Trade Issues for the ACP, March 2010' 2–5, <http://agritrade.cta.int/en/Agriculture/Commodities/Beef/Beef-Trade-issues-for-the-ACP> accessed 15 June 2015.
70 Christopher Stevens, Mareike Meyn and Jane Kennan, 'Duty-Free, Quota-Free Access: What Is It Worth?' (ODI Project Briefing Paper No.10, March 2008) 4. See also Agritrade (n 17).
71 Agritrade (n 17) 2.

Indeed, Zimbabwe has been unable to resume beef exports to the EU after suspension due to a FMD outbreak in 2001–2002, due to the strict pre-export requirements that demand that cattle in the country be identified to the farm and dip tank of origin.[72] Moreover, the stringent FMD requirements, including the requirement that a country should be declared FMD-free by the OIE in order to export live animals to the EU,[73] are the main reason why the Members of the Intergovernmental Authority for Development (IGAD) – Kenya, Ethiopia, Somalia, Sudan, Uganda, Eritrea, and Djibouti, all of which are also COMESA Members – cannot export meat products to the EU.[74]

Generally, the interpretation and implementation of the EU standards as applicable to products of animal origin, and to beef imports in particular, is uncertain and confusing. According to the Technical Centre for Agricultural and Rural Cooperation EC-ACP (CTA), some of the outstanding issues on the implementation of the EU beef import regulations are as follows:

> Will the objectives of EU regulations need to be attained in the same way in all countries?; will the EU be able to tailor requirements to country circumstances, with countries at high risk of disease facing stricter controls than those with no history of such diseases?; will all provisions of the applicable EU regulations be equally applied to production in third countries or will certain aspects be waived, providing the safety of meat destined for the EU market is not compromised, for example with regard to disposal of animal by-products?; will the exemptions to small-scale trade in animal feed between farmers within the EU be extended to small-scale feed-trading in third countries, on the basis that for feed contamination to be of concern it must affect a minimum level of total feed intake?[75]

In addition, the requirements of pre-approval of third country competent authorities and exporting establishments and the placing of responsibility for

---

72 Ibid 12. A contributory factor has been the political and economic chaos in Zimbabwe: see 'Politics, Patronage and Violence in Zimbabwe' (2013) 39 *Journal of Southern African Studies: Special Issue*.
73 European Commission, Health and Consumer Protection Directorate-General, 'General Guidance on EU Import and Transit Rules for Live Animals and Animal Products from Third Countries' 7–9.
74 Melaku G Desta, 'The Regulatory Framework for Trade in IGAD Livestock Products' (IGAD Livestock Policy Initiative, IGAD LPI Working Paper No. 07–08, 2008) 33–35.
75 Agritrade, 'Executive Brief, Beef, June 2008' 7, <http://agritrade.cta.int> accessed 15 June 2015. The EU does not clarify these uncertainties in its framework regulations, Regulations 882/2004 and 854/2004, or in its guidance document: European Union, 'General Guidance on EU Import and Transit Rules for Live Animals and Animal Products from Third Countries' (Directorate D – Animal Health and Welfare, Health and Consumer Protection Directorate-General, 17 July 2007). However, it is arguable that it may not be feasible to regulate all these details as they relate to implementation and not to food safety policy as such.

ensuring the integrity of food safety controls throughout the food chain upon the competent authorities create onerous obligations that few developing countries are able to bear. These regulations have had a debilitating effect on Least Developed Countries (LDCs):

> The ongoing investment required at both government and private-sector levels to sustain access to the EU market under increasingly strict food-safety, SPS and animal-welfare regulations, provides an important insight into why no LDC country has developed beef exports to the EU market since the introduction of duty-free, quota-free access for LDC exports in the beef sector in 2001. It would also suggest there is little prospect of new ACP beef exporters emerging in response to the duty-free, quota-free access granted under the various (I) EPAs.[76]

An important indicator of the stringency of EU food safety regulations is the fact that since 1988, the EU has banned the use of substances that have a hormonal growth-promoting effect in raising food-producing animals. This is despite the fact that the preponderance of scientific evidence affirms these substances to be harmless to human health, as against the EU's inability to demonstrate the substances' harmfulness. Furthermore, the EU's continuing ban on beef from cattle treated with growth hormones is in violation of the WTO Panel and Appellate Body rulings against such a ban in *EC – Hormones*.

4.3.2 The case of the EU–COMESA fishery products trade

The EU–COMESA fishery products trade is conducted under the duty- and quota-free regime preferential terms of the Cotonou Agreement (and its successor, the EPAs) and of the Everything But Arms (EBA) initiative.[77]

In addition to the EU general food safety requirements for products of animal origin, there are specific provisions for fishery products.[78] Marine fishery products are required to be sourced from classified production areas[79] in third countries that appear on lists drawn up and updated under similar requirements as apply to

---

76 Agritrade, 'Executive Brief, Beef, March 2010' 6, <http://agritrade.cta.int> accessed 15 June 2015.
77 Agritrade, 'Executive Brief Update 2012: ACP–EU fisheries: Market access and trade, 11 November 2012', <http://agritrade.cta.int/Fisheries/Topics/Market-access/Executive-Brief-Update-2012-ACP-EU-fisheries-Market-access-and-trade> accessed 15 June 2015.
78 For analysis of the fisheries import regulations, see United Kingdom Food Standards Agency, 'Step-by-Step Guide to Importing Fishery Products and Bivalve Molluscs from Approved Non-EU Countries to the UK, September 2014', <www.food.gov.uk/sites/default/files/import-fishery-products-sep2014.pdf> accessed 15 June 2015. See also Allan Reilly, 'European Union' in J Ryder, I Karunasagar and L Ababouch (eds) *Assessment and Management of Seafood Safety and Quality: Current Practices and Emerging Issues* (FAO Fisheries and Aquaculture Technical Paper No. 574, Rome, 2014) 306.
79 Regulation 853/2004, Annex I.

establishments.[80] Additionally, imports of aquaculture products must be specifically approved annually on the basis of a residue monitoring plan submitted by the third country in accordance with Directive 96/23.[81]

Furthermore, fishery products imports into the EU are required to meet strict conditions laid down in hygiene criteria,[82] microbiological criteria,[83] chemical contaminants criteria,[84] and veterinary residues[85] requirements.

In COMESA 14 countries produce fishery products. Out of these 14 countries, 8 countries (Egypt, Eritrea, Kenya, Madagascar, Mauritius, Seychelles, Uganda, and Zimbabwe) qualify and are permitted to export fishery products to the EU.[86] Among these eight countries, only Mauritius and Madagascar are permitted to export aquaculture products (this is because the other countries do not have a residue plan in place), and only Madagascar is permitted to export live crustaceans (e.g., lobsters, crabs, and shrimp); none are permitted to export bivalve molluscs (e.g., clams, oysters, mussels, and scallops) because these countries do not have approved and listed areas for the production of such products.[87]

According to the Food and Veterinary Office (FVO), which is the audit and inspection department of DG-SANCO, Kenya,[88] Mauritius, Madagascar, and Uganda[89] do not meet EU requirements as regards their competent authorities

---

80 Regulation 854/2004, art 13 and Annex II, ch II.
81 Council Directive 96/23/EC, arts 29–30.
82 Regulation 852/2004, arts 4 and 5 and Annexes I and II; Regulation 853/2004, Annexes I and III.
83 Regulation 2073/2005, Annex I.
84 Regulation 1881/2006, Annex, ss 3, 5 and 6.
85 Directive 96/22, arts 4, 5, 5a, 7, and 11.2, Annex II, List B and Annex III; Directive 96/23, arts 4, 7, 9, and 29–30 and Annex I.
86 The lists of approved countries, as well as their establishments and sectors, that are permitted to export fishery products to the EU are to be found at the European Commission, DG Health and Consumers, Approved establishments lists website <http://ec.europa.eu/food/food/biosafety/establishments/index_en.htm> accessed 15 June 2015.
87 Ibid.
88 The EU had previously banned the importation of fishery products from Kenya for SPS reasons four times between 1996 and 2000: see Spencer Henson and Winnie Mitullah, 'Kenyan Exports of Nile Perch: The Impact of Food Safety Standards on an Export-Oriented Supply Chain' (World Bank Policy Research Working Paper, No. 3349, June 2004) 39–43. For an analysis of the role of standards in Kenya's export strategy, see Fernando H Casquet and Victor Abiola, 'The Role of Standards under Kenya's Export Strategy' (Contribution to the Kenya Diagnostic Trade and Integration Study, The World Bank, Washington, DC, March 2005), <http://siteresources.worldbank.org/INTEXPCOMNET/Resources/Kenya_Private_Sector-Lead_Change.pdf> accessed 30 March 2015.
89 Uganda had suffered a similar fate as Kenya: its products were banned by the EU for similar reasons and for a similar period of time: see Boaz B Keizire, 'Policy Research – Implications of Liberalization of Fish Trade for Developing Countries: A Case Study for Uganda' (FAO, Rome, Project PR 26109, July 2004) 17–20. For an analysis of standards and trade in Uganda, see Steven Jaffee, 'Uganda, Standards and Trade: Experience, Capacities, and Priorities' (Paper prepared as part of the Diagnostic Trade Integration Study, The World Bank, Washington, DC, January 2006).

and food control systems, and are allowed to export fishery products because their establishments and vessels have been inspected and found to meet the EU requirements.[90] Under Article 15 of Regulation 1854/2004, fishery products from third countries that are landed directly in the EU by listed factory and freezer vessels are exempted from the official controls of the exporting country but are subject to controls by the EU Member state where they land.

For Eritrea, its competent authority and two of its establishments have been able to meet the EU requirements since 2009. However, Eritrea is presently listed in Annex II of Commission Decision 2006/766/EC, establishing the list of third countries and territories from which imports of fishery products for human consumption, other than bivalve molluscs, are permitted.[91]

It is evident that COMESA countries are severely constrained in meeting EU fishery products food safety standards. This is a result of their weak food safety capacities and their lack of institutional, technical, and scientific capacity for food quality and safety management. As a consequence, those countries that are unable to meet these fishery products food safety standards are excluded from the fishery products export trade with the EU. Moreover, exports are restricted to listed establishments. On the other hand, the EU is entitled to determine its ALOP, particularly given the susceptibility of fishery products to contamination and spoilage.

According to a report by the International Centre for Trade and Sustainable Development (ICTSD), developing countries' fisheries competent authorities are generally faced with myriad constraints:

> lack of training in Good Hygiene Practice (GHP) and Hazard Analysis Critical Control Points (HACCP); the absence of comprehensive

---

90 EU Food and Veterinary Office (FVO) Reports: European Commission, 'Final Report of a Follow Up Mission Carried Out in Kenya from 21 to 31 March 2006, In order to Assess the Public Health Controls and the Conditions of Productions of Fishery Products' (DG (SANCO)/ 2007–7302- M- FINAL) 15; European Commission, 'Final Report on a Mission Carried Out in Mauritius from 5 to 14 February 2008, In order to Evaluate the Control Systems in Place Governing the Production of Fishery Products intended for Export to the European Union (Follow Up)' (DG (SANCO)/ 2008–7668- MR- FINAL) 15; European Commission, 'Final Report of a Follow Up Mission Carried Out in Madagascar from 1 to 9 March 2007, In order to Evaluate the Control Systems in Place Governing the Production of Fishery and Aquaculture Products intended for Export to the European Union (Follow Up)' (DG (SANCO)/ 2007–7302-3 MR- FINAL) 12; European Commission, 'Final Report on a Mission Carried Out in Uganda from 31 July to 8 August 2006, In order to Assess the Public Health Controls and the Conditions of Productions of Fishery Products' (DG (SANCO)/ 8240/2006-MR- FINAL) 15. The EU reliance on establishments' compliance to permit exports illustrates the fact that the EU often relies on private actors for the fulfilment of public obligations.

91 European Commission, 'Final Report of a Mission Carried Out in Eritrea from 19 to 25 October 2010, In order to Evaluate the Control Systems in Place Governing the Production of Fishery Products intended for Export to the European Union' (DG (SANCO)/ 2010–8547- MR FINAL). Eritrea exported about eight tonnes of fishery products in 2009, mainly to the United Kingdom, Germany, and Italy.

> operational manuals and guidance related to inspection procedures at landing sites, sampling, recording and documentation for traceability and auditing of GHPs and HACCP in fish establishments; out of date regulations that fail to meet the current fish industry and international markets requirements, such as no HACCP requirements or undefined legislation related to water quality; Ineffective enforcement of regulations both at the source of the problem and, in the case of non-compliance, in courts; Inconsistent interpretation of the requirements; no monitoring programme for pesticides, bio toxins and heavy metals or other residues defined or implemented for fishery and aquaculture products; and confusion between monitoring for aquaculture products and other sources of potential hazards (. . .).[92]

Additionally, food control infrastructure is also lacking in these countries:

> Laboratories with outdated equipment and staff not fully trained in Good Laboratory Practice (GLP); Landing sites without proper hygiene facilities; Inadequate cold storage, both at establishments/capture vessels and at the point of export; The absence of a fully integrated disease reporting and monitoring system to enable preventative or remedial action to be taken quickly (. . .).[93]

Furthermore, an analysis carried out by United Nations Industrial Development Organization (UNIDO) of FVO inspections for the years 2006 to 2008 shows that non-compliance with EU fisheries food safety requirements by competent authorities, laboratories, and fishery establishments accounts for 75 per cent of all non-compliance incidents, while the rest of the requirements account for 25 per cent.[94]

Comparatively, the requirements for fishery products are more elaborate than those for horticultural products. This can be attributed to the ease with which fishery products are subject to spoilage.

For COMESA countries, and developing countries in general, the fishery products requirements present a daunting challenge, given their fundamental lack of capacity both at institutional and private sector levels.[95] The lack of capacity may serve to confine third developing countries' exports to primary products whose hygiene and microbiological criteria may be less demanding compared to those

---

[92] Martin Doherty, 'The Importance of Sanitary and Phytosanitary Measures to Fisheries Negotiations in Economic Partnership Agreements' (International Centre for Trade and Sustainable Development (ICTSD), Issue Paper No. 7, February 2010) 8.
[93] Ibid 8.
[94] Humber Seafood Institute UK, 'UNIDO FVO Inspection Analysis (Fish)' (An unpublished study quoted in Doherty M (n 92) 8.
[95] Martin Doherty and others, 'Diagnostic Impact Study of the New European Regulation 882/2004, Official Feed and Food Controls and Recommendations, Final Report' (COLECAP, March 2005) 38.

for processed products. The requirements for aquaculture products and bivalve molluscs, such as clams and mussels, appear to be particularly onerous.

The requirements for chemical contaminants and veterinary residues entail laboratory infrastructure that is lacking in most developing countries. The main hurdle faced by these countries may be not that their fishery products are unsafe, but that they are unable to verify the safety of these products. These countries are only able to export fishery products to the EU by virtue of EU technical assistance in setting up the laboratory infrastructure.[96]

Of note is the fact that FVO inspections and reports, and the resultant enforcement measures have been found to be subjective and discriminatory. In a study commissioned by the EU,[97] it was found that there were discrepancies between the level of enforcement of EU food safety standards for fisheries in Thailand and the one in Seychelles and Mauritius, with Thailand being favoured.[98] Furthermore, in a follow-up study,[99] although an FVO inspection team found that the majority of the fishing vessels supplying tuna to Thailand from Singapore and Taiwan were not on the authorised list of the registered freezer vessels, it did not suspend Thailand from its list of authorised countries as it had done in the cases of Seychelles and Mauritius for similar infringements.[100]

4.3.3 The case of the EU–COMESA horticultural products trade

Like the fisheries trade, the EU–COMESA horticultural products trade is conducted under the duty- and quota-free regime of the Cotonou Agreement (and its successor the EPAs) and of the Everything But Arms (EBA) initiative.[101]

Besides the EU general food safety requirements, certain specific provisions are applicable to horticultural products.[102] Horticultural products have to meet

---

96 One important technical assistance programme is the 'Strengthening Fishery Products Health Conditions in ACP/OCT Countries'. See website <www.sfp-acp.eu/EN/index.htm> accessed 30 March 2015.
97 Liam Campling and Martin Doherty, 'A Comparative Analysis of Cost Structure and SPS Issues in Canned Tuna Production in Mauritius/The Seychelles and Thailand: Is there a Level Playing Field?' (The Project Management Unit, Regional Trade Facilitation Programme, 18 July 2007), <http://www.rtfp.org/media/esa_fisheries__level_playing_field_in_tuna_processing_english.pdf> accessed 30 March 2015.
98 Ibid 26–28.
99 Liam Campling and Martin Doherty, 'A Comparative Analysis of Cost Structure and SPS Issues in Canned Tuna Production in Mauritius/The Seychelles and Thailand' (Follow up Study', 31 October 2007), <www.fairpolitics.nl/ . . . /Campling_&Doherty_2007_Level_Playing_Field_in_Tuna_Processing_FINAL.doc> accessed 30 March 2015.
100 Ibid 18–19.
101 Agritrade, 'Executive brief: Fruit and vegetable: Trade issues for the ACP, 01 April 2010', <http://agritrade.cta.int/Agriculture/Commodities/Horticulture/Fruit-and-vegetable-Trade-issues-for-the-ACP> accessed 30 March 2015.
102 For analysis of the EU horticultural products import regulations, see United States Department of Agriculture Foreign Agricultural Services (USDA/FAS), 'EU Food and Agricultural

requirements in traceability,[103] hygiene criteria,[104] chemical contaminants,[105] and pesticides.[106]

There are eight main exporters of horticultural products from the COMESA to the EU: Egypt, Kenya, Ethiopia, Zimbabwe, Zambia, Madagascar, Uganda, and Swaziland.[107] The major concern for COMESA countries regarding EU food safety regulations are the EU maximum residue limits for pesticides (MRLs). Under Regulation 1107/2009 only authorised pesticides may be used for plant protection, while under Regulation 396/2005 very low levels of maximum residue levels for pesticides are allowed in the EU.

Since 2011, when Regulation 1107/2009 came into force, there have been increasing Rapid Alert System for Food and Feed (RASFF) notifications and border detentions of horticultural products with above MRLs for pesticides residues.[108] In 2013 there were 99 such detentions of African products.[109] The most affected COMESA countries were Egypt and Kenya with 32 and 23 notifications respectively, most of which concerned residues of the chemical Dimethoate. The incidents led to the loss of about 25 per cent of Kenya's horticultural exports to the EU.[110] Moreover, the EU warned Kenya and Uganda that it would take strict action against their horticultural imports unless they improved their compliance with the EU phytosanitary standards.[111]

Import Regulations and Standards' (FAIRS Country Report, GAIN Report No. E80065, 12/30/2013).

103 Regulation 178 of 2002, arts 11 and 18; Regulation 852/2004, Annex I, pt A, s III.
104 Regulation 852/2004, arts 1, 3, 4 and Annex IA and arts 4.2, 5 and Annex II.
105 Council Regulation 315/93 of 8 February 1993, Laying Down Community Procedures for Contaminants in Food, OJ L 37/1, 13.2.1993; Regulation 1881/2006, arts 1 and 8–9.
106 Regulation (EC) No. 1107/2009 of the European Parliament and of the Council of 21 October 2009 concerning the placing of plant protection products on the market and repealing Council Directives 79/117/EEC and 91/414/EEC, OJ L 309/1, 24.11.2009; European Commission, 'Question and Answers: Regulation (EC) No 1107/2009 concerning the placing of plant protection product on the market' (SANCO/12415/2013, Rev. 3, 24 March 2014); Regulation (EC) No 396/2005 of the European Parliament and of the Council of 23 February 2005 on Maximum Residue Levels of Pesticides in or on Food and Feed of Plant and Animal Origin and amending Council Directive 91/414/EEC, OJ L 70/1, 16.3.2005.
107 UNCTAD (n 11) 8, 17.
108 European Commission, 'Rapid Alert System for Food and Feed (RASFF), Annual Report 2013' (RASFF Annual Report, 2013) 17–18. For analysis see Olayinka I Kareem, 'The European Union Sanitary and Phytosanitary Measures and Africa's Exports' (EUI Working Paper No. RSCAS 2014/98, 2014).
109 RASFF Annual Report 2013, 18. The products were from Egypt, Morocco, Nigeria, and Kenya.
110 Agritrade, 'New EU Maximum Residue Levels hit Kenyan Vegetable Exports, 28 April 2013', <http://agritrade.cta.int/en/Agriculture/Commodities/Horticulture/New-EU-maximum-residue-levels-hit-Kenyan-vegetable-exports> accessed 30 March 2015.
111 Agritrade, 'Increased Interceptions of 'Harmful Organisms' Overhang Some ACP Horticultural Exports to the EU, 29 September 2014', <http://agritrade.cta.int/en/Agriculture/Topics/SPS-Food-safety/Increased-interceptions-of-harmful-organisms-overhang-some-ACP-horticultural-exports-to-the-EU> accessed 30 March 2015.

Furthermore, the EU has increased its food safety controls[112] and inspection rates,[113] while it has simultaneously sought to recover full inspection costs,[114] which translate into higher inspection charges.[115] This has the consequence of increasing overall compliance costs, particularly for small-scale producers.

In general, a notable characteristic of the EU system of horticultural food safety regulations is its complexity. The regulations entail a comprehensive technology and administrative system for their implementation. Furthermore, the regulations are premised on a developed economy, with sufficient capacity for their application. Hence developing countries may find it difficult to comply with them.

Although, in form, the traceability provisions do not apply beyond the boundaries of the EU,[116] nevertheless, in effect, they require the business operator cum importer to trace food products beyond the EU; hence, third country producers are compelled to prove traceability to the EU importer as a precondition of market access into the EU.[117] This is normally achieved through Private Voluntary Standards (PVS). The FVO inspectors also require third country exporters to maintain one-step-back and one-step-forward traceability records. As such, traceability entails complex record-keeping and constitutes an administrative burden, particularly to small producers in developing countries.[118]

The requirements for HACCP and microbiological criteria for processed foods are complicated and require investment in machinery and processes; the marginal costs of implementing HACCP may be higher in developing countries, which have fewer resources, than for developed countries. Moreover, the fixed costs of

---

112 Agritrade, 'EU Food Safety Controls Increased but Fewer Non-Compliant Products from Third Countries, 11 August 2014', <http://agritrade.cta.int/en/Agriculture/Topics/SPS-Food-safety/EU-food-safety-controls-increased-but-fewer-non-compliant-products-from-third-countries> accessed 30 March 2015.

113 Agritrade, 'EU Inspection Rates Modified for ACP Floriculture and Horticulture Imports, 08 September 2013', <http://agritrade.cta.int/en/Agriculture/Commodities/Horticulture/EU-inspection-rates-modified-for-ACP-floriculture-and-horticulture-imports> accessed 30 March 2015.

114 Agritrade News (2013), 'New EU Food and Feed Controls to Include Full Cost Recovery, 07 July 2013', <http://agritrade.cta.int/Agriculture/Topics/SPS-Food-safety/New-EU-food-and-feed-controls-to-include-full-cost-recovery>

115 Agritrade, 'UK Fresh Produce Inspection Charges Increased, 23 April 2012', <http://agritrade.cta.int/en/Agriculture/Topics/SPS-Food-safety/UK-fresh-produce-inspection-charges-increased> accessed 30 March 2015. According to Agritrade, 'The increase in fees and charges is part of efforts by UK inspection services to achieve full cost recovery, and will reportedly raise the costs of import checks by 73 per cent from 2012 to 2014, with significant increases in plant passport fees, plant health licensing and services'. According to the UK Fresh Produce Consortium (FPC), 'Many sectors of the industry will struggle to absorb these costs'.

116 Guidance document Regulation 178 of 2002, 10–11. The guidance document provides that the traceability provision shall not have extra-territorial application.

117 Andrew Graffham, 'EU Legal Requirements for Imports of Fruits and Vegetables (A Suppliers Guide)' (Fresh Insights No. 1, DFID/IIED/NRI, 2006) 5.

118 Agritrade, 'Executive Brief: Fruit and Vegetable: The EU Fruit-and-Vegetable Regime, February 2009', <http://agritrade.cta.int> accessed 30 March 2015.

implementing HACCP may be prohibitive for small firms, which has resulted in a concentration of large multinational food operators in the international food trade.[119] Furthermore, HACCP does not obviate other food safety standards, but merely complements them, and as such it is an additional requirement to be met by food exporters.[120] Ultimately, these complex requirements for processed foods may result in confining developing countries to their traditional role of exporting primary products.

The EU pesticide regulations are likely to force third countries' exporters of horticultural products to use limited and higher cost pesticides or be excluded from the EU market. According to research by the South Centre:

> Many of the active substances used in developing countries are outdated, out-of-patent, low cost chemicals for which the major chemical manufacturers do not consider it worthwhile to collate the data package required for registration and authorization. Agrochemical companies have been forced to selectively defend active substances in accordance with commercial interests, focusing on those used in 'major crops' exported to large markets. None of the tropical fruits or vegetables exported by developing countries to the EU are considered to be "major crops". This gives rise to concerns that insufficient alternative treatments will be available to growers in developing countries, who are likely to be forced to use a limited range of higher cost plant protection products (. . .).[121]

The following part will examine an aspect of EU food safety that, although it is not an integral part of EU food safety standards, has nevertheless had an important impact on EU–COMESA trade. These are the EU private voluntary standards (PVS).

EU importers, in order to meet the requirements of EU food safety regulations, in particular traceability and hygiene requirements, have made compliance with PVS a prerequisite for exporters to the EU. The legitimacy of the PVS is contested. Whereas PVS are said to be voluntary, in practice they are mandatory. The EU argues that since PVS are private and voluntary they are beyond the disciplines of the SPS Agreement and Members. However, given the impact of these standards on developing countries' exports, the central question is whether PVS should fall under the disciplines of the SPS Agreement and whether national governments should be held responsible for them.

---

119 Laurian J Unnevehr and Hellen H Jensen, 'The Economic Implications of Using HACCP as a Food Safety Regulatory Standard' (1999) 24 *Food Policy* 625, 632–633.
120 William H Sperber, 'HACCP Does Not Work from Farm to Table' (2005) 16 *Food Control* 511, 514.
121 Ellen Pay, 'Overview of the Sanitary and Phytosanitary Measures in Quad Countries on Tropical Fruits and Vegetables Imported from Developing Countries' (T.R.A.D.E. Research Papers, South Centre, November 2005) 33.

4.4 Private voluntary standards (PVS) and EU food safety standards

The food business operators in the EU are responsible for food safety within their businesses, and are responsible for compliance with the requirements of food law that apply to their operations.[122] Food retailers, in order to meet their regulatory food safety obligations,[123] among other reasons,[124] have formulated their own food safety standards, known as PVS.[125] The power in the food sector in developed and emerging economies has shifted from manufacturers and producers to retailers. This shift is mainly due to the increased retail market concentration in the EU and globally. This has resulted in the emergence of food retailers as standards setters in the food industry.[126] The increased market size, together with cross-border alliances, is associated with substantial buying

---

[122] Regulation 178 of 2002, Preamble, para 30 and arts 17–19. See also Guidance document Regulation 178 of 2002. The liability of food business operators flows from breach of specific national legal requirements and not from art 17(1). See, for example, art 21 of the UK Food Safety Act of 1990, No. 16 of 1990, that provides that it shall be a defence for the person charged with a food safety offence under the Act to prove that he or she took all reasonable precautions and exercised all due diligence to avoid the commission of the offence by himself or herself or by a person under his or her control. For analysis of the role of PVS in the EU food law regime, see generally Bernd J V D Meulen (ed), *Private Food Law: Governing Food Chains through Contract Law, Self-Regulation, Private Standards, Audits and Certification Schemes* (Wageningen Academic Publishers, Wageningen, The Netherlands, 2011).

[123] Linda Fulponi, 'Private Voluntary Standards in the Food System: The Perspective of Major Food Retailers in OECD Countries' (2006) 31 *Food Policy* 6. According to the author, the majority of retailers considered avoidance of legal liability as a major motivation for PVS.

[124] Spencer Henson and Timothy Reardon, 'Private Agri-Food Standards: Implications for Food Policy and the Agri-Food System' (2005) 30 *Food Policy* 241, 246. The authors note that private standards are also used to increase profits through facilitating product differentiation, and to reduce costs and risks in their supply chains. The main cost reduction comes from using process standards to co-ordinate procurement chains and systems.

[125] See generally: Clarke Renata, 'Private Food Safety Standards: Their Role in Food Safety Regulation and their Impact' (Paper presentation at the 33rd Session of the Codex Alimentarius Commission, 2010), <http://www.fao.org/food/food-safety-quality/> accessed 30 March 2015; FAO, 'Private Standards in the United States and European Union Markets for Fruit and Vegetables: Implications for Developing Countries' (Volume 3 of FAO commodity studies), <www.fao.org/3/a-a1245e.pdf> accessed 30 March 2015. For analysis of PVS in the EU see Lawrence Busch, 'Quasi-States? The Unexpected Rise of Private Food Law' in B J V D Meulen (ed) *Private Food Law: Governing Food Chains Through Contract Law, Self-Regulation, Private Standards, Audits and Certification Schemes* (Wageningen Academic Publishers, Wageningen, The Netherlands, 2011) 51–73. See also European Commission, 'Commission Communication-EU Best Practice Guidelines for Voluntary Certification Schemes for Agricultural Products and Foodstuffs' (2010/C 341/04), O J C 341/5, 16.12.2010), <http://eur-lex.europa.eu/legal-content/EN/TXT/PDF/?uri=C ELEX:52010XC1216(02)&from=en>

[126] Nicolas Canivet, *Food Safety Certification* (FAO, Rome, 2006) 8.

power, including the ability to impose product requirements and standards on suppliers.[127]

Although PVS are said to be voluntary,[128] they are mandatory in practice since they are a requirement set by the retailers, who are the main importers of food into the EU.[129] According to the WTO Secretariat:

> Where a small number of food retailers account for a high proportion of food sales, the options for suppliers who do not participate in either an individual or collective retailer standard scheme can be considerably reduced. Furthermore, the retailer scheme may be de facto applied as the industry norm by all actors in the supply chain. Thus the choice of whether or not to comply with a voluntary standard becomes a choice between compliance or exit from the market (. . .). [130]

PVS tend to be more complex and stringent than public mandatory standards, since their scope goes beyond food safety and encompasses social economic attributes, such as animal welfare and environmental and labour conditions of

---

127 Linda Fulponi and Adeline B. Borot, 'Final Report on Private Standards and the Shaping of the Agro-Food System' (OECD, AGR/CA/APM (2006) 9/FINAL, 31-Jul-2006) 11–12. The authors estimate the increased market concentration of big retailers in OECD countries at between 60 per cent and 70 per cent of the market share. See also Julius J Okello, Clare Narrod and Devesh Roy, 'Food Safety Requirements in African Green Bean Exports and Their Impact on Small Farmers' (IFPRI Discussion Paper No. 00737, December 2007) 8. The authors term the dominance of the retailers as a 'buyer driven supply chain', which is governed by the needs of importers and retailers. This is contrasted with a 'producer driven supply chain', where the producer makes the decision on what, when, and how to produce; Jacques Trienekens and Peter Zuurbier, 'Quality and Safety Standards in the Food Industry Developments and Challenges' (2008) 113 *International Journal of Production Economics* 107, 112. According to the authors, the major aims of PVS are to improve supplier standards and consistency, and avoid product failure; to eliminate multiple audits of food suppliers/manufacturers through certification of their processes; to support consumer and retailer objectives by 'translating' these demands through the chain; and to provide concise information to assist with a due diligence defence in case of food incidents.

128 Linda Fulponi, 'Private Standard Schemes and Developing Country Access to Global Value Chains: Challenges and Opportunities Emerging from Four Case Studies' (OECD, AGR/CA/APM (2006) 20, 27 Sep 2006) 3–4. According to the author, PVS are set by retailers and coalitions of retailers (contrasted with public mandatory standards set by governments) and relate to product and process attributes. Compliance with standards is verified by third-party certification. Producers that cannot meet these standards are denied market access. The author further attributes the rise in PVS to competition among retailers; strategies to reduce in-house monitoring and inspection costs; and the globalisation of product sourcing.

129 Marinus Huige, 'Private Retail Standards and the Law of the World Trade Organisation' in Bernd J V D Meulen (ed) *Private Food Law: Governing Food Chains Through Contract Law, Self-Regulation, Private Standards, Audits and Certification Schemes* (Wageningen Academic Publishers, Wageningen, The Netherlands, 2011) 175, 177–178.

130 WTO Committee on Sanitary and Phytosanitary Measures, 'Private Standards and the SPS Agreement, Note by the Secretariat' (G/SPS/GEN/746, 24 January 2007) 3–4.

Case studies in EU–COMESA trade 153

production.[131] Furthermore, while EU food safety regulations for food of non-animal origin require 'equivalence of risk-outcome', PVS, in addition, require 'equivalence of systems'.[132] Hence, as a precondition for market access, a producer is required to meet the end product criteria of EU food safety regulations in addition to meeting the strict process criteria of PVS.[133]

PVS can be categorised into individual firm schemes, collective national schemes, and collective international schemes.[134] They can be further categorised into pre- and post-farm gate standards.[135]

The main PVS applied in COMESA–EU trade are the Global Good Agricultural Practices (GlobalGAP) standard, for pre-farm gate requirements, and the British Retail Consortium Global Standard for Food Safety (BRC) standard, for post-farm gate processing.[136]

---

131 Grace C H Lee, 'Private Food Standards and their Impacts on Developing Countries' (European Commission DG Trade Unit G2, 2006) 6. Moreover, as a precautionary measure, many retailers have extended their list of food safety requirements, including possible allergens, food contaminants, and handling and processing procedures in order to insure themselves against probable legal liability.
132 Ibid. For products of non-animal origin, EU regulations specify the characteristics of the finished product, and producers and importers are responsible for ensuring that these requirements are met. PVS, by contrast, set requirements for the entire system of production and supply, with specific instructions on production methodologies and testing procedures.
133 COLEACP, 'Private Voluntary Standards' (PIP Magazine, Issue No. 12, November 2007) 3. The magazine notes that compliance with both public and private standards in necessary in 'order to do business' with the EU.
134 For analysis of PVS categories see Bernd J V D Meulen, 'The Anatomy of Private Food Law' in Bernd J V D Meulen (ed) *Private Food Law: Governing Food Chains Through Contract Law, Self-Regulation, Private Standards, Audits and Certification Schemes* (Wageningen Academic Publishers, Wageningen, The Netherlands, 2011) 75. See also WTO (n 130) 2. Individual firm schemes are presented to the market in the form of labels that identify products as having superior characteristics to products sold by competitors – for example, Tesco supermarket's Natures Choice. Collective national schemes originate from within specific national boundaries, although they may be applicable internationally – for example, British Retail Consortium Global Standard (BRC). Collective international schemes are created and promoted from more than country and are also applicable internationally – for example, GlobalGAP.
135 Lee G C H (n 131) 10. Pre-farm gate standards cater to primary production – for example, GlobalGAP – while post-farm gate standards cater for processing requirements, – for example, BRC Global Standard.
136 Hoffmann U and Vossenaar R (eds) (n 11) 26. According to the authors, GlobalGAP is the most important private standard for GAP, while for packing/handling it is the BRC Global Standard. See also WTO Committee on Sanitary and Phytosanitary Measures, 'Private Sector Standards and Developing Country Exports of Fresh Fruit and Vegetables: Communication from the United Nations Conference on Trade and Development (UNCTAD)' (G/SPS/GEN/761, 26 February 2007) 4. According to UNCTAD, 'The EurepGAP standard seems especially relevant for many Latin American countries (such as Brazil which exports some 85 per cent of its total FFV exports, excluding nuts, to the EU market) and Africa. Conversely, South-East Asian countries export their FFV largely to regional markets, shipping only a small portion to the EU market. Therefore, the direct implications of

4.4.1 An example of a pre-farm gate PVS: The GlobalGAP standard

The Global Good Agricultural Practices (GlobalGAP) standard, formerly known as EUREPGAP,[137] was developed by a consortium of 13 retailers, mostly from the United Kingdom (UK), known as the Euro-Retailer Produce Working Group (EUREP), in 1997. It originally focused on fruits and vegetables,[138] but has since expanded to cover other products. GlobalGAP is a pre-farm gate food production quality and safety management system, which is also a business-to-business label that is not available to consumers. It provides tools for verifying good agricultural practices in a systematic and consistent way. This is done through the use of normative documents that cover general regulations, control points, and compliance criteria, and a checklist. These are applied to food safety, environmental sustainability, and worker health and safety at the farm level.[139]

The GlobalGAP standard certification is subject to a scheduled annual audit,[140] and the standard itself is subject to a triennial reviews, with the current protocol being the third version, which was launched in 2007.[141] However, GlobalGAP does not require the implementation of a HACCP system as recommended by the Codex Code of Practice on General Principles of Food Hygiene, though it requires risk assessment of inputs and at different identified stages, accompanied with the implementation of corresponding control procedures.[142]

EurepGAP requirements are likely to be less urgent for South-East Asia than for the other regions'; Anne S Poisot, 'Implementing National GAP Programmes: Key Considerations for Developing Countries' (Presentation at the FAO-UNCTAD Regional Workshop on GAP in Eastern and Southern Africa: Practices and Policies, Nairobi, Kenya, 6-9 March 2007), <www.unctad.org/trade_env/meeting.asp?MeetingID=217> accessed 15 May 2015.

137 The change of name was announced at the 8th EurepGAP Conference held in Bangkok on 6-7 September 2007.

138 John Humphrey, 'Private Standards, Small Farmers and Donor Policy: EUREPGAP in Kenya' (IDS Working Paper No. 308, July 2008) 30-31. The author notes that Global-GAP has incorporated producers and processors among its members.

139 GlobalGAP website <www.globalgap.org> accessed 30 May 2015.

140 Graffham A Karehu E and MacGregor J (n 28). For certification, a producer is required to comply with a certain number of control points. Compliance can be 'major', 'minor', or 'recommended'. A fruits and vegetable producer must comply with all the applicable major control points (if an obligation is not applicable to the producer, it must be justified) and with 95 per cent of the applicable minor control points. The audits are carried out by accredited third party auditors, who operate according to ISO 65.

141 Anne Tallontire and others, 'Governance and Agency in the Global Horticulture Chain: the Case of GlobalGAP' (Presentation at the 12th EADI General Conference: Global Governance for Sustainable Development, Geneva, 24-28 June 2008) 7. GlobalGAP version 3 is an integrated farm assurance standard composed of a core standard, with modules for different product groups: fruits and vegetables, cattle and sheep, combinable crops, dairy, flowers and ornamentals, pigs, green coffee, poultry, tea, and salmon.

142 Canivet N (n 126) 34.

Case studies in EU–COMESA trade   155

There are four options for certification under GlobalGAP:[143] individual farmer certification as option one; farmers' group certification as option two;[144] individual farmer certification under a GlobalGAP benchmarked scheme as the third option; and farmers' group certification under a GlobalGAP benchmarked scheme as option four.[145]

4.4.2 An example of post-farm gate PVS: The BRC standard

The British Retail Consortium Global Standard for Food Safety (BRC standard)[146] is a post-farm gate, business-to-business, food safety, and quality management standard based on HACCP and designed for manufacturers of all types of food products, such as canned and ready-to-eat meals and also primary products which have undergone simple processing such as boxing, packaging, washing, or trimming. The British Retail Consortium (BRC), a UK trade association representing the retail sector, developed the standard in 1998 as a one-stop criterion for food safety and quality for UK retailers and suppliers that met the requirements of EU regulations and of the UK Food Safety Act (No. 16 of 1990).

---

143 Margaret Will and Doris Guenther, 'Food Quality and Safety Standards as Required by EU Law and Private Industry: A Practitioners' Reference Book' (GTZ, Division 45, 2007) 106–115.
144 Option 1 is suitable for large scale commercial farmers who are able to demonstrate compliance with all the control points and hence meet certification requirements. Small-scale farmers, due to inadequate technical and financial resources, opt for option 2, where they can pool resources and be certified as a group. In COMESA, as at 2007, there were six countries with GlobalGAP certification; of the 606 certified farmers in Kenya, 31 were under option 1, while 575 were under option 2; in Zambia, of the 13 certified farmers, 4 were under option 1, while 9 were under option 2; in Ethiopia, all 8 certified farmers were under option 1; in Zimbabwe, all 7 certified farmers were under option 1; in Madagascar, the single certified farmer was under option 1; and in Egypt, of the 248 certified farmers, 120 were under option 1, while 128 were under option 2. See Hoffmann U and Vossenaar R (eds) (n 11) 29–30.
145 Benchmarking confers equivalence to GlobalGAP. For an analysis of GlobalGAP benchmarking, see Nigel Garbutt and Elme Coetzer, *Options for the Development of National/ Sub-regional Codes of Good Agricultural Practice for Horticultural Products Benchmarked to EurepGAP 2005* <www.unctad.org/trade_env/test1/meetings/eurepgap/EurepGAP_benchmarking_UNCTAD_November-NG.pdf> accessed 30 May 2015. For analysis of a benchmarking experience in COMESA, see Nigel Garbutt, 'Food Quality Schemes in the International Context: KenyaGAP Experiences and Lessons Learnt' (PowerPoint presentation at the Food Quality Certification Workshop, Brussels, 5–6 February 2007), <www.globalgap.org> accessed 30 May 2015. For analysis of a benchmarking experience in Latin America, see Ulrich Hoffmann and Renee Vossenaar (eds), *The Implications of Private-Sector Standards for Good Agricultural Practices: Exploring Options to Facilitate Market Access for Developing-Country Exporters of Fruit and Vegetables – Experiences of Argentina, Brazil and Costa Rica* (UNCTAD/DITC/TED/2007/2, 2008) 55–58.
146 BRC Website <www.brc.org> accessed 30 May 2015.

The BRC standard does not apply to wholesale, importation, distribution, and storage activities.[147] It requires the development of and compliance with a senior management commitment, in terms of resources needed to demonstrate commitment towards achieving the requirements of the standard; a HACCP plan, focusing on the significant product and process food safety hazards that require specific control; a quality management system that provides a framework by which the organisation will achieve the standard's requirements; and basic environmental and operational conditions that ensure production of safe food in accordance with good manufacturing practices and good hygienic practices.[148]

The BRC standard is geared towards meeting EU regulatory requirements. Hence, although Article 18 of Regulation 178 of 2002 identifies the requirement for traceability, and Article 5 of Regulation 852/2004 sets out the requirement for HACCP, neither regulation specifies how these requirements are to be met. The BRC standard verifies the existence and effectiveness of traceability and HACCP.[149]

The BRC standard generally complies with the Codex Alimentarius Code of Practice on General Principles of Food Hygiene, but has requirements that go beyond the Codex Code, such as those concerning quality control and food safety good practices.[150]

The next section will analyse the legal status of PVS in the WTO, and whether PVS are subject to the disciplines of the SPS Agreement.

---

147 Fulponi L and Battisti B A (n 106) 41. Suppliers are required to undergo certification by BRC accredited auditors. A BRC standard audit consists of a review of the suppliers' HACCP and Quality Management system plans, a factory or site inspection, check back of audit trails and further verification and document checks, and final overall evaluation.
148 BRC, 'Global Standard for Food Safety Issue 5: Summary (2008)'. According to the standard, there are fundamental requirements for certification, in default of which certification is withdrawn from an establishment. These are senior management commitment and improvement; HACCP food safety plan; corrective and preventive action; traceability; layout, production flow, and segregation; housekeeping and hygiene; handling requirements for special materials; control of operations; and training.
149 Lee G C H (n 131) 22–23. According to the author, the BRC standard meets and, on some requirements, exceeds EU regulatory requirements. For example, the BRC standard is seen to exceed EU regulations in its requirements for product control, factory environment standards, quality management system, and process control. Furthermore, although the EU regulations may not require quality management systems, these may ultimately ensure compliance with the regulations. The BRC standard may be contrasted with the GlobalGAP standard, which seeks to attain compliance with both the EU regulations and exporting country's regulations. GlobalGAP would normally refer to EU regulations where they exist, and even provide guidance on them when they are too broad. However, since the EU regulations on products of non-animal origin are based on equivalence of risk outcome, while GlobalGAP is a process certification, the two systems may be seen as complimentary.
150 Canivet N (n 126) 22. The author gives examples of quality control issues, which include handling of non-conforming products, management of the monitoring system, traceability, and management of allergens and quantity control, as well as an example of food safety good practices as the maintenance of external areas.

4.4.3 PVS and the SPS Agreement

It has yet to be determined by the WTO whether PVS are SPS standards within the scope of the SPS Agreement.[151] The issue of PVS has been an agenda item in the SPS Committee several times since 2005. Saint Vincent and the Grenadines was the first country to raise a concern regarding PVS, without any resolution. Generally, the developing countries have been concerned about the stringency and implementation costs of PVS and have argued for the disciplines of the SPS Agreement to be applied to PVS. The developed countries, in particular the EU, have taken the position that PVS, being private standards, cannot be disciplined under the SPS Agreement. The developed countries and UNCTAD have also advocated more transparency on the part of the PVS bodies and capacity-building for developing countries to meet these standards.[152]

4.4.3.1 The definition and application of an SPS standard

Arguably, the problem with confining PVS within the scope of the SPS Agreement is the fact that they encompass much more than SPS issues, and cover areas such as environmental requirements, animal welfare conditions, and labour standards. Some aspects of PVS may thus be beyond the scope of the SPS Agreement, and may fall under the scopes of other WTO Agreements, such as the TBT Agreement (for instance, in the provisions on labelling and packaging).

Although the SPS Agreement, in defining its scope under Article 1 and its application under Annex A (1) (a), does not distinguish between governmental and private standards, the Agreement is stated, under Article 2, to apply to Members, which are governments. Further, the SPS Agreement, at Annex A paragraph 1, defines SPS measures to include 'all relevant laws, decrees, regulations,

---

151 For a discussion, see Joan J Scott, *The WTO Agreement on Sanitary and Phytosanitary Measures: A Commentary* (Oxford University Press, 2007) 302–306. See also Denise Prevost, 'Private Sector Food-Safety Standards and the SPS Agreement: Challenges and Possibilities' (2008) 33 *South African Yearbook of International Law* 1.

152 For the discussion on PVS in the WTO SPS Committee, see WTO Committee on Sanitary and Phytosanitary Measures, 'Summary of the Meeting Held on 29–30 June 2005, Note by the Secretariat, Revision' (G/SPS/R/37/Rev.1, 18 August 2005) 6–7; WTO Committee on Sanitary and Phytosanitary Measures, 'Summary of the Meeting of 28 February – 1 March 2007, Note by the Secretariat' (G/SPS/R/44, 30 May 2007) 9–13; Joint UNCTAD/WTO Informal Information Session on Private Standards on 25 June 2007 <www.wto.org/english/tratop_e/sps_e/private_standards_june07_e/private_standards_june07_e.htm> accessed 30 MAY 2015; WTO Committee on Sanitary and Phytosanitary Measures, 'Summary of the Meeting of 18–19 October 2007, Note by the Secretariat' (G/SPS/R/46, 2 January 2008) 26–30; News on ad hoc working group on food safety and animal and plant health, Work on Private Food Safety and Health Standards, 26 February 2009, <www.wto.org/english/news_e/news09_e/sps_25feb09_e.htm> accessed 30 May 2015; WTO Committee on Sanitary and Phytosanitary Measures, 'Summary of the Meeting of 30–31 March 2011, Note by the Secretariat' (G/SPS/R/62, 27 May 2011).

requirements and procedures'. These are normally understood to be governments' policy implementing instruments, not private entities' instruments.

In *EC – Biotech*,[153] the Panel found that an SPS measure consists of three elements: the purpose of the measure, its legal form, and its nature.[154] Hence, for a measure to qualify as an SPS measure, it should be for any one of the enumerated purposes of Annex A (1) (a) to (d) of the SPS Agreement; it should be in the form of a law, decree, or regulation; and its nature should be that of a requirement and procedure (including end product criteria; processes and production methods; and testing, inspection, certification, and approval procedures), in accordance with the provisions of Annex A (1) of the SPS Agreement.

However, the Panels in *US – Poultry (China)*[155] and *Australia – Apples*,[156] while affirming the *EC – Biotech* Panel finding on the centrality of the 'purpose' criterion,[157] differed with it on the distinction of 'form' and 'nature' and instead interpreted the list in the last paragraph of Annex A (1) as an enumeration of five items that exemplify the type of instruments which may include SPS measures.[158]

This understanding of what constitutes an SPS measure is buttressed by the interpretation of government actions vis-à-vis private actions in *Japan – Film*,[159] where the Panel held:

> As the WTO Agreement is an international agreement, in respect of which only national governments and separate customs territories are directly subject to obligations, it follows by implication that the term measure in Article XXIII: 1(b) and Article 26.1 of the DSU, as elsewhere in the WTO Agreement, refers only to policies or actions of governments, not those of private parties.[160]

Thus, for a private action to fall under the ambit of the WTO Agreement there should at least be some governmental connection to, or endorsement of, such an action. Moreover, under the United Nations Draft Articles on Responsibility of States for Internationally Wrongful Acts, a state may only be held liable for actions of persons who are acting on its instructions, or under its direction or control.[161]

---

153 Panel Report European, *Communities – Measures Affecting the Approval and Marketing of Biotech Products*, adopted on 29 September 2006, (WT/DS291/R, WT/DS292/R, WT/DS293/R) (Panel Report, *EC – Biotech*).
154 Panel Report, *EC – Biotech*, para 7.149.
155 Panel Report, *United States – Certain Measures Affecting Imports of Poultry from China*, WT/DS392/R, adopted 25 October 2010, (Panel Report, *US – Poultry (China)*).
156 Panel Report, *Australia – Measures Affecting the Importation of Apples from New Zealand*, WT/DS367/R, adopted, as modified by the Appellate Body, on 17 December 2010 (Panel Report, *Australia – Apples*).
157 Panel Report, *US – Poultry (China)*, para 7.98; Panel Report, *Australia – Apples*, para 7.118.
158 Panel Report, *US – Poultry (China)*, para 7.100; Panel Report, *Australia – Apples*, para 7.150.
159 Panel Report, *Japan – Measures Affecting Consumer Photographic Film and Paper*, WT/DS44/R, 31 March 1998 (*Panel Report – Japan-Film*).
160 Panel Report, *Japan – Film*, para 10.52.
161 'Draft Articles on the Responsibility of States for Internationally Wrongful Acts with Commentaries' *2 International Law Commission Year Book Pt. 2 (2001)*, adopted in UN General

4.4.3.2 The scope of 'non-governmental entities'

Article 13 of the SPS Agreement provides for non-governmental entities thus: 'Members shall take such reasonable measures as may be available to them to ensure that non-governmental entities within their territories, as well as regional bodies in which relevant entities within their territories are members, comply with the relevant provisions of this Agreement (. . .)'. Article 13 may be construed as being hortatory. One possibility of implementing the Article would be to regulate the PVS setting bodies. However, this may not be viewed as reasonable or practicable, given the international operations of these bodies and the fact that their standards are voluntary and only apply among their members. Moreover, there is no definition of 'non-governmental entity' in the SPS Agreement. The question is whether 'non-governmental entity' may be construed to include the PVS-setting bodies so as to bring them under the disciplines of the SPS Agreement.

Under general public international law, state responsibility for wrongful actions of private entities arises in two instances: when it is carried out 'on the instructions of, or under the direction or control of, a state'; or for conduct that would not otherwise be attributable to a state, 'if and to the extent that the State acknowledges and adopts the conduct in question as its own'.[162] Accordingly, an act of a private entity is ascribed to the state if it was carried out under the instructions, direction, or control of the state, or where the state acknowledges and adopts such an act.

Article 4.1 of the TBT Agreement, which is akin to Article 13 of the SPS Agreement, provides for 'non-governmental standardizing bodies' rather than 'non-governmental entities'. Annex 1 paragraph 8, of the TBT Agreement defines 'non-governmental body' as a 'body other than a central government body or local government body, including a non-governmental body which has legal power to enforce a technical regulation'. It would appear, therefore, that one aspect of a non-governmental body is one to which legal powers of enforcement have been delegated. The TBT Agreement expressly provides for non-governmental bodies, such as the International Standardization Organization (ISO) and the International Electro-technical Commission (IEC), under Annexes 1 and 3, whereby it adopts the definitions and codes of good practice of these institutions. However, the SPS Agreement, under Annex A (3), only provides for inter-governmental standardizing bodies: the Codex, the OIE, and the IPPC. It follows, therefore, that whereas the role of private non-governmental entities was contemplated and provided for under the TBT Agreement, there was no such intention or provision under the SPS Agreement. Furthermore, the TBT Agreement, under Articles 3 and 8, provides disciplines in the preparation, adoption,

---

Assembly, 'Resolution 56/83, Responsibility of States for internationally wrongful acts, Annex, UN Doc. A/RES/56/83 (28 January 2002) (Draft Articles on the Responsibility of States for Internationally Wrongful Acts) Article 8. See also Antonio Cassese, *International Law* (2nd edn, Oxford University Press, 2005) 243–245.

162 Draft Articles on the Responsibility of States for Internationally Wrongful Acts, arts 8 and 11.

and application of standards and conformity assessment by non-governmental bodies. The SPS Agreement makes no such provisions.

Article 1.1(a) (1) (iv) of the WTO Agreement on Subsidies and Countervailing Measures (SCM Agreement) delineates further criteria for a non-governmental entity as follows:

> A government makes payments to a funding mechanism, or entrusts or directs a private body to carry out one or more of the type of functions (. . .) which would normally be vested in the government and the practice, in no real sense, differs from practices normally followed by governments.

Hence, private entities 'entrusted' or 'directed' by governments to carry out functions, such as subsidies, which are normally carried out by governments, fall under the disciplines of the WTO Agreements. At the bottom of this attribution is the hand of government in such entities through entrustment and direction. The Appellate Body in *US – Countervailing Duties on DRAMS*[163] further clarified the terms 'entrusted' and 'directed' thus:

> Pursuant to paragraph (iv), 'entrustment' occurs where a government gives responsibility to a private body, and 'direction' refers to situations where the government exercises its authority over a private body. In both instances, the government uses a private body as proxy (. . .).[164]

Hence, it is only in instances where a government delegates its authority to a private entity, or where a government has control over a private entity, that the actions of such entities attract the disciplines of the WTO Agreements. However, and to the contrary, PVS are set by private entities, without any government intervention, and the standards set are not legally enforceable and only complied with voluntarily.[165] Therefore, although the entities that formulate the Global-GAP and BRC standards, among other PVS, are non-governmental entities, they have not been entrusted with government authority, and they cannot therefore be brought under the disciplines of the SPS Agreement.[166] Moreover, the requirement

---

163 Appellate Body Report, *United States – Countervailing Duty Investigation on Dynamic Random Access Memory Semiconductors (DRAMS) from Korea*, WT/DS296/AB/R, 20 July 2005 (*Appellate Body Report, US – Countervailing Duties on DRAMS*).
164 Appellate Body Report, *US – Countervailing Duties on DRAMS*, para 116.
165 Ignacio Carreno and Paolo R Vergano, 'Private Voluntary Standards within the WTO Multilateral Framework' (Report submitted by the United Kingdom to the Committee on Sanitary and Phytosanitary Measures, G/SPS/GEN/802, 9 October 2007) 48, 68. According to the authors: 'It may be argued that only private entities which have been entrusted by government with the performance of certain tasks or which have otherwise a special legal status fall under the definition of non-governmental entity under the SPS Agreement'.
166 For further discussion on the relation of PVS with the SPS Agreement, see: Jan Bohanes and Lain Sandford, 'The (Untapped) Potential of WTO Rules to Discipline Private Trade-Restrictive Conduct' (Working Paper No. 56/08, Proceedings of SIEL Inaugural

for governments to take 'reasonable measures' to ensure compliance by non-governmental entities is hortatory, not mandatory, and does not provide for its implementation, and may therefore be unenforceable.

Furthermore, the SPS Committee has decided on five actions concerning PVS: to develop a working definition of private standards related to SPS, and to limit any discussions to these; for the SPS Committee, the Codex, and the OIE to inform each other regularly about their work involving PVS; for the WTO Secretariat to inform the SPS Committee of relevant developments in other WTO councils and committees; for Member states to help relevant private sector bodies in their countries that are setting standards related to SPS to understand the issues raised in the SPS Committee and the importance of the international standards of the Codex, the OIE, and the IPPC; and for the SPS Committee to explore cooperation with the Codex, the OIE, and the IPPC in developing information material underlining the importance of international SPS standards.[167] Of note is the fact that none of these five actions mandate the SPS Committee to engage with PVS as trade concerns.[168] Consequently, although PVS are set by organisations within the EU for the purposes, in part, of meeting the requirements of EU regulations, the EU may not be held liable for them.[169] Furthermore, the EU may not be able to regulate PVS because they are mainly voluntary, business-to-business standards that, in most cases, complement public regulations.[170]

Hence the dilemma of PVS is that while they play a central role in the international trade of food and agricultural products, particularly in the EU, they are not subject to the disciplines of the SPS Agreement and other international SPS standards.

Conference, Geneva, 15–17 July 2008); Spencer Henson, 'Can the WTO Deal with Private Food Safety Standards?' (Presentation made at the Workshop on Private Agri-Food Standards and a Sustainable Future for African Agriculture, London, 27–28 March 2008).

167 WTO Committee on Sanitary and Phytosanitary Measures, 'Actions Regarding SPS-Related Private Standards, Decision of the Committee' (G/SPS/55, 6 April 2011). See also, OIE, 'Resolution No. 26: Roles of Public and Private Standards in Animal Health and Animal Welfare' (Adopted by the World Assembly of Delegates of the OIE on 27 May 2010).

168 For an analysis of the functions of the SPS Committee, see Scott J (n 151) 48. See also, Andrew Lang and Joan J Scott, 'The Hidden World of WTO Governance' (2009) 20 *European Journal of International Law* 575, 590–601.

169 Lee G C H (n 131) 35. According to the author, PVS regulate commercial contracts between two voluntary parties in a free market, often reflecting consumer demands, and the EU cannot force supermarkets or retailers not to demand such standards.

170 According to the EU: 'Even if these standards, in certain cases, exceeded the requirements of EC SPS standards, the EC could not object to them as they did not conflict with EC legislation (. . .)'. See WTO Committee on Sanitary and Phytosanitary Measures, 'Summary of the Meeting Held on 29–30 June 2005, Note by the Secretariat, Revision' (G/SPS/R/37/Rev.1, 18 August 2005) 6.

4.4.4 PVS and COMESA countries

COMESA countries view compliance with PVS as conferring certain benefits, such as access to the global value chain that is essential for commercial exports to developed countries; improved efficiency in operations by reduced costs through better use of chemicals, organisation of tasks, and increased information on proper use and storage of pesticides to improve worker safety; increased information on proper use and storage of chemicals to decrease negative effects; and improved worker safety through proper attire for chemical use as well as through changes in storage procedures and separation of different tasks.[171] In enabling access to global markets, and the EU market in particular, PVS are perceived to be trade-creating.

However, PVS also pose challenges for COMESA countries. The main challenges relate to compliance costs associated with attaining compliance and verification and other fees related to system management; governance in the standards-making process, which is dominated by developed countries at the risk of not taking account of COMESA countries' interests in the process; information asymmetries resulting from lack of transparency in the standards-setting process and also lack of impact assessments of the standards; and lack of compliance capacity by some COMESA countries in terms of lack of management and organisational skills. Moreover, compliance with one importer's standards makes it costly and difficult to switch to another importer with different standards, as it would entail additional compliance costs and requirements.[172]

In general, developing countries have also challenged the legitimacy of PVS. According to one developing country:

> The proliferation of standards developed by private interest groups without any reference to the SPS Agreement or consultation with national authorities is a matter of concern and presents numerous challenges to small vulnerable economies. These standards are perceived as being in conflict with the letter and spirit of the SPS Agreement, veritable barriers to trade (which the very SPS Agreement discourages) and having the potential to cause confusion, inequity and lack of transparency.[173]

Among the trade concerns raised by developing countries in response to a survey by the WTO Secretariat concerning PVS are that the standards exceed

---

171 WTO Committee on Sanitary and Phytosanitary Measures, 'Private Voluntary Standards and Developing Country Market Access: Preliminary Results, Communication from OECD' (G/SPS/GEN/763, 27 February 2007) 4.
172 Jan Wouters, Axel Marx and Nicolas Hachez, 'Private Standards, Global Governance and Transatlantic Cooperation: The Case of Global Food Safety Governance' (2008) 11 *University of California Berkeley* 15–16.
173 WTO Committee on Sanitary and Phytosanitary Measures, 'Private Industry Standards, Communication from Saint Vincent and the Grenadines' (G/SPS/GEN/766, 28 February 2007).

national and international standards; some standards are not based on risk analysis, particularly the process standards; some standards go beyond food safety issues and encompass environmental, animal welfare, and labour standards; and the standards side-line small producers which are unable to meet the administrative requirements and compliance costs.[174]

The next part, the concluding part of the chapter, will discuss and draw conclusions from the chapter. In particular, the part will analyse the dilemma posed by food safety standards for COMESA countries. While, on the one hand, these countries lack basic SPS capacities, on the other hand, they are required to meet the most complex and stringent standards if they are to export their agricultural products to the EU.

4.5 Chapter discussion and conclusions

The impact of food safety standards in the EU–COMESA food trade is significant. Given the fact that COMESA countries enjoy preferential trade terms with the EU and, for LDCs, quota- and duty free-terms, food safety standards are the main determinants of the flow of COMESA agricultural products exports to the EU.

On the one hand, COMESA countries are beset by a number of challenges in meeting food safety standards. These countries have weak or non-existent SPS infrastructure; their SPS legislations are fragmented, scattered in various ministries, and outdated; and their food control systems are weak and disjointed. In sum, COMESA countries lack the capacity to meet basic food safety standards in their domestic markets and also in their export markets, mainly the EU.

On the other hand, the EU, which is COMESA's main exports market, poses an additional challenge to COMESA countries' exports. The EU food safety standards are not only stringent but are also, in some cases, stricter than international standards. COMESA countries' predicament is that on the one hand they are incapacitated to the extent of being incapable of compliance with international standards, while, on the other hand, they are required to meet stringent EU standards, which are, in some instances, stricter than international standards. This dilemma underlies the inability of many COMESA countries to export agricultural products to the EU and the challenges faced by those few that have managed to do so.

The EU food safety regulations are not only complex and stringent on their own account, but their implementation is also intricate and punitive for imports from developing countries. For exporters, particularly those from developing countries, navigating through these regulations is a daunting task. COMESA countries find this complex regulatory situation to be burdensome and difficult to comply with. These regulations may be impugned under Article 8 and Annex C

---

174 WTO Committee on Sanitary and Phytosanitary Measures, 'Effects of SPS-Related Private Standards – Compilation of Replies: Note by the Secretariat, Revision' (G/SPS/GEN/932/Rev. 1, 10 December 2009).

(1) (a) of the SPS Agreement (that provides for Control, inspection, and approval procedures to be undertaken and completed without undue delay and in no less favourable manner for imported products than for like domestic products).

The process of and criteria for approval and listing of third countries and their establishments for products of animal origin is lengthy, onerous, and punitive, so that few COMESA countries manage to be qualified and, among these, fewer still manage to carry out actual exports.

In the case of fishery products, most COMESA countries' fisheries competent authorities lack capacities to implement food safety control measures. Crucial food control infrastructure, such as laboratories and cold storage facilities, is lacking or inadequate. This has resulted in a high rate of rejections for COMESA countries' fishery exports, thus discouraging trade in these products.

In the case of beef products, the application and enforcement of the EU beef import regulations among EU Member states is subject to situational variations that gives rise to a degree of uncertainty and confusion among exporters. Moreover, the placing of responsibility for ensuring the integrity of food safety controls throughout the food chain upon the competent authorities creates onerous obligations that few COMESA countries are able to bear. As a result, only a few COMESA countries, and none of the LDCs, are able to export animal products to the EU, and even these few only manage to do so with the assistance of the EU.

The requirement for horticultural products exporting countries to have equivalent food control systems to those of the EU as a pre-requisite for exporting to the EU has restricted COMESA countries' exports to primary products; as opposed to processed products, which have more complex requirements. This is because most COMESA countries are unable to manage the equivalence criteria. Furthermore, the requirements for HACCP and microbiological criteria for processed foods are complicated and require investment in machinery and processes that are beyond the means of most COMESA countries. The pesticide regulations are also likely to force COMESA countries' exporters to use limited and higher costing pesticides.

The EU circumvents the disciplines of the SPS Agreement by relying on the application of PVS by EU importers for the effective implementation of its food safety regulations while at the same time disavowing liability for PVS.

Given the incapacities of COMESA countries, the burdensome nature of EU food safety regulations – especially the control inspection and approval procedures, including information requirements and procedures for sampling, testing, and certification – may be characterised as violating the spirit, if not the letter, of Article 8 and Annex C (1) (c) and (d) of the SPS Agreement (the provisions provide for limits on information requirements and the protection of the confidentiality of information). Although applied equally to both domestic as well as imported products, the practical effect of these regulations is that they disproportionately favour domestic products over products from developing countries.

The EU requirements for equivalence, which are process-based and not end product requirements, necessarily imply that third countries have to set up similar, if not the same, food safety control systems as the EU to be eligible to export to the EU. Furthermore, the practice of the FVO inspections reinforces these conditions by requiring similar, if not the same, food control systems in third countries as are to be found in the EU. Hence, in its regulations and their implementation, the EU seeks to eliminate differences in the food control systems of its food suppliers by equating these systems to its system, rather than seeing that the different systems meet its ALOP. These EU provisions and practices fail to meet the threshold of Article 4 of the SPS Agreement and are contrary to Section 4 (7) (d) of the Codex guidelines on equivalence, which provides: 'An importing country should recognise that sanitary measures different from its own may be capable of achieving its ALOP, and can therefore be found to be equivalent'.

On the other hand, COMESA countries' SPS regimes are weak and fall short of international standards. These regimes are incapable of meeting the scientific disciplines laid down in the SPS Agreement, particularly the requirement for risk analysis under Article 5. The regimes are also unable to meet the requirements for the elements of a food control system as laid down in the Codex guidelines on food control systems. Furthermore, COMESA countries' SPS regimes do not measure up to the SPS regimes of their trading partners, in particular the EU. They have to strive to achieve the food safety standards set by their export markets, especially the EU, in order to attain and maintain market access, the failure of which they stand to lose these markets.

Because of the divergence in food safety standards between COMESA countries and the EU (with the former having lower or non-existent standards, while the latter has high standards), the compliance costs are higher for COMESA countries compared to EU countries. Compliance costs are also higher for small producers compared to large producers. Therefore, compliance with the high EU food safety standards for COMESA food producers increases costs and limits their export competitiveness.

Three questions arise from the chapter discussions. First, can the COMESA countries diversify their exports into other international markets with less stringent food safety standards than the EU? Second, can the COMESA countries upgrade their food safety standards to international standards and, if denied market access, mount legal challenges against EU standards that are stricter than such standards? Third, can the COMESA countries increase their intra-COMESA trade, whose standards would be easier to meet since they all share in such standards?

The EU is COMESA's largest trading partner, for historical reasons.[175] An additional factor is the preferential trading arrangement between the EU and COMESA countries, under the Cotonou Agreement, the Economic Partnership Agreements (EPAs), and Everything But Arms (EBA) for LDCs. The preferential trading terms enhance COMESA countries' competitiveness in their exports to the EU vis-à-vis other developing countries without such preferences.

---

175 The COMESA countries are former colonies of European countries and have enjoyed preferential trading terms from their colonial days to date.

Compared to the EU, the United States (US) has relatively stricter food safety regulations in relation to horticultural products, while its food safety regulations on fishery products are less strict.[176] However, the US maintains quotas and does not have duty free access, even for the agricultural products of LDCs.[177] Similarly, Japan also maintains high tariffs and quotas for agricultural products, making African exports uncompetitive.[178] Other potential markets for COMESA countries' agricultural exports are mostly developing countries, such as India[179] and China,[180] which are also producers and exporters of agricultural products and are therefore competitors. Hence exporting to these alternative markets is neither competitive nor feasible.

An alternative solution for COMESA would be for COMESA countries to upgrade their food safety standards to international standards and, having done so, to legally challenge any denial of market access of its products by the EU. They may, as a first step, resort to requesting consultations under Article 4 of the Understanding on Rules and Procedures Governing the Settlement of Disputes, Annex 2 of the WTO Agreement (DSU) and could, depending on the circumstances, progress to requesting good offices, conciliation, and mediation under Article 4 of the DSU. The ultimate step is to request the establishment of a panel under Article 6 of the DSU. However, given the capacity constraints facing COMESA countries, this alternative can only be a long-term goal.

A second alternative solution would be to have COMESA countries to upgrade their food safety standards to international standards and to apply to the EU for a determination of equivalence. This would lead to further cooperation between the two parties that would be built on existing cooperation arrangements.

---

176 Linda R Horton and Elisabethann Wright, 'Reconciling Food Safety with Import Facilitation Objectives: Helping Developing Country Producers Meet U.S. and EU Food Requirements Through Transatlantic Cooperation' (International Food and Agricultural Trade Policy Council, IPC Position Paper – Standards Series, June 2008) 15.
177 International Food and Agricultural Trade Policy Council (IPC) and Partnership to Cut Hunger and Poverty in Africa, 'AGOA and Agriculture' (Joint Policy Brief, August 2009), <www.agritrade.org/Publications/documents/PCHPAIPC_JointPolicyBrief_Aug3.pdf> accessed 4 April 2015.
178 Lemessa Gashahun and Esmael Tilahun, 'Market Access for African Agricultural Exports: Assessment of the AoA and SPS Agreements' (Society of International Economic Law (SIEL), Second Biennial Global Conference, University of Barcelona, 8–10 July 2010). According to the authors, 44 per cent of African agricultural exports went to the EU while Japan and US shares were 4.4 per cent and 3.0 per cent respectively.
179 Ron Sandrey and Taku Fundira, 'South Africa and India: The Agricultural and Fisheries Trading Relationship' (Tralac Working Paper No. 3, 2008) 2. The authors find that India is a nominal importer of agricultural products, but is a net exporter.
180 Nelson Villoria, Thomas Hertel and Alejandro N Pratt, 'China's Growth and the Agricultural Exports of Southern Africa' (IFPRI Discussion Paper No. 00891, August 2009) 19. The authors conclude that the Southern Africa countries' agricultural exports to China are almost non-existent and that China's growth has not stimulated Southern Africa agricultural exports.

A third alternative solution would be to increase intra-COMESA trade. Since the COMESA countries are mostly producers and exporters of agricultural products, which are mainly primary commodities and horticultural products, and most of their imports are manufactured products, the potential for intra-COMESA trade is limited, owing to the lack of diversification of products and competitiveness vis-à-vis other international producers, such as the EU, India, and China. However, in order to realise the full potential of intra-COMESA trade, supply-side constraints and other non-tariff barriers also need to be addressed.[181]

---

181 Alemayehu Geda and Haile Kebret, 'Regional Economic Integration in Africa: A Review of Problems and Prospects with a Case Study of COMESA' (2007) 17 *Journal of African Economies* 357, 372–374. See also: UNCTAD, 'Economic Development in Africa Report 2013: Intra-African Trade: Unlocking Private Sector Dynamism' (UNCTAD/ALDC/AFRICA/2013, 2013) 51–57; Alberto P Perez and John S Wilson, 'Why Trade Facilitation Matters to Africa' (2009) 8 *World Trade Review* 379, 383–400; United Nations Economic Commission for Africa (UNECA), 'Assessing Regional Integration in Africa: Enhancing Intra-African Trade' (United Nations Publications, Addis Ababa, Ethiopia, 2010) 64–65; Onsando Osiemo, 'Last Frontier: Sanitary and Phytosanitary Standards and Technical Regulations as Non-Tariff Barriers in Intra-African Trade' (2015) 23 *African Journal of International and Comparative Law* 174.

5 Towards a model for co-operation in food safety standards in EU–COMESA trade

Sanitary and phytosanitary capacity-building constitutes an essential component of the Economic Partnership Agreements currently being negotiated between the European Union and a number of African countries and regions. The aim is to provide a sound, legal and regulatory framework that will allow the necessary capacity to be built in order to ensure African produce can gain access to European Union markets.[1]

Africa looks forward to joint programmes [with the EU] in the establishment of a food safety institution, a functional competent authority that is fully supported for border inspections, rapid alert and monitoring to strengthen our food control systems.[2]

Great powers are more likely to achieve regulatory coordination at their preferred level of standards. Their power affects the location of regulatory coordination in two ways. First, their market size can alter the incentives of actors such that their preferred outcome becomes the only equilibrium. Second, the threat of economic coercion can accelerate the lock-in effect of coordinating at the great power's ideal point.[3]

5.1 Introduction

Chapter 2 analysed the EU food safety regime, which was found to be stringent and non- negotiable. Chapter 3 analysed COMESA countries' food safety systems and found them to be weak or non-existent, and in any event non-compliant with EU and international standards. Chapter 4 analysed and highlighted COMESA

---

1 John Dalli, EU Commissioner for Health and Consumer Policy, Speech at a High-Level Conference on Better Training for Safer Food, 18 November 2010, Brussels, <http://ec.europa.eu/food/training_strategy/docs/1819112010_btfs_conf_speech_commissioner_jd.pdf> accessed 13 October 2015.
2 Rhoda P Tumusiime, Commissioner, Department for Rural Economy and Agriculture, African Union Commission, Speech at a High-Level Conference on Better Training for Safer Food, 18 November 2010, Brussels, <http://ec.europa.eu/food/training_strategy/docs/1819112010_btfs_conf_speech_commissioner_tumusiime.pdf> accessed 13 October 2015.
3 Daniel W Drezner, 'Globalization, Harmonization, and Competition: The Different Pathways to Policy Convergence' (2005) 12 *Journal of European Public Policy* 841, 849.

countries' concerns and challenges with the EU food safety standards. Most COMESA countries find it difficult – and for certain products, such as beef, impossible – to meet EU non-negotiable food safety standards. The main cause of these difficulties is the fact that, due their different levels of development, the two parties have different levels of standards: the EU has a high level of food safety standards which are not negotiable, while COMESA countries have low or non-existent standards. Hence it is difficult for COMESA countries to have equivalence and mutual recognition agreements on sanitary or phytosanitary matters, which serve to facilitate trade in agricultural products, with their main trading partner, the EU. This situation poses the question of how COMESA countries can establish and enhance their trade in food products under this standards divide.

As a first step, there is a need for the upgrading of national food safety control systems in COMESA countries to at least international standards, in order to meet internal[4] as well as external, mainly EU, food safety standards. The upgraded national food safety control systems, particularly when they are based on regional or international standards or on common regulatory objectives, may then be used as building blocks for a COMESA food control system.[5]

A COMESA food control system will in turn reinforce national food control systems. The regional system will do this by formulating and supervising regional best practices and by providing reference laboratories and capacity building for members.[6] Furthermore, a regional system will enable members to have a common position in international standards-setting organisations and therefore influence the formulation of international standards.

COMESA does not have a comprehensive SPS policy; neither does it have a food safety policy nor a food control system.[7] The COMESA Regulations on the

---

4 The Rome Declaration on World Food Security and the World Food Summit Plan of Action for the millennium development goals, 13–17 November 1996, Rome, Italy (The Rome Declaration), <www.fao.org/docrep/003/w3613e/w3613e00.htm> accessed 13 April 2015. The internal requirements are the need for food security: adequacy, which refers to quantity and sufficiency; nutritional quality; and food safety.
5 Mwamakamba L and others, 'Developing and Maintaining National Food Safety Control Systems: Experiences from the WHO African Region' (2012) 12 *African Journal of Food, Agriculture, Nutrition and Development* 6291.
6 Margaret Will, 'Harmonisation and Mutual Recognition of Regulations and Standards for Food Safety and Quality in Regional Economic Communities: The Case of the East African Community (EAC) and the Common Market for Eastern and Southern Africa (COMESA)' (Report for Deutsche Gesellschaft für Internationale Zusammenarbeit (GIZ), 2012) 76–94, <www.giz.de/Themen/en/SID-9AB3B99F-4F6F1263/dokumente/giz2012-Food-safety-and-quality-standards-and-regulations.pdf> accessed 13 April 2015. For further analysis see Enrique A Carroll, *Regional Approaches to Better Standards Systems* (World Bank Policy Research Working Paper No. 3948, Washington, DC, 2006). The author advocates for a gradual upgrading of national and regional standards to international standards.
7 COMESA appears to be pursuing its SPS issues under the umbrella of promoting agricultural marketing. Food safety is seen as a component of this wider strategy and not an independent issue. See COMESA Agricultural Marketing Promotion and Regional Integration

Application of Sanitary and Phytosanitary Measures (COMESA SPS Regulations)[8] do not specifically address food safety and neither do they provide for a food control system. However, the Regulations provide for some elements of food control, such as the Green Pass, under Article 7 of the Regulations, which will be a regional SPS certification system for food and agricultural products, allowing for free movement of these goods within COMESA; and, under Articles 15, 16, and 17 of the Regulations, which establish regional accreditation bodies, reference laboratories, and satellite laboratories. These provisions provide a basis for formulating a COMESA food safety control system.

As a solution to the COMESA countries' conundrum, this chapter proposes an SPS legal framework to be employed to facilitate trade in food and agricultural products between the EU and COMESA. It does this in three steps. First, it proposes the assessment and upgrading of COMESA countries' food safety control systems to international standards. Second, it proposes a legal framework for a COMESA food control system based on the COMESA SPS Regulations. A similar initiative is underway at the continental level under the African Union (AU). The AU has initiated a process for the creation of an African Food Safety Authority (AFSA); a Rapid Alert System for Food and Feed (RSFF); and an AU Food Safety Management Coordination System (AU-FSMCS).[9] Third, having established the COMESA food control system, it proposes a joint EU–COMESA food safety control system that would act as a bridge between the two systems and thus enhance trade.

The chapter proceeds as follows. Part two will first examine capacity building tools that may be applicable to COMESA countries. Foremost among these tools is the FAO capacity building needs assessment and a set of internationally accepted benchmarks for each of the food control system's elements. The needs assessment is a tailor-made exercise for each individual country to assess the current status of its food control system, the desired future for the system, and the capacity needed to achieve that desired future. The chapter proposes to apply the needs assessment tool following the 'hierarchy of trade-related SPS management functions', a tool developed by the World Bank that is used to prioritise capacity building needs. The needs assessment is followed by an examination of the three models for food control institutions as provided by the Food and Agricultural Organization of the United Nations (FAO) with a view to determining an ideal model for COMESA countries. Part three proposes a legal framework for a COMESA food control system based on the COMESA SPS Regulations together with its core elements of

---

Project (AMPRIP), <http://famis.comesa.int/index.php?option=articles&task=viewarticle&sid=4> accessed 13 April 2015.

8 COMESA Regulations on the Application of Sanitary and Phytosanitary Measures (COMESA Legal Notice No. 310 of 2009, Official Gazette, Vol. 15, No. 5, 8 December 2009).

9 See 'Proceedings and Presentations at the AU Continental Workshop on the establishment of Food Safety Authority at the AU; a Rapid Alert System for Food and Feed-RASFF; and a Food Safety Management Coordination Mechanism', 29–30 October 2012, Kigali, Rwanda <www.au-ibar.org/> accessed 13 April 2015.

regulatory framework and organisation structure. It also examines its basic functions of inspection, certification, and laboratory services. Part four will examine the legal basis of the proposed EU–COMESA food safety control system together with its core requirements. The part examines the SPS provisions in the EU-ACP countries EPAs with a view of extracting useful lessons towards the EU–COMESA food control system. Part five proposes a joint EU–COMESA food safety control system and its key structures and functions. The chapter concludes in part six with a discussion and the conclusions drawn from the chapter.

5.2 Tools for upgrading COMESA national food safety control systems

5.2.1 Capacity building needs assessment

As a preliminary step, the capacities[10] of COMESA national food control systems have to be assessed to determine the full extent of their weaknesses and their food safety capacity building needs.[11] Capacity building needs assessment is an important initial step in the upgrading of national food control systems because it identifies major systemic strengths and weaknesses and formulates strategies to address the shortcomings. The process is a step-by-step exercise, beginning with consultations and dialogue with stakeholders, including producers, consumers, and food processors, and culminating in a capacity building programme and activities addressing the components of the national food control system.[12]

---

10 Capacity is defined as the ability of individuals and organisations or organisational units to perform functions effectively, efficiently, and sustainably. See United Nations Development Programme (UNDP), 'Capacity Assessment and Development in a Systems and Strategic Management Context' (Technical Advisory Paper No. 3, January 1998, United Nations Development Programme (UNDP), New York) x.

11 Food safety and quality capacity has been defined as 'the ability of individuals, organisations and systems along the farm-to-table continuum to perform appropriate functions effectively, efficiently and sustainably in order to ensure the safety and quality of food for domestic consumption and export'. See United Nations Food and Agricultural Organization (FAO), *Strengthening National Food Control Systems: Guidelines to Assess Capacity Building Needs* (FAO, Rome, 2006) 5, <www.fao.org/righttofood/kc/downloads/vl/docs/AH433.pdf> accessed 13 April 2015.

The Guidelines further define capacity building as

> the process through which relevant stakeholders from farm to table (including government agencies, food enterprises and consumers) improve their abilities to perform their core roles and responsibilities, solve problems, define and achieve objectives, understand and address needs, and effectively work together in order to ensure the safety and quality of food for domestic consumption and export. Capacity building in food safety and quality therefore encompasses a continuous process of improvements that are specific to existing capability and identified needs.

12 FAO (n 11) gives detailed procedures on the conduct of the exercise of capacity building needs assessment for each of the core components of a food control system. Key requirements for the exercise are the tools and techniques used to carry out the exercise, such

A prerequisite for the exercise is technical assistance, in the form of expertise and funding.

According to FAO,[13] the capacity building needs assessment process involves a five steps procedure:

1. Seeking the support of key stakeholders and agreeing on the goals, objectives, and process to carry out the assessment; this leads to the establishment of terms of reference for the exercise.
2. A situation analysis, entailing a review of existing capacity and performance of the food control system.
3. The establishment of the desired goals and objectives of the exercise.
4. The identification and prioritisation of the capacity building needs.
5. The consideration of options to address identified needs and the development of a capacity building action plan.

The assessment includes a number of international benchmarks 'that provide a descriptive guide of what countries should aim to achieve in each of the core components of a national food control system'.[14] The FAO has additionally endeavoured to develop best practices in capacity building needs assessment through regional workshops, the outcomes of which could be used to develop individual country best practices.[15] For COMESA countries, capacity building needs assessments that have already been carried out in Kenya, Uganda, Tanzania, Rwanda, and Zambia serve to further illustrate the needs assessment

---

as focus group discussions; SWOT (strength, weaknesses, opportunities threats) analysis; regulatory impact assessment; and cost benefit analysis.

13 FAO, *Strengthening National Food Control Systems: A Quick Guide to Assess Capacity Building Needs* (FAO, Rome, 2007) 6, <ftp://ftp.fao.org/docrep/fao/010/a1142e/a1142e00.pdf> accessed 13 April 2015.

14 Ibid:

> By defining acceptable indicators and performance standards, the benchmarks will enable officials involved in the capacity building needs assessment process to: learn from internationally accepted good practices and broad guiding principles; pursue continuous improvements in policy making and service delivery; and improve efficiency and effectiveness within each of the components of a national food control system.

15 FAO, 'Report of FAO International Training Workshop on Assessing the Capacity Building Needs of National Food Control Systems, 28 November to 1 December 2006, Rome, January 2007', <ftp://ftp.fao.org/ag/agn/food/meetings/2006/fao_tot_workshop.pdf> accessed 13 April 2015; FAO, 'Report of FAO Sub-Regional Workshop for East Africa: Strengthening National Food Control Systems, 4–8 December 2006, Bagamoyo, Tanzania, <ftp://ftp.fao.org/ag/agn/food/meetings/2006/tanzania_ws_report.pdf> accessed 13 April 2015; FAO/STDF, 'Post Workshop Report: Strengthening Capability to Assess the Capacity Building Needs of Food Control Systems and Develop Capacity Building Action Plans in Developing APEC Member Economies, Beijing, China, from 19–23 November, 2007', <http://www.standardsfacility.org/files/Project_documents/Project_Grants/STDF_173_Post_workshop_report.pdf> accessed 13 April 2015.

process and also provide benchmarks for the exercise.[16] Furthermore, their terms of reference and the situation analysis – steps 1 and 2 – may be deemed to have been carried out in the FAO/WHO Regional Conference on Food Safety for Africa of 2005.[17] Regional representatives met and reviewed the existing capacity and performance of the regions' and national food control systems and documented these in the report. The Conference, in line with step 3 (formulation of goals and objectives), passed a resolution on a Five-Year Strategic Plan for Food Safety in Africa.[18]

---

16 Spencer Henson, 'Review of Case Studies and Evaluations of Sanitary and Phytosanitary Capacity: Kenya, Tanzania and Uganda' (Report presented at an STDF Aid for Trade workshop on 30 September 2007 in Dar es Salaam, Tanzania), <www.uneca.org/eca_programmes/trade_and_regional_integration/events/aidfortrade/docs/Synthesis-SPSevaluations%20_Henson.pdf> accessed 14 April 2015; WTO Committee on Sanitary and Phytosanitary Measures, 'Overview of SPS Needs and Assistance in Eight Least Developed Countries: Note by the Secretariat' (G/SPS/GEN/900, 4 February 2009); Mulat Abegaz, *Assessment of the Capacity of Food Safety and Quality in Zambia* (Working Paper Prepared for the World Bank, June 2006) 9, <http://siteresources.worldbank.org/INTRANETTRADE/Resources/Topics/Standards/Zambia_annexes.pdf> accessed 14 April 2015. For an overview of the needs assessment tools, see: Standards and Trade Development Facility (STDF), '*SPS-Related Capacity Evaluation Tools: An Overview of Tools Developed by International Organizations* (WTO, 2009), <www.standardsfacility.org/files/various/STDF_Capacity_Evaluation_Tools_Eng_.pdf> accessed 14 April 2015; WTO Committee on Sanitary and Phytosanitary Measures, 'Overview of SPS Capacity Evaluation Tools, Note by the Secretariat' (G/SPS/GEN/821, 18 February 2008); WTO Committee on Sanitary and Phytosanitary Measures, 'UNIDO SPS-Related Capacity Evaluation Tools – A Brief Overview, STDF Workshop on SPS Capacity Evaluation Tools, 31 March 2008' (G/SPS/GEN/826, 14 March 2008).
17 FAO/WHO, 'Final Report, Regional Conference on Food Safety for Africa, 3–6 October 2005, Harare, Zimbabwe', <www.fao.org/docrep/meeting/010/a0215e/a0215e00.htm> accessed 14 April 2015. See also, WHO, Regional Committee for Africa, 'Food Safety and Health: Situation Analysis and Perspectives, Report of the Regional Director, Fifty-third session, Johannesburg, South Africa, 1–5 September 2003' (AFR/RC53/12 Rev.1, 19 June 2003).
18 FAO/WHO (n 17) 134–144. The strategic plan consists of recommendations encapsulated into nine core elements: food safety policies and programmes; legislative and institutional aspects; standards and regulations; food inspection programmes and techniques; food analysis and food safety testing laboratories; monitoring food-borne diseases and the safety of foods on the market; participation in Codex; communication and stakeholder involvement (including industry officials and consumers); and national, regional, and international cooperation. Furthermore, the WHO regional committee for Africa recommended a Food Safety and Health: A Strategy for the WHO African Region, whose guiding principles and priority interventions would include 'country ownership and leadership; holistic and risk-based actions; inter-sectoral cooperation and collaboration; community participation; individual responsibility; and participation of women and communities; formulation and implementation of policies and regulations; capacity building in food borne disease surveillance and inspection; and health education'. See WHO, Regional Committee for Africa, 'Food Safety and Health: A Strategy for the WHO African Region, Report of the Regional Director, Fifty-Seventh session, Brazzaville, Republic of Congo, 27–31 August 2007' (AFR/RC57/4, 25 June 2007) 4–5.

5.2.2 The hierarchy of trade-related SPS management functions

Identifying and prioritizing capacity building needs, in line with step 4 of the FAO capacity building needs assessment process, may be a difficult task given the region's countries' numerous multiple deficiencies in their food control systems. One way of simplifying and thus illuminating the task is to cluster the food control system's functions in order of priority. This is best illustrated by the World Bank's Hierarchy of Trade-Related SPS Management Functions, which are in a four-tiered pyramid structure.[19]

At the base of the pyramid are the first-tier functions of awareness and recognition. These are the fundamentals of the food control system, without which it will not function. The awareness and recognition functions entail stakeholders – producers, processors, transporters, retailers, technocrats, regulators, and so on – to appreciate the importance and relevance of food safety and their role in the food control system in order for it to function.

A second-tier fundamental function is the application of risk management good practices at the primary production level. This arises from awareness and recognition functions and involves good agricultural practices (GAP), good manufacturing practices (GMP), and HACCP (with other related quality management systems, such as ISO 22000). These involve the practice of basic hygiene, proper usage and storage of pesticides, and good record keeping. Together with awareness and recognition, risk management good practices can effectively manage many potential SPS risks.[20]

Since not all SPS risks may be managed at the decentralised primary production level, a third-tier function – that of a regulatory framework and institutional structures – is placed at the centre of the pyramid. Proper regulations and institutional structures provide for oversight and collective action that entails basic research; surveillance systems; quarantine and emergency management systems; scientific testing; verification systems; technical skills; technical equipment; well-defined procedures; and recurrent funding.

The apex of the pyramid is dedicated to SPS diplomacy. SPS diplomacy involves the higher realms of food control systems: membership and participation in the WTO, Codex, etc.; multilateral and bilateral SPS relations; and regional SPS engagements on harmonisation, equivalence, etc. This function requires high levels of technical expertise, which is generally lacking among developing countries.

The functions at the bottom of the pyramid represent the basis for the system. The functions towards the top of the pyramid represent added value and improvements upon the foundation functions. Thus, the lower the function in the pyramid, the more important it is to the system. Consequently, capacity building will have the highest impact when directed at the lower functions and,

---

19 Steven Jaffee (ed), *Food Safety and Agricultural Health Standards: Challenges and Opportunities for Developing Country Exports* (World Bank Report No. 31207, Washington, DC) 129–133.
20 Ibid 129.

optimally, ought to be directed at the higher functions only after addressing the lower functions.[21]

From the World Bank's prioritisation model, the assessment of capacity building needs of COMESA countries should begin with the awareness and recognition function, followed by each of the other functions up the pyramid.

5.2.3 Discussion

The capacity building needs assessment and the prioritisation of the food control management exercises begin with an examination of a country's current food control status, followed by the identification of its desired future status. Between the current status and the desired future lies the gap or need that needs to be filled. Once the capacity building need is identified, the last stage is its prioritisation in accordance with the hierarchy of food management functions.

The upgrading of a national food control system is a multifaceted exercise. For a developing country, priority would lie with the awareness and recognition function: that is, stakeholders' awareness of the importance and relevance of food safety and their role in the system. Priority will then go up the pyramid depending upon a particular country's situation. The needs assessment exercise will also be dependent upon each country's situation analysis, with each country's objectives and goals being dependent on its institutional capacities. Hence, for one country, the end result of the exercise might be the adoption of a capacity building action plan, while for another country it might be a food safety compliance action plan, centred on one or several high risk or high-gain export-oriented products.

An important food control management function is that of the application of risk management good practices at the primary production level. This is a second tier function, after awareness and recognition, but together these two functions can effectively manage many potential food safety risks. Moreover, these two functions are cost effective as they do not require heavy capital investment. Hence, for developing countries, the export of primary products to developed countries can be accomplished cost effectively by the attainment of these two

---

21 Ibid. According to Jaffee, the output of priority setting can vary:

> In countries with a strong trade focus and relatively strong institutions dealing with SPS management, the product could be a National SPS Management Strategy and Action Plan, providing a comprehensive picture of the strengths and weaknesses of national food safety and agricultural health systems and laying out a subset of priority measures – policy and regulatory reforms, investments, and so on – to be undertaken, over the short (one year) to medium (three years) terms. In the less well developed economies, where institutional capacity is weaker or more fragmented, a more modest output in the form of an Industry or Supply Chain Standards Strategy or a Standards Compliance Action Plan would normally suffice. This Action Plan could center on one or several high risk/high gain export-oriented sub-sectors. Hybrid outputs could also be envisaged. These would combine one or more industry action plans with an analysis of priority actions in specific cross-cutting technical or administrative fields (i.e. WTO accession requirements, accreditation and certification systems, plant health risk management).

176   *Towards a model in EU–COMESA trade*

functions. Consequently, capacity building will have the highest impact for developing countries when directed at the lower functions and, optimally, ought to be directed at the higher functions only after addressing the lower functions.

The following part builds upon the foregoing tools and examines pathways to upgrading national food control systems through an analytical framework based on known benchmarks. The part will examine the basic requirements for the upgrading of the core elements of food control systems, in line with the World Bank's hierarchy of functions, as may be applicable to COMESA.

5.2.4   *An analytical framework for examining core elements of national food control systems*

From the foregoing capacity building needs assessment and the prioritisation of the food control management exercises, the question arises: What are the core elements of a food control system and how may these be prioritised for purposes of analysis and upgrading? This question will be answered by delineating key analytical categories from the foregoing analyses and by developing a common conceptual framework that may serve as a guideline for the upgrading of COMESA food control systems.

The analytical framework adopts, as its key analytical categories, the elements identified by the FAO, and accepted by its Members, as the building blocks of a national food control system: food law and regulations; food control management; inspection services; laboratory services; and information, education, and communication training.[22] Furthermore, these categories are analysed based on international benchmarks as provided for under the SPS Agreement, the Codex, the FAO, and the WHO, and as applied in the EU food control system. Moreover, the hierarchy of management functions is applied in order to prioritise the various management functions for purposes of analysis.

5.2.4.1   *Information, education, and communication (IEC)*

Information, education, and communication (IEC) may be defined as

> the process of developing, packaging and disseminating appropriate messages to specific audiences to increase their knowledge, skills and motivation to make decisions that enhance food safety and quality. IEC provides a means for the government agency(s) involved in food control management to engage in dialogue with diverse stakeholders along the food chain – including consumers and their organizations, the food industry, industry associations, grassroots organizations, etc. – about food safety and quality issues.[23]

---

22   FAO/WHO, *Assuring Food Safety and Quality: Guidelines for Strengthening National Food Control Systems* (Food and Nutrition Paper No. 76, FAO, Rome, 2003) 6–9.
23   FAO (n 11) 107. According to FAO, IEC may be applied to

> increase awareness and knowledge among consumers about ways they can enhance food safety and quality for themselves and their families; promote the adoption of good

IEC creates awareness and public participation and as such assists in the implementation of food policy.[24] This entails the provision of well-researched and packaged information and educational programmes for consumers, officials, and workers in the food industry; training of trainers' programmes; the provision of reference materials and manuals; and the training of inspectors and laboratory analysts.[25]

For COMESA countries, awareness and recognition of the significance of SPS matters, and food control in particular, are important for public health,[26] food security,[27] and trade in food.[28] Informing and educating the general public and the consumer about food safety will strengthen the culture of food hygiene and good food handling. The current situation, where food safety standards are only emphasised for export products and not for domestic trade,[29] renders the SPS capacities of developing countries unsustainable as they are limited to the export sectors, and not domestic markets. Food hygiene and good food handling education needs to be established for the domestic market also for developing countries' SPS capacities sustainability. Additionally, public officials need education and training on SPS and food safety in order to enable them to develop informed policies and also to provide for the budget to implement food safety policies.[30] Educating and training public health officials, laboratory technicians, food inspectors, and other technical personnel is equally important.

5.2.4.1.1 BENCHMARKS FOR IEC

The EU policy and regulations on consumer information policy are a practical benchmark for national IEC policies.[31] These EU provisions require public consultations with all stakeholders during the preparation, evaluation, and revision of

---

agricultural, manufacturing, hygiene and handling practices (including HACCP) by the food industry; and obtain information from different stakeholders (including consumers and their organizations and the food industry) that can be used to support decision-making processes, planning and implementation of official food control management activities.

24 Jessica Vapnek and Melvin Spreij, *Perspectives and Guidelines on Food Legislation, with a new Model Food Law* (FAO Legislative Study No. 87, FAO, Rome, 2005) 118. According to the authors:

Professional groups as well as the general public can benefit from activities designed to promote awareness and increase knowledge of food control and food safety issues in the country. For the former group, conferences, workshops and publications are useful avenues to explore; for the latter, the media, fact sheets, posters, videos, rural radio and educational programmes in school can enhance awareness of food safety and consumer issues among the public.

25 FAO/WHO (n 22) 9.
26 WHO (n 18) 2.
27 The Rome Declaration (n 4).
28 Countries have market access for safe food only.
29 Henson S (n 16).
30 In particular, the politicians need to be well informed on the importance of SPS matters to the national economy so that they can formulate policies and enact legislation that enhances SPS systems.
31 European Commission, 'White Paper on Food Safety, Brussels, 12 January 2000' (COM (1999) 719 final) 31–33; Regulation 178 of 2002, arts 8, 9, 10, 38, 41 and 50.

food law. The provisions guarantee communication of risk management decisions, input from the public on the scientific processes, and dissemination of opinions of the scientific committees of the EFSA. Furthermore, the provision for a Rapid Alert System for notification of direct or indirect risks to human health deriving from food or feed is a critical component of a modern food control system.

Under Regulation 22 of the COMESA SPS Regulations,[32] COMESA Members are enjoined to consult the public and private sectors on SPS issues. There is no provision for an institution or forum where such consultations are formalised. However, there is a Web-based COMESA food and agricultural marketing information system that provides information on COMESA SPS Regulations, animal disease status, a plant disease and pest list, and food safety status and important food safety threats.[33] Additionally, the African Union Interafrican Bureau for Animal Resources (AU-IBAR) provides SPS information to national SPS contact points.[34] There is no provision for a Rapid Alert System in the COMESA SPS Regulations. However, a referential guide on a Rapid Alert System for Food and Feed has been developed by the African Organization for Standardization (ARSO).[35]

According to the FAO, there are 10 benchmarks for IEC.[36] First, the food control agency has a policy for IEC-related to food safety and quality targeting external audiences such as consumers, consumer organisations, the food industry, professional associations, etc. Second, there is a programme for planning, developing, and implementing IEC activities in a coordinated manner. Third, there are accessible IEC materials, preferably in local languages. Fourth, the food control agency has an adequate number of trained staff with appropriate IEC skills. Fifth, there is access to appropriate equipment, such as computers, printers, mobile education units, audio-visual equipment, and financial resources. Sixth, the staff of the food control agency actively pursues IEC with external stakeholders, including the mass media. Seventh, there is involvement of relevant groups, such as agricultural extension officers; local communities; public health workers; the food industry; and social, religious, and academic institutions, in IEC activities. Eighth, there is regular collection of data and information about consumer behaviour, attitudes, concerns, and dietary patterns. Ninth, there exists a system for risk communication, particularly during food emergencies. Tenth, there is a system to evaluate the performance and impact of IEC materials and

---

32 Regulations on the Application of Sanitary and Phytosanitary Measures, COMESA Legal Notice No. 310 of 2009, Official Gazette, Vol. 15, No. 5, 8 December 2009 (COMESA SPS Regulations).
33 COMESA Food and Agricultural Marketing System <http://famis.comesa.int/> accessed 15 May 2015.
34 African Union Interafrican Bureau for Animal Resources (AU-IBAR) <www.au-ibar.org/> accessed 15 May 2015.
35 African organization for standardization (ARSO) <www.arso-oran.org/> accessed 15 May 2015.
36 FAO (n 11) 112.

programmes. However, these benchmarks may only be applicable to COMESA once a food safety agency is formed and subject to adaptation to the socioeconomic environment of COMESA.

5.2.4.2 Food control management: Good practices for hygiene and safety

Food control management is defined as

> the continuous process of planning, organizing, monitoring, coordinating and communicating, in an integrated way, a broad range of risk-based decisions and actions to ensure the safety and quality of domestically produced, imported and exported food for national consumers and export markets as appropriate. Food control management covers the various policy and operational responsibilities of competent government authorities responsible for food control. These include the development and implementation of food control policies, strategies and plans that reflect the government's commitment to food safety and quality and provide a sound framework for food control activities.[37]

Some of the activities of food control management are mandatory, such as policy formulation and enactment of regulations. However, other activities involve the promotion of voluntary codes and guidelines of good practices (GPs) in agriculture (GAP), hygiene (GHP), and manufacturing (GMP), including HACCP.

As a second-tier function in the pyramid of priorities, good practices at the primary production stage have a huge potential to effectively manage risks, and thus impact positively on the food management system. GAPs reflect national development priorities and agronomic conditions, promote the production of safe and healthy foods, improve workers' health and safety, and reduce environmental impacts. Furthermore, GAPs assist farmers and exporters in meeting the regulatory and private-sector requirements of domestic and international markets, and as such are used to secure access to markets.[38] The challenges faced by farmers in implementing GAPs include little base knowledge of GAPs; lack of financial independence; subsistence living; poor rural infrastructures; variable access to irrigation; poor record-keeping skills; difficulty of access to unadulterated inputs, such as seeds; poor quality of irrigation water; and lack of proper advice on appropriate use and application of agrochemicals.[39]

---

37 FAO (n 11) 18.
38 WTO Committee on Sanitary and Phytosanitary Measures, 'Private Sector Standards and Developing Country Exports of Fresh Fruit and Vegetables: Communication from the United Nations Conference on Trade and Development (UNCTAD)' (G/SPS/GEN/761, 26 February 2007) 6.
39 Nigel Garbutt and Elme Coetzer, *Options for the Development of National/Sub-Regional Codes of Good Agricultural Practice for Horticultural Products Benchmarked to EUREPGAP* (Consultation Draft, September 2005) 26, <www.unctad.org/trade_env/test1/

For COMESA countries, the main challenge of GAPs is not their practice per se, but their benchmarking process by the private standards bodies. The benchmarking process for GAPs is complex and burdensome. The requirements for record keeping, traceability, storage of chemicals, and hygiene practices involve complex processes and documentation that need the farmer to be literate and disciplined to a degree that is not common in developing countries. Furthermore, certification involves costs: the initial set-up capital costs and recurrent costs, in addition to audit costs, in order to confirm compliance.

Moreover, different export markets may involve different certification processes, adding to the complexity and costs. COMESA countries, given their poverty, illiteracy levels, and their small farming methods, are challenged by the requirements of GAPs. Hence, in practice, GAPs are mainly applied to farming that is geared towards exports, but not to locally traded produce. Furthermore, even in export farming, the small farmers are reliant on the large multinational farming companies and international donors to assist them in implementing GAPs.[40] As such, for most small farmers, GAPs may not be sustainable in the long term.

5.2.4.2.1 BENCHMARKS FOR GOOD PRACTICES FOR HYGIENE AND SAFETY

The requirements for good practices for hygiene and safety would include the following: first, clarity in market demand and support – i.e., target markets and key actors; second, established stakeholder coordination mechanisms, such as a steering committee or task force; third, a concerted and clear strategy, such as interfacing different objectives and capacities of actors; fourth, appropriate standards and documentation that are adapted to national circumstances and legal requirements; fifth, reliable inspection, certification, and laboratory services that are to be established or strengthened; and sixth, supportive infrastructure and capacity building, such as farm infrastructure, training, and service providers.[41] GAPs schemes are either owned by the private sector or governments. As a result there is no internationally accepted GAP.[42]

---

meetings/eurepgap/EurepGAP_benchmarking_UNCTAD_November-NG.pdf> accessed 15 May 2015.

40 Ulrich Hoffmann and Renee Vossenaar (eds), *Private-Sector Standards and National Schemes for Good Agricultural Practices: Implications for Exports of Fresh Fruit and Vegetables from Sub-Saharan AfricaExperiences of Ghana, Kenya, and Uganda* (UNCTAD/DITC/TED/2007/13, Geneva, 2008). This may be a factor in the declining numbers of small scale farmers involved in contract farming for the export market.

41 Anne S Poisot, 'Implementing National GAP Programmes: Key Considerations for Developing Countries' (Presentation at the FAO-UNCTAD Regional Workshop on GAP in Eastern and Southern Africa: Practices and Policies, Nairobi, Kenya, 6–9 March 2007), <www.unctad.org/trade_env/meeting.asp?MeetingID=217> accessed 15 May 2015.

42 Despite its dominance and prevalence, GlobalGAP is as yet to be recognised as a GAP benchmark. However, FAO is in the process of developing an international framework for GAPs. See FAO Committee on Agriculture, 'Development of a Framework

The benchmarking process may be time-consuming and might imply the need to introduce into existing national GAPs new requirements that may not be particularly relevant or appropriate to local conditions, which may create obstacles to small growers. Moreover, GAPs look to the equivalence of process, while the SPS Agreement looks to the equivalence of outcomes.[43] As a consequence, there is no internationally accepted benchmark for GAPs. However, there are internationally accepted national GAPs, developed in Chile, Brazil, Argentina, Kenya, and Malaysia, among others,[44] which may be looked at for benchmarks.

5.2.4.3 Food inspection and certification

Food inspection is defined by the Codex as 'the examination of food or systems for control of food, raw materials, processing and distribution, including in-process and finished product testing, in order to verify that they conform to requirements'.[45] The inspection and certification is carried out by accredited agencies.[46] The Codex has further defined certification as 'the procedure by which official certification bodies and officially recognised bodies provide written or equivalent

---

    for Good Agricultural Practices, Seventeenth Session Rome, 31 March–4 April 2003' (COAG/2003/6, March 2003), <ftp://ftp.fao.org/docrep/fao/meeting/006/y8704e.pdf> accessed 15 May 2015.
    FAO is developing a set of 10 component groups of generic indicators and practices of GAP. These include aspects related to soil and water management; crop and fodder production; crop protection; animal production and health; harvesting and on-farm processing and storage; on-farm energy and waste management; human welfare, health, and safety; and wildlife and landscape. See also the 'FAO Good Agricultural Practices' website <www.fao.org/prods/GAP/index_en.htm> accessed 15 May 2015.
43 Grace C H Lee, *Private Food Standards and Their Impacts on Developing Countries* (European Commission DG Trade Unit G2, 2006) 6, <http://tradeinfo.cec.eu.int/doclib/docs/2006/march/tradoc_127969.pdf> accessed 15 May 2015. This interpretation of equivalence of GAPs is considered to be necessary if buyers are to have confidence in the comparability of different standards. See also Garbutt N and Coetzer E (n 39) 11.
44 See, for example, UNCTAD, *Food Safety and Environmental Requirements in Export Markets: Friend or Foe for Producers of Fruit and Vegetables in Asian Developing Countries?* (UNCTAD/DITC/TED/2006/8, Geneva, 2007); UNCTAD, *The Implications of Private-Sector Standards for Good Agricultural Practices: Exploring Options to Facilitate Market Access for Developing-Country Exporters of Fruit and Vegetables – Experiences of Argentina, Brazil and Costa Rica* (UNCTAD/DITC/TED/2007/2, Geneva, 2007); UNCTAD, *Report of the Expert Meeting on Enabling Small Commodity Producers and Processors in Developing Countries to Reach Global Markets* (TD/B/COM.1/EM.32/3, Geneva, 2007); UNCTAD, *Challenges and Opportunities Arising from Private Standards on Food Safety and Environment for Exporters of Fresh Fruit and Vegetables in Asia: Experiences of Malaysia, Thailand and Viet Nam* (UNCTAD/DITC/TED/2007/6, Geneva, 2008), <www.unctad.org/trade_env/projectCTF.asp> accessed 15 May 2015.
45 Codex, 'Guidelines for the Design, Operation, Assessment and Accreditation of Food Import and Export Inspection and Certification Systems' (CAC/GL 26–1997).
46 Ibid. Accreditation is the procedure by which a government agency having jurisdiction formally recognises the competence of an inspection and/or certification body to provide inspection and certification services.

assurance that foods or food control systems conform to requirements'.[47] Food inspection is an essential service for the implementation of the food control system.[48] Depending on the food control system, inspection services may be centralised or spread over various ministries and agencies.

COMESA lacks a competent authority capable of carrying out inspections on production facilities and food products and providing official certification of compliance with food safety requirements. COMESA countries' food control systems are weak and lack inspection capacity. This has resulted in food inspection activities being concentrated on export products, to the detriment of products destined for national markets. A starting point would be the establishment of national food control systems, followed by the establishment of a centralised food control system at the regional level. This would be followed by the setting of harmonised standards and the setting up of inspection services.

5.2.4.3.1 BENCHMARKS FOR INSPECTION AND CERTIFICATION

The benchmarks for inspection and certification may not be applicable to the existing situation in COMESA. A major weakness, in terms of inspection and certification, is the lack of a database of food premises that categorises premises according to risk and also includes food inspection records so as to enable inspection and certification. However, the benchmarks may be applicable, to a limited extent, to the existing exports certification services.

There are 15 FAO benchmarks for food inspection and certification services.[49] First is the existence of documented policies and procedures for risk-based inspection, including sampling of domestically produced, imported, and exported food. Second is the existence of a national database of food premises that categorises them according to risk and includes food inspection records. Third is a system for the collection, reporting, and analysis of information related to food inspection.

---

47 Ibid. Certification of food may be, as appropriate, based on a range of inspection activities, which may include continuous on-line inspection, auditing of quality assurance systems, and examination of finished products.

48 FAO/WHO (n 22) 7–8. Some of the responsibilities of inspection involves are

> inspecting premises and processes for compliance with hygienic and other requirements of standards and regulations; evaluating HACCP plans and their implementation; sampling food during harvest, processing, storage, transport, or sale to establish compliance, to contribute data for risk assessments and to identify offenders; recognizing different forms of food decomposition by organoleptic assessment; identifying food which is unfit for human consumption; or food which is otherwise deceptively sold to the consumer; and taking the necessary remedial action; recognizing, collecting and transmitting evidence when breaches of law occur, and appearing in court to assist prosecution; encouraging voluntary compliance in particular by means of quality assurance procedures; carrying out inspection, sampling and certification of food for import/export inspection purposes when so required; in establishments working under safety assurance programmes such as HACCP, conduct risk based audits.

49 FAO (n 11) 72.

Fourth is the planning, implementation, and monitoring of food inspection activities based on high, medium, and low risk criteria. Fifth is an adequate number of officers authorised to carry out work outlined in food legislation. Sixth, food inspectors have suitable qualifications, training, and experience, consistent with their authorisation under food legislation. Seventh is access to adequate resources, facilities, equipment, and supplies for food inspection. Eighth, reliable transportation and communication systems ensure delivery of inspection services and transmission of samples to laboratories. The ninth benchmark is consistency, fairness, and honesty in the implementation of food inspection. Tenth, there are documented procedures for the collection and submission of food samples to official food control laboratories, the request for analysis, and reporting of results. Eleventh, there are documented procedures to respond to and manage food emergencies. Twelfth, there are documented procedures for the investigation and management of outbreaks of food-borne illnesses. Thirteenth, there are documented procedures to respond to consumer complaints. Fourteenth, there are documented procedures for food inspection as part of a quality management system. Fifteenth is a mechanism for review and evaluation of the food inspection system.

The EU Regulation 882/2004 on official controls performed to ensure the verification of compliance with feed and food law, and hence inspection and certification, provides practical benchmarks for best practices in the application of the FAO benchmarks on inspection and certification.[50] Further, and more comprehensively, benchmarks are provided by the Codex principles and guidelines.[51]

---

50 Regulation (EC) 882/2004 of the European Parliament and of the Council of 29 April 2004 on official controls performed to ensure the verification of compliance with feed and food law, animal health and animal welfare, [2004] OJ No L 191, 28.5.2004 (Regulation 882/2004); European Commission, 'Guidance Document: On Certain Key Questions Related to Import Requirements and the New Rules on Food Hygiene and on Official Food Controls' (SANCO/1446/2005 Rev. 2014 (PLSPV/2005/1446/1446R4-EN. doc); European Commission, 'Guidance Document: On Official Controls, Under Regulation (EC) No 882/2004, Concerning Microbiological Sampling and Testing of Foodstuffs' (Brussels, 13 November 2006), <http://ec.europa.eu/food/safety/official_controls/legislation/docs/sampling_testing_en.pdf>

51 Codex: Principles for Food Import and Export Inspection and Certification (CAC/GL 20–1995); Guidelines for the Design, Operation, Assessment and Accreditation of Food Import and Export Inspection and Certification Systems (CAC/GL 26–1997); Guidelines for Food Import Control Systems (CAC/GL 47–2003); Principles and Guidelines for the Exchange of Information in Food Safety Emergency Situations (CAC/GL 19–1995); Guidelines for the Exchange of Information between Countries on Rejections of Imported Foods (CAC/GL 25–1997); Guidelines for the Development of Equivalence Agreements Regarding Food Import and Export Inspection and Certification Systems (CAC/GL 34–1999); Guidelines on the Judgment of Equivalence of Sanitary Measures Associated with Food Inspection and Certification Systems (CAC/GL 53–2003); Guidelines for Design, Production, Issuance and Use of Generic Official Certificates (CAC/GL 38–2001); Principles for Traceability/Product Tracing as a Tool within a Food Inspection and Certification System (CAC/GL 60–2006).

5.2.4.4 Food control laboratory services

Food control laboratories are a necessary component of a food control system, particularly for the implementation and enforcement of food legislation. The laboratories perform tests on food samples for physical, chemical, and microbiological contamination in order to verify the safety and quality of food to enable the appropriate risk management actions. The number, location, and functions of laboratories are dependent upon the food control system, the volume of work to be carried out, and the resources available.[52] Moreover, the recording of microbiological contamination is important in the collection of epidemiological data, which is important in planning, implementing, and assessing food-borne disease control.[53]

Articles 15, 16, and 17 of the COMESA SPS Regulations provide for the establishment of regional accreditation bodies, reference laboratories, and satellite laboratories. The provisions on the establishment of COMESA reference and satellite laboratories are similar to Articles 32 and 33 of EU Regulation 882/2004, which establish EU and national reference laboratories. Moreover, three regional laboratories, in Zambia, Mauritius, and Kenya, have been designated as referral laboratories.[54] Under the COMESA Agricultural Marketing Promotion and Regional Integration Project (AMPRIP), COMESA has begun the establishment of the region's laboratories. AMPRIP rehabilitated 3 SPS reference and 12 national laboratories and procured laboratory equipment for 15 laboratories. The COMESA SPS technical committee has also been set up and procured SPS surveillance equipment for 15 countries.[55]

---

52 FAO/WHO (n 22) 8. Laboratories require considerable capital investment and maintenance costs.
53 Kabwit Nguz, 'Assessing Food Safety System in Sub-Saharan Countries: An Overview of Key Issues' (2007) 18 *Food Control* 131, 134.
54 COMESA, 'Victoria Declaration of the Fifth Meeting of the COMESA Ministers of Agriculture held in Victoria, Mahe, Seychelles, 14–15 March 2008' (Victoria Declaration) para 15, <http://famis.comesa.int/pdf//VICTORIA_Declaration_2008_English.pdf> accessed 15 May 2015.
   The COMESA agricultural ministers declared as follows:

   > In order to adequately address issues of SPS, three Regional Referral Laboratories be designated as follows: a. The Veterinary Laboratory at the Central Veterinary Research Institute in Lusaka, Zambia, for Animal Health; b. The Food Technology Laboratory of Mauritius for Food Safety; and c. The Plant Health Laboratory at the Kenya Plant Health Inspectorate Service (KEPHIS) Plant Quarantine Station in Nairobi, Kenya, for Plant Health.

   See also Science with Africa, 'COMESA establishes 3 laboratory centres' (e-Newsletter, Issue No. 7, February 2011, Lusaka), <www.uneca.org/sciencewithafrica/swa1/enewsletter/content_feb_2011/ScienceInAfrica.pdf> accessed 15 May 2015. The newsletter confirmed the setting up of the laboratories.
55 COMESA, 'COMESAS Agricultural Marketing Promotion and Regional Integration Project (AMPRIP)', <http://famis.comesa.int/index.php?option=articles&task=viewarticle&sid=4> accessed 15 May 2015.

5.2.4.4.1 BENCHMARKS FOR LABORATORY SERVICES

COMESA countries have at least one national accredited laboratory each, in addition to the three regional laboratories. Laboratory tests and certification are requirements for export products and are therefore essential for horticultural, beef, and fish exports. Within COMESA there is a paucity of accredited laboratories. These need to be increased. Furthermore, there is a lack of an accreditation service within COMESA: these services are sourced from South Africa or the EU. COMESA regional laboratories are better placed to pool resources such as personnel and equipment, and to gain accreditation for certification purposes.

The Codex has laid down five benchmarks for laboratory services.[56] The first is compliance with the general criteria for testing laboratories laid down in ISO/IEC Guide 17025, on general requirements for the competence of calibration and testing laboratories.

Second is participation in appropriate proficiency testing schemes for food analysis which conform to the requirements laid down in the International Harmonized Protocol for the Proficiency Testing of (Chemical) Analytical Laboratories.

Third, whenever available, there is use of methods of analysis which have been validated according to the principles laid down by the Codex.

Fourth is use of internal quality control procedures, such as those described in the Harmonized Guidelines for Internal Quality Control in Analytical Chemistry Laboratories.

Fifth, the bodies assessing the laboratories referred to above should comply with the general criteria for laboratory accreditation, such as those laid down in the ISO/IEC Guide 58:1993, on calibration and testing laboratory accreditation systems – general requirements for operation and recognition.

The FAO has elaborated on the five Codex benchmarks for laboratory services.[57] First, there should be an adequate number of suitably located food control laboratories to support the food control system with reference laboratories, such as for contaminants or food-borne disease organisms.

Second, there should be a documented procedure for the approval and accreditation of official food control laboratories according to international standards and a network of official food control laboratories, accredited to carry out specific analytical tests, and for appellate purposes as necessary. These laboratories are to be staffed with an adequate number of food analysts with suitable qualifications, training, experience, and integrity; management staff; and support staff.

Third, there should be official food control laboratories that have adequate infrastructure, facilities, equipment, supplies, and reference materials, and access to calibration and maintenance, and that have an operating quality assurance programme,

---

56 Codex Guidelines for the Assessment of the Competence of Testing Laboratories Involved in the Import and Export Control of Food (CAC/GL 27–1997).
57 FAO (n 11) 90. See also Kenneth L Rosebaum, 'Legislative Drafting Guide-A practitioner's view' (FAO Legal papers Online, No. 64, February 2007), <www.fao.org/legal/prs-ol/paper-e.htm> accessed 15 May 2015.

including participation in inter-laboratory proficiency testing with validated analytical methods wherever available and based on a manual of official analytical methods and Standard Operating Procedures.

Fourth, there should be effective linkages between official food control laboratories and the food control system, including food inspection, the public health system for food-borne disease surveillance, and any other relevant laboratories.

Of note is that the EU has adopted these benchmarks in its provisions for official laboratories.[58] These may therefore provide a tested practical approach to adopting these benchmarks for laboratory services.

5.2.4.5 Food legislation

Food legislation (or food law) is the complete body of legal texts (laws, regulations, and standards) that establish broad principles for food control in a country, and that governs all aspects of the production, handling, marketing, and trade of food as a means to protect consumers against unsafe food and fraudulent practices.[59]

Food legislation is not only limited to mandatory, legally enforceable laws. It also encompasses voluntary and preventive standards and schemes such as the GAPs, GMPs, and GHPs. The core elements of food legislation are the farm to table approach and its risk analysis base, which ensure the supply of safe food.

There is a low uptake of recommended modern food safety laws and policies by COMESA countries and developing countries generally.[60] This may be indicative of a lack of awareness and recognition of the important role of food control systems, and legislation, in the overall economy of countries, more particularly in countries' exports. It may also be a reflection of bureaucratic inertia, with current systems unwilling to change or forgo some of their powers. Equally, the slow pace of change could be a reflection of a clash of policy and legislative cultures, between the Western global models and African models mired in a mixture of models from their traditional past as well as from their recent colonial legacies. The costs of modernizing the legislation may not be much, but those of implementation could be substantial, and this fact could make governments, already financially strained, move slowly on food safety legislative reforms. With better education, information, and training on SPS matters, countries will begin to appreciate the importance of SPS legislation. These countries will also require technical assistance in the formulation and implementation of their SPS legislation.

---

58 Regulation 882/2004, art 12.
59 FAO (n 11) 39. For analysis, see Jessica Vapnek, 'Legislative Implementation of the Food Chain Approach' (2007) 40 *Vanderbilt Journal of Transnational Law* 987.
60 FAO/WHO Food Standards Programme, *FAO/WHO Coordinating Committee for Africa, Eighteenth Session: Submissions by Uganda and Malawi* (Accra, Ghana, 24–27 January 2009), <www.codexafrica.org/en/downloads.htm> accessed 16 May 2015. Most countries' food safety laws are outdated and not harmonised with the SPS Agreement's principles, nor Codex standards, and do not conform with any of the FAO model laws.

5.2.4.5.1 BENCHMARKS FOR FOOD LEGISLATION

According to the FAO/WHO,[61] food legislation should provide for a high level of health protection and accurate, clear definitions to increase consistency and legal security; be based on good quality, transparent, and independent scientific advice; include provision for the use of precaution and the adoption of provisional measures where an unacceptable level of risk to health has been identified and where full risk assessment could not be performed; include provisions for the right of consumers to have access to accurate and sufficient information; provide for tracing of food products and for their recall in case of problems; include clear provisions indicating that primary responsibility for food safety and quality rests with producers and processors; include an obligation to ensure that only safe and fairly presented food is placed on the market; recognise the country's international trade obligations; and ensure transparency in the development of food law and access to information.

Moreover, food legislation should remain basic and horizontal, leaving the details to regulations, rules, and schedules. This will make amendments and updates easier.

Good regulatory practices are necessary for the enactment of effective food legislation. The following are the common principles of Good Regulatory Practice. Good regulations should:

(a) serve clearly identified policy objectives and be effective in achieving those objectives;
(b) have a sound legal and empirical basis;
(c) produce benefits that justify costs, considering the distribution of effects across society and taking economic, environmental and social effects into account;
(d) minimise costs and market distortions;
(e) be clear, simple, and practical for users;
(f) be consistent with other regulations and policies;
(g) be transparent to both regulators and those affected by regulation;
(h) be based on international or national standards that are harmonised to international standards, except where legitimate reasons for deviations exist;
(i) reference only those parts of a standard that represent minimum requirements to fulfil the desired objectives;
(j) be least trade restrictive to achieve the desired objectives;
(k) be performance based rather than prescriptive;
(l) accord equal treatment to products of national origin and like products imported from Member states; and
(m) be subject to review to maintain flexibility and adaptability to changes.[62]

---

61 FAO/WHO (n 22) 6–7 and Annex (6) 54–57, for guidelines for developing a national food law.
62 OECD Reference Checklist for Regulatory Decision-Making; OECD Guiding Principles for Regulatory Quality and Performance. <www.oecd.org> accessed 16 May 2015.

These practices may provide benchmarks for food legislation. Good regulatory practices may be emulated from, for illustrative purposes, the practices of ASEAN,[63] the EU,[64] and the United Kingdom,[65] taking into account the different circumstances of developing countries, in particular COMESA countries. Regulatory Impact Assessment (RIA)[66] and Cost Benefit Analysis (CBA)[67] legislative tools may also be used to analyse current or potential legislation. These tools may be used to identify and quantify impacts of current and proposed legislation.[68]

---

63 ASEAN Good Regulatory Practice (GRP) Guide. <www.aseansec.org/> accessed 16 May 2015.
64 European Commission Better Regulation Home page. <http://ec.europa.eu/governance/better_regulation/index_en.htm> accessed 16 May 2015.
65 The Better Regulations Task Force, 'Principles of Better Regulation' (2003), <http://archive.cabinetoffice.gov.uk/brc/upload/assets/www.brc.gov.uk/principlesleaflet.pdf> accessed 16 May 2015.
66 Scott H Jacobs, 'An Overview of Regulatory Impact Analysis in OECD Countries' in Deighton R Smith and Scott H Jacobs (eds) *Regulatory Impact Analysis: Best Practices in OECD Countries* (OECD, Paris, France, 1997) 13, 13–14. RIA is defined as

> a decision tool, a method of i) systematically and consistently examining selected potential impacts arising from government action and of ii) communicating the information to decision-makers. Both the analysis and communication aspects are crucial. It is a flexible tool. Its objectives, design, and role in administrative processes differ among countries and even among regulatory policy areas. RIA then is an adjunct to good decision-making (. . .).

For analysis see: Delia Rodrigo, 'Regulatory Impact Analysis in OECD Countries: Challenges for Developing Countries' (Paper prepared for the South Asian Third High Level Investment Roundtable, Dhaka, Bangladesh, June 2005), <www.oecd.org/dataoecd/21/52/35258511.pdf> accessed 16 May 2015.
67 FAO (n 11) 134. CBA is defined as 'attempts to measure the actual costs of different regulatory options to strengthen capacity and the value of these improvements for different stakeholders (consumers, food industry, government, etc.), and to measure whether the benefits exceed the costs'. For further analysis, see also Spencer Henson and Oliver Masakure, 'Guidelines on the Use of Economic Analysis to Inform SPS Related Decision Making' (STDF/Coord/291/Guidelines, 6 November 2009), <www.standardsfacility.org/files/EconomicAnalysis/STDF_Coord_291_Guidelines_22Jan10.pdf> accessed 19 June 2015; Julie A Caswell, 'Expanding the Focus of Cost-Benefit Analysis for Food Safety: A Multi-Factorial Risk Prioritization Approach' (2008) 21 *Innovation: The European Journal of Social Science Research* 165; Xavier Irz, 'The Cost-Benefit Analysis of Food Safety Policies: Is it useful?' (2008) 21 *Innovation: The European Journal of Social Science Research* 159; Stephanie Krieger, Gerhard Schiefer and C A Da Silva, *Costs and Benefits in Food Quality Systems: Concepts and Multi Criteria Evaluation Approach* (FAO, Rome, 2007).
68 However, according to FAO (n 11) 134–135, there are notable challenges to the use of these tools, especially for developing countries:

> The expertise, resources and/or information required may not always be readily available. Sometimes there may be limited data, or data that exists may be fraught with assumptions that may create uncertainty as to the outcome of adopting a specific regulatory option. For instance, limited data on the incidence of food-borne illnesses makes it difficult to accurately assess the current costs and economic impact of food borne illness, as well as to quantify the economic benefits to government and the general public of new food safety regulations that may reduce the incidence of food-borne illness. In other cases, it may be difficult to predict how regulations will actually affect industry and/or consumer behaviour.

The FAO benchmarks for food legislation are that such legislation[69] protects consumer health and consumers' interests; defines the roles and responsibilities of government agencies responsible for food control; provides rules and regulations for a science-based food control system; has definitions to ensure consistency and legal security; is based on risk analysis; ensures transparency in the development of food regulations and standards; incorporates checks and balances; defines enforcement powers and procedures; provides for appropriate enforcement and control measures; provides that primary responsibility for food safety and quality rests with producers and processors; ensures that only safe and fairly presented foods are placed on the market; provides for accurate and sufficient information on food products; provides for the approval, registration, or licensing of food premises; defines the appointment of authorised officers; provides for the tracing of food products and their recall in case of problems; and recognises the country's international trade obligations. However, small and medium enterprises merit special consideration.[70]

5.2.5 Levels of government intervention in food control systems

Food legislation is not the only, and at times, the optimum intervention in food control. Private Voluntary Standards (PVS), including voluntary and preventive standards and schemes such as the GAPs, GMPs, GHPs, and HACCP, have become the norm for food control, rather than the exception. Public–private partnerships (PPPs) to enhance SPS capacities serve to improve the quality and delivery of SPS services both at the national and regional levels.[71] The appropriate level of government intervention in food control management may vary: from leaving the market to find the solution, to industry self-regulation, provision of information by governments, education campaigns, labelling requirements, to direct regulation. According to the co-regulation model, there are six levels of government intervention in food safety governance.[72]

---

69 FAO (94) 134–135.
70 Charlotte Yapp and Robyn Fairman, 'Factors Affecting Food Safety Compliance within Small and Medium-Sized Enterprises: Implications for Regulatory and Enforcement Strategies' (2006) 17(1) *Food Control* 51. The authors postulate that SMEs face a myriad of legislation compliance barrier including the lack of trust in food safety legislation and enforcement officers; a lack of motivation in dealing with food safety legislation; and a lack of knowledge and understanding.
71 STDF, 'Promoting a Partnership Approach to Enhance SPS Capacity' (STDF Briefing Note No. 6, November 2010), <www.standardsfacility.org/TAPPP.htm> accessed 19 June 2015. The paper gives the example of Uganda, where the competent authority has a partnership with a private laboratory, whereby the latter provides support to verify pesticide residues and heavy metals to facilitate fish exports. See also Clare Narrod and others, 'Public-Private Partnerships and Collective Action in High Value Fruit and Vegetable Supply Chains' (2009) 34 *Food Policy* 8.
72 Marian G Martinez and others, 'Co-Regulation as a Possible Model for Food Safety Governance: Opportunities for Public-Private Partnerships' (2007) 32 *Food Policy* 299, 301. The authors argue for a bigger role for public–private partnerships in food control systems. With the onus of implementing food legislation increasingly being shifted to food operators, co-regulation is increasing.

Government intervention increases from level one to level six. Level one is non-intervention: there is no government action as its intervention may be unnecessary or may have unintended consequences.

Level two is more positive action: the self-regulation by the food industry. This involves voluntary codes of practice, such as farm assurance schemes or retailers' proprietary quality assurance schemes.

The third level is co-regulation. Co-regulation involves both legislation and self-regulation or some form of direct stakeholders' participation in the regulatory decision-making process. Co-regulation has the advantages of the predictability and binding nature of legislation, with the flexibility of self-regulatory approaches. Co-regulation is a good illustration of Public Private Partnership in governance.

Level four is information and education: assembling and publishing evidence to inform the public debate, information, and advice to consumers.

Level five is the incentive-based structures involving practices such as rewarding desirable behaviour by the private sector and creating market incentives for investments in food safety.

Level six, direct intervention, is the traditional government regulatory authority involving direct regulation, public enforcement and monitoring, and sanctions and penalties.

Hence, although the traditional route for government intervention in food control systems is by regulation, over time these other forms of interventions have evolved depending upon the circumstances of individual countries. The choice of a particular intervention will depend on the needs and priorities of a country as identified in the country's needs assessment and on the prioritisation of such needs in accordance with the hierarchy of food management functions.

5.2.6 Discussion

There is no clear path for the upgrading of COMESA countries' food control systems. A first necessary step is the prioritisation of each country's food control capacity building needs. Given the scarcity of resources among these countries, a necessary condition for the upgrading exercise is the provision of co-coordinated, tailor-made, and targeted technical assistance from the developed countries and from international organisations such as the Standards and Trade Development Facility (STDF). In order to have proper coordination and to achieve efficiencies and economies of scale, a regional upgrading strategy would need to be followed.

Hence, strategies like the adoption of regional food safety policies, best practices, reference laboratories, and certification bodies will need to be considered. The cost of the needs assessment and prioritisation exercises and the subsequent upgrading, in accordance with the above benchmarks, is prohibitive for most developing countries. This necessitates technical assistance from developed countries and through agencies such as the STDF facility.[73] However, a major drawback of such assistance is the question of the sustainability of the resultant capacities beyond the aid period. It is arguable whether such aid-dependent capacities are sustainable in the long term, beyond the aid period. However, capacity assessment tools and analytical frameworks provide coherent means for the examination of countries' food control systems and a basis upon which their upgrading may be undertaken.

An important consideration would be the determination and recognition of the dichotomy between food control management for national markets and for export markets. The distinction between the two systems already exists in practice, where food for the export markets is subjected to higher food safety standards in line with the requirements of those markets, whereas food for the national market is subjected to lower food safety standards. Recognition of this division, subject to commensurate food hygiene and good food handling education for the domestic market, will enable the development of different, but appropriate, food safety policies that cater for the two standards systems and create efficiencies in the utilisation of resources in the upgrading exercises. For instance, the implementation of good practices for food hygiene and safety may be the main strategy for food for the national market, while in addition, the implementation of food inspection, laboratory services, and certification would be the main strategy for food for the export market.

With increasing emphasis being placed on information, education, and communication, there will be increasing awareness of food safety standards. Awareness creation will be a foundation upon which food control systems may be built. Hence, the upgrading of COMESA countries' food control systems will be a gradual, long-term exercise, the progress of which will vary from country to country, and which would require the overall leadership of COMESA.

The next part will examine models for institutional aspects of food control systems. These institutions are the authorities that administer the food control system and enforcement mechanisms through inspections and certifying laboratories.

5.2.7 Models for food control institutions

One of the main functions of food legislation is to define powers under the food control system and the exercise of such powers, as well as by whom they are to be exercised. This translates to the creation of institutions under the system, their different jurisdictions, and their powers and duties.[74] In particular, the

---

73 WTO SPS Committee, 'Update on the Operation of the Standards and Trade Development Facility, Note by the Secretariat' (G/SPS/GEN/1075, 18 March 2011).
74 For an analysis of the institutional aspects of food legislation, see Ellen Vos and Frank Wendler (eds), *Food Safety Regulations in Europe: A Comparative Institutional Analysis*

food legislation will provide for the authority or authorities that will administer the food control system and enforcement mechanisms through inspections and certifying laboratories. Three administrative models for food control systems have emerged: the multiple agencies system, the single agency system, and the integrated system. This part examines these models, and their advantages and disadvantages, for the purposes of proposing any one such model for COMESA countries.

5.2.7.1 Multiple agencies food control system

The multiple agency food control system is based on sectoral agencies that cater for various food industry sectors, such as fisheries, meat and meat products, fruits and vegetables, etc. These agencies are semi-autonomous, and may be either voluntary or mandatory, but are based on the food legislation or sectoral regulations.[75] The sectoral agencies result in multiple agency food control systems. Under such systems, food control responsibilities are shared among government ministries, and the various agencies fall under separate ministries, such as trade, health, agriculture, fisheries, etc.[76] Multiple agencies are the norm, particularly among developing countries.[77]

According to the FAO,[78] multiple agencies suffer from a lack of overall coordination (resulting in incoherence, leading to over-regulation or time gaps in adequate regulatory activity) and clear lines over mandates and jurisdiction of the various agencies managing food control (leading to duplication of functions and inefficiencies). Moreover, the different ministries have differing levels of expertise and resources, leading to uneven implementation of food safety policies and regulations. Ultimately, multiple agencies suffer from a conflict between the objectives of public health and those of facilitation of trade and industry development. This results in an overall reduction in the confidence of both domestic and export markets in the credibility of the food control system.

(Intersentia, Antwerp, 2006); Christopher Ansell and David Vogel (eds), *What's the Beef? The Contested Governance of European Food Safety* (The MIT Press, Cambridge, Massachusetts, 2006) chs 6–8; United States Government Accountability Office, 'Food Safety: Experiences of Seven Countries in Consolidating their Food Safety Systems' (GAO-05-212, February 2005), <www.gao.gov/cgi-bin/getrpt?GAO-05-212> accessed 16 June 2015.

75 FAO/WHO (n 22) 14.
76 There is further fragmentation where local authorities also have a role in the system.
77 Reilly A, 'Defining the Responsibilities and Tasks of Different Stakeholders Within the Framework of a National Strategy for Food Control' (Paper prepared for the Second FAO/WHO Global Forum of Food Safety Regulators, Bangkok, Thailand, 12–14 October 2004) 4, <www.foodsafetyforum.org/global2/documents_en.asp> accessed 16 June 2015; A N Mutukumira and David J Jukes, 'The Development of National Food Safety Control Systems in Sub-Saharan Africa – Issues and Opportunities'(In Proceedings of Food Africa Conference) 5–9, <www.worldfoodscience.org/pdf/Mutukumira_AfricaWFS.pdf> accessed 16 June 2015.
78 FAO/WHO (n 22) 14.

However, there may be strong social and political reasons for maintaining the system.[79] Moreover, the FAO proposes having one ministry coordinate the activities of the whole multiple agencies system and a food board in order to mitigate some of these drawbacks.[80]

5.2.7.2 Single agency food control system

Under the single agency food control system, all the powers and duties under a food control system are placed under the authority of one agency.[81] According to the FAO,[82] the single agency system has a number of advantages. First, the system applies protection measures uniformly, leading to harmonisation. Second, the system has the capacity to respond quickly to emerging challenges and the demands of the domestic and international markets, leading to more streamlined and efficient services, benefiting industry and promoting trade. Third, the system has the ability to act quickly to protect consumers, improve cost efficiency, and have a more effective use of resources and expertise.[83]

The main drawbacks of the single agency system are its initial disruptive actions when human and physical resources have to be relocated from diverse ministries and agencies to the centralised structure. This will entail financial costs and disruption of control, particularly during the early period of the exercise.[84]

---

79 Vapnek J and Spreij M (n 24) 185. According to the authors:

> Because food control systems do more than foster food safety (they also ensure fair trade practices and promote export trade), in some situations there can be strong reasons for developing or maintaining a system in which there is strong sectoral control. There may also be a desire to assign responsibility to local authorities who usually have a better sense of the local food trade and who may be able to respond more rapidly to food emergencies in their areas.

80 Ibid 231–253. The second version of the FAO model law (which provides for a multiple agencies food control system) provides for a ministry that is in charge of the enforcement and implementation of the Act and a food board that is responsible for advising the minister on all matters relating to food.
81 The main proponents of this system are the EU, Australia and Canada.
82 Vapnek J and Spreij M (n 24) 197. FAO advocates for the single agency system because it 'best serves the goals of integration and will best achieve a food chain approach to food safety while eliminating inconsistencies, overlaps and gaps. (. . .) Human health is too important to leave to the vicissitudes of regional or local variations in control'.
83 FAO/WHO (n 22) 15.
84 Vapnek J and Spreij M (n 24) 169–170. The authors contrast the single agency system with the multiple agency system, and find the latter more onerous:

> By contrast, relying on the multiple agency approach is less expensive and causes minimal disruption but its success depends first on the clear definition of each entity's sphere of influence, and second on the good will of the various entities engaged in food control. Where the delineation of responsibilities under the food law (and via agreements between entities) is insufficiently specific, or where there is no desire on the part of the entities involved in food control to collaborate and to streamline operations, such a system is unlikely to succeed.

The single agency is overseen by a responsible minister, who in turn is advised by a management board, which in turn is advised by scientific committees and a consultative committee. Hence the single agency system is resource-intensive and elaborate, which may explain why its application is mostly limited to developed countries.

5.2.7.3 Integrated food control system

The integrated food control system is an intermediate system between the multiple agencies and single agency systems. It is a system in which, instead of shifting the authority from multiple agencies to a single agency, the authority is spread among the existing agencies, whereby there is more coordination and collaboration among the agencies with a supra-ministerial authority overseeing and coordinating the operations of the whole system.[85] The system has several levels of operation. Level one is concerned with formulation of policy, risk assessment and management, and development of standards and regulations. Level two is charged with coordination of food control activity, monitoring, and auditing. Level three covers inspection and enforcement. Level four is in charge of education and training.[86]

The functions for levels one and two are assigned to the supra-ministerial authority, while the functions for levels three and four remain with existing sectoral agencies and ministries.[87] Hence, the authority will establish policy and coordinate the activities of the system, while the line ministries and sectoral agencies will exercise enforcement, inspection, and education and training functions.

According to the FAO,[88] the integrated system is advantageous in that it does not do away with the functions of the ministries and sectoral agencies, which may be undesirable for social and political reasons. Furthermore, the system provides coherence in the national food control system and is politically more acceptable, as it does not disturb the day-to-day inspection and enforcement role of other agencies. Moreover, by separating risk assessment and risk management functions, the integrated system leads to objective consumer protection measures which enhance confidence and credibility in the domestic and export markets. Ultimately, the system may be more cost-effective in the long term.

5.2.8 Discussion

Each food control system needs a food control institution at its centre. The nature of such an institution will depend on each country's circumstances. Developing countries' food control systems are predominantly multiple agencies systems.

---

85 Vapnek J and Spreij M (n 24) 169.
86 FAO/WHO (n 22) 15.
87 Vapnek J and Spreij M (n 24) 185.
88 FAO/WHO (n 22) 15–16.

There is minimal coordination among these agencies, leading to duplication of mandates and inefficient execution of duties that ultimately result in loss of confidence in the systems. The multiple agencies system is archaic and is a leftover from past colonial systems. The FAO proposal for a coordinating ministry and a food board may not necessarily resolve these issues and may end up creating yet more bureaucracy in the systems. The upgrading of such a system would entail the merging of functions in a number of agencies and ministries and capacity building in resources such as laboratories and inspection and certification services that can be utilised by all agencies in common.

The single agency system, with its harmonisation effect and ability to respond quickly, is a better system than the multiple agencies system. The European Food Safety Authority (EFSA) is a prime example of such a system. Its main disadvantage is that it is a resource-intensive system, and hence unsuitable for developing countries which lack resources. A major lesson from the single agency system is the advantage of uniform application of regulations in food safety and rapid responses to food safety emergencies. A further lesson may be the setting up of such an agency at the regional level to formulate regional harmonised policies, leaving the enforcement to national agencies.

The integrated food control system is an attempt to marry the multiple and single food control systems. It fails in this objective as the resultant system is more unwieldy than the multiple agency system, while it lacks the harmonising effect of the single agency system. The inter-ministerial authority is a poor substitute for the individual ministries' authority under the multiple agencies system, and the food safety authority of the single agency system. The inter-ministerial authority's coordinating and supervisory functions may be difficult to implement given the independence of the sectoral agencies, which may be reluctant to cede any of their powers to it. Moreover, with the inspection and enforcement functions shared between the line ministries and sectoral agencies, the system may be unable to respond quickly to food safety emergencies.

The challenge of inadequate resources, and hence prioritisation, lies at the centre of the lack of institutional structures for food control among COMESA countries. Faced with numerous challenges – public health, education, infrastructure, etc., and having inadequate resources – COMESA countries are often hard pressed to prioritise their expenditures and are more often than not forced to use firefighting strategies: tackling only those issues that are pressing and of the moment.[89] Under such circumstances, food control is often relegated to the periphery of priorities. It only gains on the priority list with emergencies, such as

---

[89] For analysis, see: Alemayehu Geda and Haile Kebret, 'Regional Economic Integration in Africa: A Review of Problems and Prospects with a Case Study of COMESA' (2007) 17 *Journal of African Economies* 357; UNCTAD, 'Trends in World Commodity Trade, Enhancing Africa's Competitiveness and Generating Development Gains: Note by the UNCTAD Secretariat' (UNCTAD/DITC/COM/2005/7).

the EU ban on fish imports from the Lake Victoria region of East Africa.[90] Alternatively, food control tends to emerge on the priority list with donors' interest in one or more elements of the system. Inevitably, the food control system and its institutions have therefore tended to develop haphazardly, dependent upon the availability of sporadic resources, or emergencies, or donor interest. Hence the prevalence of the multi-agency version of food control systems among COMESA countries.

Reforms to the COMESA countries' food control systems will have to take into account three factors: the political underpinnings of the systems; the socio-economic environment in which the agencies are functional; and the availability of resources to make such reforms sustainable in the long term. A starting point for such reforms could be the creation of a regional authority with overall supervisory authority over national agencies, coupled with an expert advisory board that would render technical advice to the national agencies. Emphasis should be placed on the simplicity and coherence of structures with a view to reducing operational costs and enhancing efficiency.

Ultimately, for purposes of upgrading the COMESA countries' food control systems, these model institutional structures may be viewed as providing a menu of what a food control agency may consist of, but leaving the choice of components to individual countries.

The next part will discuss a proposal for a COMESA Food Control System (CFCS) based on the COMESA SPS Regulations and incorporating lessons drawn from the discussion on the upgrading of national food control systems.

5.3 The COMESA food control system (CFCS)

A regional food control system should be anchored on a sound policy. The CFCS policy will adopt the objectives of food safety: protecting public health by reducing the risk of food-borne illness; protecting consumers from unsanitary, unwholesome, mislabelled or adulterated food; contributing to economic development by maintaining consumer confidence in the food system and providing a sound regulatory foundation for national, regional, and international trade in food; and promoting fair trade practices. Furthermore, the policy will emphasise the core concepts of food control: a comprehensive, integrated, farm-to-table approach; strategies based on risk analysis; transparency that ensures positive interaction among all stakeholders; application of the principle of prevention throughout the food chain from farm to table; establishment of emergency procedures and rapid alert systems to facilitate withdraw or recall of products; and establishment of

---

90 Mbithi S Mwikya, 'Trade Issues and Policy Coherence in Fisheries: A Developing Country Perspective' (Paper presented at OECD Workshop on Policy Coherence for Development in Fisheries, Paris, France, 24–25 April 2006, COM/AGR/DCD/PCDF/2006/5) 9. The EU imposed a series of bans on exports from the Lake Victoria region between 1996 and 2000. Some of the bans were mainly based on reported outbreak of cholera and salmonella in some settlements in some part of Lake Victoria coast.

guidelines for the exchange of information in food control emergency situations and on rejections of imported food.[91]

Due to the scarcity of resources within COMESA, the CFCS policy will advocate the use of Codex standards and Codex risk assessments as carried out by its various committees, appropriately adapted to local conditions. A good model for the CFCS in this regard is the Association of Southeast Asian Nation (ASEAN) food safety programme.[92] ASEAN has established eight working groups, along the lines of the Codex working groups, whose mandate is the development of principles and standards relating to food control: ASEAN Sectoral Working Group on Livestock (ASWGL); ASEAN Sectoral Working Group on Fisheries (ASWGF); ASEAN Sectoral Working Group on Crops (ASWGC); ASEAN Experts Group on Food Safety (AEGFS); ACCSQ – Prepared Foodstuff Product Working Group (ACCSQ-PPWG); ASEAN Task Force on Codex (ATFC); ASEAN Working Group on Halal (AWG Halal); and Ad-hoc Working Group on Food Irradiation (AWGFI). These working groups have so far produced the ASEAN Harmonised Food Control and Safety Requirements and Principles that are largely adaptations of the Codex standards and principles.[93]

In addition to formulating common definitions of terms, concepts, procedures, and processes, the CFCS policy will advocate the promotion of education, information, and training and the practice of voluntary codes and guidelines of good practices (GPs) in agriculture (GAP), hygiene (GHP), and manufacturing (GMP), and HACCP, given their pivotal roles in the food control system. Finally, the CFCS policy will have an action plan and a timeline for its implementation.

5.3.1 *The CFCS regulatory framework*

Food legislation is not only limited to mandatory, legally enforceable laws. It also encompasses voluntary and preventive standards and schemes such as the GAPs, GMPs, and GHPs. The core elements of food legislation are the farm-to-table approach and its risk analysis base, which ensure the supply of safe food.[94] However, there is a low uptake of recommended modern food safety laws and policies by COMESA countries.[95]

---

91 FAO/WHO (n 22) 10–16.
92 ASEAN website: <www.aseansec.org.> accessed 20 June 2015. ASEAN is a political and economic organisation of 10 Southeast Asian countries. It was formed on 8 August 1967.
93 ASEAN Food Safety Network, 'ASEAN Progress on the Harmonization of Food Control and Safety Requirements and Principles, 4 June 2015', <www.aseanfoodsafetynetwork.net/CurrentIssueDetail.php?CIId=119> accessed 20 June 2015.
94 FAO, *Strengthening National Food Control Systems: Guidelines to Assess Capacity Building Needs* (FAO, Rome, 2006) 39, <www.fao.org/righttofood/kc/downloads/vl/docs/AH433.pdf> accessed 20 June 2015.
95 FAO/WHO, 'FAO/WHO Coordinating Committee for Africa, Eighteenth Session, Accra, Ghana, 24–27 January 2009: Submissions by Uganda and Malawi', <www.codexafrica.org/en/downloads.htm> accessed 20 June 2015. Most countries' food safety laws are outdated

A good model for the CFCS regulatory framework is the EU food safety regulatory regime: the framework Regulation 178 of 2002; the hygiene regulations: 852/2004, 853/2004, and 854/2004; and the official controls Regulation 882/2004.

Based on the EU model, the CFCS food control regulatory framework (the food law) will formally establish the food control system by providing for all the components necessary for the system to function and the principles, obligations, and definitions that will be applicable in the system. The food law will encapsulate the food safety principles and provide for procedures and processes for the implementation of the integrated, farm-to-table approach.[96] The food law should ensure a high level of protection of human life and health and of consumer interests, including fair practices in food trade.

Like the in the EU, the CFCS food law will cover both exports and imports. There should be special care to avoid the food law breaching the disciplines of the SPS Agreement. The food law should not discriminate between imports and exports; it should not be more trade restrictive than necessary; and it should not constitute a disguised restriction on international trade.

The CFCS food law will lay out, in general terms, the responsibilities of the various parties in the food control system, such as the implementation of traceability and GAPs by primary producers; the implementation of GMPs and HACCP by food processors; refrigerated vehicles by transporters; hygiene practices by business operators; and awareness for consumers.[97] The details of such responsibilities will be taken up by the more detailed sectoral laws that may be enacted and when necessary, as will important aspects of food safety, such as animal welfare and health; food hygiene; food contaminants; pesticides and veterinary medicines residues in food; radioactive contamination; food additives; food flavourings; food packaging; and food irradiation.

The COMESA Green Pass will be tailored for food safety, animal health, and plant health. The food law could provide for the COMESA Green Pass for food safety by laying down requirements for food safety; setting criteria for national Green Pass authorities; and setting the procedures for enforcement by national food safety authorities, under the overall supervision of the COMESA Food Safety Authority (CFSA). Alternatively, the food law could reaffirm the principle of mutual recognition and its applicability to Green Passes once issued by a Member country.[98]

---

and not harmonised with the SPS Agreement's principles, nor Codex standards, and do not conform with any of the FAO model laws.

96 Of necessity this will also include feed produced for, or fed to, food-producing animals. Hence the food law shall provide for both food and feed safety requirements. However, there will be need for a separate more comprehensive feed safety law, given its non-food aspects.

97 FAO/WHO (n 22) 6–7 and Annex (6) 54–57.

98 This would entail mutual trust in the competencies of national laboratories and certification bodies. This in turn will require that accreditation bodies be operational and acceptable by national bodies.

For purposes of harmonisation, the CFCS food law will adopt the Common Regulatory Objectives (CRO) concept (CRO refers to a set of regionally agreed upon standards and product requirements and their product coverage); and the Reference to Standards Principle (RSP) (the RSP is a requirement in the CRO that products that meet the referenced international or regional standards are deemed to have met the region's standards and will therefore be free to circulate in the region.).[99]

Good regulatory practices are necessary for the enactment of effective food legislation. Good regulatory practices promote the use of several regulatory tools such as the following: impact assessment (IA) of proposed legislation; simplification of existing legislation (through codification, recasting, and repeal); consultation procedures on drafting proposals; screening and withdrawal of pending proposals; and monitoring and reducing administrative burdens.

Good regulatory practices may be emulated from, for illustrative purposes, the practices of ASEAN,[100] the EU,[101] the OECD,[102] and the United Kingdom,[103] taking into account the different circumstances of developing countries, in particular COMESA countries.

Furthermore, CFCS food law will apply other regulatory tools such as Regulatory Impact Assessment (RIA)[104] and Cost Benefit Analysis (CBA)[105] to analyse current or potential legislation. These tools may also be used to identify and quantify impacts of current and proposed legislation.[106]

---

99 United Nations Economic Commission for Europe (UNECE), 'International Model for Technical Harmonization Based on Good Regulatory Practice for the Preparation, Adoption and Application of Technical Regulations via the Use of International Standards', <www.unece.org/trade/wp6/Recommendations/Rec_L.pdf> accessed 20 June 2015. Although the UNECE model is meant for technical regulations, it lends itself easily to other types of regulations. Its main advantage is that once adopted regionally, the regions' members' standards become easier to harmonise. See also, ISO/IEC, 'Using and Referencing ISO and IEC Standards to Support Public Policy, 2014', <www.iso.org/> accessed 20 June 2015.
100 ASEAN, 'Good Regulatory Practice (GRP) Guide', <www.aseansec.org/> accessed 20 June 2015.
101 European Commission Better Regulation Guidelines, <http://ec.europa.eu/governance/better_regulation/index_en.htm> accessed 20 June 2015.
102 OECD, 'Reference Checklist for Regulatory Decision-Making and OECD Guiding Principles for Regulatory Quality and Performance', <www.oecd.org> accessed 20 June 2015.
103 The Better Regulations Task Force, 'Principles of Better Regulation' (2003), <http://archive.cabinetoffice.gov.uk/brc/upload/assets/www.brc.gov.uk/principlesleaflet.pdf> accessed 20 June 2015.
104 See (n 66).
105 See (n 67).
106 However, according to FAO (n 10), there are notable challenges to the use of these tools, especially for developing countries:

> The expertise, resources and/or information required may not always be readily available. Sometimes there may be limited data, or data that exists may be fraught with assumptions that may create uncertainty as to the outcome of adopting a specific

5.3.2 The CFCS organisational structure

Given the lack of SPS capacity, both human and physical, within the region and its members, and the lack of an organisation to implement the region's food control system, the COMESA Food Safety Authority (CFSA) needs to be top-heavy with the necessary capacities. To a large extent the CFSA will need to exercise command and control powers in order to implement the system. However, given the region's different political regimes and their differing socioeconomic statuses, the region's risk management aspect of food control will be a daunting challenge for any organisation. A good model would be the EU, where the EFSA carries the mandate for risk assessment while the Commission has the mandate for risk management.

Hence, for the system to be effective, the risk management aspects of the system will be undertaken by the COMESA Council of Ministers, while the CFSA will implement most of the other food control functions.

It is proposed that the single agency food control model, where all the powers and duties under a food control system are placed under the authority of one agency, be adopted for the CFSA.[107] The COMESA Council of Ministers will exercise overall oversight of the food control system. Under the COMESA SPS Regulations, the Council of Ministers is specially vested with powers, through regulations, or directives, or codes of practice, to implement and enforce the Green Pass and to ensure the effective operation of regional reference laboratories, regional satellite laboratories, and national SPS related laboratories.[108] The COMESA Committee on Agriculture, composed of national ministries in charge of agriculture, will have the responsibility of implementing the food safety policy and regulations and supervising the activities of the CFSA.[109]

There will be a Management Board, to be composed of representatives of national food control systems, which will be in charge of the operations of the CFSA. The Scientific Committees and Consultative Committee, both composed of scientists and technical personnel from national food safety agencies, will provide technical and scientific advice to the Management Board and the CFSA. The CFSA will be

---

regulatory option. For instance, limited data on the incidence of food-borne illnesses makes it difficult to accurately assess the current costs and economic impact of food borne illness, as well as to quantify the economic benefits to government and the general public of new food safety regulations that may reduce the incidence of food-borne illness. In other cases, it may be difficult to predict how regulations will actually affect industry and/or consumer behaviour.

107 FAO/WHO (n 22) 15; Vapnek J and Spreij M (n 24) 197. FAO advocates for the single agency system because it 'best serves the goals of integration and will best achieve a food chain approach to food safety while eliminating inconsistencies, overlaps and gaps (. . .) human health is too important to leave to the vicissitudes of regional or local variations in control'. See also art 21.2 of the COMESA SPS regulation, which provides for the SPS unit to be located at the Secretariat.
108 COMESA SPS Regulations, art 18.
109 COMESA SPS Regulations, art 21 vests the Committee on Agriculture with the responsibility of implementing the Regulations.

under the management of a CEO. The CFSA will have four main departments: food analysis surveillance; food standards; food inspection; and support services and communication. The national food control agencies will form a bottom layer, below the CFSA and its departments, which does not signify subordination, since officers from these agencies will be involved in the committees of CFSA. The CFSA will be assigned the roles of risk assessment and risk communication,[110] while the risk management function will be assigned to the COMESA Council of Ministers.

The CFSA will cooperate with the national food safety authorities, which will play a supporting role and be implementers of the decisions of the CFSA.

5.3.3 The CFCS inspection and certification

Inspection and certification services[111] are essential functions in a food control system. However, there is a general lack of qualified food safety inspectors in the COMESA. Hence a regional inspectorate service, with enough qualified personnel and equipment, will boost the region's food safety controls. A regional food inspectorate service, with operation criteria and control guidelines, will benefit from the pooled resources of the region, especially in research and training, and will also enhance national inspectorate services through shared resources and coordination of activities.

With intensified education and communication[112] among stakeholders in the system, producers should be mainly responsible for food safety through the practice of GAPs, GHPs, GMPs, and HACCP. In turn, the inspectorate services will concentrate on monitoring and controlling risks, auditing the food control system, and training.

The COMESA Green Pass (CGP)[113] is a commodity-specific certification system that would play a crucial role in the certification process within the CFCS. The CGP certification system provides for the registration of enterprises eligible for the Green Pass. Once issued with a CGP, enterprises are allowed to trade their products freely within the region. Eligible enterprises

---

110 The CFSA will, of necessity, have other administrative supervisory and coordinating functions. Some of these functions will be informed by the envisaged functions of the SPS unit under COMESA SPS regulations, art 21 (2):

> provide appropriate technical guidance to Member States on SPS matters; facilitate capacity building in SPS matters at both National and Regional levels; facilitate the collection and dissemination of technical information on SPS matters to the Member States; advise the Technical Committee on Agriculture on any request for accreditation as a National Green Pass Issuing Authority; Coordinate all regional programmes and institutions related to SPS matters; Coordinate and support the work of regional reference and satellite laboratories.

111 Codex Guidelines for the Design, Operation, Assessment and Accreditation of Food Import and Export Inspection and Certification Systems (CAC/GL 26–1997).

112 Communication would include early warning systems and rapid alert infrastructure that exploit the use of modern technology. It would be much more cost effective to have such infrastructure at the regional level rather than each country striving to have its own.

113 COMESA SPS Regulations, arts 7–13.

will be subject to monitoring and evaluation for conformity with eligibility criteria and requirements.[114] Of note is the fact that enterprises that do not meet the criteria will be assisted by the CGP authorities to fulfil the requirements. This will be an important function of the CFSA, as it will enhance the capacities of key stakeholders in the food safety system. Moreover, the national CGP authorities will themselves be evaluated by the CFSA for adequacy of resources to carry out certification functions; the effectiveness of their monitoring and surveillance systems; the effectiveness of their emergency preparedness systems; and the effectiveness of their traceability systems. This will serve to strengthen the national authorities.

The inspection and certification systems, both as a department of the CFSA and at the national level, should be in accordance with Codex principles and guidelines[115] and EU regulations.[116]

5.3.4 The CFCS reference laboratories

Laboratories are at the centre of the food control system. The CFCS is based on risk analysis, a major part of which is the risk assessment carried out in laboratories. Given the lack of enough accredited laboratories in the COMESA region, a centralised and well-coordinated system of laboratories will play a key role in ensuring food safety in the region and in assuring export markets of the safety and quality of COMESA produce.

Food control laboratories are a necessary component of a food control system, particularly for the implementation and enforcement of food legislation. The laboratories perform tests on food samples for physical, chemical, and microbiological contamination in order to verify the safety and quality of food to enable the appropriate risk management actions. The number, location, and functions of laboratories will be dependent upon the food control system, the volume of

---

114 The criteria and requirements are the food safety standards and good practices as per international or regional standards.
115 Codex: Principles for Food Import and Export Inspection and Certification (CAC/GL 20-1995); Guidelines for the Design, Operation, Assessment and Accreditation of Food Import and Export Inspection and Certification Systems (CAC/GL 26-1997); Guidelines for Food Import Control Systems (CAC/GL 47-2003); Principles and Guidelines for the Exchange of Information in Food Safety Emergency Situations (CAC/GL 19-1995); Guidelines for the Exchange of Information between Countries on Rejections of Imported Foods (CAC/GL 25-1997); Guidelines for the Development of Equivalence Agreements Regarding Food Import and Export Inspection and Certification Systems (CAC/GL 34-1999); Guidelines on the Judgment of Equivalence of Sanitary Measures Associated with Food Inspection and Certification Systems (CAC/GL 53-2003); Guidelines for Design, Production, Issuance and Use of Generic Official Certificates (CAC/GL 38-2001); Principles for Traceability/Product Tracing as a Tool within a Food Inspection and Certification System (CAC/GL 60-2006).
116 EU Regulation 882 of 2004, arts 10 and 30.

work to be carried out, and the resources available.[117] Moreover, the recording of microbiological contamination is important in the collection of epidemiological data, which is important in planning, implementing, and assessing food-borne disease control.[118]

Articles 15, 16, and 17 of the COMESA SPS Regulations provide for the establishment of regional accreditation bodies, reference laboratories, and satellite laboratories. The provisions on the establishment of COMESA reference and satellite laboratories are similar to Articles 32 and 33 of EU Regulation 882/2004, which establish EU and national reference laboratories. Moreover, three regional laboratories, in Zambia, Mauritius, and Kenya, have been designated as referral laboratories.[119] Under the COMESA Agricultural Marketing Promotion and Regional Integration Project (AMPRIP), COMESA has begun the establishment of the region's laboratories.[120]

The Regional SPS Reference Laboratories (RSPSRLs), provided for under the COMESA SPS Regulations,[121] would also be utilised by the CFSA for food safety risk assessment. The RSPSRLs are a network of laboratories, both at the regional and sub-regional (satellite) levels.[122]

The RSPSRLs, working closely with the regional scientific and consultative committees, will be able to improve the safety and quality of the food traded within and outside COMESA. The RSPSRLs should be set up and operate in accordance with Codex standards[123] and EU regulations.[124]

The system of RSPSRLs compares well with the ASEAN Food Reference Laboratories system (AFRLs). However, under AFRLs the laboratories are assigned specific areas of expertise: mycotoxins; pesticide residues; genetically modified organisms; veterinary drug residues; heavy metals and trace elements; microbiology; food contact materials; food additives; and environmental contaminants. Moreover, AFRLs connects the regional laboratories directly to the national laboratories and without providing for satellite laboratories.[125] The EU has a

---

117 FAO/WHO (n 22) 8. Laboratories require considerable capital investment and maintenance costs.
118 Nguz K (n 53) 134.
119 Victoria Declaration (n 54).
120 COMESA (n 55).
121 COMESA SPS Regulations, art 16.
122 COMESA SPS Regulations, art 17.
123 Codex has formulated a number of guidelines on the establishment and operation of laboratories. See Codex list of standards: <www.codexalimentarius.net/web/standard_list.do?lang=en> accessed 30 June 2015.
124 Under Regulation 882 of 2004, art 12, the EU recognises as equivalent only official laboratories assessed and accredited in accordance with the following standards: EN ISO/IEC 17025 on General requirements for the competence of testing and calibration laboratories; EN 45002 on General criteria for the assessment of testing laboratories; and EN 45003 on Calibration and testing laboratory accreditation system-General requirements for operation and recognition.
125 ASEAN Food Safety Network, 'ASEAN Food Reference Laboratories (AFRLs), 9 July 2015', <www.aseanfoodsafetynetwork.net/CurrentIssueDetail.php?CIId=121> accessed 30 June 2015.

similar but wider and longer list of EU Reference Laboratories (EURLs) with a corresponding larger mandate under Regulation 882/2004.[126]

5.3.5 Discussion

Most developing countries need to upgrade their SPS standards in order to participate more effectively in international trade. For the resource-poor countries of the COMESA region, the regional approach to standardisation appears to be the optimal option in upgrading their food safety standards. Regional standards that are implemented by a regional food safety authority, such as the CFSA, have a number of advantages: they are cost-effective, as countries pool their resources to address their common standards issues; they enhance the SPS capacities of the Member countries through education and training and by sharing services, such as inspection and certification, and infrastructure, such as laboratories; they inspire confidence and trust in export markets in the region's food safety standards and thus increase trade; they help speed up the harmonisation of standards by prescribing one set of standards for all Members; and they enable the Member countries to present common positions in international forums and hence influence the setting of international standards.

The EU is the largest market for COMESA food products. COMESA exports mainly comprise fish and fishery products and fresh fruits and vegetables. These facts have two implications. First, COMESA food safety standards, whether they are international or regional standards, have to be aligned with EU food safety standards. Second, the applicable EU food safety standards are mainly those related to traceability and GHPs, GAPs, and HACCP; although EU food safety standards may generally be regarded as being complex and costly to implement, those for fish and fishery products and fresh fruits and vegetables mainly relate to traceability, hygiene, and good practices. As such, these standards are not complex and do not have high implementation costs. Instead, they require well-informed and trained producers for their implementation. The challenge for COMESA is therefore how to inform, train, and educate its food safety stakeholders on traceability, good hygiene, and good agricultural practices.

The CFSA will need to give first priority to the function of information, communication, education, and training. The second priority area will be the training of producers on traceability and GHPs, GAPs, and HACCP. The third priority area will be the legislation of regulations and standards that will take into account the regions' and its Members' unique political and socioeconomic circumstances, and the international standards and EU standards. The rest of the food control system's functions will then follow in order of priority as will be required.

The upgrading of the region's and national SPS standards and infrastructure will require technical assistance and cooperation from international organisations

---

126 European Commission, 'EU Reference Laboratories', <http://ec.europa.eu/food/safety/official_controls/legislation/ref-labs/index_en.htm> accessed 30 June 2015.

and developed countries. The STDF,[127] the World Bank,[128] and the EU[129] are some of the major sources of technical assistance. International agencies and donors will likely find it easier and more efficient to deal with the CFSA rather than individual countries, although these too will continue to require assistance. However, care must be taken to avoid duplication of activities and to ensure that capacity building is prioritised in accordance with COMESA priorities.[130]

As a result of the pooled resources, shared regional inspection, certification, and laboratory services will be crucial in the effective implementation of the food control system. Because of the generally weak or non-existent national food safety infrastructures, shared services will be relied upon to ensure that the system functions well. Because of its enhanced resources, the CFSA authority will not only be pressed to set standards, but also to police their utilisation by Member countries. For an effective regional and national SPS diplomacy strategy, the CFSA will have to engage with international organisations and with multilateral and bilateral partners as representative of the region's and Members' interests.

The upgraded national food safety authorities will have a key role in implementing the CFCS policies and regulations within their jurisdictions. In particular, they will be responsible for the fundamental role of education, information, and communication within their borders. They will also be key players in inspection and certification roles under their jurisdictions. Furthermore, the national authorities will be represented in the Management Board and also in the Consultative Committee and Scientific Committees. Ultimately, the creation of the CFSA and the formulation of regional SPS standards obviate the need for utilizing mutual recognition and equivalence as standardisation tools within the COMESA region.

However, as standardisation will necessarily be a gradual process over a period of time, there will still be a need for the determination of equivalence of national conformity and certification systems in the interim period – although this may not be necessary if countries were to have confidence and trust in each other's certification systems and institute a mutual recognition regime.

---

127 See, for example, WTO Committee on Sanitary and Phytosanitary Measures, 'Update on the Operation of the Standards and Trade Development Facility: Note by the Secretariat' (G/SPS/GEN/1075, 18 March 2011); WTO Committee on Sanitary and Phytosanitary Measures, 'SPS Technical Assistance Activities in 2009: Information from the Secretariat' (G/SPS/GEN/956, 6 July 2009).
128 See, for example, WTO Committee on Sanitary and Phytosanitary Measures, 'Sanitary and Phytosanitary (SPS) Standards: The World Bank's Analytical and Support Programme: Communication from the World Bank' (G/SPS/GEN/520, 20 October 2004).
129 See, for example, European Commission, 'Aid for Trade Monitoring Report 2010, Brussels, 21.4.2010' (SEC (2010) 419 final). See also Regulation 882 of 2004, art 50, on support for developing countries. The EU undertakes to help developing countries food and feed control systems through such activities as joint projects and training of developing countries' control officials.
130 COMESA SPS Regulations, art 19 provides for mutual support and coordination. The provision affirms the technical assistance provisions of the SPS Agreement and advocates for regional and national efforts at securing technical assistance.

The next part, will propose a path for building an EU–COMESA Food Control System (ECFCS). Based upon the foregoing analyses, the next part first explores the possibility of placing the ECFCS within the EPA's framework, before opting for a separate structure.

5.4 Towards an EU–COMESA food control system

In Chapter 4, the EU food control system was analysed and the implications for food imports from COMESA countries were examined. An important lesson that emerges from that analysis is that the high EU food safety standards are not negotiable. The only options open for countries wishing to export food into the EU are either to have similar standards to the EU or to have standards that may be deemed to be equivalent. For COMESA countries, given their incapacities, the former option is not possible; they can only aspire to the latter option.

Hence COMESA countries can only hope to continue with their food exports to the EU by upgrading their standards, to be deemed equivalent by the EU. However, given the difficulties in achieving harmonisation, recognition of equivalence, or mutual recognition, an option for these countries to achieve equivalence would appear to be through a free trade agreement (FTA) with the EU that provides for SPS norms and procedures.[131]

Nine out of the 19 COMESA countries have executed the Economic Partnership Agreements (EPAs) with the EU, under the Cotonou Partnership Agreement (CPA).[132] Madagascar, Mauritius, Seychelles, and Zimbabwe have signed the interim EPA under the Eastern and Southern Africa (ESA) group; Burundi, Kenya, Rwanda, and Uganda have ratified the EPA under the East Africa Community (EAC) group; while Swaziland has ratified the EPA under the Southern African Development Community (SADC).[133] Among the regions that have executed EPAs are as follows: SADC;[134] The Economic Community of West

---

131 For a discussion of EU policy on FTAs (including SPS provisions), see Stephen Woolcock, 'European Union Policy Towards Free Trade Agreements' (ECIPE Working Paper No. 03/2007), <www.ecipe.org/pdf/EWP-3-2007.Pdf> accessed 30 June 2015.
132 Except Egypt and Libya, which are not parties to the Cotonou preferential agreement. The rest of the countries will continue to trade under the Everything But Arms (EBA) preference regime. For full texts of the EPAs see European Commission, Economic partnerships website: <http://ec.europa.eu/trade/policy/countries-and-regions/development/economic-partnerships/> accessed 30 June 2015.
133 Isabelle Ramdoo, 'Comparing EAC, SADC and ECOWAS EPAs: What Can ESA EPA Draw from Them?' (ECDPM Presentation, Harare, Zimbabwe, 24–25 November 2014) 3–4, <http://ecdpm.org/publications/comparing-eac-sadc-ecowas-epas/> accessed 30 June 2015.
134 Ibid. Out of the seven countries forming the SADC EPA negotiation group, six countries have ratified the EPA: Botswana, Lesotho, Swaziland, Namibia, South Africa, and Mozambique. Angola failed to do so. Tanzania left the both the SADC EPA group and the ESA EPA group.

African States (ECOWAS);[135] ESA;[136] East African Community (EAC);[137] Central Africa States;[138] Caribbean Community states plus the Dominican Republic (CARIFORUM);[139] and Pacific states (Pacific).[140] An examination of the SPS provisions of these EPAs may provide lessons for an EU–COMESA food control framework.

5.4.1 The SPS provisions in the EPAs

The SPS provisions of the EPAs[141] are similar in form to other EU FTAs' SPS provisions.[142] The EPAs' SPS provisions re-affirm the principles and objectives of the SPS Agreement and its three international standards-setting organisations. Their main objectives are the fostering of cooperation in SPS matters between the parties in order to increase their trade and investments, and assisting the developing countries to harmonise their intra-regional SPS standards and increase their SPS capacities in order to meet the EU's standards.[143]

The EPAs further provide for the designation of competent authorities by the parties; the re-affirmation of the principle of transparency and information exchange, which entails the setting up of early warning systems and epidemiological surveillance; and cooperation and technical assistance to enhance regional collaboration and integration and the SPS capacities of the developing countries.[144]

---

135 Ibid. All the ECOWAS countries have ratified the EPA.
136 Ibid. In the ESA grouping: Madagascar, Mauritius, Seychelles, and Zimbabwe have signed the interim EPA, while Comoros and Zambia have initialled the interim EPA.
137 Ibid. All the EAC countries have ratified the EPA.
138 Ibid. In Central Africa, only Cameroon has signed an interim EPA.
139 Ibid. All the CARIFORUM countries, except Haiti, have signed the EPA.
140 Ibid. In the Pacific region only Fiji and Papua New Guinea have signed an interim agreement and only Papua New Guinea has ratified it.
141 The SPS provisions are to be found in ch two, title v of the EAC EPA; ch 9 of the SADC EPA; ch 7 of the CARIFORUM EPA; and pt two, ch 3 of the ECOWAS EPA; Proposed title II of the ESA EPA; ch 4 of Central Africa EPA; and ch 5 of Pacific EPA. For an analysis of the interim EPAs see Sanoussi Bilal and Christopher Stevens (eds), *The Interim Economic Partnership Agreements between the EU and African States: Contents, Challenges and Prospects* (Policy Management Report 17, ECPDM, Maastricht, 2009), <www.ecdpm.org/pmr17> accessed 30 June 2015.
142 Bettina Rudolff and Simons Johannes, 'Comparing EU Free Trade Agreements: Sanitary and Phytosanitary Standards' (ECDPM InBrief 6B, July 2004, ECPM-CTA), <www.ecdpm.org/inbrief6b> accessed 30 June 2015. According to the authors, EU bilateral agreements' SPS provisions differ in four main respects: 'the extent to which they reaffirm WTO rules; the emphasis on cooperation on SPS measures; the adoption of a general exception clause similar to GATT art XX; and the specification of technical assistance in SPS issues'. However, most of these provisions are general and shallow, mainly with emphasis on cooperation on SPS matters.
143 EAC EPA, art 30; CARIFORUM EPA, arts 52–54; SADC EPA, arts 60–64; ESA EPA, art 31; ECOWAS EPA, arts 32–33; Central Africa EPA, art 40; and Pacific EPA, art 34.
144 EAC EPA, art 32; CARIFORUM EPA, art 55–59; SADC EPA, art 59–64; ESA EPA, arts 35–36; ECOWAS EPA, arts 25–33; Central Africa EPA, arts 45–46; Pacific EPA, arts 38–40.

The EPAs, like other EU FTAs, affirm the principles and objectives of the SPS Agreement. They provide for cooperation on SPS matters, and they advocate harmonisation of SPS standards or determination of equivalence.[145] The EPAs also go further than most EU FTAs, except the EU–Chile Association Agreement, in providing for technical assistance on SPS matters.[146] Moreover, the SADC, ESA, and Pacific EPAs provide for Committees to monitor and review the implementation of the Agreements in a similar manner to the EU–Mexico Global Agreement and the EU–Chile Association Agreement.[147]

However, the EPAs fail to provide for procedural specifics that go beyond the SPS Agreement's provisions. The EPAs do not provide for the process of equivalence determination; guidelines for imports verifications, checks, and certification; time schedules for internal reporting and consultations; or the approval of establishments. These omissions may be attributed to the nature of these agreements. However, the fact that the provisions are similar to many other EU FTAs may be an indication that the EU is not in favour of provisions that go further than those of the SPS Agreement. An alternative would be negotiations on determination of equivalence, as in the Mexico and Chile FTAs, but this may prove a daunting task for the COMESA countries, given their incapacities.[148]

5.4.2 Lessons from the SPS provisions in the EPAs

The EPAs, by providing for harmonisation and equivalence, have gone further than most EU FTAs. However, the provisions for implementation are not sufficiently specific on details such as procedures for determination of equivalence, which is likely to result in non-implementation of these provisions, unless such procedures are provided for in the final EPAs.

Furthermore, given the disparities in the economies of the COMESA countries vis-à-vis the EU countries, it may ultimately not be feasible to harmonise their respective food control systems. However, with technical assistance, COMESA countries may be able to establish equivalence in food safety in their export products to the EU. This would imply a two-tier food control system: one for

---

145 EAC EPA, arts 34–35; CARIFORUM EPA, art 56; SADC EPA, art 57; ESA EPA, art 34; ECOWAS EPA, arts 28 and 33; Central Africa EPA, art 46 (the EPA sets a time limit of four years for the completion of harmonisation within the region); Pacific EPA, art 37 (the EPA provides for equivalence instead of harmonisation).
146 EAC EPA, art 32; CARIFORUM EPA, art 53; SADC EPA, art 64; ESA EPA, art 35; ECOWAS EPA, art 33; Central Africa EPA, art 47; and Pacific EPA, art 34.
147 SADC EPA, art 62; ESA EPA, art 40; and Pacific EPA, art 42.
148 Mexico and Chile may be termed as emerging economies and as such can afford the costs of upgrading their food control systems to be equivalent to the EU system. On the other hand, COMESA countries consist of developing and least developed countries which may not afford the costs of equivalence.

the export products that is equivalent to EU standards, and another for locally traded, non-export products.¹⁴⁹

There is significant importance attached to transparency and information exchange. The EPAs have provided for notification of SPS measures, scientific opinions on food safety, and collaboration on SPS matters, to enable parties to meet each other's SPS standards. These provisions are also to be found in Article 7 and Annex B of the SPS Agreement. Transparency is particularly important as regards control, inspection, and approval procedures, where these are preconditions for market access. The issue raised by these provisions relates to the lack of capacity by COMESA countries to effectively utilise the provisions. These countries lack effective inquiry points and competent authorities, and as such may be unable to utilise information that is provided, and may not be able to provide useful information themselves.¹⁵⁰ These shortcomings should be factored in the proposed food control systems and appropriate implementation rules and procedures should be provided.

The EPAs singularly lack provisions for practical implementation of the SPS provisions. It appears that the EU would prefer implementation aspects to be negotiated outside the EPAs. In the Euro-Mediterranean Association Agreements,¹⁵¹ negotiations have been ongoing concerning administrative, procedural, and institutional aspects of the FTAs. The lack of institutional and administrative

---

149 A further implication is the prioritisation of resources and development of strategies to cope with food safety standards. See Ronaldt Thoen, Laurens Vlaar and Jacco Kaarsemaker, *Structure and Dynamics of the European Market for Horticulture Products and Opportunities for SSA Exporters, Final Report* (VEK Adviesgroep B.V. and The World Bank African Region Sustainable Development, June 2004) 85, <www.hubrural.org/IMG/pdf/european_market_for_horticulture_products_eng.pdf> accessed 1 July 2015. The authors argue, in the case of horticultural development, that such development cannot be based on a traditional development continuum (emerging, nascent, immature, and mature) but on the existence or non-existence of a minimum set of basic and advanced production factors. There should be aprioritizing on regional crop combinations, based on their strengths and weaknesses. See also Spencer Henson and Steven Jaffee, 'Understanding Developing Country Strategic Responses to the Enhancement of Food Safety Standards' (2008) 31 *The World Economy* 548. The authors argue that one of the strategies for coping with food safety standards is to choose not to comply with the food safety standards in a particular market:

> This implies switching customers, in the case of a private standard, or exiting particular export markets. The exporter may choose to substitute products for which food safety standards are less costly to meet. Such a strategy might be employed where compliance will yield a fundamental loss of competitiveness and/or negative economic and social impacts, where resources might be better spent elsewhere and/or where profitable alternative markets exist that have less demanding standards, for example, the higher quality segments of domestic markets.

150 See, for example, FAO/WHO, *Coordinating Committee for Africa Eighteenth Session: Submissions by Malawi and Uganda* (Accra, Ghana, 24–27 January 2009), <www.codexafrica.org/en/downloads.htm> accessed 1 July 2015.
151 See FTAs between the EU and Algeria; Egypt; Israel; Jordan; Lebanon; Morocco; Palestinian Authority; Syria; Tunisia; and Turkey. Agreements available at <http://ec.europa.eu/trade/issues/bilateral/regions/euromed/aa_en.htm> accessed 1 July 2015.

provisions in the EPAs renders them impractical and uncertain until these aspects are included or concluded. Future endeavours on SPS cooperation should strive to have these aspects included in the negotiations and enacted in the final agreement. Nonetheless, the disparities in negotiating capacity between the EU and the developing countries are notable.

5.4.3 Discussion

From the foregoing analyses it appears that a closer, more practical engagement, as envisaged for the EU–COMESA food control framework, may not sit comfortably within the main provisions of the EPA framework. The SPS provisions in the EPA framework are general and applicable to all SPS measures; the provisions provide for SPS principles and are not specific to any product. The specific requirements of the EU–COMESA Food Control System (ECFCS) may therefore not fit well in the EPA framework. On the other hand, other than through the EPAs, it appears there is no feasible alternative for the anchoring of an EU–COMESA SPS legal framework. The alternative of negotiating a separate specific agreement on the EU–COMESA food control legal framework is not feasible given the fact that even the very general EPAs have taken a long time to negotiate.

It is therefore proposed that, in so far as food safety is concerned, the optimal basis for the ECFCS be as a protocol or annex to the EPAs. Furthermore, the ECFCS should be based on the determination of equivalence. This is informed by the fact that the EU already provides for equivalence under its food import conditions.[152] Moreover, it is under these equivalence provisions that COMESA countries have been exporting food products to the EU.

5.4.4 Factors for consideration in the ECFCS

Under Article 11 of Regulation 178 of 2002, food imported into the EU must comply with EU food law or with equivalent conditions. The responsibility for ensuring the food safety of imported food lies with the EU food business operator, under Article 17 of the said Regulation. For purposes of identifying those along the food chain and for recall and withdrawal purposes, the food business operator is enjoined under Article 18 of the Regulation to maintain a one-step-back and one-step-forward traceability system. Under Article 19 of the Regulation, the food operator is required to withdraw from the market all unsafe food and to inform the authorities immediately of such action.

The EU's main responsibility is the outcome – that the food marketed is safe – while the food operator's responsibility is to ensure such an outcome by developing a food safety system. Hence the food business operators, which are mainly supermarkets, are responsible for the safety and quality of their food inputs, the conduct of their suppliers, and the safety of consumers, and are forced to come

---

152 Regulation 178 of 2002, art 11.

up with private voluntary standards (PVS) in order to ensure that the EU's food safety standards are met (among other reasons).[153]

The shifting of food safety responsibility to the food business operator has led to several consequences for food control. First, while the responsibility for ensuring food safety lies with food business operators, the competent authorities have the responsibility for establishing food control systems to verify compliance with the food law. Second, because products of animal origin generally present higher food safety risks than those of non-animal origin and are hence subject to strict controls, food business operators are more concentrated in the importation of food of non-animal origin, mainly fresh fruits and vegetables. Hence, with the exception of fish and fishery products, COMESA countries are predominantly exporters of fresh fruits and vegetables.[154] This has been to the detriment of exports of foods of animal origin. Third, and as a result of the foregoing, the EU's food control system is more attuned to and geared towards compliance by food operators and establishments rather than the third countries' competent authorities or their food control systems.[155] Fourth, COMESA countries that export products to the EU have a two-way division in their food control systems: one catering to horticultural products that are largely based on PVS,[156] and another catering to products of animal origin that is based on public mandatory standards.[157]

An important factor to be noted is that whereas the EU has a developed food control system with harmonised food safety standards, COMESA is at the initial stage of both establishing a food control system and developing harmonised food safety standards. Coupled with this is the fact that the EU countries have a shared history of many centuries and hence have common sociocultural values and developed economies; on the other hand, COMESA countries are creations

---

153 Regulation 178 of 2002, Preamble para 30 provides: 'A food business operator is best placed to devise a safe system for supplying food and ensuring that the food it supplies is safe; thus, it should have primary legal responsibility for ensuring food safety (. . .)'.
154 Patrick Labaste (ed), *The European Horticulture Market Opportunities for Sub-Saharan African Exporters* (World Bank Publications No. 63, Washington, DC, 2005) 46. The author points out that PVS have replaced public mandatory standards in the conduct of horticultural trade due to the close relationships between supermarkets and their suppliers – the so called 'license to produce' and 'license to deliver' protocols.
155 This is borne out by the fact that even where countries' Competent Authorities and their food control systems do not meet EU requirements, the EU will still allow imports based on the listing of their establishments.
156 This arises from the demand by importers that producers of horticultural products be EUREPGAP certified for primary production and be BRC certified for minimally processed products. However, these products still require the phytosanitary certificate issued by the Competent Authority.
157 This arises from the requirement of guarantees by third countries, under Regulation 882 of 2004, art 48, before such countries can be included in the list of approved countries from which imports of products of animal origin are permitted. The paucity of exports of products of animal origin from COMESA countries could be explained, in part, by the inability of these countries to provide the EU with the requisite guarantees.

of colonialism, with minimal common sociocultural values and poor economies. Hence, in as much as it would be simple for COMESA to emulate the EU food control system, it may not be practicable. COMESA needs to develop a food control system that is suitable for its unique circumstances; nevertheless, there are valuable lessons to be learnt from the EU experience.

5.5 The EU–COMESA food control system (ECFCS)

To be noted at the outset is the fact that the ECFCS will be an addition to, and not a substitute of, the existing EU–COMESA food trade regime. The main objective of the ECFCS will be to achieve equivalence with the EU food control system for the COMESA food control system for agricultural and food products exports to the EU. The framework would ensure the equivalence of the COMESA hygiene practices, its implementation of HACCP principles, its official controls, and the registration and approval of food establishments.[158] This would be achieved by providing COMESA with technical and financial assistance and promoting technology transfer, for the development of the necessary infrastructure and capacities for food control; addressing issues arising from EU food control measures through technical assistance and capacity building activities on agreed priority sectors and products; promoting COMESA harmonisation of food control measures and the development of appropriate regulatory frameworks and policies; facilitating the participation of COMESA food control officials in EU food control training and standards-making processes; and promoting linkages, joint ventures, and joint research and development between COMESA and EU institutions and laboratories.

5.5.1 The ECFCS structure

On the basis of its nature and objectives, the ECFCS will consist mainly of technical and administrative personnel for its implementation. Moreover, given the fact that COMESA food imports form a minor percentage of EU food imports, although they are a major percentage of COMESA exports, the structure for the ECFCS will, of necessity, be simple and sparse. The ECFCS will consist of two main organs: the Joint Food Control Committee (JFCC) and the Joint Scientific Committee (JSC). With these two organs in place, other organs can be created on an ad hoc basis, depending on need. Of note is that ECFCS will be complementing the existing infrastructure under Regulation 852 of 2004.

---

158 Regulation 852 of 2004 makes it mandatory for food business operators to implement good hygiene practices, including HACCP principles, at all stages of production, processing, and distribution of food. These requirements are applicable to food imports also. The registration and approval of establishments is mandatory under Regulation 853 of 2004.

5.5.1.1 The Joint Food Control Committee (JFCC)

The organisational structure will be headed by the Joint Food Control Committee (JFCC), composed of the representatives from the EFSA, the CFSA, and nominees of COMESA countries' food control authorities. The composition of the JFCC will be informed by the fact that these are the people most involved with food safety issues and regulation at the regional and national levels. The JFCC will be the steering organ of the ECFCS. The main function of the JFCC will be policy formulation and to set the agenda for the ECFCS. This will necessarily involve prioritizing food control issues, developing work plans, and negotiating for resources. JFCC functions on information and transparency will include setting up a modern information centre, preferably computer-based, with a database and information on food safety that will provide information on changes to food safety measures which may affect products of export interest to COMESA countries; establishing an early warning system and rapid alert system for food safety issues; notifying of food control measures; and coordinating consultations and exchange of information on notification and application of food control measures.

The JFCC's technical assistance and capacity building functions will include setting up training programmes in food safety for public inspectors and certifying personnel, aimed at building the public sector capacity for regulating, monitoring, and certification of compliance with food safety measures; providing private sector commodity producers and processors, aimed at building private sector capacity to comply with food control requirements; creating sustainable enquiry points and competent authorities in COMESA and the training of their personnel and staff; enabling COMESA countries to update and develop adequate legislative and regulatory instruments; and setting up institutional and operational mechanisms for the implementation of the ECFCS.

5.5.1.2 The Joint Scientific Committee (JSC)

The Joint Scientific Committee (JSC) will be composed of scientific officers from the EFSA, the CFSA, and national food control authorities. The main function of the JSC will be to render scientific opinions on food safety matters arising in the ECFCS. More significantly, the JSC will undertake the determination of equivalence where there are differences between the EU and COMESA food control measures. As such its function will be that of a scientific arbiter in situations of scientific differences.

A critical function of the JSC will be that of a forum where the transfer of scientific knowledge and technology from the EU to COMESA takes place through training and working sessions involving both EU and COMESA scientists. It is to be hoped that over time, the JSC will bring about harmonisation of the EU and COMESA food control systems. In order to be effective the JSC will need to form special scientific panels from amongst its members to carry out its functions.[159] Such panels could be concerned with additives and flavourings; pesticide

---

159 These would be similar to the scientific panels of EFSA. See Regulation 178 of 2002, art 28.

residues; GMOs; biological hazards; contaminants; plant health; and animal health, among other items.

The JSC's other functions will include strengthening COMESA Regional Accreditation Bodies, including setting up training programmes for laboratory auditors; setting up inter-laboratory testing and validation programmes, accreditation of laboratories in accordance with the EU and Codex standards, as well as the provision of continuous training programmes for laboratory specialists; implementing measures in COMESA countries aimed at improved food risk management at production and processing levels; strengthening COMESA reference laboratories in animal health, plant protection, and food safety; and creating linkages with EU reference laboratories, including training, technology transfer, and joint ventures.

5.6 Chapter discussion and conclusions

Food safety standards are a product of culture. Different cultures give rise to different standards.[160] Thus there are differing food safety standards across the countries. Food safety standards, per se, are deemed to be inalienable sovereign rights.[161] However, since this right has been shown to be subject to abuse, the disciplines of the SPS Agreement are brought into play so that standards that fall foul of these disciplines are adjudged to be inconsistent with the requirements of the SPS Agreement and are required to be brought into conformity with such requirements. The right to set one's food safety standards finds further expression under Article 3.3 of the SPS Agreement, wherein countries have a right to set their own level of appropriate protection (ALOP), but are still subject to the disciplines of the Agreement; foremost amongst them in this regard are the disciplines of risk assessment.[162]

The EU has a sovereign right to set its ALOP. As COMESA's biggest trading partner, and consisting of developed countries vis-à-vis COMESA's developing countries, the EU is in a position to influence the standards in the food trade between the two regions. In the EU's bilateral relations, harmonisation and equivalence have often been predominantly towards EU standards.[163] It therefore

---

160 Marsha A Echols, 'Food Safety Regulation in the European Union and the United States: Different Cultures, Different Laws' (1998) 4 *Columbia Journal of European Law* 525.
161 This right is reaffirmed by the SPS Agreement, preamble para 1.
162 *Appellate Body Report, EC – Hormones*, para 177:

> The requirements of a risk assessment under Article 5.1, as well as of 'sufficient scientific evidence' under Article 2.2, are essential for the maintenance of the delicate and carefully negotiated balance in the SPS Agreement between the shared, but sometimes competing, interests of promoting international trade and of protecting the life and health of human beings. We conclude that the Panel's finding that the European Communities is required by Article 3.3 to comply with the requirements of Article 5.1 is correct (. . .).

163 See, in particular, art 61 of the EU–South Africa Trade, Development and Cooperation Agreement (TDCA); art 56 of the EU–Tunisia FTA and art 40 of EU–Morocco FTA.

appears that COMESA has little choice but to harmonise its food safety standards towards the EU's standards in order to maintain market access for its food exports to the EU. COMESA countries can do this through the determination of equivalence. The EU practice of unilateral determination of equivalence for countries wishing to export food products to the EU has taken root and is anchored in the EU hygiene regulations.

Faced with numerous challenges – public health, education, infrastructure, etc., and having inadequate resources – COMESA countries are often hard-pressed to prioritise their expenditures and are more often than not forced to use firefighting strategies: tackling only those issues that are pressing and of the moment.

The reforms to the COMESA countries' food control systems will have to take into account three factors: the political underpinnings of the systems; the socioeconomic environment in which the agencies are functional; and the availability of resources to make such reforms sustainable in the long term. In order for COMESA countries to maximise their benefits under the EU equivalence and also improve their food security, they need to upgrade their food control systems.

COMESA countries also need to prioritise their food control functions in accordance with the World Bank model:[164] the information, communication, and education function takes first priority; the application of good practices for hygiene and safety, such as GAPs/GHPs/GMPs/HACCP, comes second; suitable and applied regulation come third; laying down institutional structures and clearly defining roles in the system come fourth; technical management functions, such as construction and maintenance of laboratories and inspection and certification services, come fifth; and lastly come the SPS diplomacy functions, such as participation in regional and international organisations. The prioritizing of functions is not a cut-and-dried process; it is adaptable to suit an individual country's circumstances, taking into account regional strategies.

Further, in the upgrading process, COMESA countries need to adopt the recommendations of the FAO/WHO guidelines for developing national food control systems.[165] Of particular significance are the main recommendations on

---

> Compliance with EU food law or its equivalence is a requirement for food imports into the EU. Regulation 178 of 2002, art 11 of provides:
>
>> Food and feed imported into the Community for placing on the market within the Community shall comply with the relevant requirements of food law or conditions recognised by the Community to be at least equivalent thereto or, where a specific agreement exists between the Community and the exporting country, with requirements contained therein.
>
> Regulation 852 of 2004, art 10 makes it mandatory that imported food shall comply with its detailed hygiene requirements including the implementation of HACCP principles. Regulation 853 of 2004, art 6 makes it mandatory that imported food of animal origin emanates from approved/listed countries and establishments listed under and in accordance with Regulation 854 of 2004, arts 11, 12, 13, and 14. There is no reference to international standards in these EU regulations; importers are required to comply or demonstrate equivalence.

164 Jaffee S (ed) (n19).
165 FAO/WHO (n 22).

the enactment of a national food law, elements of the food control system, and the provision for a food control agency to oversee the system. The hybrid agency model recommends itself for national food control systems, while the single agency model, appropriately adapted, recommends itself at the regional level.[166]

A key strategy among COMESA countries is that of a regional food control system. The COMESA food control system will benefit from pooled resources and economies of scale. In particular, its system of reference laboratories and common inspection and certification services will not only enhance food control at the regional level, but also build the capacities of national systems by creating backward linkages with national systems and by developing regional capacity enhancing initiatives and training programmes.

In addition to other avenues of technical assistance, the COMESA food control system, through the CFSA, will be a focal point for EU technical assistance under Article 50 of Regulation 882 of 2004. Under the said Article, in order to ensure that developing countries are able to comply with the provisions of the Regulation, the EU undertakes to provide the following:

> (b) assistance with providing the information referred to in Article 47,[167] if necessary by Community experts; (c) the promotion of joint projects between developing countries and Member states; (d) the development of guidelines to assist developing countries in organising official controls on products exported to the Community; (e) sending Community experts to developing countries so as to assist in the organisation of official controls; (f) the participation of control staff from developing countries in the training courses referred to in Article 51. (. . .) promote support to developing countries with regard to feed and food safety in general and compliance with feed and food standards in particular, in order to build the institutional capacity required to meet the requirements referred to in Articles 5,[168] 12,[169] 47 and 48.[170]

An effective way of ensuring that COMESA countries meet the EU equivalence requirements is through the ECFCS. As a forum between the two parties, the system will ensure a faster channel of communication and information transfer between the EU and COMESA on food safety matters. As a vehicle of cooperation between the parties, the system will facilitate more effective technical cooperation through technology transfer and technical training of personnel.[171]

---

166 Ibid 15–16. See also Vapnek J and Spreij M (n 24) 169–170.
167 Information relating to national food control systems.
168 Pertaining to the delegation of specific tasks related to official controls.
169 Concerning the designation and accreditation of official laboratories.
170 Relating to specific import conditions for listing third countries and conditions to be met by their guarantees.
171 The EU 'Better Training for Safer Food in Africa' initiative, under the EU–Africa Strategy, could form a basis for future cooperation for the ECFCS. Better Training for Safer Food

The upgrading of the COMESA food control system will be more efficient under the ECFCS, since it will be better coordinated and geared towards meeting the EU equivalence requirements. COMESA food control resources will also be more effectively utilised since the region's food control needs will be prioritised and resources allocated accordingly. As a result of the ECFCS, there will be a gradual improvement in the food safety standards in the COMESA region, which will lead to better food security in the region and increased trading opportunities with the EU.

---

in Africa is aimed at strengthening national, regional, and pan-African SPS capacity of competent authorities in areas such as control, surveillance, legislation, management, and inspection. The initiative focuses on international standards and GSPs and GMPs in relation to food safety, animal health, animal welfare, and plant health. Website available at <http://ec.europa.eu/food/training_strategy/index_en.htm> accessed 4 August 2015.

The EU–Africa strategy has as its main objectives to strengthen the SPS capacity of the officials of the African Union Community, Regional Economic Communities, and specialised bodies; to share information and policy advice on rules and procedures; to strengthen the official controls of feed and food systems; and to initiate discussions on the rehabilitation and modernisation of testing and certification laboratories. Website available at <www.africa-eu-partnership.org/> accessed 4 August 2015.

6 Conclusions

The real 21st century trade issues are standards and rules in areas such as safety, health, or consumer protection.[1]

6.1 Introduction

The importance of COMESA countries' agricultural products and food exports to the EU cannot be gainsaid. The EU is the biggest market for these COMESA products. SPS standards, particularly food safety standards, are generally a challenge to developing countries' trade in these products.[2] On the one hand is the EU, consisting of highly developed and industrialised countries with high food safety standards. On the other hand, you have poor, underdeveloped countries in COMESA with few or non-existent standards striving to export agricultural and food products to the EU.

The export of agricultural products offers an avenue for combating poverty and increasing incomes in developing countries, among them COMESA Members.[3] Though granted quota- and duty-free preferences by the EU, COMESA Members are unable to maximise their exports to the EU because of the hurdle posed by EU food safety standards. How to overcome this 'standards challenge' is the central problem of this book.

This chapter follows up with the objectives that were set out in the Introduction and summarises the findings of the book. Part one summarises and draws conclusions on the SPS Agreement. Part two summarises and draws conclusions

---

1 Pascal Lamy, 'EU Trade Commissioner, in the Financial Times, 7 September 2004', quoted in: Maggie X Chen and Aaditya Mattoo, *Regionalism in Standards: Good or Bad for Trade?* (World Bank Publications No. 3458, 2004) 1.
2 Christine Chemnitz, 'The Impact of Food Safety and Quality Standards on Developing Countries Agricultural Producers and Exports' (PhD thesis, Faculty of Agriculture and Horticulture at Humboldt-University, Berlin, 2012), <http://edoc.hu-berlin.de/dissertationen/chemnitz-christine-2011-11-15/PDF/chemnitz.pdf> accessed 30 August 2015.
3 World Bank, *World Development Report 2008: Agriculture for Development* (World Bank, Washington, DC, 2007), <https://openknowledge.worldbank.org/handle/10986/5990> accessed 30 August 2015.

on the EU food safety regime. Part three summarises and draws conclusions on the COMESA food safety standards. Part four draws conclusions on the proposed EU–COMESA Food Control System (ECFCS).

6.2 The SPS Agreement

Both developed and developing countries have an interest in promoting fair food safety standards in the international trade of horticultural, beef, and fisheries products. On the one hand, as exporters, they both have an interest that these standards are no more stringent than necessary, and that these standards are not protectionist in their intent or application. On the other hand, as importers, they are both concerned that their food safety standards will ensure that imports of these products do not pose unacceptable risks to the health and life of people, plants, or animals.

Because developing countries are 'standards takers' while developed countries are 'standards makers', developing countries perceive developed countries' standards as protectionist, serving as barriers to their food and agricultural trade, more particularly to the detriment of small producers. Despite the fact that standards play a positive role in overcoming market failures, the perception persists that standards are barriers to trade, which is further reinforced by the standards' complexity and lack of harmonisation. Moreover, the standards' compliance costs are higher for developing countries than for developed countries.

To address these perceptions and to act as a 'yard stick' for Member countries' standards, the SPS Agreement is anchored on scientific disciplines for SPS standards, as provided for under Article 2.2: 'based on scientific principles and is not maintained without sufficient scientific evidence (. . .)'. Furthermore, the scientific disciplines of the SPS Agreement are anchored on the concept of risk assessment, as defined under Annex A, paragraph 4. Article 5.7 of the SPS Agreement provides for situations where there is insufficient relevant scientific evidence. In such situations it allows for conditional provisional SPS measures. On the other hand, in order to minimise differences in SPS standards, harmonisation of SPS standards is one of the long-term objectives of the SPS Agreement.

Cognizant of the developing countries shortcomings, the SPS Agreement has specific provisions to cater for these constraints. It provides for technical assistance, under Article 9; special and differential treatment, under Article 10; a reasonable adaptation period, under paragraph 2 of Annex B; special notification requirements, under paragraphs 8 and 9 of Annex B; and delayed implementation of the Agreement, under Article 14.

Generally, the SPS Agreement has not lived up to the high expectations of WTO Members, especially developing countries. Despite the SPS Agreement, developing countries continue to face challenges from the standards of developed countries. The developing countries see developed countries' standards as too stringent, inappropriate, not based on international standards, and of protectionist intent. The adjudicated disputes arising from the SPS Agreement serve to illustrate the deep-rooted problems involving SPS standards. The SPS Agreement's reliance on scientific evidence as a basis for SPS measures has also proved controversial, not least because of the uncertainty of science itself.

Furthermore, the SPS Agreement's special and differential treatment (SDT) provisions, which are intended to enable developing countries to comply with and benefit from the disciplines under that Agreement, contain no binding obligations. The SDT provisions are mostly unenforceable as they are expressed in imprecise and hortatory language. Even where these provisions are couched in mandatory terms, this may not be sufficient to make them enforceable. Since the SDT provisions that are meant to enable developing countries to integrate into the system are unenforceable, this has resulted in increasing legal inequality between developed and developing countries and creates an imbalance in the WTO rule-based system.

Although the SPS Agreement encourages Members to use international standards, guidelines, or recommendations, there is no distinction between them in the SPS Agreement as to their relative normative value and status. There is also no specific procedure set out concerning how these standards, regulations, and recommendations are to be established.

From a Global Administrative Law perspective, the lack of transparency and unequal participation of most developing countries in the international standardisation process raises issues of the legitimacy of the process and its final outcomes, the standards themselves. The issue of legitimacy gives ground for charges of a democratic deficit being levelled at the international standards-setting organisations. Moreover, the process has resulted in international standards that are inappropriate to the developing countries' situation and which require infrastructure that is not available in those countries. A further consequence is that international standards which reflect the interests of developing countries are slow to develop. Furthermore, given the dominant role played by the developed countries in the international standards-setting process, in addition to their developed technology, international standards are similar to the standards of developed countries, and hence developed countries' costs of compliance are lower compared to those of developing countries, further marginalizing the latter.

Moreover, the process of international standards-setting has become increasingly politicised since the advent of the SPS Agreement, with its harmonisation provisions encouraging conformity with international standards. This has resulted in making the adoption of standards a more complex and time-consuming process. Further, although the Codex standards are meant to be scientifically sound, the scientific expert system that sets these standards lacks transparency, does not conform to the scientific principles of independence and objectivity, and does not provide opportunities for debates among scientists on controversial issues. The Codex does not provide information on how it manages scientific controversies; hence there is no avenue for assessing its conclusions concerning the extent to which they may be contested in a peer review, or how minority views among experts are dealt with. The standards-setting system lacks accountability and gives rise to a democratic deficit that jeopardises the legitimacy and credibility of the Codex.

Additionally, the SPS Agreement faces many challenges to be overcome if it is to achieve its objectives. The major challenges are the slow harmonisation process; the controversy concerning the place of science in risk analysis; the problems faced by developing countries in meeting developed countries' standards; and the persistence of developed countries' SPS standards as non-tariff barriers to developing countries' exports.

6.3 EU food safety standards

A point that emerges clearly is that, given the EU's history of food safety scares, the EU stringent food safety standards are not negotiable. The BSE crisis exposed the shortcomings that had hitherto bedevilled the EU food safety policy and institutions. As a result of the crisis, the EU came up with a new policy on food safety which would be anchored on scientific principles and based upon a comprehensive, integrated approach that would take into account traceability of feed and food and their ingredients; risk analysis; and the precautionary principle and other legitimate factors. The new policy orientation led to the enactment of Regulation 178 of 2002 – the EU General Food Law.

The EU food safety regulations apply equally to domestic and imported food products. The food business operator, such as a supermarket food retailer or food processor, is required to ensure the safety of foods imported by the business by ensuring that it complies with EU regulations, and must withdraw from the market all non-conforming food. Furthermore, food business operators are required to comply with the general and specific hygiene requirements, the Hazard Analysis Critical Control Points system (HACCP) requirements and official controls, and registration and approval.

EU food imports are only allowed upon compliance with the relevant food safety regulations or from countries deemed to have equivalent food control systems. For the third country's food control system to be considered equivalent, it is audited by the Food and Veterinary Office (FVO) for the following: food legislation; the organisation of its competent authority; the training of staff in the performance of official controls; the resources, including diagnostic facilities, available to the competent authority; the existence and operation of documented control procedures and control systems based on priorities; and the extent and operation of official controls on imports of animals, plants, and their products.

From the analysis of EU food safety standards several lessons emerge. First, food safety institutions should be unified and centralised in order to avoid duplication of efforts in policy formulation and implementation and to foster policy coherence and focus. Second, Member states of an FTA should be limited in their choice of implementing forms and methods of food safety regulations. This limits the room for divergent and probable protectionist implementation of such regulations. Third, there is need to build confidence in FTA food safety regulations, and also in Member states' conduct of mandated functions under the food safety policy.

222 Conclusions

The EU is a selective policy recipient of international standards. These standards are taken into account in the adoption of the EU's SPS regulations so long as they are compatible with the EU's food safety objectives. Furthermore, apart from the protection of human life and health, the EU's food safety objectives go further, to include the protection of consumers' interests; fair practices in food trade; the protection of animal health and welfare; and plant and environmental health.[4] The EU's food safety objectives are also intended to achieve the EU's general objective of free movement of food and feed. On the other hand, the Codex standards have as their objective the protection of the consumer and the facilitation of international trade, while the objective of the SPS Agreement is the prevention of SPS measures from becoming unnecessary barriers to trade. As a result of these differences in policy orientation, the EU's food safety standards tend to be more stringent than the Codex standards.

The EU food safety standards pose a dilemma. The EU, by taking into consideration 'other legitimate factors' in its risk management decisions breaches the Codex provisions on 'criteria for consideration of the other factors referred to in the Second Statement of the Principle'. In the Codex, the 'other factors' may not be in conflict with the scientific evidence supporting the measure, and the factors should be acceptable worldwide or on a regional basis. However, it is precisely because the EU wishes to go 'beyond science' in its risk management that it invokes these 'other factors'. If these factors are to be compliant with the scientific evidence, they are rendered superfluous. Furthermore, since other Members of the WTO may object to these factors, they cannot receive worldwide acceptance.

Moreover, whereas under Article 7 of the SPS Agreement provisional measures are to be reviewed within a reasonable time, under Article 7(2) of Regulation 178 of 2002 the review is not so bound, and the precautionary measure may be taken in situations of lasting uncertainty. Hence the precautionary principle as applied in the EU under Article 7 of Regulation 178 of 2002 is not the equivalent of the provisional measure envisaged under Article 5.7 of the SPS Agreement, and as such it may be challenged under the provisions of the SPS Agreement.

Given the incapacities of developing countries, and in particular COMESA countries, the burdensome nature of EU food safety standards – especially the control inspection and approval procedures, including information requirements and procedures for sampling, testing, and certification – may be characterised as non-conforming to the spirit, if not the letter, of Article 8 and Annex C (1) (c) and (d) of the SPS Agreement since, although applied equally to domestic as well as imported products, in practice their effect is disproportionately in favour of domestic products as compared to products from developing countries.

Furthermore, the EU requirements for equivalence, which are process-based and not end product requirements, necessarily imply that third countries have to set up similar, if not the same, food safety control systems as the EU to be eligible to export to the EU. Furthermore, the practice of the FVO inspections reinforces

---

4 Regulation 178 of 2002, art 5.1.

these conditions by requiring similar, if not the same, food control systems in third countries as are to be found in the EU. These EU provisions and practices may fail to meet the threshold of Article 4 of the SPS Agreement and may be impugned under Section 4 (7) (d) of the Codex guidelines on equivalence, which provides: 'An importing country should recognise that sanitary measures different from its own may be capable of achieving its ALOP, and can therefore be found to be equivalent'.

Moreover, particularly from developing countries' perspectives, the EU food safety standards are complex and stringent not only in their formulation but also in their application. The EU standards appear to be burdensome to developing countries, and in particular COMESA countries. Compliance with the EU standards entails the setting up and operation of sophisticated food control systems that are beyond the capacities of most developing countries, especially COMESA countries. This is evidenced by the EU standards for horticultural and animal products. This has resulted in a two-tier standards system in COMESA exporting countries: one that is strict that is geared towards meeting the strict EU standards and the other one that is low for products destined for the domestic market.

The burdensome nature of the stringency of the EU food safety standards is manifested in horticultural products by the requirement for exporting countries to have equivalent food control systems in addition to requirements for HACCP and microbiological criteria. This results in most developing countries restricting their exports to primary products that have fewer requirements, as opposed to processed products with more complex requirements.

On the other hand, the stringency of the EU food safety standards in animal products is manifested in the process of and criteria for approval and listing of third countries and their establishments that is lengthy, onerous, and punitive, so that few developing countries, including COMESA countries, manage to be qualified and, among these, fewer still manage to carry out actual exports.

Further, the EU appears to be circumventing the disciplines of the SPS Agreement by relying on PVS and their implementation by food business operators to effect implementation of its food safety regulations while at the same time disavowing liability for them. This is illustrated by the EU traceability and HACCP requirements. Although Article 18 of Regulation 178 of 2002 provides for the requirement for traceability, and Article 5 of Regulation 852/2004 sets out the requirement for HACCP, neither regulation specifies how these requirements are to be met. In order to meet the requirements of these regulations the BRC standard verifies the existence and effectiveness of traceability and HACCP.

6.4 COMESA food safety standards

There is an EU–COMESA food safety standards dilemma: while, on the one hand, the EU's food safety standards are found to be burdensome for developing countries and their conformity to international standards to be contested; on the other hand, COMESA countries are found to have a weak institutional framework, with slow and inefficient decision-making procedures coupled with a lack

224 Conclusions

of capacity to deliver on core mandates by community institutions. Yet the two entities are determined to trade with each other in food products.

COMESA food control systems (encompassing food legislation; food control management; food inspection; official food control laboratories; and food safety and quality information, education, and communication) are weak and fall short of international standards. These systems are incapable of meeting the scientific disciplines laid down in the SPS Agreement, particularly the requirement for risk analysis under Article 5 of the Agreement. The systems are also unable to meet the requirements for the elements of a food control system as laid down in the Codex guidelines on food control systems.

COMESA Members' SPS regimes do not measure up to the SPS regimes of their trading partners, in particular the EU. Furthermore, SPS management and enforcement institutions at the national and regional level are weak or mostly non-existent. The weakness or lack of SPS management and enforcement institutions at the regional level in COMESA may be attributable to the poor economic climate prevailing across most of Africa.

These circumstances result in a standards 'gap' between the EU and COMESA, where compliance with EU standards is out of reach for most COMESA countries, except with the aid of technical assistance. COMESA Member countries' trade concerns with EU food safety standards are mainly centred on their lack of capacity to meet the requirements of these standards, rather than their legality. Their strategies for dealing with the challenge posed by the EU standards have been to find ways and means of compliance.

On the other hand, the compliance costs of EU food safety standards serve to accentuate the lack of capacity of COMESA countries, particularly for small-scale farmers. Whereas the EU is able to set food safety standards which its Members are able to meet, these standards are required to be met by developing countries, including COMESA countries, without taking into account their abilities to meet the costs of compliance. Even where non-recurrent costs, such as infrastructure, have been met, the recurrent costs, such as chemicals in laboratories, might prove difficult to meet. Hence, although the impact of compliance costs may not be precisely determined, it is a justified fear that compliance costs may be detrimental to COMESA countries' exports. COMESA countries have mostly relied on technical assistance to overcome these challenges.

The incapacities of COMESA countries are legion. The COMESA countries have outdated and piecemeal legislation. The legislation does not adequately tackle current and emerging food safety problems in relation to pesticide residues, food additives, contaminants, and biotoxins. The legislation is often scattered over several uncoordinated statutes and without implementation strategies, leading to high levels of default in implementation.

Furthermore, a majority of food safety standards in COMESA countries relate to product specifications. Only a limited number of standards cover sampling and testing methods, labelling, or other matters that are of more relevance to trade. Even where standards have been harmonised regionally, few are adopted nationally, thus limiting their effectiveness. Most of the standards are based on Codex standards, which are often not appropriate to some national circumstances. Some countries experience difficulty in adapting Codex standards to meet national needs due to lack of technical expertise. Furthermore, although some countries have standards based on Codex, they have difficulty in monitoring the implementation of these standards or lack laboratory facilities to verify compliance of food samples with relevant standards.

Most COMESA countries lack clear food safety policies, leading to a paucity of coordinated and sustainable food control management systems. Moreover, most countries in the region do not appreciate the major public health and economic implications of food safety, and as a consequence food safety remains a low priority in national policy-making. As a result, essential elements of food control management are inadequate, or non-existent.

Moreover, most food inspection services in COMESA are underfunded, while the food inspectors are poorly trained, poorly paid, and tasked with additional functions over their core functions. These services are often located in the capitals and major cities, with little, if any, control exercised in small towns and rural areas. Moreover, few countries in COMESA have efficient national import/export inspection and certification systems.

Similarly, official food control laboratories in most COMESA countries are weak and fail to meet the Codex criteria for such laboratories. Most of these laboratories do not have the capacity to test for chemical contaminants and biotoxins, and many of them are not accredited.

6.5 A food control system for EU–COMESA food products trade

As a solution to the 'standards divide' in the EU–COMESA food trade, this book proposes a three-pronged solution. First, the book proposes a framework for a needs assessment and upgrading of national food control systems in COMESA.

The second proposal is for a COMESA food control system (CFCS) based on the premise that a regional food control system with regional standards has the following advantages: it is cost effective, as countries pool their resources together to address their common standards issues; it enhances the SPS capacities of the Member countries through education and training and by sharing services such as inspection and certification, and infrastructure such as laboratories; it inspires confidence and trust in export markets in the region's food safety standards and thus increases trade; it helps speed up the harmonisation of standards by prescribing one set of standards for all members; and it enables the Member countries to present common positions in international forums and hence influence the setting of international standards. Additionally, the formulation of regional food safety standards obviates the need for utilizing mutual recognition and equivalence as standardisation tools within the COMESA region.

A final proposal is for the EU–COMESA Food Control System (ECFCS). It is proposed that the ECFCS be based on the determination of equivalence and that it be in the form of an annex or protocol in the EPA framework. The main

226 *Conclusions*

objective of the ECFCS would be to achieve equivalence with the EU food control system for the COMESA food control system for export products to the EU by ensuring the equivalence of COMESA hygiene practices, its implementation of HACCP principles, its official controls, and the registration and approval of food establishments.

6.6 Final remarks

Since the inception of the GATT in 1947, international trade norms have pursued, as their main objective, the liberalisation of international trade through streamlining and disciplining the rules of market access. Having settled the modalities of disciplining tariffs, standards, both technical and SPS, remain as major barriers to market access.

Hence both the TBT and the SPS Agreements are aimed at disciplining standards in international trade. Both Agreements have as their main objective the harmonisation of Members' standards, which they seek to achieve by exhorting Members to base their standards on international standards; it is only by default that the other disciplines in the Agreements are resorted to.

The primary discipline for SPS standards is that they must conform to the norms set by the SPS Agreement. As a result, although WTO Members are free to set their own SPS standards, these standards are required to be based on risk assessment. Similarly, regional standards are also required to be based on risk assessment. In default of basing their SPS standards on risk assessment, countries and regions are liable to consultations and dispute settlement proceedings under Article 11 of the SPS Agreement and further under the provisions of Articles XXII and XXIII of GATT 1994, as elaborated and applied by the Dispute Settlement Understanding (DSU).

According to the WTO Secretariat, as at the end of the year 2014, 42 disputes had cited the SPS Agreement in their requests for consultations,[5] and a total of 368 specific trade concerns were raised in the SPS Committee between 1995 and the end of 2013.[6] Hence, it is evident that national SPS standards continue to give rise to trade concerns in international trade. Moreover, given the fact that the number of trade concerns is far higher than the number of disputes, it appears that WTO Members prefer to settle their trade concerns at the consultative stage rather than at the formal dispute stage.[7] Furthermore, so far, in all the adjudicated disputes under the SPS Agreement, the Panels and Appellate Body have ruled against the impugned Member standards. Thus it may be concluded that that the norms set by the SPS Agreement have served to discipline Members' SPS

---

5 WTO website: <http://www.wto.org/english/tratop_e/dispu_e/dispu_agreements_index_e.htm?id=A19#selected_agreement> accessed 15 September 2015.
6 WTO Committee on Sanitary and Phytosanitary Measures, 'Specific Trade Concerns, Note by the Secretariat, Revision' (G/SPS/GEN/204/Rev.14, 4 March 2014) 5.
7 Francis Snyder, 'Reflections on the Hidden Jurisprudence of the WTO' (2013) 2 *Peking University Transnational Law Review* 162.

Conclusions 227

standards. To the extent that Members' non-conforming SPS standards may be said to impact negatively on international trade, the disciplines of the SPS Agreement may be viewed as impacting positively on international trade.

Under Article XXIV of GATT 1994, regional trade agreements (RTAs) are recognised as trade facilitating arrangements. Good examples of such arrangements are the EU and COMESA. Indeed, under Article 35(2) of the Cotonou Agreement, the promotion of regional integration is the basis for EC-ACP trade relations. However, it is evident that whereas the EU's SPS standards are based on the EU's chosen level of protection, which is, at times, higher than that of international standards, COMESA as a region and its Member countries have scanty SPS standards. Furthermore, COMESA lacks an SPS infrastructure, unlike the EU, which has an elaborate one.

These disparities, coupled by the underdeveloped status of COMESA vis-à-vis the EU, serve as a barrier to EU–COMESA trade in agricultural products. As a result of COMESA's non-conformity with international SPS standards, its exports to the EU and to the rest of the world are curtailed, perpetuating its poverty, as increasing trade serves to alleviate poverty.

Thus, as proposed in this book, in order for COMESA to improve its exports to the EU and to the rest of the world, it should, as a first step, upgrade its standards and SPS infrastructure to international standards. The upgrade will qualify COMESA to ask the EU for a determination of equivalence under Article 4 of the SPS Agreement. Alternatively, as proposed in this study, the upgrade will enable COMESA to effectively participate in the EU–COMESA Food Control System.

Index

Africa 2; agriculture in 3, 6–7, 17, 107–9, 110–11, 218; food control systems in 114; *see also* African Union (AU); Common Market for Eastern and Southern Africa (COMESA); specific countries in Africa
African Organization for Standardization (ARSO) 178
African Union (AU) 6–7, 170; African Food Safety Authority (AFSA) 170; Food Safety Management Coordination System (AU-FSMCS) 170; Interafrican Bureau for Animal Resources (AU-IBAR) 178; Rapid Alert System for Food and Feed 170
Agreement on Subsidies and Countervailing Measures (SCM Agreement) 160
Agreement on Technical Barriers to Trade (TBT Agreement) 29, 226; Annex 1 159; Annex 3 159; Article 2.12 46; Article 3 159–60; Article 4.1 159; Article 8 159–60
Agreement on the Application of Sanitary and Phytosanitary Measures (SPS Agreement) 3, 5, 8, 16, 28–37, 219–21, 226; Annex A 20, 30, 32, 33, 38, 45, 46, 76n126, 157, 158, 159, 219; Annex B 41–2, 45, 46, 48, 209, 219; Annex C 163–4, 222; Article 1 157; Article 2 157; Article 2.2 30, 31, 33, 35, 219; Article 2.3 39n147, 92; Article 3.1 38, 39, 40, 46–7, 74; Article 3.2 38, 39, 40, 47; Article 3.3 14, 37, 40, 56, 74, 84, 214; Article 4 39, 165, 223, 227; Article 5 37, 75, 125, 165; Article 5.1 30, 31, 33, 34, 35, 36, 37, 40, 53, 78; Article 5.2 30, 34, 37, 40; Article 5.3 30, 34, 40; Article 5.4 40, 54; Article 5.5 37, 40, 54; Article 5.6 30–1, 37, 40; Article 5.7 30, 35, 36, 37, 40, 84, 85, 91, 92, 219, 222; Article 5.8 40; Article 7 48, 209, 222; Article 8 163, 164, 222; Article 9 41, 42, 219; Article 9.2 42, 57; Article 10 41, 219; Article 10.1 43–4, 57; Article 10.2 44, 45, 57; Article 10.3 44; Article 10.4 44–5; Article 11 58, 226; Article 13 159; Article 14 42, 219; developing countries, provisions for 41–6; dispute resolution procedures 27; disputes under 11–15; harmonisation under 37–9, 41, 46, 58; preamble 19n41, 37–8, 41, 46, 84; precautionary principle and 84–5; private volunteer standards and 157–61; scientific disciplines of 30
agriculture: in Africa 3, 6–7, 17, 107–9, 110–11, 218; in Asia 17; importance of trade in 3, 17; subsidies for 18
Agritrade 142, 143
Alemanno, Alberto 78n134
Algeria 101
Alpharma Inc. v. Council of the European Union 92n214
anthrax 101
appropriate level of protection (ALOP) 51, 214
Argentina 14, 15, 181
Artegodan GmbH and Others v. Commission 87, 90
ASEAN *see* Association of Southeast Asian Nations (ASEAN)
Asia: agriculture in 17; *see also* specific countries in Asia
Asselt, Margolein B A V 91n208
Association of Southeast Asian Nations (ASEAN) 96, 108, 188, 197, 203; Harmonised of Food Control and

Safety Requirements and Principles 197; working groups 197
AU *see* African Union (AU)
Australia – Apples 12, 14, 158
Australia – Salmon 11, 12, 31, 32, 33, 37, 39n147

barriers to trade 4–5, 10–11, 18–19, 131, 132–3, 137; *see also* Sanitary and Phytosanitary Measures (SPS standards)
beef, trade in 12, 126, 129, 140–43, 164
Benin 114
Biret International v. Council 95
Botswana 140, 141
botulism 101
Bovine Spongiform Encephalopathy (BSE) 60
Brazil 181
British Retail Consortium Global Standard for Food Safety (BRC standard) 20, 153, 155–6, 160
Brown, Lester 109n45
Burundi 107, 206

Canada – Continued Suspension 11–12, 14, 32, 35, 52, 80
capacity building, definition of 171n11
Caribbean Community (CARICOM) 96
Caribbean Community states plus the Dominican Republic (CARIFORUM) 207
CARICOM 96
Carreno, Ignacio 160n165
Cartegena Protocol on Biosafety to the Convention on Biological Diversity 37n138
Central Africa States 207
Chaoimh, Eadaoin N 90n202
Charlier, Christophe 64n28
chemical poisoning 2, 101
Chile 181
China 2, 15, 166
Chiquita Brands International, Inc. and Others v. Commission of the European Communities 96
cholera 101
Codex Alimentarius Commission (Codex) 5, 25, 45, 46, 121, 161, 165, 185, 223; Code of Practice on General Principles of Food Hygiene 154, 156; Criteria for Consideration of the Other Factors referred to in the Second Statement of Principle 81; Definitions of Risk Analysis Terms Related to Food Safety 72; EU use of standards 72–4; General Principles of Food Hygiene 48; Guidelines for the Design, Operation, Assessment and Accreditation of Food Import and Export Inspection and Certification Systems 116, 120, 181; precautionary principle and 85–7; Principles and Guidelines for National Food Control Systems 113; Principles for Food Import and Export Inspection and Certification 118, 183; Procedural Manual 38n142, 76n123, 77n127, 112n63; standards of, use of 39, 41, 70, 71, 72–4, 75, 116, 197, 224–5; Statements of Principle Concerning the Role of Science in the Codex Decision-Making Process and the Extent to Which Other Factors are Taken Into Account 72, 77, 81; transparency of procedures 27, 50; Working Principles for Risk Analysis for Application in the Framework of the Codex Alimentarius 72, 85–6, 87; Working Principles for Risk Analysis for Food Safety for Application by Governments 86–7
COMESA *see* Common Market for Eastern and Southern Africa (COMESA)
COMESA Food Control System (CFCS) 196–206; Common Regulatory Objectives (CRO) 199; Cost Benefit Analysis (CBA) 199; Food Safety Authority (CFSA) 198, 200; Green Pass (CGP) 198, 201; inspection and certification 201–2; laboratories 202–4; organisational structure 200–1; Reference to Standards Principle (RSP) 199; Regional SPS Reference Laboratories (RSPSRLs) 203; regulatory framework 197–9; Regulatory Impact Assessment (RIA) 199
COMESA Regulations on the Application of Sanitary and Phytosanitary Measures (COMESA SPS Regulations) 111–12, 169–70, 200; Article 7 170; Article 15 170, 184, 203; Article 16 170, 184, 203;

Article 17 170, 184, 203; Article 21 201n110; Article 22 178
COMESA Treaty 103, 106, 111; Article 50 111; Article 113 111; Article 132 111; Green Pass 111, 170
Commission v. Denmark 88n195
Commission v. Germany (Rheinheitsgebot) 73, 75
Common Market for Eastern and Southern Africa (COMESA) 3, 102–11, 184n54; Agricultural Marketing Promotion and Regional Integration Project (AMPRIP) 124, 184, 203; Authority 103–4, 105; Comprehensive Africa Agricultural Development Programme (CAADP) 124; Council of Ministers 103, 104, 105, 200; Court of Justice 103, 104–5, 106; Customs Union 103; establishment of 102–3; food inspections in 119–20; food safety control systems 8–9, 112–26, 169, 223–5; Free Trade Area (FTA) 103; harmonised standards of 122, 125; institutional framework of 103–5; laboratories in 121–2, 123, 184; and PVS 162–3; Secretariat 103, 104, 105–6, 123; socioeconomic aspects of 106–11; *see also* COMESA Regulations on the Application of Sanitary and Phytosanitary Measures (COMESA SPS Regulations); EU–COMESA trade
Comoros 106, 107
compliance costs 134–7
Cost Benefit Analysis (CBA) 188, 199
Cote d'Ivoire 132
Cotonou Agreement 126, 128, 140, 143, 147, 165, 206; Article 35(2) 227
Creutzfeldt-Jakob Disease (nvCJD) 60
Criminal Proceedings v. Leon Motte 74–5
Criminal proceedings v. Michel Debus 73
Criminal Proceedings v. Sandoz BV 74

Democratic Republic of Congo 101, 106
developing countries: agriculture importance in 3, 17; participation by 44–5; special and differential treatment of 43–4, 45–6, 54–7; SPS Agreement provisions for 41–6; SPS standards for 4–5, 15; technical assistance for 42–3
Directive 96/23 144

Djibouti 107, 142
Doha Ministerial Decision 56
Doherty, Martin 145–6

East African Community (EAC) 125, 206, 207
Eastern and Southern Africa (ESA) 206, 207
EC – Bananas 96
EC – Biotech 11, 13, 35, 43, 57, 70, 71, 96, 97–8, 158
EC – Hormones 11, 12, 14, 33, 34, 37, 38, 39, 49, 53, 54, 58, 70, 76, 78, 79, 79n147, 96, 97, 98, 143, 214n162
Economic Community of West African States (ECOWAS) 96, 117–18, 206–7
Economic Partnership Agreements (EPAs) 128, 140, 143, 147, 165, 206; SPS provisions in 207–8
ECOWAS *see* Economic Community of West African States (ECOWAS)
EC – Poultry (US) 1–2, 12, 13, 48
EFTA v. Norway 89n199
Egypt 1, 144, 148
EPA *see* Economic Partnership Agreements (EPAs)
equivalence 51–2, 164–5, 166
Eritrea 142, 144, 145
Escherichia coli (E. Coli) 1
Ethiopia 109, 121, 142, 148
EU *see* European Union (EU)
EU–Chile Association Agreement 208
EU–COMESA Food Control System (ECFCS) 225–6; factors to consider in 210–12; Joint Food Control Committee (JFCC) 212, 213; Joint Scientific Committee (JSC) 212, 213–14; structure of 212–14
EU–COMESA trade 1, 3, 6–7, 102, 127–67, 225; beef trade 126, 129, 140–43, 164; fishery products trade 120, 129, 143–7, 164; horticultural products trade 129, 132, 147–50, 164; importance of 204, 218; model to improve 168–217; needs assessment in 171–6; private voluntary standards in 151–63; regulatory gap in 137–50
EU–Mexico Global Agreement 208
Euro-Mediterranean Association Agreements 209
European Food Safety Authority (EFSA) 8, 62, 63, 64, 65–9, 195; Advisory

232 *Index*

Forum 68; Executive Director 68; Management Board 68; Scientific Committee 66, 68, 69; Scientific Panels 66, 68, 69
European Union (EU) 1, 108, 188; Commission Decision 2006/766/EC 145; 'Communication on Consumer Health and Food Safety' 87; Communication on the Precautionary Principle 88, 89, 91n209; Directorate General for Health and Consumers (DG SANCO) 117, 119, 144; 'Final Report on a Mission Carried Out in Egypt from 22 to 31 January 2007 Concerning Controls of Pesticides in Food of Plant Origin intended for Export to the European Union' 137n41; 'First Written Submission in EC – Measures Affecting the Approval and Marketing of Biotech Products' 27; Food and Veterinary Office (FVO) 119, 144, 149, 165, 221; food control management in 117; food inspections in 119; food safety standards of 8, 61–2, 69–94, 87–9, 113–14, 221–3; Green Paper on the General Principles of Food Law 88; laboratories in 121; National Reference Laboratories (NRLs) 121; RASFF Annual Report 2013 2; Reference Laboratories (EURLs) 121, 204; risk analysis in 72, 75–81; Standing Committee on the Food Chain and Animal Health (SCFCAH) 117; US, trade with 1–2; *see also* EU–COMESA trade; European Food Safety Authority (EFSA); Treaty on the Functioning of the European Union (TFEU); specific countries in Europe; specific regulations
Euro-Retailer Produce Working Group (EUREP) 154
Everything But Arms (EBA) 126, 128, 140, 143, 147, 165

FAO *see* Food and Agriculture Organization (FAO)
Federation de l'industrie de l'huilerie de la CEE (Fediol) v. Commission 95
fishery products, trade in 12, 120, 129, 143–7, 164, 166
fish mouse 101
Five-Year Strategic Plan for Food Safety in Africa 173

food, definition of 112n63
Food and Agriculture Organization (FAO) 5, 75, 102, 108, 116n85, 119, 122, 170; *Assuring Food Safety and Quality: Guidelines for Strengthening National Food Control Systems* 112n64, 182n48, 187, 192, 200n107; diagnostic tool of 42; food control system core pillars 114; Regional Conference on Food Safety for Africa of 2005 173; risk assessment by 72; *Strengthening National Food Control Systems: Guidelines to Assess Capacity Building Needs* 171n11, 172, 172n14, 176, 176n23, 178, 179, 182, 185, 188nn67–8, 189, 199n106; technical assistance by 42–3
food control, definition of 112
food control management 116–18, 179–81; benchmarks for 180–1; definition of 116n85, 179
food control system: COMESA 112–22; definition of 113; elements of 114–22; food control management 116–18, 179–81; food legislation 115–16, 186–9; government intervention in 189–90; inspection 118–20, 181–3; integrated model 194, 195; laboratories 120–22, 184–6; models for 191–4; multiple agency model 192–3, 194–5; risk management 116–18; single agency model 193–4, 195
food inspection 118–20, 181–3; benchmarks for 182–3; definition of 118, 181
food legislation/law 115–16, 186–9; benchmarks for 187–9; definition of 113
foot-and-mouth disease (FMD) 14, 141, 142
France 113
free trade agreement (FTA) 206
fruits, trade in 12–13, 14, 129

General Agreement on Tariffs and Trade of 1947 (GATT) 4, 10, 16, 71, 226
General Agreement on Tariffs and Trade of 1994 (GATT 1994) 29, 38, 40, 41, 47; Article XX 28; Article XXII 226; Article XXIII 226; Article XXIV 227
genetically modified organisms (GMOs) 70, 97

Germany 113
global administration law (GAL) 25–8, 48, 220; definition of 26
Global Good Agricultural Practices (GlobalGAP) 20, 153, 154–5, 160
good agricultural practices (GAP) 174, 179, 181
good hygiene practices (GHP) 145, 179
good manufacturing practices (GMP) 174, 179
Good Regulatory Practice 187

Harmonized Guidelines for Internal Quality Control in Analytical Chemistry Laboratories 185
Hazard Analysis Critical Control Point (HACCP) 139, 145, 149, 154, 156, 174, 179, 221
Heiskanen, Veijo 28n79, 47n180
Henson, Spencer 130–1, 136, 209n149
Henson, Steven 138n41
Hepatitis A 101
Hierarchy of Trade-Related SPS Management Functions 170, 174–5
horticultural products, trade in 12–13, 14, 129, 132, 147–50, 164, 166
Howse, Robert 10n5

India 166
information, education, and communication (IEC) 176–9; benchmarks 177–9; definition of 176
Ingco, Merlinda D 17n36
inspection *see* food inspection
Intergovernmental Authority for Development (IGAD) 142
International Centre for Trade and Sustainable Development (ICTSD) 145–6
International Electro-technical Commission (IEC) 159
International Harmonized Protocol for the Proficiency Testing of (Chemical) Analytical Laboratories 185
International Office of Epizootics (OIE) 5, 25, 41, 43, 45, 46, 161; diagnostic tool of 42; mediation procedures 26–7; Terrestrial Animal Health Code 38n143, 141; trainings by 42
International Plant Protection Convention (IPPC) 5, 25, 41, 45, 46; dispute settlement procedures 25; Phytosanitary Capacity Evaluation (PCE) 42; preamble 38n144; trainings by 42

International Standardization Organization (ISO) 159; ISO 17025 123, 185; ISO/IEC Guide 58:1993 185
IPPC *see* International Plant Protection Convention (IPPC)

Jacobs, Scott H 188n66
Jaffee, Steven 130–1, 134n32, 136, 175n21, 209n149
Japan 166
Japan – Agricultural Products 11, 12–13, 31, 35, 36, 40
Japan – Apples 11, 13, 31, 36, 52, 85, 90
Japan – Film 158
Josling, Timothy E 20n43, 21n45

Kenya 101, 117, 124, 132, 172, 181, 206; beef exports by 140, 141, 142; fishery exports by 120, 144; horticultural exports by 109, 148; laboratories in 125, 184, 203
Klinke, Andreas 76n123

laboratories, food control 120–22, 123, 184–6; benchmarks for 185–6
land-locked least developed countries (LLDCs) 107
Least Developed Countries (LDCs) 107, 128, 143, 165
Léon van Parys NV v. BelgischeInterventie- en Restitutiebureau (BIRB) 96
Libya 106
Lome Convention 140
Lome IV 140

McCarthy, Colin 110n50
Madagascar 140, 141, 144, 148, 206
Maertens, Miet 23n55, 133n30, 135
Malawi 103, 121
Malaysia 181
Mali 114
Mauritius 101, 106, 107, 144, 147, 184, 203, 206
maximum residue limits for pesticides (MRLs) 70, 148
Mehdi, Shafaeddin 134n32, 135n34
MERCOSUR 96, 108
Meulen, Bernd van der 96
Monsanto Agricoltura Italia SpA and Others v. Presidenza del Consiglio dei Ministri and Others 73, 88n194
Mozambique 101

multilateral environmental agreement (MEA) 82
mushroom poisoning 101

Nakajima All Precision Co. Ltd. v. Council 95
Namibia 141
Nash, John D 17n36
needs assessment 170, 171–6
Nigeria 101
non-governmental body, definition of 159

OIE *see* International Office of Epizootics (OIE)
Opel Austria v. Council of the European Union 94
Orden David 20n43, 21n45

Pacific states 207
Peel, Jacqueline 78n142, 79
pesticide poisoning 2, 101
Pfizer Animal Health SA v. Council of the European Union 73, 75, 80, 88n194, 97
Phytosanitary Capacity Evaluation (PCE) 42
Portugal v. Council 95–6
poultry, trade in 1–2, 13–14
precautionary principle 37, 77, 82–94; Codex and 85–7; definition of 82, 88; EU food safety standards and 87–9; SPS Agreement and 84–5
Preferential Trade Area for Eastern and Southern Africa (PTA) 102
Prevost, Denise 16n31, 79n143
Private Voluntary Standards (PVS) 9, 20, 149, 150, 151–63, 189, 211; BRC standard 20, 153, 155–6, 160; and COMESA countries 162–3; GlobalGap standard 20, 153, 154–5, 160; non-governmental entities in 159–61; and SPS Agreement 157–61
Proceedings for Compulsory Reconstruction v. Smanor SA 73
PTA Treaty 102–3; Article 50 102
public-private partnerships (PPPs) 189

Queen, The v. The Minister for Agriculture, Fisheries and Food and the Secretary of State for Health, ex parte: Fedesa and Others 97
Queen, The v. The Minister for Agriculture, Fisheries and Food and the Secretary of State for Health, ex parte: National Farmers' Union and Others 79n146
Qureshi, Asif H 55–6

Racke GmbH & Co. vis the Hauptzollamt Mainz 94
Rapid Alert System for Food and Feed (RASFF) 148, 170, 178
regional trade agreements (RTAs) 112, 123, 227
Regulation 178 (2002) (EU) 8, 61, 62, 63–4, 66, 85, 90, 92, 114, 115, 138, 198, 221; Article 1 65; Article 3.1 75; Article 5 65, 66, 73; Article 7 77, 88, 89, 91, 222; Article 8 65, 66; Article 9 66; Article 10 66; Article 11 139n52, 210, 215n163; Article 13 66; Article 16 66; Article 17 210; Article 18 156, 210, 223; Article 19 210; Article 22 65; preamble 65–6, 211n153
Regulation 258/97 (EU) 73
Regulation 396/2005 (EU) 148
Regulation 852/2004 (EU) 138, 198, 212; Article 5 156, 223
Regulation 853/2004 (EU) 138, 198
Regulation 854/2004 (EU) 138, 198; Article 11 141; Article 12 141
Regulation 882/2004 (EU) 138, 183, 198, 204; Article 32 184, 203; Article 33 184, 203; Article 50 216
Regulation 1107/2009 (EU) 148
Regulation 1854/2004 (EU) 145
Regulatory Impact Assessment (RIA) 188, 199
Renn, Ortwin 76n123
Rio Declaration 82
risk analysis: definition of 63; EU standards for 72, 75–81
risk assessment 31–2, 78–80; additives, contaminants or toxins 32, 33; appropriateness of 33–4; definition of 63, 76; entry, establishing or spread of pests or diseases 32–3; factors in 34
risk management 116–18; definition of 63–4, 77
Roberts, Donna 20n43, 21n45
Rwanda 107, 172, 206

Sadeleer, Nicholas D 90n201
Saint Vincent and the Grenadines 157
Sanitary and Phytosanitary Measures (SPS standards) 3, 4–6, 10–11; application of 30–1; basis of measures

Index 235

29, 31–2, 33–5; definition of 20, 157–8; of developed countries 4–5, 15; of developing countries 4–5, 15; harmonisation of 22, 37–41, 46, 47–51; impact on trade of 22–3, 130–7; level of protection higher than 40; phased introduction of new 44; precautionary principle and 82–94; provisional measures 35–6; significance of 17–28; as trade barrier 4–5, 15, 18–19; voluntary 20
Scoones, Ian 141
Senegal 101, 132
Seychelles 106, 107, 144, 147, 206
Singapore 147
Somalia 142
South Africa 101, 114
South Centre 150
Southern African Development Community (SADC) 206
special and differential treatment (SDT) 43–4, 45–6, 54–7
Spreij, Melvin 177n24, 193n79, 193n82, 193n84
SPS Agreement *see* Agreement on the Application of Sanitary and Phytosanitary Measures (SPS Agreement)
SPS Committee 161; 'Guidelines to Further the Practical Implementation of Article 5.5' 76n123
SPS standards *see* Sanitary and Phytosanitary Measures (SPS standards)
standard, definition of 20
Standards and Trade Development Facility (STDF) 5, 43, 45, 190, 205
Sudan 106, 121, 142
Swaziland 107, 121, 140, 141, 148, 206
Swinnen, Johan F M 23n55, 133n30, 135
Szajkowska, Anna 62n16

Taiwan 147
Tanzania 101, 117, 125, 172
TBT Agreement *see* Agreement on Technical Barriers to Trade (TBT Agreement)
TBT Committee 51
Technical Centre for Agricultural and Rural Cooperation EC-ACP (CTA) 142
TFEU *see* Treaty on the Functioning of the European Union (TFEU)
Thailand 147

trade: SPS standards as catalyst to 131–2; *see also* barriers to trade
Treaty of Amsterdam (ToA) 75
Treaty on the Functioning of the European Union (TFEU) 61; Article 11 87; Article 12 87; Article 34 62, 75; Article 35 62; Article 36 62, 74, 75, 100; Article 114(4) 75, 100; Article 168 90; Article 169 90; Article 191 87, 89–90; Article 218 94
Trebilcock, Michael J 10n5
Trouwborst, Arie 90n201
typhoid fever 101

UEMOA 123
Uganda 101, 103, 107, 114, 117, 142, 172, 206; fishery exports by 120, 144; horticultural exports by 148; laboratories in 125
Understanding on Rules and Procedures Governing the Settlement of Disputes (DSU) 26, 226; Article 4 166; Article 6 166; Article 11 52
United Kingdom (UK) 113, 188; Food Safety Act (No. 16 of 1990) 155
United Nations: Conference on Trade and Development (UNCTAD) 5, 107, 108–9, 153n136, 157; Draft Articles on Responsibility of States for Internationally Wrongful Acts 158; Economic Commission for Africa (UNECA) 109–10; Industrial Development Organization (UNIDO) 146; *see also* Food and Agriculture Organization (FAO)
United States (US) 1–2, 166
US – Animals 12, 14
US – Clove Cigarettes 46
US – Continued Suspension 11, 14, 32, 35, 52, 80
US – Countervailing Duties on DRAMS 160
US – Poultry (China) 12, 13–14, 158

Valceschini, Egizio 64n28
Van den Bossche, Peter 16n31, 79n143
Vapnek, Jessica 177n24, 193n79, 193n82, 193n84
vegetables, trade in 129
Vergano, Paolo R 160n165
Vienna Convention 46
Vogel, David 24n57
Vos, Ellen 91n208

West African Economic and Monetary Union (UEMOA) 123
WHO *see* World Health Organization (WHO)
Wilson, John S 136n38
Wolmer, William 141
World Bank 5, 43, 110–11, 124–5, 205; Hierarchy of Trade-Related SPS Management Functions 170, 174–5; standards as catalyst theory 131
World Health Organization (WHO) 5, 75, 122; *Assuring Food Safety and Quality: Guidelines for Strengthening National Food Control Systems* 112n64, 182n48, 187, 192, 200n107; diagnostic tools of 42; 'Food Safety and Health: A Strategy for the WHO African Region' 173n18; Regional Conference on Food Safety for Africa of 2005 173; Regional Office for Africa 101; risk assessment by 72; technical assistance by 42–3
World Trade Organization (WTO) 4, 41, 103; Agreement on Subsidies and Countervailing Measures (SCM Agreement) 160; Committee on Sanitary and Phytosanitary Measures 152, 161n170, 162; Committee on Trade and Development 45; Dispute Settlement Body (DSB) 106; Fourth Ministerial Conference (2001) 45; Secretariat 42, 152, 161, 162–3, 226; SPS Committee 76n123; Standards and Trade Development Facility (STDF) 5, 43, 45, 190, 205; trainings by 42; Understanding on Rules and Procedures Governing the Settlement of Disputes (DS) 26, 166, 226; *see also* Agreement on the Application of Sanitary and Phytosanitary Measures (SPS Agreement); Sanitary and Phytosanitary Measures (SPS standards)
WTO *see* World Trade Organization (WTO)

Yassin Abdullah Kadi and Al Barakaat International Foundation v. Council of the European Union and Commission of the European Communities 95

Zambia 101, 106, 107, 121, 172; horticultural exports by 109, 148; laboratories in 184, 203
Zimbabwe 101, 107, 206; beef exports by 140, 141, 142; fishery exports by 144; horticultural exports by 148